THE RECOVERY
OF RHETORIC

Knowledge: Disciplinarity and Beyond

Series Editors: Ellen Messer-Davidow, David R. Shumway, David J. Sylvan

Knowledges: Historical and Critical Studies in Disciplinarity
Edited by Ellen Messer-Davidow, David R. Shumway, and David J. Sylvan

The Recovery of Rhetoric: Persuasive Discourse and Disciplinarity in the Human Sciences
Edited by Richard H. Roberts and James M.M. Good

THE RECOVERY
OF RHETORIC

Persuasive Discourse and Disciplinarity
in the Human Sciences

Edited by

R.H. Roberts

and

J.M.M. Good

University Press of Virginia
Charlottesville and London

First published 1993 by
Bristol Classical Press
an imprint of
Gerald Duckworth & Co. Ltd

First published 1993 in the United States of America by
the University Press of Virginia
Box 3608 University Station
Charlottesville, VA 22903

Library of Congress Cataloging-in-Publication Data

The Recovery of rhetoric : persuasive discourse and disciplinarity in
    the human sciences / edited by R. H. Roberts and J. M. M. Good.
        p. cm. -- (Knowledge, disciplinarity and beyond)
    Includes bibliographical references and indexes.
    ISBN 0-8139-1455-8 (cloth). -- ISBN 0-8139-1456-6 (pbk.)
    1. Rhetoric. 2. Knowledge, Theory of. I. Roberts, R. H.
(Richard H.) II. Good, J. M. M. (James M. M.) III. Series.
P301.R347 1993
808--dc20   92-39541
                                                                 CIP

Printed in Great Britain by
The Cromwell Press, Melksham, Wiltshire

Contents

Acknowledgements

We wish to acknowledge the valuable assistance and support of our colleagues in the Centre for the History of the Human Sciences in Durham in the preparation of this volume. In particular, Irving Velody gave helpful advice. Arthur Still provided us at an early stage with a set of clarificatory definitions of interdisciplinarity for which we would also like to express our appreciation.

Our contributors have also given generously of their time and energy. Brian Vickers made his way from Zürich to Durham and in doing so lent a distinctive impetus to the whole lecture series. Others made lengthy journeys in the winter months of 1989-90 and all were exemplary in their ability to produce their final texts well within the contractual time limit.

We are grateful for the financial support of the General Lectures Committee of the University of Durham without which the public lecture series 'Rhetoric and the Human Sciences' would not have taken place. In addition, we wish to thank the Research and Initiatives Committee for providing funds which enabled Richard Roberts to attend the biennial conference of the *International Society for the History of Rhetoric* which took place in Göttingen in September 1989. It thus proved possible to extend the range of the volume by the inclusion of papers by Michael Cahn, Walter Rüegg and Philippe-Joseph Salazar.

We should like to thank the editors of the *Knowledge: Disciplinarity and Beyond* Series, Ellen Messer-Davidow, David Shumway, and David Sylvan, and an anonymous reader, all of whom made many helpful comments on the first draft of this book.

In Durham we are much indebted to Mrs Margaret Hall and Miss Paula Nisbett of the Department of Psychology who word processed the text of *The Recovery of Rhetoric* with outstanding care, patience and understanding. We should like to thank Mr Henry Lupton who provided valuable help with the bibliography, and Ms Gesine Leo who undertook a first draft translation of Professor Rüegg's paper. Thanks are due to Mr Alan MacFarlane for assistance with proof-reading.

We are grateful to the editors of *History of the Human Sciences* for permission to republish Professor Billig's paper.

Last, but not least, we express thanks to our wives, Audrey and Halusia, and to our children, Anthony, Jane and Katharine, who have withstood yet more parental absenteeism with patience and good humour.

Richard H. Roberts
James M.M. Good
Durham, September, 1992

Notes on Contributors

Michael Billig is Professor of Social Science at the University of Loughborough. His main interests include social psychology and the study of ideology. Recent books include *Arguing and Thinking* (Cambridge: University Press, 1987); *Ideological Dilemmas* (London: Sage, 1988); *Ideology and Opinions* (London: Sage, 1991); and *Talking of the Royal Family* (London: Routledge, 1991).

Michael Cahn has taught at the University of Konstanz for seven years and has held a visiting appointment in Austin, Texas. His *Kunst der Überlistung Studien zur Wissenschaftsgeschichte der Rhetorik* (Munich: Wilhelm Fink Verlag) was published in 1986. Further essays on the disciplinary constitution of rhetoric through rhetorical means have appeared in *Rhetorica, Helikon* and *Argumentation*. He has also published on literature and science, literary theory, and on the history of the book in *Der Druck des Wissens* (1991). He has recently moved to Cambridge.

David E. Cooper is Professor of Philosophy at the University of Durham and an Honorary Senior Research Fellow at King's College, University of London. His interests include Continental Philosophy, Philosophy of Language, and Asian Philosophy. His several books include Metaphor (Oxford: Blackwell, 1986) and Existentialism – A Reconstruction (Oxford: Blackwell, 1990), and (as Editor) The Blackwell's Companion to Aesthetics. He is currently writing an introduction to world philosophies.

James M.M. Good teaches Social Psychology and is Co-Director of the Centre for the History of the Human Scinces at the University of Durham. He has published in a wide variety of areas of psychology and has a particular interest in the impact of American pragmatism on the human sciences and the development of social psychology as an interdisciplinary field. He was a founder member of the Durham Research Group for the History of the Human Sciences.

Donald M. McCloskey is Professor of Economics and of History at the University of Iowa. He is author and editor of many books including *The Rhetoric of Economics* (Wisconsin: University of Wisconsin Press, 1986) and (with John Nelson and Allan Megill) the ground-breaking collection *The Rhetoric of the Human Sciences: Language and Argument in Scholarship and Public Affairs* (Madison: University of Wisconsin Press, 1987). He is founder and Co-Director of the Project on the Rhetoric of Inquiry.

Ann Moss is Reader in French at the University of Durham. She is currently writing a book on the history and role of commonplace-books in Early Modern Europe and has published extensively on Renaissance literary commentary, sixteenth-century French poetry, the hymnology of the Renaissance and Reformation and Renaissance rhetoric.

John S. Nelson is Professor of Political Science and Co-Director of the Project on the Rhetoric of Inquiry at the University of Iowa. In his current work he is addressing political communication and myth. Professor Nelson's many publications include co-editing *The Rhetoric of the Human Sciences: Language and Argument in Scholarship and Public Affairs* (Madison: University of Wisconsin Press, 1987).

Richard H. Roberts is Professor of Divinity and Director of the Institute for Religion and the Human Sciences at the University of St Andrews and has published books on Ernst Bloch and Karl Barth. He was M.B. Reckitt Research Fellow in the Department of Religious Studies at Lancaster University where he organised the project *Religion and the Resurgence of Capitalism* and he is now planning a project on globalisation and world religions.

Hilary Rose is Professor of Social Policy, University of Bradford and Director of the West Yorkshire Centre for research on Women. Currently she is attached to the Swedish Collegium for the Advanced Study of the Social Sciences at Uppsala where she is working on a book on science and gender.

Walter Rüegg is Emeritus Professor of Sociology at the University of Berne. He is general editor and co-author of *A History of the University in Europe* in four volumes (Cambridge: University Press, 1991ff.) and his main publications are *Anstösse, Aufsätze und Vorträge zur dialogischen Lebensform* (Frankfurt a.M., 1973); *Bedrohte Lebensordnung, Studien zur humanistischen Soziologie* (Zürich und München, 1973); and *Zementierung oder Innovation, Effizienz von Hochschulsystemen.*

Philippe-Joseph Salazar is Professor of French Languge and Literature at the University of Cape Town and Dean of the Arts Faculty. He is Corresponding Member of the Collège International de Philosophie for South Africa. He studied with Roland Barthes, Emmanuel Levinas and Marc Fumaroli and holds a doctorate in cultural anthropology (Sorbonne) and a *doctorat d'État* from the Sorbonne on the moral tradition in Europe (1590-1720). His major publications are *Ideologies de l'opera* (Paris: Presses Universitaires de France, 1980), *L'intrigue raciale* (Paris: Méridiens Klincksieck, 1989) and an edition of Jacques Amyot's *Projet d'éloquence royale* (Paris: Les belles lettres, 1992). He is preparing a book on the rapport between the Scripture and the birth of anthropological thought in the French academies of the Classical Age.

Herbert W. Simons is Professor of Rhetoric and Communications at Temple University. His interests are divided between the study of scholarly rhetorics and of communication and Professor Simons' books include the edited collections: *Rhetoric in the Human Sciences* (London: Sage, 1989); with Trevor Melia, *The Legacy of Kenneth Burke* (Madison: University of Wisconsin Press, 1988); and *The Rhetorical Turn* (Chicago: 1990).

Brian Vickers is Professor of English Literature and Director of the Centre for Renaissance Studies at the Eidgenössische Technische Hochschule, Zürich and was founding President of the International Society for the History of Rhetoric. He has published many books on Shakespeare, the history of early science, and classical and renaissance rhetoric. Professor Vickers' monumental *In Defence of Rhetoric* (Oxford: University Press, 1988) is the standard historical introduction to the rhetorical tradition.

Foreword

For many readers, the title of this book may be puzzling. Rhetoric has been studied for thousands of years; disciplinarity, though, is a far more recent phenomenon. How, except anachronistically, can one speak of the 'recovery' of rhetoric as a means of analysing disciplinarity? To this question, Richard Roberts and James Good respond in two ways.

First, they point out how important rhetoric has been for the constitution of various 'human sciences' disciplines as such. It turns out that disciplines were constructed, legitimated, and institutionalised by means of persuasive discourses directed at particular audiences. Moreover, human sciences continue to be maintained by rhetorical means; this can be seen, for example, in their episodic internal debates over epistemology and field distinctions.

On the other hand, Roberts and Good argue that by attending to rhetoric in the human sciences, scholars can begin to move away from boundaries and distinctions that characterise disciplinarity. If all disciplines are revealed to operate by means of rhetoric, then their conceptual and methodological autonomy appears as a persuasive argument, not as a timeless and necessary condition. This in turn can lead to the 'undisciplining' of the human sciences and, perhaps more generally, to a unification of certain disparate aspects of contemporary life.

'The Recovery of Rhetoric' thus turns out to be a critical tool, useful in showing how disciplines are constituted and implicitly, how knowledge could be formulated in an alternative manner. Yet to pose matters in this way is to raise two other questions: why should knowledge be configured in an alternative fashion? and could rhetorical analysis aid in such reconfiguration? On these issues, the essays in this volume are, perhaps inevitably, diffuse.

What is wrong with disciplinarity? Is the problem really that 'specialisation and fragmentation' are 'disabling'? One might in fact argue, along more Foucauldian lines, that the numerous boundaries, the subtle distinctions, and the sedulous training inherent in any discipline are constructive: they yield objects of study, methods of analysis, scholars, students, journals, and grants. From a certain point of view, disciplines are narrow or imbalanced; nonetheless, they represent an achieved coherence, a bringing together of otherwise disparate parts. The rhetorical means by which this coherence is accomplished is in fact a major theme of the essays in Part III of this volume.

Seen in this way, the problem with disciplinarity is not that it is disabling but in fact the reverse: disciplinarity is overly enabling. Instead of splitting a formerly

x

unified body of knowledge into disparate and dispersed splinters, disciplinarity constitutes novel and previously unimagined knowledges out of hitherto separated bits and pieces. 'Interdisciplinarity', as Good points out in his essay on social psychology, is simply another, more grandiose, disciplinary 'quest'. In this sense, using rhetorical analysis to argue for 'grand theory' is tantamount to recovering an old disciplinary dream.

Could a rhetorical focus more critically move beyond disciplinarity? We could start to answer this question by considering the periodic attempts at 'recovering' rhetoric discussed by a number of the authors in the first two parts of this volume. Such recuperative attempts, we learn, take the form of manipulative appropriation: an idealised past and a certain set of techniques said to have been codified in that past are used, quite self-consciously, to argue for a new configuration of knowledge. (Rather, one might think, like the various contemporary projects on rhetoric evoked – and exemplified – by Roberts and Good.) Rhetoric, though historically ancient, is thus timeless in its potential applicability. It follows, then, that the disciplinarity of the human sciences is a phenomenon made possible by the use of rhetoric at a particular historical moment. That moment – one in which various institutions and skills are applied to and developed with regard to a disparate and heterogeneous set of populations – is arguably still with us.

From this perspective, the claimed wholeness and timeless applicability of rhetoric are perfect instruments of disciplinarity. If rhetoric really is as ancient and unified as it is often presented, small wonder that it has been used as a kind of disciplinary soldering iron to unite previously separate people and phenomena. One well might wonder whether a focus on rhetoric, as thus conceived, could ever aid in finding alternatives to disciplinarity.

Clearly, our arguments point in favour of a certain kind of fragmentation. Instead of building up ever broader disciplines or 'interdisciplines', might it not be better to valorise and take seriously other types of knowledge? Consider, for example, chautauquas, public health comic books, or union organising videos: none of these was assembled as a discipline or was argued for by the means studied in this volume. Nor can we easily imagine an agenda in which these knowledges are brought together in an inter- or multi-discipline. A move toward such alternative ways of knowing may be the best way to achieve the 'undisciplining' of knowledge called for by Roberts and Good.

At this point, it is useful to recall that rhetoric in the ancient Greek world was not quite as unified or universal as Renaissance or other 'recuperators' made it seem. Rhetoric differed markedly by the social class of the orators, by the arenas (assembly, trial courts, theatre) in which they spoke, and by the extent to which their audiences were 'ideologically hegemonic'. Indeed, even during the relatively brief classical era in ancient Athens, there were important innovations in rhetorical practices.[1] Theorisation of those practices was every bit as diverse; witness, in this regard, the differences between Plato and Aristotle. We should expect that in our own era, rhetorical analysis can be just as disparate and just as innovative as it was 2 500 years ago. The arguments used in and on behalf of non-disciplinary forms of knowledge seem different from those connected with the human sciences; why presume that both kinds of arguments should be analysed in the same fashion?

If the potential of this volume is to be fulfilled, the essays that follow are best read somewhat 'against the grain'. Such an anti-intentionalist – dare we say anti-rhetorical? – stance may turn out to be the best way of recovering rhetoric.

Ellen Messer-Davidow
David R. Shumway
David J. Sylvan
1992

Note

1. Ober, Josiah, *Mass and Elite in Democratic Athens: Rhetorical Ideology and the Power of the People* (Princeton: Princeton University Press, 1989).

INTRODUCTION

Persuasive Discourse In and Between Disciplines in the Human Sciences

James M.M. Good (University of Durham) and
Richard H. Roberts (University of St Andrews)

...looking at things rhetorically forces you to find connections across different fields of study, to unite theory and practice, to find bridges between the academy and what goes on outside it. It also reminds you of the immense debt we owe to the past.[1]

The principal concern of this book is the widespread and growing interest in the nature and function of rhetoric as such, and in the rhetorical analysis of the discourse of many disciplines in the human sciences. *The Recovery of Rhetoric* reflects the responses of a wide range of the human sciences as they come to terms with threats to the project of modernity, and as they attempt to locate and sustain themselves rhetorically as disciplines in the 'postmodern condition'.[2] A further goal of this volume is to bring together contrasting examples of contemporary rhetorical inquiry, drawing upon work in continental Europe, Britain and North America. We believe that our contributors demonstrate that there are both analytical and emancipatory dimensions in the constitution and practice of the human sciences which are only made fully apparent through rhetorical analysis.

The title of this book identifies four recurring themes: the 'recovery of rhetoric'; the nature of persuasive discourse; disciplinarity; and the human sciences. First, we are concerned with the widespread evidence of a revival of interest in many forms of rhetoric, sufficient, we believe, for us to write of its 'recovery' (despite the ambiguities latent in this claim). Second, we employ the term 'persuasive discourse' so as to draw attention away from the sometimes pejorative and inappropriate connotations conveyed by the term 'rhetoric' as such. Third, we examine the processes by which disciplines establish themselves and assert their credibility through the generation of 'commonplaces'. We also see the way in which rhetorical analysis can show how the discourses and the practices of the human sciences both enact and conceal the persuasive strategies essential to the establishment of knowledge about the human world. Fourth, we employ the term 'human science' as opposed to the more familiar 'social science' to embrace the full range of disciplines required to make sense of the human condition.

Intensive engagement with the complex of issues surrounding the 'recovery of rhetoric' indicates that the term 'rhetoric' itself has within the past decade been broadened to such a degree that the more sensitive purists have considerable and sometimes justified difficulty in recognising this expanding penumbra as rhetoric in the traditional sense. We thus begin with a number of assumptions: that rhetoric is, in terms of a minimal but classic definition, the art or science of persuasion; that it initially received its categories and distinctions from the Sophists, Aristotle, Cicero, Isocrates and Quintilian, developments which were later taken up and applied in the Renaissance; and that these categories and distinctions have now re-emerged in what Chaïm Perelman and Lucie Olbrechts-Tyteca have designated as the 'New Rhetoric'.

Rhetoric, however, has always been more than merely the art of persuasion. Michael Cahn will later remind us that rhetoric implies a theory of speaking and of language, and that it also represents certain philosophical assumptions about the nature of humanity. Indeed, the 'recovery of rhetoric' is also a recovery of the essential inter-relatedness of the humanities and the social sciences. In this volume our use of the term 'human sciences' follows the example of our colleagues Arthur Still and Irving Velody in the opening editorial of the journal *History of the Human Sciences*:

> 'Human sciences', like the German *Geisteswissenschaft*, encompasses a number of different disciplines, including sociology, psychology, anthropology, and linguistics. Unlike 'social sciences' it suggests a critical and historical approach which transcends these specialisms and links their interests with those of philosophy, literary criticism, history, aesthetics, law, and politics.[3]

In this Introduction we begin by noting some of the landmarks in the history of rhetoric and then identify a variety of perspectives in the contemporary study of rhetoric. This is followed by a consideration of the role of rhetoric in the emergence and development of autonomous disciplines in the human sciences. A consequence of this emergence is disciplinary specialisation and the fragmentation of knowledge. We briefly examine the way in which disciplines control the organisation and production of knowledge, noting especially the role of disciplinary boundaries in such regulation and control. We go on to discuss in rhetorical terms the resultant attempts to cross disciplinary boundaries by means of interdisciplinary inquiry. This leads to a brief review of the possibilities for the re-integration of the human sciences. We conclude this introductory chapter with the formulation of some 'commonplaces' which capture the discursive dimension in the human sciences and identify some current debates which we believe would benefit from a more thorough rhetorical analysis.

The history of rhetoric and its contemporary concerns

Rhetoric once enjoyed a central place in the syllabus of the first three liberal arts, the medieval *trivium* of grammar, dialectic and rhetoric. After a decline, it recovered its vitality in the Renaissance, but then with the Enlightenment it again entered into a long, painful and complex descent from its position of power and influence. One of our major concerns is the nature and significance of the 'occultation' of rhetoric, its decline into apparent invisibility, a process that attended the evolution and differentiation of the human and social sciences in the nineteenth and twentieth centuries. It is the absence of an effective awareness of the full potential of rhetoric which facilitates contemporary trivialisation in the 'mere rhetoric' of media discourse. The present 'recovery of rhetoric' has, however, a history that is yet to be written (indeed some sceptics might argue that the event has yet to come to pass). In consequence, the present collection should be regarded as soundings taken in waters as yet only partially charted. What our contributors do demonstrate, nevertheless, is that there is a great variety of responses to the revival of the rhetorical tradition and its rediscovery in guises that on first inspection might appear a-rhetorical. It is our belief as editors that this diversity in mode and place of response and rediscovery is in fact underlaid by a number of common features. Indeed, such features have encouraged us to conclude this Introduction with a summary of some general prospects for rhetorical inquiry into the sometimes fragmented disciplines of the human sciences.

It is possible to differentiate at least five major clusters of activity in the present-day study of rhetoric and use of rhetorical analysis, but these distinctions should be understood as a heuristic convenience and not as mutually exclusive categories. The first cluster is the historical and linguistic study of classical and Renaissance rhetoric powerfully represented by, for example, the *International Society for the History of Rhetoric* and its journal *Rhetorica*. A second prominent locus of research is associated with the preparation of the multi-volume *Historisches Wörterbuch der Rhetorik* under the editorial control of Walter Jens and Gert Ueding in the University of Tübingen. This magisterial work will examine all aspects of rhetoric, historical and contemporary. A third area of activity is what takes place in the many departments of rhetoric and communication, primarily in the United States, where rhetorical methods are still formally taught as the means of improving pragmatic powers of persuasion and of self-presentation in a highly competitive environment where personal skills are at a premium. A fourth area is the renewed interest in rhetoric evident in literary theory and literary criticism where, for example, Wayne Booth's *Modern Dogma and the Rhetoric of Assent* and his later *The Rhetoric of Fiction* acquired paradigmatic status and stimulated much interest. The fifth area, and that most immediately relevant to the present discussion, is the 'rhetoric of (and in) the human sciences', a development closely associated with the POROI project[4] at the University of Iowa and with the programme initiated at Temple University.[5]

Both these North American centres of activity reflect the second generation application and development of the so-called 'New Rhetoric' of Perelman and

Olbrechts-Tyteca, and the less clearly defined but no less pervasive influence of the polymathic oeuvre of Kenneth Burke. It is our intention to seek out some of the common ground shaped by these broadly distinguished areas of activity, all of which are in differing ways reflected in the contents of this collection. Contributors to this volume share at least the following: a confidence in the power of language to construe the human condition, enabled by an awareness of the limits and the possibilities of the rhetorical construction of discourse; and a concern with some of the excesses of deconstruction.

The disciplinary turn: rhetoric and the emergence of the human sciences

What becomes apparent from the contributions to this volume is that rhetoric has played a central part in the formation, development and legitimation of the emerging human sciences in the course of the nineteenth century. If we are to understand the present-day classifications and hierarchies of the various disciplines in the human sciences, then it is essential to examine their rhetorical constitution. In this section we illustrate some of these relationships with respect to the development of just one of the human sciences – psychology. We believe this to be an appropriate choice: the discipline of psychology still embodies many features of the legacy of Cartesian philosophy, such as for example, an individualistic, representational theory of mind, together with the notion of an isolated knower faced with the task of acquiring reliable knowledge about other minds on the basis of private experience.[6] Psychology thus wrestles with a variety of the dualisms that have dominated the intellectual life of many of the human sciences during the past three centuries: body/mind, subject/object, individual/collective, organism/environment, fact/value, biological/social, knowledge/action, and so on. Despite the interdisciplinary character of cognitive science (the dominant tradition in contemporary academic psychology, referred to as 'the mind's new science' by Howard Gardner[7]), psychology as a whole remains predominantly an individualistic, reductionist and mechanistic enterprise. It remains an undertaking which, as is noted by Michael Billig below, neglects social and contextual factors and fails to transcend traditional dualisms by means of the development of 'mutualist' perspectives.[8]

The emergence of scientific psychology is frequently traced to the late nineteenth century, when it (along with other emerging human sciences such as anthropology and sociology) became differentiated or 'emancipated' as a discipline from studies in philosophy, history, sensory physiology, medicine and literature. The differentiation of the human sciences can be profitably examined in terms of processes of 'professionalisation', and in certain cases 'certification'.[9] It is clear, however, that these processes were by no means completed until well into the twentieth century.[10] The metaphor of emancipation is, moreover, deceptive. As Mitchell Ash has recently remarked:

But the liberation of psychology, such as it was, was nowhere a simple matter of one

4

part of philosophy or of medicine, reaching a certain stage of development and then splitting off more or less inevitably and developing further on its own, supported by independent institutions. Instead we are dealing here with complex processes of conceptual construction, reconstruction, and transformation, which took place in various historical settings. The successful institutionalization of some kinds of psychological thinking was only one of these processes; it did not end psychology's intellectual and social embeddedness, but only changed its structure.[11]

It is our contention that even today, psychology together with other human sciences retains an intellectual and social embeddedness, a condition of intellectual dependency which rhetorical inquiry helps disclose. Disciplinary histories can also provide us with examples of rhetorics of legitimation which are currently employed in both the constitution and the perpetuation of the autonomy of disciplines. These rhetorics form an important part of the practices of disciplinary specialisms. In the writing of disciplinary histories, key events or figures are troped as 'founding fathers', 'choice-points', or 'points of inflection'. These tropes are embedded in the narratives which are the vehicle for the disciplinary historian's reconstruction of the emergence of a discipline. In the textbooks of the history of psychology, for example, the founding of Wilhelm Wundt's Leipzig laboratory provides the 'point of inflection', the 'epistemological break' in a process of rhetorical reconstruction of the emergence of a discipline.[12] Wundt is thus seen as a 'founding father' in the emergence of a new discipline, rather than just an 'ancestor' in its pre-history.[13] In his paper in this volume, Michael Cahn cogently and reflexively applies such a rhetorical analysis to the discipline of rhetoric itself. The task of legitimation can thus be seen to be pervasive in the human sciences.[14]

Such a task takes on an added significance given the endemic nature of crisis in the human sciences. For example, Sigmund Koch (one of the most ardent critics of the natural science pretensions of psychology) points to the contestable epistemological and ontological assumptions about both the nature of the person and the methods by which reliable knowledge about her might be acquired.[15] In today's postmodern intellectual culture, such metaphysical talk may well be frowned upon; but debates about 'foundations' do still take place, postmodernists and poststructuralists notwithstanding, and these provide a rich vein for rhetorical analysis.[16] Indeed, it was just the absence of such debates in the physical sciences and their prevalence in the social sciences that provided the impetus for Thomas Kuhn's analysis of scientific paradigms.[17] Jeffrey Bergner in his analysis of modern social science argues that it is characterised by a formalism founded in a very definite and specific understanding of the relation between concepts and reality. This is an understanding in which concepts are seen as being constitutive of social and psychological reality.[18] Such concepts are embodied in the persuasive discourses of the human sciences, discourses which encourage and foster a false disciplinary self-sufficiency and disguise the intellectual 'embeddedness' referred to above.

Although our discussion above has concentrated on the role of rhetoric in the 'disciplining of knowledge' during the emergence of the human sciences, this volume and the book series which it inaugurates, also reflect the growing awareness of the ways in which disciplinary knowledge is not only 'embedded' in linguistic and social practices but is also 'organised around, and actually located within machines, standardised techniques and practices, and skills'.[19] The chapters in Part III also clearly illustrate how power relations permeate even the most ordinary of everyday disciplinary activities. Various factors have contributed to this awareness – the impact of Foucauldian analyses, of sociological studies of science, and of discourse analysis, for example – each revealing a variety of ways in which rhetoric is centrally involved in the constitution of disciplines and in the production of the 'internal relationship' of knowledge and power.[20]

Interdisciplines, territorial boundaries and re-integration in the human sciences

With the growth of disciplinary specialisation and fragmentation there has also developed a increasing concern about the disabling consequences of disciplinary boundaries. This has led to ever more frequent demands for the weakening of such boundaries and for the development of modes of interdisciplinary inquiry. There is as yet little consensus as to how intellectual activity which crosses disciplinary boundaries should be described.[21] A variety of prefixes is available, the most prominent of which are multi-, cross-, inter- or trans-disciplinarity. At the outset of our rhetoric project, Arthur Still (one of the editors of *History of the Human Sciences*) wrote an open letter setting out a classification scheme for different types of border crossing which identified the following:

1 *Multi-disciplinarity* – where specialists attach themselves to a common project in order to further their own interests (Still sees the voyage of the Beagle as a paradigm of this kind of multi-disciplinarity).

2 *Interdisciplinarity* – where expertise from more than one discipline is required in order to achieve a common aim (e.g., neuroscience, cognitive science, discourse analysis).

3 *Cross-disciplinarity* – where individuals from different disciplines tend to get together because they have common interests. Still puts it nicely as follows: 'Cross-disciplinarity...is what is left over when the cake of knowledge is sliced into disciplines and your sympathy with cross-disciplinary urges will depend upon whether you believe it to be half the cake or just a few crumbs'.[22] We share Still's view that cross-disciplinarity can be a source of innovatory teaching and research initiatives 'appropriate to a world in which the traditional boundaries have become a crippling restriction'.[23]

In her recent extensive review of the origins, nature and achievements of interdisciplinarity, Julie Klein adds a fourth term – trans-disciplinarity.[24]

4 *Trans-disciplinarity* – conceptual frameworks that transcend the narrow scope of 'disciplinary world views, metaphorically encompassing the several parts of material handled separately by specialized disciplines'.[25] In trans-disciplinarity, disciplinary barriers are broken through and disciplines become subordinate to the larger framework. Klein cites peace research, human population biology and broad

applications of rhetoric as examples of such trans-disciplinarity.

There is, however, a rhetoric employed in relation to the crossing of disciplinary boundaries – there is talk of 'sharing' and 'borrowing', of 'bridge-building' and 'integration'. Geopolitical metaphors abound – 'trespassing', 'property rights', and 'territorial struggles' feature prominently in the literature of cross-disciplinary work.[26] Klein argues that there is also a rhetorical opposition between disciplinarity and interdisciplinarity: disciplines are sometimes seen as providing the necessary tools for interdisciplinary work; inter-disciplines are sometimes seen as being on the verge of becoming 'undisciplined if there is no organized pay-off for the constant critical selection of ideas, theories and data'.[27] Trans-disciplinary fields may even begin to acquire some of the characteristics of disciplines – special languages, systems of apprenticeship, 'invisible networks' and specialist journals.

Reflecting on interdisciplinary education in the late 1980s, Klein notes that there are grounds for both optimism and pessimism:

> ...interdisciplinary programs have been limited in three major ways: by the lack of a long-standing tradition for interdisciplinary education, by the power of disciplinary and departmental boundaries, and by the influence of conditions outside the university.[28]

On a more positive note, she cites evidence that undergraduate interdisciplinary programmes (in the United States at least) are numerous, spanning all four years of the curriculum and linked with the revitalisation of the liberal arts. Within the human sciences, examples of candidates for successful interdisciplinary work cited by Klein include Edward Said's *Orientalism*,[29] the study by Robert Bellah and his co-authors, *Habits of the Heart*,[30] Robert Darnton's *The Great Cat Massacre*[31] and Hayden White's *Metahistory: The Historical Imagination in Nineteenth Century Europe*.[32] Further examples might be provided by John Shotter and Kenneth Gergen's *Texts of Identity*[33] and Jonathan Potter and Margaret Wetherell's *Discourse and Social Psychology*.[34]

An example of the innovation which can occur at the margins and intersections of disciplines as a consequence of the move to interdisciplinarity is provided by some recent work in the multi-disciplinary field of cognition. Thus students of cognition within psychology, anthropology and sociology increasingly now recognise the folly of attempting to study cognition independently of its social and cultural context. Indeed social and cultural factors are now coming to be seen as constitutive of psychological processes. This is how Michael Cole, a leading exponent of this 'ethnographic' approach to cognition, has put it:

> We cannot avoid the centrality of culturally organized experience in the operation, not to say the *definition* of human psychological processes. If culture and individual functioning are inextricably interwoven...if the properties of interaction (and hence of the individual) emerge in the course of its own production, new kinds of observations, and new theories that are neither *psychological* nor *anthropological* in currently understood senses of those terms must be created.[35] [emphasis in original]

In other words we have here a reminder of the 'embeddedness' noted above by

Ash. But more than this is involved. Cole is pointing to the need for a new kind of knowledge to emerge, knowledge which is neither anthropological nor psychological but which is genuinely interdisciplinary. What is being called for here is nothing short of an attempt to develop a 'culture-inclusive' human science that eschews exclusive dependence upon the individualistic and decontextualised studies of the laboratory.[36] In other words we need to cultivate what Clifford Geertz has recently called an 'outdoor psychology'.[37] Such a view of cognition is, moreover, seen as being 'seamlessly distributed across persons, activity and situations',[38] a mutualist view which is far removed from the lonely Cartesian spectator of the world, alienated from the sphere of action.

In order to transcend Cartesian dualisms and to escape the conceptual straight-jackets of the disciplinary institutions in which they are grounded, we believe it to be necessary to embrace a more mutualist perspective[39] and to foster a tactical and provisional 'undisciplining' of the human sciences.[40] This view is consonant with Serge Moscovici's recent proposals (and with those of Philippe-Joseph Salazar, see later) for dealing with the 'crisis of the representation of the social' in the human sciences by means of 'a flexible union of sociology, economics, psychology, history'.[41] We consider that such 'flexible unions' of currently disparate human sciences may go some way towards countering the adverse consequences of disciplinary specialism alluded to previously. It is also likely to foster the conditions conducive to creative innovation at the margins and intersections of disciplines, through the process Mattei Dogan and Robert Pahre call 'hybridization'.[42] The chapters in the final part of this book provide a variety of illustrations of the operation of rhetorical factors in the 'boundary work'[43] of disciplines and in 'flexible unions' of putatively autonomous disciplines.

Having discussed the role of rhetoric in the emergence of the human sciences and in the legitimation of disciplinary claims, the nature of interdisciplinarity, and the need for re-integration in the human sciences, we are now in a position to formulate some theses which focus and generalise what we consider to be an emerging consensus concerning the discursive dimension in the human sciences. It seems to us appropriate to present these in a rhetorical genre.

Some 'commonplaces' of the recovery of rhetoric in the human sciences

1 *Rhetorical analysis does not merely offer a deconstructive insight into the power-play implicit in disciplinary discourse but also exposes constructive procedures common to all the human sciences. In consequence, the human scientist becomes aware of the inescapable role of rhetorical procedures not only in the practice of her discipline but also in its constitution.*

Earlier in this chapter we drew attention to the way in which disciplinary histories provide examples of rhetorics of legitimation which are employed in both the constitution and the perpetuation of the autonomy of disciplines. Cahn also shows how rhetoric constitutes itself as a discipline and simultaneously disguises the rhetorical conditions of its disciplinary existence. Such disciplinary practices in the human sciences are described in several chapters in this and cognate studies. Moreover, as Herbert Simons clearly shows, such practices are also to be found in the natural and medical sciences. We do not believe, however, that this acknowledgement of the role of discursive practices in science requires the acceptance of the sociological reductionism of the 'strong programme in the sociology of science'.[44]

2 *The recovery of rhetoric in the human sciences has contributed to a recovery of the 'person' in disciplines which have largely been dominated by positivistic natural science paradigms.*

Such a recovery of the 'person' is reflected in the prevalence of notions of agency, intention and narrative in recent work. Whilst there is a noticeable element of individualism in such developments, the growing recognition of the dialogic aspects of thinking (discussed by Billig in Part III) serves to counter this tendency.[45] Moreover, the practitioner faces a dilemma, because theorists of postmodernity have asserted the fragmentation of subjectivity and individual identity, expressing reservations about the appropriateness of any 'action-centred model' for a critical social theory.[46] That is to say a belief in the possibility of radical social change is undermined. Such theorists nonetheless frequently take for granted some notion of the self as agent, reflexive, and capable of effective action in pursuit of self-determined goals.

3 *Whilst rhetoric is essential to the constitution of disciplines in the human sciences it also tends to foster a false sense of disciplinary self-sufficiency.*

We have already suggested earlier in this chapter that the social organisation of knowledge in the university can be a major obstacle to fruitful intellectual inquiry in the human sciences. In this context we have seen that the crossing of disciplinary boundaries has been, and will continue to be, of value in overcoming such an obstacle. A variety of strategies is available to counter the false self-sufficiency of disciplinary inquiry. Nevertheless we believe that interdisciplinary activity needs to be *constructed* and that this involves a demanding, collective exploration of the self-constituting strategies of the disciplines involved. Such an exploration is an enterprise fraught with fear when this exposes, as it must do, the slender bases of the security upon which the cultural identities of disciplines may rest. In our experience these endeavours tend to attract first of all a hard core of determined individuals already operating in at least two spheres of discourse; the real challenge lies in inducing those locked (often unconsciously) into totalising and self-justifying autonomous rhetorics to participate in acts of mutual disciplinary divestiture. This self-conscious 'undisciplining' of the human sciences again involves the kind of 'flexible union' called for by Moscovici.[47]

4 *The analysis of persuasive discourse in the human sciences offers accounts of*

relationships between authors/researchers, discourses, and audiences. In so doing it reveals intentions, justifications, and consequences. The human sciences, understood rhetorically, can thus be seen to be moral sciences, and to have, moreover, an emancipatory or critical dimension.

With the recovery of the 'person' in the human sciences, there has been a recovery of moral and political perspectives, of rights and obligations, power and subordination, reasons and excuses. Critical and emancipatory dimensions are now to be found in many of the human sciences. The postmodern shift away from the search for foundations, laws, and attempts to ground justice in rationality, however, poses a major challenge to the development of an emancipatory human science. David Harvey has recently suggested that postmodernity may be characterised by a resort (even a return) to rhetoric, but it is our contention that, rightly understood as a comprehensive and sophisticated mode of analysis, rhetoric can do much to counter the fragmenting and relativistic aspects of the postmodern condition. Thus contemporary rhetoric may contribute to the rehabilitation of 'grand theory' (and indeed critical theory).[48]

> 5 *Rhetorical inquiry with its deconstructive and constructive capabilities is reflexive; the practitioner becomes more fully aware that every intellectual construction in the human sciences is historically and culturally enmeshed, yet replete with the possibility of innovation.*

A significant feature of contemporary human science is the widespread recognition of a need to apply its concepts to an analysis of its own practices. Such reflexivity is enhanced through the analysis of persuasive discourse. In writing disciplinary histories, for example, we are now aware of the perils of both 'presentism' and 'historicism'.[49] Yet some degree of 'presentism' is inescapable, since we can never step outside our conceptual frameworks, or escape historical determination. A rhetorical reflexivity may nonetheless foster an 'enlightened presentism' and avoid the more obvious illusions of progressivism. Rhetorical analysis can thus make us more aware of 'the things we think with'.[50]

Some prospects for rhetorical analysis

In this final section we draw attention to the wider implications of our rhetorical analyses for the theory and practice of the human sciences.

Community and the citizenship debate

A frequent theme of recent discussions has been the relationship between rhetoric and the notion of community. Alasdair MacIntyre's *After Virtue* has often served as a catalyst for such debates and raises important questions about the relationship between biography, social role, narrative, and social structure, which draw attention (as MacIntyre sees it) to the need to 'construct local forms of community in which the intellectual and moral life can be sustained through the new dark ages which are already upon us'.[51] At various points in this volume the importance of rhetoric for the health of a participatory democracy and its political culture is noted; this is further confirmed by the recent revival of interest in the role of rhetoric in the fostering of citizenship.[52] Such developments have to face postmodern challenges, like that of Richard Rorty, whose rigid dichotomy between private irony and public hope permits no theoretical grounding for, or means of adjudicating between, the 'final vocabularies' in terms of which we debate new forms of community.[53]

The relationship between the Academy and society

As was noted above, a rhetorical approach can contribute to the development of an emancipatory human science which is aware of the social constitution of knowledge, yet sensitive to the moral and intellectual imperatives posed by the demands for effective social action.

A rhetorical approach therefore goes beyond disciplinary reflexivity to reveal the external conditions of the constitution of any discipline and its modes of operation.[54] In our view, attention should be focused upon the Academy and its historic obligation to ensure that debate continues between rival intellectual traditions,[55] despite the imposition of line-management practices in education in Britain and elsewhere. Whilst we do not subscribe to MacIntyre's views about the final incommensurability of such traditions,[56] we nonetheless endorse his attempt to revive the ideals of the Scottish preliberal university where:

> ...conceptions of and standards of rational justification are elaborated, put to work in the detailed practices of enquiry, and themselves rationally evaluated, so that only from the university can the wider society learn how to conduct its own debates, practical or theoretical, in a rationally defensible way.[57]

MacIntyre points out how the preliberal university was successful in promoting an educated public, thus he raises anew important questions about the 'social role of the man of knowledge',[58] a matter with which the Pragmatist philosophers such as John Dewey and G.H. Mead were also much exercised.[59] MacIntyre also shows how the rhetorical dimension of the Scottish Enlightenment, classically represented by such a figure as Adam Smith, contributed much to the success of a broadly-based, intelligently interdisciplinary tradition. Such a tradition continues to this day in Scottish education, despite the demands of disciplinary specialisation and the current political urge to transform all education into training.

The politics of globalisation and postmodernity

The tendency of the world socio-economic system (i.e., world capitalism) to promote a global culture (a process often understood as 'globalisation'[60]) on the one hand, and intense local resurgences of ethnic, religious, and national identities[61] on the other, presents a tension scarcely manageable within the parameters of the 'market' and conventional political activity. We have already noted in this chapter how ancestral identities draw upon long-standing traditions and their respective narratives and myths of origin. Rhetorical analysis can help us understand and interpret both the processes whereby the identities spring into life and the conflicts between the local and the global. A central factor in this political dimension is the ever clearer articulation of the narratives of gender which run, implicitly or explicitly, through the issues to which we allude.[62]

New technology and the transformation of persuasive discourse

These socio-political processes are, moreover, promoted and disseminated by global media and information technology. With the development and the availability of widespread access to electronically-mediated communication – electronic messaging (e-mail), fax messages, telephone and video conferencing, and electronic data banks, a new kind of discourse is arising in which the boundaries between the subject and the world are changing and in which 'the body is no longer an effective limit on the subject's position'.[63] Mark Poster has recently proposed the concept of 'mode of information' as a way of periodising history in terms of variations in the structure of symbolic exchange and of noting how contemporary culture 'gives a certain fetishistic importance' to information.[64] Poster's aim is to bring poststructuralist theory to bear on the phenomena of electronically-mediated communication. A new kind of persuasive discourse is at work in such communication, involving multiple and often anonymous authors and audiences and often resulting in powerful, frequently global, consequences, as was abundantly evident in the Gulf War. The control of access to these resources has educational and political implications which are now becoming increasingly apparent.

Transcending dualisms: beyond the realism/relativism debate

Rhetorical awareness allows for a fuller account of agency in the human sciences that moves beyond disciplinary boundaries (whilst respecting them in the fullest way) precisely because it accounts for the mutually shared principles integral to the constitution of all human endeavour of this kind.[65] We therefore consider that the recovery of rhetoric may permit the development of a form of *rhetorical pragmatism* in the human sciences, the full implications of which await further exploration. In this form of pragmatism there would be a recognition of the role of discursive factors in the constitution of knowledge; but as Charles Taylor has recently maintained, such a social epistemology should not be allowed to 'command ontology'.[66] A rhetorical analysis recognising the dialogical character of thinking is also more likely to contribute to successful 'conversations' between rival intellectual traditions. In this respect, it is helpful to recall Michael Billig's remarks about the enduring message of the Platonic dialogues: 'Socrates never persuades anyone, but yet he does not leave things just as they had been...both have formulated new thoughts...they agree to continue the argument on some other occasion'.[67]

Epilogue: rhetoric and the emancipatory imperative

As we have already emphasised, any serious consideration of the role of rhetoric in the human sciences must come to terms with the way in which knowledge is embodied in disciplinary rhetorics and practices. An analysis of the latter requires a detailed examination of the relationship between institutions, discourse, legitimacy and power. Thus, for example, in a review of the Iowa edited volume, *The Rhetoric of the Human Sciences*, John Peters Durham expressed his concern about the way in which some 'rhetorics' of inquiry served only to foster *disciplinary* interests, while they 'left the status quo of disciplines intact'.[68] We believe that the present collection of papers goes some way beyond this, in that it both clarifies and demonstrates the relevance of rhetorical analyses for such questions of power, knowledge and legitimacy. We also consider that the following chapters contain ample evidence of the central role of dialogue and persuasive strategies in the human sciences. As we have seen, the issues confronted in a rhetorical approach are not merely conceptual or clarificatory. These issues impinge upon fundamental problems inherent in the constitution of disciplines and of the objects of their inquiry, as well as exposing the necessary interactions between disciplines which must be constructed when problems in the real world have to be solved.

We have seen how rhetorical inquiry reveals common features in widely dispersed spheres of discourse. Central to a rhetorical approach is the expectation that every act of constitution and communication in a discipline is capable of explanation in terms of rhetorical categories. These expose the intentions and strategies of the communicator, the construction of the subject matter communicated, and the nature of the audience that receives the communication and which, in traditional terms, undergoes persuasion.

It is our view that the rhetorical approach allows us to proceed beyond the merely analytical and comparative appraisal of disciplines. It also encourages what we have called the 'undisciplining' of the human sciences. A rejection of a view of the human sciences as differentiated and fully autonomous is necessarily reinforced by the rhetorical method, properly understood. Furthermore, the application of a rhetorical perspective in the consideration of agency exposes the operation of intention and thus promotes a concern with accountability and justification. Any tendency to take refuge in forms of disciplinary foundationalism or quasi-fundamentalism is in principle checked. Nonetheless, it is also apparent that an acknowledgement of the role of rhetoric in the establishment of disciplinary commonplaces, in effect presuppositions constitutive of a sphere of discourse, is central to the arguments of many of our contributors. An explicit recognition of the dialogical character of the rhetoric of the human sciences promotes the likelihood that conflicting tendencies are held in balance.

In conclusion, we are optimistic about the positive potential of analyses of persuasive discourse in the human sciences. It should by now be apparent that rhetorical analysis can, in principle, have a variety of beneficial consequences – especially through its disclosure of the continuing need for 'grand theory' and its revelation of emancipatory possibilities. Far from relinquishing 'grand narratives', we share Anthony Gidden's view that there is an urgent need for the development of 'totalising theories with critical intent'.[69] Moreover, Roy Bhaskar (citing the young Marx at the end of his fine essay on scientific explanation and human emancipation) writes as follows:

If human beings, and social forms in general, are emergent from but conditioned by nature, then there is at least the possibility that the human sciences provided that they 'do not anticipate the new world dogmatically, but rather seek to find the new world through criticism of the old', could still be of some benefit to the greater majority of human kind.[70]

This assessment we fully endorse: awareness of the constructive and deconstructive power of the 'recovery of rhetoric' will enable such a process of discovery of a 'new world' and its possibilities.

Notes

1. Leith, D., and Myerson, G., 'The kernel of wisdom' *Times Higher Educational Supplement* (9 February 1990) p. 21.

2. In his discussion of the 'postmodern condition', J.-F. Lyotard emphasises 'incredulity toward metanarratives' (Lyotard, J.-F., *The Postmodern Condition* [Manchester: Manchester University Press, 1984]). With the alleged failure of the project of modernity, legitimation in terms of the grand narratives of classical social theory is no longer seen to be necessary. For some recent discussions of the transformation of modernity and its relation to postmodernity see R. Boyne and A. Rattansi (eds), *Postmodernism and Society* (Basingstoke: Macmillan, 1990); D. Harvey, *The Condition of Postmodernity* (Oxford: Blackwell, 1989); Z. Bauman, *Intimations of Postmodernity* (London: Routledge, 1992); A. Giddens, *Modernity and Self-Identity: Self and Society in the Late Modern Age* (Cambridge: Polity Press, 1991); S. Seidman and D.G. Wagner (eds), *Postmodernism and Social Theory: The Debate over General Theory* (Cambridge, MA: Blackwell, 1992); the special issue of *Theory, Culture & Society* vol. 2, no. 3 (1985) on *The Fate of Modernity* and B. Smart, 'On the disorder of things: Sociology, postmodernity and the end of the "social" ' *Sociology* 24 (1990) pp. 397-416.

3. *History of the Human Sciences* 1 (1987) p. 1.

4. This Iowa Project on the Rhetoric of Inquiry (POROI) involves the extension of rhetorical analysis to many disciplines and has already led to the commissioning of some thirty books.

5. See H.W. Simons (ed.), *Rhetoric in the Human Sciences* (London: Sage, 1989) for a recent example of the proceedings of one of the regular Temple University conferences on the general topic of discourse analysis.

6. A valuable account of of the development of 'representational cognitivism' is to be found in A.W. Still, 'The biology of science: An essay on the evolution of representational cognitivism' *Journal for the Theory of Social Behaviour* 16 (1986) pp. 251-67. Marjorie Grene ends her sympathetic study of Descartes with an attempt to provide a perspective on perception which could enable progress beyond 'the crippling Cartesian heritage' (Grene, M., *Descartes* [Brighton: Harvester Press, 1985]). As a way out of the dualistic Cartesian impasse she draws upon the theory of perception of J.J. Gibson (Gibson, J.J., *The Ecological Approach to Visual Perception* [New York: Houghton Mifflin, 1979]; Reed, E.S., and Jones, R. [eds], *Reasons* *for Realism: Essays of J.J. Gibson* [Hillsdale: Erlbaum, 1982]). For a cogent analysis of the explanatory role of individual mental representations in psychology and for an illustration of a 'non-individualistic conception of explanatory kinds' see T. Burge, 'Individualism and psychology' *Philosophical Review* XCV (1986) pp. 3-45.

7. In H. Gardner, *The Mind's New Science: A History of the Cognitive Revolution* (New York: Basic Books, 1985).

8. Over the course of this century there have been a number of attempts to overcome such dualisms and to develop a 'mutualist' psychology (see J.M.M. Good and A.W. Still, 'Mutualism in the Human Sciences: Towards the implementation of a theory' *Journal for the Theory of Social Behaviour* 22 (1992) pp. 105-28. These attempts derive from a variety of sources – American pragmatism (see D.N. Shalin, 'Pragmatism and social interaction' *American Sociological Review* 51 [1986] pp. 9-29), the later philosophy of Wittgenstein (see M. Chapman and R.A. Dixon [eds], *Meaning and the Growth of Understanding: Wittgenstein's Significance for Developmental Psychology* [New York: Springer-Verlag, 1987]), existentialism (see M. Merleau-Ponty, *Phenomenology of Perception* [London: Routledge and Kegan Paul, 1962] and D.E. Cooper, *Existentialism: A Reconstruction* [Oxford: Blackwell, 1990]), the 'ecological psychology' of J.J. Gibson (see E.S. Reed, *James J. Gibson and the Psychology of Perception* [New Haven: Yale University Press, 1988] and A. Costall and A.W. Still, *Cognitive Psychology in Question* [Brighton: Harvester Press, 1987]), and most recently the deconstructionists (see I. Parker, *The Crisis in Modern Social Psychology – and How to End it* [London: Routledge, 1989] and I. Parker and J. Shotter, *Deconstructing Social Psychology* [London: Routledge, 1990]).

9. See W.R. Woodward, 'Professionalization, rationality, and political linkages in twentieth-century psychology', in M.G. Ash and W.R. Woodward (eds), *Psychology in Twentieth-Century Thought and Society* (Cambridge: Cambridge University Press, 1987); and D. Ross, 'The development of the social sciences' in A. Oleson and J. Voss (eds), *The Organization of Knowledge in Modern America, 1860-1920* (Baltimore: Johns Hopkins University Press, 1979).

10. This view is convincingly documented in W.R. Woodward and M.G. Ash (eds), *The Problematic Science: Psychology in Nineteenth Century Thought* (New York: Praeger, 1982).

11. M.G. Ash in W.R. Woodward and M.G. Ash (eds), op. cit., p. 347.

12. See J.M.M. Good and A.W. Still, op. cit. On the dangers of the search for 'origins' and of the retrospective imposition of disciplinary boundaries see R. Smith, 'Does the history of psychology have a subject?' *History of the Human Sciences* 1 (1988) pp. 147-77.

13. The contrast between 'ancestors' and 'founders' is usefully explored in R.M. Farr, 'The international origins of a science: Social psychology' *British Psychological Society History and Philosophy of Psychology Newsletter* no. 8 (1989) pp. 13-21. For an alternative view of such tropes in writing disciplinary histories see J.M.M. Good and A.W. Still, *British Psychological Society History and Philosophy of Psychology Newsletter* no. 8 (1989) pp. 22-7. A more general discussion of social factors in the 'domains of construction' of scientific psychology is to be found in

K. Danziger, *Constructing the Subject: Historical Origins of Psychological Research* (Cambridge: Cambridge University Press, 1990).

14. For a discussion of the variety of functions of disciplinary histories see W. Lepenies and P. Weingart, 'Introduction', in L. Graham, W. Lepenies, and P. Weingart (eds), *The Functions and Uses of Disciplinary Histories* (Dordrecht: Reidel, 1983). 'In battles for supremacy in a field', note Lepenies and Weingart, 'in times of uncertainty of orientation, or in conflicts over the truth claims of contradicting schools of thought a history of the discipline serves to rearrange the relative impact of past achievements, the proper evaluation of founding fathers and disciplines, heroic discoveries and consequential mistakes. Histories thus serve to legitimate new paradigms and delegitimate old ones.' (Lepenies and Weigart, op. cit. p. xvii.)

15. See S. Koch, 'Reflections on the state of psychology' *Social Research* 38 (1971) pp. 669-709.

16. Some examples of recent debates about foundations in psychology are J. Margolis, P.T. Manicas, R. Harré and P.F. Secord, *Psychology: Designing the Discipline* (Oxford: Blackwell, 1986); M.E. Jaeger and R.L. Rosnow, 'Contextualism and its implications for psychological inquiry' *British Journal of Psychology* 79 (1988) pp. 63-75; and I. Parker, *The Crisis in Modern Social Psychology – and How to End It* (London: Routledge, 1989).

17. Kuhn, T.S., *The Structure of Scientific Revolutions* (Chicago: University of Chicago Press, 1962).

18. See J.T. Bergner, *The Origin of Formalism in Social Science* (Chicago: University of Chicago Press, 1981).

19. Rouse, J., 'Policing knowledge: Disembodied policy for embodied knowledge' *Inquiry* 34 (1991) p. 358. Over the past few decades a number of lines of work have converged on a view of knowledge as embodied. The work of Foucault has been the most influential in showing how the embodied investigator has been produced by techniques of manipulation and formation (Foucault, M., *L'archéologie du savoir* [Paris: Gallimard 1969], *The Archaeology of Knowledge* [trans. A. Sheridan; London: Tavistock, 1972]; Foucault, M., *Surveiller et punir* [Paris: Gallimard, 1975] *Discipline and Punish* [trans. A. Sheridan; London: Tavistock, 1977]). Foucault's views about embodied knowledge were influenced by his teacher Merleau-Ponty. The influence of the latter is also reflected in recent work (see M. Johnson, *The Body in the Mind: The Bodily Basis of Meaning, Imagination and Reason* [Chicago: University of Chicago Press, 1987]). See also J. Rouse, *Knowledge and Power: Toward a Political Philosophy of Science* (Ithaca: Cornell University Press, 1987); S. Fuller, *Social Epistemology* (Bloomington: Indiana University Press, 1988); and D.R. Shumway and E. Messer-Davidow, 'Disciplinarity: An introduction' *Poetics Today* 12 (1991) pp. 201-25.

20. See J. Rouse, op. cit., especially chs 1 and 7; S. Fuller, 'Disciplinary boundaries and the rhetoric of the social sciences' *Poetics Today* 12 (1991) pp. 301-25 and R.H. Brown, 'Poetics, politics and professionalism in the rise of American psychology' *History of the Human Sciences* 5 (1992) pp. 47-61.

21. See W. Bechtel, 'The nature of scientific integration', in W. Bechtel (ed.), *Integrating Scientific Disciplines* (Dordrecht: Martinus Nijhoff, 1986); J.T. Klein,

Interdisciplinarity: History, Theory and Practice (Detroit: Wayne State University Press, 1990); *Group for Research and Innovation in Higher Education, Interdisciplinarity* (London: Nuffield Foundation, 1975); R. Holland, *Self and Social Context* (London: Macmillan, 1977).

22. Still, A.W., letter dated 1 December 1988.

23. Still, A.W., op. cit.

24. Klein, J.T., op. cit.

25. Klein, J.T., op. cit., p. 66.

26. Klein, J.T., op. cit., ch. 4, 'The rhetoric of interdisciplinarity'.

27. Boulding, K.E., 'Peace research' *International Social Science Journal* 29 (1977) p. 604, quoted in J.T. Klein, op. cit.

28. Klein, J.T., op.cit., p. 179.

29. Said, E., *Orientalism* (New York: Pantheon, 1978).

30. Bellah, R.N., Madsen, R., Sullivan, W.M., Swidler A., and Tipton, S.M., *Habits of the Heart: Individualism and Commitment in American Life* (Berkeley: University of California Press, 1985).

31. Darnton, R., *The Great Cat Massacre and other Episodes in French Cultural History* (London: Allen Lane, 1984).

32. White, H., *Metahistory: The Historical Imagination in Nineteenth Century Europe* (Baltimore: Johns Hopkins University Press, 1973).

33. Shotter, J., and Gergen, K.J. (eds), *Texts of Identity* (London: Sage, 1989).

34. Potter, J., and Wetherell, M., *Discourse and Social Psychology: Beyond Attitudes and Behaviour* (London: Sage, 1987).

35. Cole, M., 'Cross-cultural psychology: A combined review' *American Psychologist* 26 (1981) p. 334.

36. The term is from Jan Valsiner and refers to a 'research paradigm [within developmental psychology] that is primarily directed towards explaining how culture organises the conditions for children's development, and how children assimilate these conditions, and simultaneously accommodate to them'. See J. Valsiner (ed.), *Child Development in Cultural Context* (Toronto: Hogrefe and Huber, 1989). Michael Cole has been in the forefront of attempts to establish a 'cultural psychology', drawing extensively on the work of Soviet psychologists (especially Vygotsky) – see M. Cole, 'Cultural psychology: A once and future discipline?', in J.J. Berman (ed.), *Nebraska Symposium on Motivation, 1989: Cross-cultural Perspectives* vol. 3 (Lincoln: University of Nebraska Press, 1990); for a related (and perhaps more heavily anthropological) approach see J.W. Stigler, R.A. Shweder, and G. Herdt (eds), *Cultural Psychology: Essays on Comparative Human Development* (Cambridge: Cambridge University Press, 1989). Shweder sees the current need for the development of a 'cultural psychology' as a reflection 'of one of the pitfalls of the "cognitive revolution" of the 1960s, the failure of the cognitive revolution to develop an adequate theory of the person'(Shweder, 1989, in Stigler, *et al.*, op. cit., p. 1).

37. Geertz, C., *Local Knowledge: Further Essays in Interpretive Anthropology* (New York: Basic Books, 1983).

38. For one illustration of such an 'outdoor' psychology see J. Lave, *Cognition* *in Practice: Mind, Mathematics and Culture in Everyday Life* (Cambridge: Cambridge University Press, 1988).

39. See note 8.

40. The notion of 'postdisciplinarity' has also emerged from similar expressions of concern about the consequences of disciplinary specialism (cf. R. Markley, 'Complex dynamics: Literature, science, and postdisciplinarity' *Poetics Today* 12 [1991] pp. 337-46).

41. See S. Moscovici, 'Questions for the twenty-first century' *Theory, Culture and Society* 7 (1990) pp. 1-19.

42. Dogan, M., and Pahre, R., *Creative Marginality: Innovation at the Intersections of Social Science* (Boulder: Westview Press, 1990).

43. The term is from Steve Fuller. See S. Fuller, *Social Epistemology* (Bloomington: Indiana University Press, 1988).

44. For a recent discussion of the rhetoric of science see Gillian Beer and Herminio Martin's Introduction to the special issue of *History of the Human Sciences* on *Rhetoric and Science* (Beer, G. and Martins, H., 'Introduction' *History of the Human Sciences* 3 [1990] pp. 163-75); a representative sample of views about the relative merits of epistemological and sociological explanations of scientific events is to be found in a symposium on 'Deconstructing quarks' which is focused on a paper by Paul Roth and Robert Barrett with responses and replies from a number of leading sociologists of science, including Trevor Pinch, Steve Fuller and Andy Pickering (*Social Studies of Science* 20 [1990] no. 4).

45. Billig, M., *Arguing and Thinking: A Rhetorical Approach to Social Psychology* (Cambridge/Paris: Cambridge University Press/Editions de la Maison des Sciences de l'Homme, 1987); on Bakhtin's contribution to the development of the 'dialogical' approach see M. Holquist, *Dialogism: Bakhtin and his World* (London: Routledge, 1990); for mutualist approaches to the study of dialogue see I. Leudar and C. Antaki, 'Completion and dynamics in explanation seeking', in C. Antaki (ed.), *Analysing Everyday Explanation: A Casebook of Methods* (London: Sage, 1988); and I. Markova and K. Foppa (eds), *The Dynamics of Dialogue* (London: Harvester Wheatsheaf, 1990).

46. See R. Boyne and A. Rattansi, 'The theory and politics of postmodernism: By way of an introduction', in R. Boyne and A. Rattansi (eds), *Postmodernism and Society* (Basingstoke: Macmillan, 1990); M. Poster, *The Mode of Information: Post-structuralism and Social Context* (Cambridge: Polity Press, 1990); E.E. Sampson, 'The challenge of social change for psychology: Globalization and psychology's theory of the person' *American Psychologist* 44 (1989) pp. 914-21; P. Waugh, *Feminine Fictions: Revisiting the Postmodern* (London: Routledge, 1989).

47. In discussing the personal characteristics of the interdisciplinary individual Klein comments as follows:

> Research on career patterns supports the widely held belief that senior faculty are the most likely and perhaps the best suited for interdisciplinary activities. They are the ones who can risk time out of the disciplinary mainstream, and they are the ones who often need new challenges'. [Klein, op. cit., p. 182]

and she goes on to note that:

> Certain character traits have also been associated with interdisciplinary individuals, among them reliability, flexibility, patience, resilience, sensitivity to others, risk-taking, a thick skin, and a preference for diversity and new social roles. [ibid. pp. 182-3]

48. Axel Honneth provides a valuable overview of the vicissitudes of critical theory (Honneth, A., 'Critical theory', in A. Giddens and J. Turner [eds], *Social Theory Today* [Cambridge: Polity Press, 1987]). An edited collection on *Habermas and Modernity* (Bernstein, R.J. [ed.], *Habermas and Modernity* [Cambridge: Polity Press, 1985]) discusses Habermas' attempt to sustain the project of modernity in face of postmodernist attacks; for more recent assessments of Habermas (including his recently translated *Philosophical Discourse of Modernity*) see D.M. Rasmussen, *Reading Habermas* (Oxford: Blackwell, 1990); S.K. White, *The Recent Work of Jürgen Habermas: Reason, Justice and Modernity* (Cambridge: Cambridge University Press, 1988); see also P. Dews, *Logics of Disintegration: Post-structuralist Thought and the Claims of Critical Theory* (London: Verso, 1987); S. Crook provides a powerful plea for a post-foundationalist radical social theory which can both maintain the 'accountability' of enquiry while also facing up to the contingency of value. See S. Crook, *Modernist Radicalism and its Aftermath: Foundationalism and Anti-foundationalism in Radical Social Theory* (London: Routledge, 1991).

49. The terms are those of George Stocking. See G. Stocking, 'On the limits of "presentism" and "historicism" in the historiography of the behavioral sciences' *Journal of the History of the Behavioral Sciences* 1 (1965) pp. 211-7.

50. See R. Darnton, *The Great Cat Massacre and other Episodes in French Cultural History* (London: Allen Lane, 1984).

51. MacIntyre, A., *After Virtue: A Study in Moral Theory* (London: Duckworth, 1981) p. 245.

52. See R.N. Bellah, *et al.*, *Habits of the Heart: Individualism and Commitment in American Life* (Berkeley: University of California Press, 1985); J. Shotter, 'Rhetoric and the recovery of civil society' *Economy and Society* 18 (1989) pp. 149-66; M. Billig, 'Conservatism and the rhetoric of rhetoric' *Economy and Society* 18 (1989) pp. 132-48 and D. Leith and G. Myerson, *The Power of Address: Explorations in Rhetoric* (London: Routledge, 1989).

53. In R. Rorty, *Contingency, Irony, and Solidarity* (Cambridge: Cambridge University Press, 1989); for two strongly contrasted reactions to Rorty's views about the contingency of self, language and community see R.J. Bernstein, 'Rorty's liberal utopia' *Social Research* 57 (1990) pp. 31-72 and S.S. Wolin, 'Democracy in the discourse of Postmodernism' *Social Research* 57 (1990) pp. 5-30; on the political implications of his position see J. Burrows 'Conversational politics: Rorty's Pragmatist apology for liberalism', in A. Malachowski, *Reading Rorty* (Oxford: Blackwell, 1990) and C. West, 'Afterword: The Politics of American Neo-Pragmatism', in J. Rajchman and C. West (eds), *Post-Analytic Philosophy* (New York: Columbia University Press, 1985).

54. A valuable account of the contemporary significance of reflexivity is to be found in H. Lawson, *Reflexivity: The Postmodern Predicament* (London: Hutchinson, 1985).

55. See A. MacIntyre, *Three Rival Versions of Moral Enquiry* (London: Duckworth, 1990).

56. In A. MacIntyre, *Whose Justice? Which Rationality?* (London: Duckworth, 1988).

57. MacIntyre, A., *Three Rival Versions of Moral Enquiry* (London: Duckworth, 1990) p. 222.

58. The term is from F. Znaniecki, *The Social Role of the Man of Knowledge* (New York: Columbia University Press, 1940); for two recent views of the social and political responsibilities of academics and intellectuals see R. Hariman, 'The rhetoric of inquiry and the professional scholar', in H.W. Simons (ed.), *Rhetoric in the Human Sciences* (London: Sage, 1989); and I. Maclean, A. Montefiore, and P. Winch (eds), *The Political Responsibility of Intellectuals* (Cambridge: Cambridge University Press, 1990).

59. See H. Joas, *G.H. Mead: A Contemporary Re-Examination of his Thought* (Cambridge: Polity Press, 1985); and R.J. Bernstein, *Philosophical Profiles: Essays in a Pragmatic Mode* (Cambridge: Polity Press, 1986).

60. A recent issue of *Theory, Culture and Society* is devoted to this topic. See M. Featherstone, 'Global culture: An introduction' *Theory, Culture and Society* 7 (1990) pp. 1-14.

61. For a valuable collection of recent views see R. Boyne and A. Rattansi (eds), op. cit. Gary Wickham provides a cautious assessment of the politics of postmodernism in 'The political possibilities of postmodernism' *Economy and Society* 19 (1990) pp. 121-49, emphasising the need to focus on specific sites of analysis and engagement (for example, of feminist or cultural politics).

62. See, for example, Hilary Rose (in Part IV of this volume), S. Lovibond, 'Feminism and postmodernism', in R. Boyne and A. Rattansi (eds), op. cit. and P. Waugh, op. cit.

63. See M. Poster, *The Mode of Information: Poststructuralism and Social Context* (Cambridge: Polity Press, 1990). There has been considerable effort devoted to the task of clarifying ways in which electronically-mediated communication differs from face-to-face communication. For some examples see J. Siegel, V. Dubrovsky, S. Kiesler, and T. McGuire, 'Group processes in computer-mediated communication' *Organizational Behaviour and Human Decision Processes* 37 (1986) pp. 57-87; B.W. Hesse, C.M. Werner, and I. Altman, 'Temporal aspects of computer-mediated communication' *Computers in Human Behavior* 4 (1988) pp. 147-65; and D.E. Murray, 'Composition as conversation: The computer terminal as medium of communication', in L. Odell and D. Goswami (eds), *Writing in Nonacademic Settings* (New York: Guilford Press, 1985). We are grateful to Charles Crook for some of these references and for numerous invaluable discussions concerning the socially-distributed nature of cognition.

64. M. Poster, op. cit., pp. 5-6. In this introductory chapter Poster explores the theoretical conditions for understanding the 'new configurations of the subject'.

65. Recent helpful discussions of attempts to strike a balance between the rival claims of modernity/postmodernity and realism/relativism are to be found in S.K. White, *The Recent Work of Jürgen Habermas: Reason, Justice and Modernity* (Cambridge: Cambridge University Press, 1988) and J. Margolis, 'Postscript on Modernism and Postmodernism, both' *Theory, Culture and Society* 6 (1989) pp. 5-30. The juxtaposition of 'rhetoric' and 'realism' is to be found in a number of recent works. For example, in R.H. Brown, *Society as Text: Essays on Rhetoric, Reason and Reality* (Chicago: University of Chicago Press, 1987); R.H. Brown, *Social Science as Civic Discourse* (Chicago: University of Chicago Press, 1989); J. Margolis, *Pragmatism without Foundations: Reconciling Realism and Relativism* (Oxford: Blackwell, 1986); and J. Margolis, op. cit. (1989). Elsewhere one of the authors has suggested the term 'ecological realism'; see J.M.M. Good and A.W. Still, 'Ecological psychology as a theory of social cognition', in A. Gellatly, D. Rogers, and J. Sloboda (eds), *Social Worlds of Childhood* (Oxford: Clarendon Press, 1989).

66. In C. Taylor, 'Rorty in the epistemological tradition', in A. Malachowski (ed.), *Reading Rorty* (Oxford: Blackwell, 1990).

67. Billig, M., 'Conservatism and the rhetoric of rhetoric' *Economy and Society* 18 (1989) pp. 132-48.

68. Review of *The Rhetoric of the Human Sciences*, J.S. Nelson, A. Megill, and D.N. McCloskey (eds) (Madison: University of Wisconsin Press, 1987); *Theory and Society* 18 (1989) pp. 555-60.

69. Giddens, A., *Times Higher Educational Supplement* (January 1992).

70. Bhaskar, R., 'Scientific explanation and human emancipation', in R. Bhaskar, *Reclaiming Reality: A Critical Introduction to Contemporary Philosophy* (London: Verso, 1989) p. 114.

PART I

The History and Formation of Rhetoric
as a Discipline

The first section of this book contains three accounts of episodes in the historical formation of rhetoric. In the opening chapter, Brian Vickers expounds his conception of the 'recovery of rhetoric',[1] in a way which exposes his basically conservative orientation: salvage of a 'sunken ship' is in order. Rhetoric has had previous periods of eclipse which are compellingly portrayed through the myth of Arethusa's transformation from nymph into the submerged stream which resurges elsewhere as a fountain. This image of displacement informs Vickers' account of phases in the history of rhetoric. Thus the reappearance of rhetorical influence after the fall of the Roman Empire in education and in the Church permits him to outline the contextual factors that determine the forms and functions that rhetoric is likely to adopt. So, for example, the original role of rhetoric as the means of sustaining a political culture in the public oratory of the Greek polis was redundant in the wholly non-democratic setting of the feudal Middle Ages where it became the stock-in-trade of a professionalised legal class. Throughout, Vickers urges upon the reader the importance of rhetoric to the health of a participatory democracy. This construal of rhetoric as indispensable to healthy political life emphasises the manifest contradiction between Vickers' 'high' view of classical rhetoric (and its repeated rebirths) and the contemporary public currency of such expressions such as 'mere rhetoric' often used to identify virtually all forms of exaggerated or unsupported political intervention.

Vickers shows that the 'recoveries' of rhetoric by Petrarch and Erasmus furnish contrasting modes of appropriation, and that both 'unabashedly use rhetoric for their own purposes'; but that, Professor Vickers argues, 'is what it is there for'. It is readily apparent where Vickers' sympathies lie, but he does not perhaps fully confront the problem of the ethics of rhetorical construction and intervention which all proponents of the art inherit from the dispute between Aristotle and Plato. The repeated 'recoveries' of rediscovered forms of classical rhetoric are readily demonstrable through the historical approach adopted by Vickers. Other writers in this collection, especially Walter Rüegg and Philippe-Joseph Salazar, show that in reality the situation is far more complex: the repudiation and substitution of rhetoric by 'science' may itself be understood both as an explicit and implicit rhetorical strategy in equally valid ways.

Indeed, it is once more on the grounds of contingent necessity that Chaïm Perelman and Lucie Olbrechts-Tyteca engage in their 'recovery' of rhetoric some four centuries later. In a brief summary of a long and complex work, Vickers shows how an alternative to the universalisation of formal logical argument along Cartesian lines could be developed which allowed for the reintegration of mind and will and for the reintroduction of the ethical into formal scientific discourse. Vickers touches in conclusion upon the evils of advertising and the manipulative character of current political propaganda. Clearly much more could be said about the ambiguity of rhetoric which Vickers exploits as a means of construction and as a subversive agent of deconstructive criticism.

In ch. 2, Ann Moss shows how Renaissance rhetoric was concerned both with the generation of cogent discourse and with the proliferation of figures of speech. As such, it had to defend its legitimate sphere of influence over against the fields of dialectic and grammar. The field of rhetoric was 'the probable, the truth-like; its aim, not certainty beyond rational doubt, but the agreement of the listener or reader to believe in the case presented'. In positive terms, it is remarkable how close this early modern use seems to lie to the interests of the New Rhetoric; negatively, how easy it is for rhetoric to skirt poetic composition, the manufacture of fictions. Moss shows how the commonplace book, as the ever-enlarging receptacle of commentary upon received wisdom, had the capacity to facilitate discovery. Moreover, this use signals a turn to self-referentiality in literature, and the emergence and development of the genre presages changes in the conception both of the self and of the discipline as such.

In the final chapter in this section, Michael Cahn draws our attention to the implicit, yet necessary, structure of rhetoric's own act of self-constitution as a professional pursuit and discipline at a stage before the successive 'recoveries' outlined in the first chapter. This is not merely an account of the origin of an art that must conceal itself if it is to succeed; Cahn is concerned to make more ambitious claims about the strategies involved in the self-constitution of disciplines. Given the self-involving nature of rhetoric and the consequent close identification between the art and the individual practitioner, he asks how was it that rhetoric constituted itself as a institutional discipline. His answer involves the careful examination of the function of the indirect tropes employed by the practitioner: language; the contingency of the moment (*kairos*); and the direct, authority-assertive tropes of the *techne* or disciplinary skill; nature; and lastly the strategy of self-concealment, the *ars est artem celare*. These are combined together to show how rhetoric both constitutes itself as a discipline, and yet, simultaneously, how it makes us forget the conditions of its disciplinary existence. This is a demanding presentation of aspects of the ambiguity that attends any recourse to rhetoric: the attainment of efficaciousness (in other words powerful discourse) involves concealment, and thus, by implication, a necessary deceit. It will become apparent that this pattern of empowerment and concealment is a central and recurring feature of the both the constitution and the subsequent practices of the human sciences.

1. Professor Vickers' choice of title and the ideas of the editors happily (and independently) coincided.

1

The Recovery of Rhetoric:
Petrarch, Erasmus, Perelman

Brian Vickers (ETH Zürich)

I

To speak of a 'recovery' of rhetoric is to treat an intellectual system as if it were a sunken ship that had been located by divers a hundred fathoms deep, and slowly winched to the surface, some parts still intact, others lost altogether, others having suffered a 'sea-change'. The comparison is partly just, since there have been periods where rhetoric seems to have disappeared from human consciousness, and (to generalise a little) there have been at least two phases of recovery. The great period of rhetoric was from its first formulation in Greece in the fifth century BC, through its triumph in politics and education within the Greek domain, to its adoption by the Romans in the first century BC and its spread through the Empire – a single span of eight hundred years halted by the fall of that empire and the triumph of the barbarians. Rhetoric as a system had been born out of social need – a series of legal disputes in the Greek towns of Sicily over the ownership of land, following the expulsion of the tyrants which had necessitated the codification of court-room speeches.[1] But over these eight centuries it rose to become the central discipline in education, affecting 'all public utterances' and indeed all intellectual activity (*IDR* 11). The Greeks exported rhetoric to Rome, the Romans exported it to the whole of the civilised world. In his fifteenth satire Juvenal commented ironically that

> today the whole world
> Has its Graeco-Roman culture. Smart Gaulish [French] professors
> Are training the lawyers of Britain: even in Iceland
> There's talk of setting up a Rhetorical Faculty.[2]

Indeed, Roman influence in Britain ultimately produced the first English rhetoric book, the Venerable Bede's *Liber Schematorum et Troporum (Book of Schemes and Tropes*, ca. AD 701),[3] and Durham must be counted among the first centres for rhetorical studies in these islands.

Reference to Bede, and to the persistence of rhetoric after the fall of the Roman Empire, shows that we cannot in fact limit the metaphor of 'the recovery' of rhetoric to the sinking of a ship, an absolute, once-and-for-all event, clearly locatable in time and space. Perhaps it would be better to invoke an ancient myth, reworked by Ovid, telling how the nymph Arethusa, bathing in the river Alpheus, was pursued by a river god. In order to 'escape his embrace, she was transformed by Diana into a stream which, descending into the ground, rose again as a fountain in the far-off island of Ortygia, on the Sicilian coast', near Syracuse.[4] In the same way rhetoric has descended into the ground only to reappear in unexpected places and unpredictable times. The Venerable Bede, working in the monasteries of Wearmouth and Jarrow, drew most of the material in his rhetoric book from the Latin grammarians Donatus (ca. AD 350) and Diomedes (late fourth century AD), and the encyclopaedist Isidore of Seville (ca. AD 570-636). The *Etymologia* of the last-named was one of the main sources for the knowledge of rhetoric in the Middle Ages, and drew both on Donatus and on the *Institutiones divinarum et saecularum litterarum* of Flavius Cassidorus Senator (AD 480-575), which itself derived from the *Artis Rhetoricae libri tres* of Fortunatianus (third century),[5] which in turn drew on – but I break off the chain! Looking back from Bede, then, takes us through several centuries of Roman teaching in grammar and rhetoric. Looking on from him we see his pupil Archbishop Egbert founding a school at York, whose pupils included Alcuin (ca. AD 735-804). Alcuin was summoned by the Emperor Charlemagne in AD 782 to become headmaster of his palace school, teaching for 22 years in the Frankish schools.[6] Among Alcuin's pupils was Rabanus Maurus, author of an influential treatise on the role of rhetoric in the Church, the *De institutione clericorum* (AD 819), and from this tradition a rhetorical culture developed on the continent which returned to England 'three hundred years later in the person of John of Salisbury'.[7]

Two traditions enabled rhetoric to reappear, Arethusa-like, after the collapse of the Roman Empire: one was education, the other Christianity. In education, the fact that rhetoric (along with grammar and dialectic – the three disciplines of the Trivium which constituted the first stage of instruction) also formed one of the Seven Liberal Arts, meant that whatever vestiges of Graeco-Roman culture survived the Dark Ages, it still held tenaciously to its part. The rhetorical treatises produced after the fall of Rome are brief, giving only a sketchy account of the role of rhetoric in political or civic life, and serving mostly as manuals of expressive devices, the figures and tropes. At the same time the two classical rhetoric books to survive into the Middle Ages (the youthful Cicero's highly schematic *De inventione* and the anonymous *Rhetorica ad Herennium*), both dating from ca. 87-84 BC and typifying the vogue for tidy classification so common in the Hellenistic period, attracted a veritable army of commentators. John Ward estimates that more manuscripts of these two books survive than of any other classical texts, and that thousands of copies and commentaries were in circulation.[8] These treatises were also pillaged by writers on rhetoric, from Donatus to Alcuin and beyond.

The other main route in which rhetoric reached the Middle Ages was through the Church. A key figure here was St Augustine, whose *De doctrina christiana* (ca.

26

AD 396-426) argued that a knowledge of tropes was essential to the understanding of the Bible (III.xxix). In the fourth and last book Augustine settled much Christian misgiving about the use of pagan learning, and validated the use of classical rhetoric in the composition of sermons.[9] His book was drawn on by the early Christian writers on rhetoric – Cassiodorus (who, commenting on the Psalms, pointed out many rhetorical figures), Bede, and Rabanus Maurus – and it remained a basic text for the whole development of mediaeval preaching.[10] Simultaneously rhetoric was taking hold in Byzantium in a movement which culminated in Michael Psellus founding in the mid-eleventh century a university curriculum based solely on rhetoric.[11] Rhetoric, like the rest of the Greek intellectual heritage, was also taken up in Arabic culture, but with less far-reaching consequences for the mediaeval West, where – in contrast, for example, to mathematics, astronomy, or alchemy – rhetoric still had an unbroken tradition.[12]

Yet the apparent continuity of the rhetorical tradition conceals major and far-reaching differences. Along with other elements of verbal culture, rhetoric was subject to a series of changes which had a restricting effect, so much so that the dominant impression we gain when comparing medieval to classical rhetoric is one of fragmentation. To begin with, many of the major texts – Cicero's *Orator, Brutus*, and to all intents and purposes, *De Oratore* – had disappeared; others (notably Quintilian's *Institutio oratoria*) survived in badly damaged form. More damaging, due to the virtual disappearance of the historical context, was the lost understanding of the role of rhetoric in Greek and Roman political life. Mediaeval commentators who came across a word like 'civic' in the prooemium to *De inventione* had no idea of its socio-political implications. The disputes within the basic curriculum – the so-called 'Battles of the Liberal Arts' – meant that rhetoric suffered first of all at the hands of grammar, which took over some parts of the rhetorical curriculum, for example, the figures of speech, and metrics, and taught them as philological entities detached from literary texts. Rhetoric was also invaded by logic or dialectic, when they appropriated such crucial elements of the total rhetorical scheme as the commonplaces, definitions, proof, and the major techniques of argumentation. Logic rapidly became the leading discipline in the universities, virtually eclipsing rhetoric. Simultaneously, theology took over some parts of rhetoric, especially moral and political questions. The virtual disappearance of democracy, through which political debate could in principle determine governmental decisions, meant that the oratory of the forum and law-courts suffered oblivion in the Middle Ages. We can already trace a shift from Greece, where political speaking was the right and in some cases the unavoidable duty of any citizen in the *polis*, to Rome, where pleading in law-courts became the prerogative of professional advocates. In the Middle Ages, which lacked knowledge of the speeches of Demosthenes and Cicero, and had no concept of democratic political institutions, any reference to public oratory was likely to be ignored, treated with puzzlement, or elided into some other topic.

The gradual breaking-up of the rhetorical tradition in this period shows all too clearly how rhetoric flourishes or declines according to the demands that a society makes on it.[13] If you give central importance to democracy and to participation in political decision-making, then eloquence will cover the whole field of human activity. Banish democracy, professionalise legal practice, and oratory becomes either the possession of a few highly-educated, specially-trained speakers, or merely a subject to be studied in schools. But whereas for Quintilian, in the first century AD, the educational status of rhetoric still included political activity, literature, ethics, and humane studies in general, a thousand years later rhetoric had become fragmented and divided up between various types of specialism. Readers approached rhetorical treatises, and indeed literary works themselves, in a ruthlessly utilitarian way. Users raided such works in order to provide a stock of reusable quotations, *sententiae* taken out of their context, and put to the strangest uses in works of theology, logic, or philosophy. Since the practical role of rhetoric had almost disappeared, users were left with a collection of theoretical pronouncements which could be re-applied to various pragmatic goals. Virtually the only survival of rhetoric as a spoken art was in the composition of sermons. But the clerics who studied the many preaching-manuals (not parish priests, who had a much lower education, but professional preachers) did so to compose a specific sermon, to improve their preaching technique, or to make use of the proliferating compilations of *sententiae*. These manuals were not read by anyone else in society; nor did the clerics interest themselves in any other branch of rhetoric.

The fragmentation of rhetoric into theoretical pronouncements to be dismantled and re-applied, resulted in a compartmentalisation of rhetoric for the use of clearly-defined social groups, each operating within its own domain. Historians traditionally distinguish three main *artes*: the *ars praedicandi*, the *ars poetriae* ('preceptive grammar, or the Rhetoric of Verse-Writing', as J.J. Murphy calls it), and the *ars dictaminis*, the art of letter-writing.[14] The arts of poetry were composed by professional teachers of grammar, who limited themselves to teaching schoolboys how to write Latin verse, often in the most mechanical terms. Their concern was with poetic composition in the narrowest sense: the choice and arrangement of words in a verse-line, sentence structure, and in embellishment. Interest in content or effect, for example, invention, plot, structure, persuasion, yielded to a concern with verbal forms. The *artes poetriae* list the rhetorical figures purely as lexical items. (These rhetorical figures were always seen in classical rhetoric as compressed emotional states with the clear function of representing the feelings of a speaker or character and of arousing similar feelings in the reader or listener.) They are put on the same level as, say, adjectives ending in *-osus*, or *-ilis*, unrelated to meaning or feeling. The art of *dictamen* similarly concerned itself with form: the forms necessary to draw up legal documents; the proper form of a letter to be written by an inferior to a superior – requesting a favour, competing for secular or ecclesiastical office, or just asking for money. Such manuals depended not on theory but on specimen letters and varying forms of address. Here too, energy became channelled into such matters as the proper *salutatio* (or greeting-formula), word-order and the right way to end a sentence. The complex unity of classical rhetoric shrank to a series of rules divorced from a political, social, or cultural context; rules which could be put into practice by the pupil just as mechanically as his master set them down.

II

This progressive fragmentation of rhetoric in the Middle Ages requires us to revise our metaphor from Ovid. The stream Alpheus continues to flow, but in ever-narrowing channels, and with increasingly brackish water. It does not disappear altogether, but it has been cut off from any fresh sources. The recovery of rhetoric in the Renaissance was brought about by a rediscovery of those sources, a joining up of currents separated from each other over the preceding five centuries, and a tapping of the great reservoirs of Greek and Roman history. The person responsible for inaugurating this process of recovery was Francesco Petrarca (AD 1304-74), as his followers quickly and generously perceived. It was Petrarch, 'my teacher', as Boccaccio proudly wrote in 1370, who 'cleansed the fount of Helicon, swampy with mud and rushes, restoring its waters to their former purity,...reopened the Castalian cave...restored Apollo to his ancient temple and brought back the Muses, soiled by rusticity, to their pristine beauty. Then he ascended to the topmost peaks of Parnassus'.[15] Petrarch's gesture, in having himself crowned with a laurel wreath on the Capitoline Hill of Rome in 1341, was a deliberate appropriation of the supremacy of the poet in classical culture. A generation later, and in more temperate terms, Leonardo Bruni celebrated Petrarch as the first 'who recognised and restored to light the ancient elegance of style which was lost and dead'. Bruni can now give an explanation for his success:

> ...he saw and opened the way to this perfection by recovering the words of Cicero, by enjoying them, by understanding them, and by adapting himself as much as he could...

so much so that he surpassed Virgil, who wrote no prose, and Cicero, who wrote no poetry, by achieving excellence in both forms of writing.[16]

Bruni's tribute is historically correct, for Petrarch led the discovery of classical texts which made it possible for the first time to reconstruct an accurate picture of Roman, and to a lesser extent, Greek society. He discovered a manuscript of the *Pro Archia*, Cicero's celebrated defence of poetry, at Liège in 1333, spurring other humanists to scour the libraries of monasteries and convents. In 1345 Petrarch discovered three collections of Cicero's letters in the Chapter Library of Verona: *Ad Atticum*, *Ad Brutum*, and *Ad Quinctum Fratrem*. The remaining collection, the *Ad Familiares*, was copied for Coluccio Salutati in the 1390s, while Leonardo Bruni and Poggio Bracciolini found sixteen more orations by Cicero. The most spectacular discovery was made in 1416 by Poggio during the Council of Constance. Bored by its discussions, he went on a search of the Abbey of St Gall and found, in a monk's cell at the foot of a tower, a complete Quintilian, 'safe and unharmed, though covered with mould and filthy with dust'. Five years later Gerardo Landriani, Bishop of Lodi, found a complete manuscript of Cicero's *De Oratore*, *Orator*, and *Brutus*.[17] Petrarch's greatest service to the inauguration of humanist studies was to

29

inspire the search that, within a century, had restored most of the major texts in classical rhetoric.

Petrarch also led the way in recovering the main justification for rhetoric, its social and ethical value. In the *De inventione* (1.2.2-3; 1.4.5) Cicero, inspired by a passage in Isocrates, had praised rhetoric as a civilising factor in human society, which had transformed men 'from wild savages into a kind and gentle folk' by the use of 'reason and eloquence', *ratio* and *oratio*. Rhetoric, Cicero wrote, plays a crucial role in society, for it preserves the community, 'renders life safe' and protects virtue, so that as mankind most excel animals 'by having the power of speech'; the orator, who 'excels men in that ability by which men excel beasts', is to be especially valued (*IDR* 10-11). Petrarch worshipped Cicero's mastery of language: 'Rhetoric was the queen of the Arts for him, and Cicero the king of rhetoricians'.[18] Emulating Cicero, he collected his own 'Familiar Letters'. Written between 1325 and 1366 (and rather self-consciously edited for publication from 1345 onwards), the *Rerum Familiarum Libri XXIV* was an epoch-making exercise in *imitatio*, which shows how well Petrarch had re-assimilated Latin culture.[19] Petrarch never wrote a treatise on rhetoric, but in his letters – which resemble informal essays on recurring issues in life – we find many of the *topoi* of the Ciceronian tradition. In his moral philosophical works (especially *De officiis*, 'On duties'), Cicero had repeated the case made so often in his rhetorical works, that speech was a God-given faculty to be cultivated and used for the public good, in defence of justice and liberty, against evil and oppression. So, in one of his earlier letters, Petrarch writes that 'the care of the mind calls for a philosopher, while the proper use of language requires an orator'. He urges that

> ...we correct not only our life and conduct, which is the primary concern of virtue, but our language usage as well...by the cultivation of eloquence. Our speech is not a small indicator of our mind, nor is our mind a small controller of our speech. Each depends upon the other but while one remains in one's breast, the other emerges into the open. The one ornaments it as it is about to emerge and shapes it as it wants to; the other announces how it is as it emerges. People obey the judgment of one, and believe the opinion of the other. Therefore both must be consulted, so that [the mind] will be reasonably strict with [speech], and [speech] will be truthfully magnificent with [the mind]. [I.9; 1.47]

Petrarch's Ciceronian model of the person is based on the inherent unity between thought and speech, and between speech and action. In order to 'speak seriously, austerely, judiciously and, most importantly, uniformly' (alluding to the classical concept of *decorum*, but also to ethical constancy), he declares, 'our desires [must] first order themselves', a task that only 'a wise man' is capable of. If the personality and desires are not brought into harmony and consistency, the resulting 'disorder will be reflected in our conduct and in our words' (ibid.). This model of the person as a being capable of achieving a coherent unity between language and mind goes through Renaissance culture. As John Hoskins wrote, in one of the most intelligent rhetoric books of the Renaissance:

The conceits of the mind are pictures of things and the tongue is interpreter of those pictures. The order of God's creatures in themselves is not only admirable and glorious, but eloquent.

Speaking 'unskilfully', then, would not be so shameful if 'only the tongue were disgraced by it'. But 'disordered speech' damages 'the right proportion and co- herence of things in themselves', as well as revealing the speaker's inner disorder. That man's mind cannot

...be thought in tune whose words do jar, nor his reason in frame whose sentences are preposterous; nor his fancy clear and perfect whose utterance breaks itself into fragments and uncertainties.[20]

The breakdown of coherence between mind and words was a fruitful theme for comedy in the Renaissance, as in *Love's Labour's Lost*, or – with more disturbing overtones – in the plays of Ben Jonson.

The function of rhetoric, all humanists believed, is not only to reveal our psychic and moral balance (or lack of it) but also to develop our powers of communication, for the good of others. Even if we did not need eloquence, Petrarch continues, we would have to acquire some ability to communicate, and 'great toil would yet be necessary for the sake of those with whom we live. For without doubt, our conversa- tion would be of great assistance to their minds' (I.9; 1.48). At this point Petrarch imagines a friend objecting that it would be more effective to provide examples of virtue by our own behaviour, so that others ' "would be seized by the urge to imitate. For we are aroused...in much better fashion...through the stimulus of deeds rather than of words" '. Petrarch admits the exemplary effect of virtuous behaviour, but he refuses to accept the dichotomy between deeds and words. Eloquence on its own can be of great help to 'the progress of human life', as we see in everyday existence, when people are 'suddenly turned from a most wicked way of life to the greatest modesty through the spoken words of others!'. Alluding to the prooemium of *De inventione,* with its praise of rhetoric's civilising power and its use of the fables of Orpheus and Amphion, two mythological figures 'able to inculcate gentleness and patience in all things', Petrarch urges that skill in rhetoric – by which he means written communication – 'permits us to be useful to those living in distant regions', and to do 'much good to our posterity' (I.9; 1.49).

Petrarch has in effect equated rhetoric with ethics, assigning to it the functions of praising virtue, furthering 'the greater love of God and the hatred of sin', and 'the investigation of new ideas'. Even if we are so selfish that 'no sense of charity towards our fellow men drives us', he writes, 'I would still consider the study of eloquence to be of the greatest aid to ourselves...'. He justifies this statement by citing his own personal experience, the value 'to me in solitude [of] certain familiar and famous words not only grasped in the mind but actually spoken orally, words with which I am accustomed to rouse my sleepy thoughts'. Presenting himself both as reader and writer, Petrarch reaffirms the inevitable union between ethics and eloquence, describing his own writings as 'more suited to my ailments, just as the sensitive hand of a doctor who is himself ill is placed more readily where he feels the pain to be'. In his own compositions the 'salutary words', restoring his moral health, 'fall tenderly upon my ears...and transfigure my insides with hidden powers' (1.49-50).

Petrarch's concept of rhetoric, in this early and programmatic epistle, rests on two principles: that rhetoric is inherently good, designed to help others according to the Christian notion of charity; and that it is effective in moving the emotions. This second idea, summed up in the verbs *movere* and *flectere*, was perhaps the greatest legacy of Latin rhetoric to the Renaissance, being adopted everywhere, in rhetorical theory and practice, in poetics, music, and even painting.[21] It is no accident that Petrarch should have devoted a whole epistle to *'the notable effects of eloquence and of music'* (III.22; 1.169-71). All the examples he quotes from Greek and Roman history show the power of eloquence in an admirable light, pacifying barbarians, winning over tyrants, softening the cruelty of executioners. In a letter advising a friend to continue his studies of civil law, despite Petrarch's own aversion to the subject ('I wasted seven entire years in such study'), and his contempt for present-day lawyers (who care nothing for 'the origin of justice and the first lawyers', being only interested in profit, thus reducing law to the status of 'the mechanical arts'), he recalls with nostalgia the ancient world, when 'lawyers and orators enjoyed great fame'. To have mastered both disciplines, to be able to 'join the power and beauty of skilful speech' to a knowledge of the complexities of the law, and to be able to draw on both spontaneously when under fire from one's adversaries, requires great talent. But it is only possible, Petrarch insists with a truly Ciceronian notion of function-ality, if one possesses 'an eloquence befitting the matter at hand, effective, adorned, and capable of arousing minds'. The men who 'have excelled in the art of oratory', such as Demosthenes, Isocrates and Aeschines among the Greeks, Cicero, Crassus and Julius Caesar among the Romans, 'have enjoyed great glory and were justifiably said to control events through their eloquence and to hold sway over the minds of men' (XX.4; 3.132-8). Rhetoric works!

This 'exquisite eloquence' becomes the main topic in several letters, such as one distinguishing true eloquence from mere loquaciousness: 'one is a matter of quality, the other of quantity' (VI.7; 1.326), or several letters concerned with questions of style. In an amusing account of contemporary ecclesiastical vanities, Petrarch de-scribes a humiliation that he suffered from the Roman Curia due to an error of *decorum* on his part, being accused of having a 'style...too lofty for the humility required of the Roman See'. This pompous accusation gives rise to a discussion of the three styles as defined by Cicero (XIII.5; 2.189-95). Between friends, he writes later, no special style is needed, for 'great love needs no artificial eloquence', only sincerity (XVIII.8; 3.56-9). The question of individual style and the limits of *imitatio* are discussed in a letter to Boccaccio where Petrarch disclaims any desire to proclaim himself a wholly original poet. Horace, Juvenal, Virgil and others boast of having opened up a new genre or new style, but 'I am one', Petrarch writes, 'who delights in imitation and not in sameness, in a resemblance that is not servile, where the imitator's genius shines forth rather than his blindness or his ineptitude' (XXII.2; 3.211-15). Here, too, Petrarch laid the basis for a more enlightened concept of *imitatio* that was shared by many Renaissance writers.[22]

Petrarch in this way extends the rhetorical tradition, becoming a model for future writers just as he modelled himself on those he most admired, above all Cicero. The praise of Cicero is a frequent topic in these letters, within decent bounds: 'I shall revere and admire, yet not adore, our Cicero, and not as a god but as a man with a divine intellect' (XVIII.14; 3.66-7). Yet while celebrating Cicero's writings, Petrarch feels compelled to criticise 'his weak character' and 'his inconstancy in friendship', his 'serious and destructive quarrels upon slightest provocation', and 'his childish mania for wrangling, all of which are so unseemly in a philosopher' (XXIV.2; 3.314-16). In one of the famous letters he addressed to dead writers (XXIV.3; 317-18) he rounds on Cicero bitterly: '...O rash and ill-fated elder, why did you choose to become involved in so many quarrels and utterly useless feuds? Why did you forsake that peaceful ease so befitting a man of your years, your profession, and your fate?' Yet in the next letter, also to Cicero, he begs pardon, and makes amends by praising this 'great father of Roman eloquence' on behalf of all writers in Latin,

> ...for it is with the waters from your wellsprings that we irrigate our fields, frankly admitting that we are sustained by your leadership, aided by your judgments, and enlightened by your radiance.... Under your auspices...we have achieved whatever writing skills and principles we possess. [XXIV.4; 3.319-21]

The recovery of Cicero had enabled Alpheus to flow again.

The influence of rhetoric on Petrarch extended from the early to the mature works, affecting his concept of speech, his own practice of style, and even his very way of thinking and arguing. Anyone who studies Petrarch's moral-philosophical works will frequently find him at one point advising participation in social and communal life, at another arguing in favour of retirement, or even monastic life. This duality has posed a problem to those modern historians who approach his work in ignorance of the rhetorical tradition and dismiss it as 'a heap of contradictions'.[23] But Petrarch is only following out the rhetorical practice of arguing both sides of a case, *in utramque partem disserere*, and following the basic injunction in all manuals of rhetoric that a speech must be adapted to the specific audience to which it is addressed, to their capabilities, life-interest, and concerns. In fact, Petrarch applied exactly the same process to rhetoric itself, in a late and once-popular work, the *De remediis utriusque fortunae* (or 'Remedies against the two types of fortune, good and bad'), completed in 1366.[24] This collection of 253 dialogues is directed against the dangers of prosperity (in Book One) and adversity (in Book Two), with Reason as the main speaker in both books. In Book One, Reason speaks with (or rather rebukes) Joy and Hope; in Book Two, Sorrow and Fear. Petrarch's aim is the traditional Stoic and Christian one of preparing the mind or soul against all the dangers of this life, teaching it not to be in love with transitory pleasures or vanities when life goes well, nor to be cast down by suffering when life goes badly.

In the ninth dialogue of Book One, Joy revels in his mastery of eloquence, describing it in a series of formulaic sentences: 'Myne eloquence is flowing and swift' – 'Myne eloquence is very shynyng' – 'The plentie of my eloquence is very great'. To each of these sentences Reason delivers some devastating comments, while Joy continues on the same track, evidently oblivious to the corrections being administered. Reason states that eloquence 'must be tempered with holynesse and wysedome…. For no man can be a true oratour, that is to say, a maister of eloquence, unless he be a good man' (fo. 9a). This is a familiar principle from classical rhetoric, and Reason duly cites the famous definitions of Cato, '*An Oratour is an honest man, skilful in speaking*', and Cicero, that '*Eloquence…is nothyng els but wisedome, speaking copiously*' (fo. 9b). Without wisdom and virtue, the eloquence of 'a deceiptful man' would be like 'the payntyng of a harlot, or sugred poyson, or the strength of a frentike person' (ibid.). Warming to the task, Reason cites

> …the saying of a certaine wyse man, *that life & death are in the power of the tongue*. The tongues, not of one man onely, but of a certaine many, have overthrowne whole commonwealthes, & wil overthrow hereafter. The tongue is the worst and most hurtful member of an evil person. (fo. 10a)

Since, as history teaches us, 'eloquence hath dwelt among infinite vices', lacking virtue it is 'noisome and hurtful' (ibid.). The unambiguous excellence of eloquence in the *Familiar Letters* is now severely qualified.

The matching dialogue in Book Two (no. 101) is even more critical of rhetoric. Here Sorrow complains that 'I lacke eloquence' – 'I cannot speake' – only for Reason to comfort him by damning the supposed gift that he lacks: 'Thou lackest one of the instruments to get hatred,…for many have perished through eloquence', as history amply records. Even those who have not been in danger have wasted their time studying the art, for

> …in all the worlde there is nothing so vayne, for which so many labours, so long watchynges are willyngly undertaken: this flickering breath so exerciseth mens mindes, as though there were some vertue [*innate power*] in their wordes. [fo. 294a]

Where now is the praise of eloquence, attainable by diligent study, imitating the best masters? This dehortation from eloquence systematically inverts many of Petrarch's earlier principles. When Sorrow complains 'I am voyde of wordes', Reason responds: 'Apply thy mind unto deedes: For in wordes there is breath, & labour, and speeche, and in deedes, quietnesse, vertue, and felicitie' (ibid.). Previously, Petrarch had rejected that dichotomy, insisting on the continuity between thought and action. And whereas he had earlier conceived of the mind as being organically linked to its expression in speech, now a wedge is driven between them. Do not 'weary thy tongue in vayne', Reason urges, but suffer 'other men to speake, & understand thou, forsomuch as there is a more secrete, and delicate pleasure in the meditation of the minde than in the utterance of the tongue, beyng both of longer continuance, & also havyng in it more quietnesse, & less envie' (fo. 294b). The same advice is given in the next dialogue (no. 102), '*Of losse of the tongue and speeche*', namely 'hold thy peace', and so keep out of trouble. For you can still please God with your heart (fo. 295a-296b).

Petrarch the Christian, then, re-enacts the split between *cor* and *lingua* which, so his great master Cicero alleged, had first been made by Socrates, beginning that disastrous split between philosophy and rhetoric from which we still suffer.[25] Petrarch re-enacts this divorce in the name of Christianity, but in so doing he goes counter to the teachings of St Augustine, Cassiodorus, and all those who argued for a properly Christian eloquence. It is hard to know which played the major part in Petrarch's thinking at this stage in his life, the Stoic principle of countering prosperity and adversity with their opposites, or medieval Christianity with its strong desire to propagate a *contemptus mundi*.

I cannot resolve the contradiction between Petrarch's two attitudes to eloquence, and rather take it as establishing an axiom or self-evident truth in the history of rhetoric, namely that the recovery of this discipline is always an act of selection, including some elements, rejecting others. For one thing, the very scope of rhetoric is immense – ranging from highly technical treatises on 'topics' (sources of argument) to detailed consideration of court-room strategies (the *Ad Herennium*, Cicero, Quintilian), and from elaborate classification of stylistic types and effects (Hermogenes, Longinus, Demetrius) to what seems to modern readers an unnecessarily minute classification of all possible modes of praise literature (the *Peri epideiktikon* of Menander the Rhetor). So vast is the range of rhetoric that no-one in later times could possibly need it all. In making a selection, then, these influential pioneers in the recovery of rhetoric express a personal choice, made for personal ends. They unabashedly use rhetoric for their own purposes – but that is what it is there for.

III

To highlight the individual nature of Petrarch's dualism, let us briefly consider another Renaissance figure involved in the recovery of rhetoric, Desiderius Erasmus (ca. AD 1469-1536). Unlike Petrarch, who never wrote a rhetoric-book, Erasmus wrote – or rather compiled – many, for every level of user. There are the educational treatises on how to teach beginning students, in which the humane attitudes of Quintilian are joined to the humanist pedagogy formulated in fifteenth-century Italy by Guarino, Vittorino da Feltre and others.[26] Erasmus writes discussions of the basic educational processes, *De ratione studii ac legendi interpretandique auctores liber* (1511), *De pueris statim ac liberaliter instituendis declamatio* (1529), and elementary treatises such as *De recta latini graecique sermonis pronuntiatione dialogus* (1528). He defends liberal studies, uniting classical culture and Christianity, in *Antibarbarorum liber* (1520). He outlines in copious detail the techniques of achieving *copia*, or 'fullness of expression' in Latin style, in the *De duplici copia verborum ac rerum commentarii duo* (1512). The desire to be of practical use, giving his readers all possible tools for literary composition, led to Erasmus issuing compilations which were meant as source-books, great magazines or repertories of classical literature, digested into order, such as the *Parabolae sive similia* (1514), the

Apophthegmata (1531), and above all that great collection of proverbs, the *Adagiorum Collectanea* (Paris, 1500), the first edition containing 818 adages, vastly expanded as the *Adagiorum Chiliades* (1508), containing 3 260 adages with essay length commentaries. This collection was constantly expanded during eight successive editions, until the final version in 1536 contained 4 151 adages.[27] Not content with compiling general treatises on education, and vast storehouses for writers, Erasmus also produced books dealing with specific genres, both secular – the *De conscribendis epistolis* (1522) and *Conficiendarum epistolarum formula* (1519/20) – and religious, the *De ratione concionandi* or *Ecclesiastes* (1535), a manual on preaching.[28] By contrast with the fragmented readership of medieval rhetoric, Erasmus wrote treatises on grammar, the arts of poetry, letter-writing, and sermon-writing, and clearly expected that readers of one book would need to know the others. In his own person he incarnated the reunification of rhetoric brought about in the Renaissance.

In all his writings, Erasmus drew freely on the classical authors he admired most, Cicero and Quintilian. He modelled himself on their work, in questions of style, argument and literary structure.[29] He advised his readers to read the whole of classical literature twice, once for the content, and once for the style, and certainly fulfilled his own injunction. So total is his absorption of the rhetorical tradition that there is no possibility of his turning against it, as Petrarch had done. Certainly Erasmus will mock abuses of rhetoric, such as in the slavish imitation of Cicero's style, exposed in his *Dialogus Ciceronianus* (1528), and errors of thought and speech, in several of the *Colloquia* (1519), those spirited dialogues which started off as models for good Latinity and developed into another form of personal essay. But for Erasmus, rhetoric is an essential element in the education of man and the proper functioning of society. For him, as for all the humanists, man is distinguished from animals by the gift of speech (*GRE* 1.53), and he echoes the familiar praise of eloquence which resounded from Isocrates and Cicero to Quintilian and Lorenzo Valla (*GRE* 1.62-71). The misuse of language, he writes in *Lingua* (1525), has always produced violence and evil, from the lies told to Adam by Satan to the wars of the present day (*GRE* 1.73-4). But although aware of this negative side, Erasmus gives it comparatively little emphasis. All his efforts go into instructing the teacher how to apply rhetoric to his classroom interpretations of classical authors, and to inspire his pupils to imitate rhetorical techniques in their school compositions (*GRE* 1.509-26). Erasmus' own published commentaries on classical texts are primarily geared towards rhetoric (*GRE* 526-41). They point out the rhetorical genus involved, whether in prose or verse (both are subsumed under rhetoric) and indicate the parts of an oration that lie behind the structure of so many literary works. They also draw attention to their use of emotional persuasion with a matching emphasis on *movere*, singling out individual rhetorical figures, and so on.

All this is rather to be expected from a humanist several generations later than Petrarch, grappling with the practicalities of mastering rhetoric in reading and composition. Where Erasmus the Christian differs from the elder Petrarch, however, is in refusing any dichotomy between pagan rhetoric and Christian values. Taking as his model the St Augustine of *De doctrina Christiana*, in annotating the New Testament

Erasmus goes out of his way to indicate all its beauties of style, showing how it frequently uses *movere*, pointing out specific figures of speech (*GRE* 1.548-53). Rejecting the four-fold allegorical interpretation in medieval exegesis, Erasmus insists on the essential simplicity of the Biblical text (1.558-62, 568-79) which is only expressed in an indirect manner through the use of tropes: 'the largest part of understanding the Gospels depends on the tropes' (1.563). Since, like other rhetoricians, Erasmus believed that everyday language is full of tropes,[30] he found it inevitable that Christ, putting on human nature, should have used these resources (1.564-5). So he picks out for special attention the tropes *synecdoche*, *hyperbaton*, *hyperbole*, and *hypallage*, all means with which Holy Writ had enriched meaning (1.565-8). Rhetoric, he insists, is fundamental to understanding the scriptures (1.579-86). Even in his *Paraphrases*, expanded versions of Biblical texts, Erasmus introduced all kinds of rhetorical devices, following his own teachings in the *De copia*, as Jacques Chomarat has shown (1.593-604, 618-32, 645-7). In the *Psalms*, needless to say, he finds many forms of rhetoric (1.672-7).

Chomarat's extremely detailed study of Erasmus' grammar and rhetoric, to which all future students will be indebted, has discussed in an apparently exhaustive manner the Dutch humanist's teachings on 'style and the art of composition' (Part 4, ch. 5: *GRE* 2.712-843), and on the oratorical genres, covering in turn the colloquies (Part 5, ch. 1: 2.849-930), the declamation (ch. 2: 2.931-1001), the letter (ch. 3: 2.1002-52), and the sermon (ch. 4: 2.1053-1155). Most of this material derives centrally from the rhetorical tradition, the only surprise being Erasmus' breadth of reading and inexhaustible energy in making his knowledge available to the reader in the most coherent and useful manner. But the *Ecclesiastes* deserves more attention, partly as a salutary contrast to Petrarch's dualism, partly as an indication of how anyone recovering classical rhetoric does so for their own ends. The work is divided into four books, and in his Preface Erasmus announces that the first will discuss the difficulty and greatness of preaching. 'In the second and third I adapt to the needs of preaching the precepts of rhetoric, dialectic, and theology.' The fourth book is an outline of the main ideas contained in scripture, and where the preacher can find them (*GRE* 2.1059-60). Book Two, then, starts with *inventio*, which Erasmus describes as the most important process in rhetoric, and which he sees as 'embracing both *elocutio* and *dispositio*'. Of the three aims of eloquence, *docere* must come first, while *delectare* is the least, *flectere* or *movere* the most important. He sets out the parts of a sermon (simply applying the five-part model from the classical oration), reviews the *loci* for the deliberative and epideictic genres, analyses forms of argument and proof, and ends by saying that in the conclusion of the sermon the preacher must appeal to the audience's *affectus*, inflaming his listeners to Christian piety (2.1063-6). Once more rhetoric has recovered its unity between form, content, and purpose.

In Book Three, Erasmus first deals with the two remaining parts of the five *officia oratoris*, *memoria* and *actio* or gesture. He again criticises the useless artificialities of mnemotechny (*GRE* 1.514ff, 2.1066), and refuses to lay down any general rules for gesture, allowing each preacher to retain his individuality. He then returns to his main interest, the style of the sermon and the effect that it should have, being simultaneously *vehemens*, *iucunda*, and *copiosa*. He invokes *amplificatio* not in the distorted medieval sense of making a composition longer[31] but in the true classical sense of heightening the emotional level, distinguishing moderate from violent feelings, and listing the ways of achieving this effect: appealing to the imagination, using the appropriate figures and tropes, above all metaphor, 'which holds the first place among all the qualities of style' (*GRE* 2.1066-8). The fourth book analyses the subjects most frequently met in sermons: the celestial hierarchies, God, the law (divided into the law of nature, the law of Moses, and the new law of the evangelists), the virtues and vices, and a miscellaneous section of topics which he calls '*Sylva*' (2.1069-71). As this brief synopsis shows, Erasmus has fully integrated classical and Christian sources. The whole aim of a sermon is to make men and women practise the *philosophia Christi*, to turn their souls to the love of celestial things (2.1096), and in this process Quintilian and Cicero are indispensable. Indeed Erasmus sometimes takes over their very words, substituting a Christian for a pagan expression. The Christian orator can now be defined as a *vir pius dicendi peritus* (2.1103-7).

Erasmus' assimilation of classical rhetoric is so total – as he said of himself in 1523, '*Erasmus nihil docuit nisi eloquentiam*' ('Erasmus taught nothing but eloquence') (*GRE* 1.21) – that we can hardly speak of a 'recovery', rather of a repossession or personal refashioning in the values and forms of rhetorical humanism. Many readers will admire Erasmus' tolerance, especially when set against the heated and pitiless controversies waged by Luther, Tyndale, Sir Thomas More and others, those verbal battles which imitated and fed into the wars of religion. True to his detestation of war and cherishing of peace, in his absorption of rhetoric Erasmus retained the essential quality of persuasion, namely its status as an alternative to absolutism, tyranny, and all forms of violence. In the *Ecclesiastes*, as elsewhere, Erasmus opposes all those who practise dogmatism (theological or otherwise), and use fear and persecution, albeit disguised as religion (*GRE* 2.1118-53). The virtues he prefers are *humanitas* and *caritas* (2.1160-1), which are given a prominent place in his rhetoric. As Chomarat puts it, 'Le désir de persuader est l'âme de l'éloquence; elle exclut la contrainte, la violence et la peur; celles-ci n'entraînent jamais l'adhésion sincère qui doit être libre'. As against the 'menaces and condemnations' too often used by religion to safeguard its institutions and ritual practices, Erasmus sets a church based on peace and concord, which will not persecute heretics but 'try to persuade by means of persuasion'. Erasmus

> ...pratique donc et prêche cette vertue nouvelle dans le monde chrétien, mais qui découle de la nature même de l'art de persuader: la tolérance; celle-ci est à la fois moyen et fin, elle n'est autre en effet que le respect des personnes.... [2.1162-3]

The orator adapts his speech to his audience, uses all the verbal and emotional resources in his power to plead the cause that he holds to be right, but still does not attempt to impose his will on his hearers. They are free to assent, or refuse.

IV

I have chosen to emphasise this quality in Erasmus' repossession of rhetoric because I feel that he gained a more profound understanding of the *ethos* of persuasion than did his illustrious predecessor, Petrarch. But also because it links Erasmus with a later stage in the recovery of rhetoric, one very close to us, the *Nouvelle Rhétorique* of the Belgian scholar Chaïm Perelman and Lucie Olbrechts-Tyteca.[32] Leaping in this manner over four centuries, in which rhetoric traced a course of irresistible rise followed by inevitable decline,[33] we see again how the recovery of rhetoric takes on a specific shape according to the needs and purposes of its user.

Perelman records that as a student in Belgium he experienced the very last course taught in rhetoric, the discipline being dropped from the school curriculum in 1929.[34] Twenty years later, having written a doctoral dissertation on Gottlob Frege and a monograph on justice, he realised with some surprise that modern formal logic was entirely unable to discuss the questions of value involved in any legal system. To remedy this alarming gap he began to work out a new treatise on argumentation, and in 1958 he published with his collaborator Olbrechts-Tyteca a substantial work which has since attracted great interest.[35] The starting-point of this treatise is the authors' rejection of the system that has come to dominate modern logic, and indeed much of science, Descartes' *Discourse on Method*. Descartes 'made the self-evident the mark of reason, and considered rational only those demonstrations which, starting from clear and distinct ideas, extended, by means of apodictic proofs, the self-evidence of the axioms to the derived theorems' (*NR* 1). This geometrical model for a rational science is supposed to 'elaborate a system of necessary propositions which will impose itself on every rational being, concerning which agreement is inevitable', and disagreement, therefore, is 'a sign of error' (*NR* 2). In a formal demonstration we begin with axioms and end with theorems (*NR* 490). Formal logic limits itself to 'a set of conventions that are well founded in a field of purely theoretical knowledge' (*NR* 132), and it aspires towards the condition of mathematics, a self-contained system which is 'no longer related to any rational evidence', but can freely manipulate its own 'artificial language', laying down 'which are the axioms...which are the rules of transformation'. The main concern of Cartesian logic is 'to avoid doubt and ambiguity', striving towards 'unquestionable univocity' (*NR* 13). This desire for 'a universal language' makes 'clarity of concepts' the great ideal, 'forgetting that this very clarity may stand in the way of other functions of language' (*NR* 133).

The system elaborated by Descartes and those who followed him, such as Kant, 'accepts only purely logical proof, and excludes from philosophy all argument that does not absolutely compel acceptance' (*NR* 29). Indeed, it not only excludes such arguments, it rejects as 'irrational' all elements that are not self-evident. Perelman and Olbrechts-Tyteca object that

Whether these elements consist of obstacles to be surmounted – such as imagination,

39

passion, or suggestion – or of suprarational sources of certitude such as the heart, grace, [or] intuition, this conception introduced a dichotomy, a differentiation between human faculties, which is completely artificial and contrary to the real processes of our thought. [*NR* 3]

What the Cartesian system does is to make an unjustified limitation of the human faculty of reasoning and proving to the domain of the self-evident, to be instantly accepted, without further discussion. By identifying their system with the 'rational' and rejecting all others as 'irrational', Cartesians have operated a binary category designed to privilege one pole of the opposition and discredit the other. The dichotomy of Cartesian systems, reason/unreason, is an either/or and corresponds (to use the distinctions developed by Gregory Bateson and Anthony Wilden)[36] to the working of a digital computer (like an adding-machine), a movement through discontinuous steps which includes the options yes/no, on/off. Rhetoric, however, resembles the analog computer (like a clock), marked by continuous functions along the scale of less/more, and lacking the option yes/no.

The model that the new rhetoric offers is not a 'yes/no' but a 'more/less' one, where the essence of argumentation is its use of 'discursive techniques allowing us *to induce or to increase the mind's adherence to the theses presented for its assent*' (*NR* 4). The audience's 'adherence' or agreement is the crucial element, which has by nature a 'variable intensity' (ibid.), greater or less according to their prior convictions and the success of the orator in increasing or reversing them. The coherence of this new rhetoric to the tradition of the old can be seen from a very similar statement at the outset of the anonymous but influential *Rhetorica ad Herennium* (ca. 87-84 BC):

> The task of the public speaker is to discuss capably those matters which law and custom have fixed for the uses of citizenship, and to secure as far as possible the agreement of his hearers.[37] [1.2.2]

Its author, no less than Aristotle or Cicero, would have welcomed the assertions of their successors, almost two millennia later, that a theory of argumentation should study speakers' 'action on minds by means of discourse', those 'argumentative structures' that can only be analysed verbally, neither by laboratory experiments, nor with the reductive, a priori techniques of the sciences (*NR* 9-10). Argumentation, they write, 'aims at bringing about an action which is the result of a deliberate choice among several possibilities, without previous agreement on a criterion by which to evaluate the solutions' (*NR* 46). The speaker has to establish the criteria of choice by argument, and in order to bring about change he or she must act on the will as well as the mind, seeing both as interdependent. As Perelman and his collaborator argue, the

> ...traditional distinction between action on the mind and action on the will..., which presents the first kind of action as completely impersonal and timeless and the second as completely irrational, is based on an error and leads to an impasse. The error is that of conceiving man as made up of a set of completely independent faculties. The

impasse consists in removing all rational justification from action based on choice, and thus making the exercise of human freedom absurd. [*NR* 46]

Argumentation, by contrast, 'allows us to understand our decisions', involving as they do adherence freely given (ibid.).

The domain of argument, then, is the possibility of various reactions, varying decisions. To 'the detractors of rhetoric', such as Plato in the *Phaedrus*, for whom 'there was but a single truth in every matter' (*NR* 45), the open-mindedness of the rhetor can only be a sign of weakness or duplicity. In fact, they argue, a speaker's wanting to persuade us reveals his or her essential modesty, not claiming access to the Gospel truth, nor aspiring to an authority that would place their words 'beyond question' (*NR* 16). Rhetoric recognises that no statement is assured 'uncontroverted, universal agreement' (*NR* 67); and that all discourse confronts 'the necessity for interpretation' (*NR* 126), for the construction of models of understanding, notions which are 'malleable' rather than 'univocal'. For this reason 'the conclusions of an argument' are not binding in the way that a mathematical proof is, but can be questioned in the light of further experience (*NR* 132), or opposed arguments (*NR* 461). The process of persuasion, unlike the artificially isolated system in demonstrative proofs, '*assumes the existence of an intellectual contact*' between speaker and audience, 'an effective community of minds' (*NR* 14), and therefore involves 'a constant interaction among all its elements', speaker, audience, situation (*NR* 190). The determining element, these modern rhetoricians argue, is actually the audience, not the speaker – a point seen by Aristotle and Demosthenes[38] long ago – for it is 'the audience which has the major role in determining the quality of argument and the behavior of orators' (*NR* 24). Plato recognised this truth, and in his desire to damn rhetoric and rhetoricians limited its 'audience to an incompetent mob' (*NR* 25). But of course 'argumentations can be addressed to every kind of audience' (*NR* 7).

The centrality of the audience has immediate consequences for the speaker, and for his discourse. The prime quality required of him at all times is adaptability. Whatever change an argument intends to bring about is only possible 'if there is a continuous adaptation of the speaker to his audience' (*NR* 23). This implies that he knows them, appreciates their social functions and roles (*NR* 21), is aware that for them, as for himself, 'hopes and desires determine our beliefs' (*NR* 61) and that their 'intensity of adherence' depends on the force of his arguments (*NR* 461). It is to the forms of argumentation, then, their starting-point, elaboration, proper use, and range of effect that the two authors devote their main energy in a treatise running to over 500 pages. I shall not attempt to summarise it, but if I may follow my rule that every recovery of rhetoric implies a selection from the whole corpus, I would like to pick out one topic (one of many, in fact) where this new rhetoric links up with the old, since it is one to which I have devoted special attention, the functional nature of rhetorical figures.[39] Their principle, that 'argumentation is an action which always tends to modify a pre-existing state of affairs' (*NR* 54), leads them to see all the elements of discourse as a totality. Where a bad tradition used to see rhetoric as merely a 'technique' for presenting ready-made ideas, 'as an art of expressing thought', reducing its status to the merely formal, they object:

> We rebel against this conception, which is at the source of the degeneration, sterility, and verbalism of rhetoric as well as of the contempt generally felt for it. We refuse to separate the form of a discourse from its substance, to study stylistic structures and figures independently of the purpose they must achieve in the argumentation. [*NR* 142]

Their refusal to separate constituent parts does not, happily, lead to the monism of Benedetto Croce, who was finally unable to talk about any part other than 'the whole'.[40]

Their discussion of 'rhetorical figures and argumentation' (*NR* 167-71) starts with the seldom-quoted but essential observation of the Roman orator Latro, as recorded by Seneca (*Controversiae*, Book 1, Pref. para. 24), that 'the figures were not invented as ornaments'. Then they quote a traditional explanation of the function of the figure *hypotyposis* (*demonstratio*) as being to place the thing, or person described 'under our eyes', so making it more vivid, present to our mind. As they rightly say, this characteristic makes the figure 'a persuasive factor' in the speech, not ornamental but functional; and they utter a caveat which has been largely ignored by most modern historians of rhetoric:

> If the argumentative role of figures is disregarded, their study will soon seem a useless pastime, a search for strange names for rather farfetched and affected turns of speech. [*NR* 167]

(That is indeed prophetic of how the figures have been discussed.) Perelman and Olbrechts-Tyteca, by contrast, believe that our goal in studying the tropes and figures should be 'to show *how and in what respects the use of particular figures is explained by the requirements of argumentation*' (*NR* 168). For them, a figure is argumentative 'if it brings about a change of perspective', winning 'the adherence of the hearer to this argumentative form' (*NR* 169). Discussions of particular groups of figures punctuate the following 300 pages, and it would repay study to follow up their analyses of 'figures for increasing the feeling of presence' (*NR* 171-9, 504), those expressing tautology and contradiction (217-18), specific devices such as *hyperbole* and *litotes* (290-1), *antimetabole* (428-9), paradox and *oxymoron* (443-4), *hyperbaton* and other figures dislocating conventional order as a sign of disordered emotion (456-7), figures acting to express restraint and moderation (467), culminating in renunciation (487), and many others. The excellence of *The New Rhetoric* lies in its combination of a clearly articulated over-all argument with an abundance of illustrations from antiquity to the present day, and a never-failing sense of practicality.

The final element I should like to pick out links their rhetoric with that of Erasmus, or Aristotle, and sets it firmly against Plato. Whereas Plato could talk about the need to use both persuasion and compulsion in governing the state, or just compulsion alone,[41] Perelman and Olbrechts-Tyteca insist throughout that argumentation is 'a substitute for...physical force', compulsion or violence (*NR* 54-5). That is, the adherence of the audience is gained or lost according to the performance of the speaker, on an issue not yet settled, to a public willing to be persuaded, because 'listening to someone implies readiness to eventually accept his viewpoint' (*NR* 17). As against the exclusive categories of a Plato or a Descartes, they 'combat uncompromising and irreducible philosophical oppositions presented by all kinds of absolutism: dualisms of reason and imagination, of knowledge and opinion, of irrefutable self-evidence and deceptive will...' (*NR* 510), in effect all the weapons used by such philosophers to cripple their adversaries. As they say, most importantly

> ...the assertion that whatever is not objectively and indisputably valid belongs to the realm of the arbitrary and subjective creates an unbridgeable gulf between theoretical knowledge...and action,

the one being legitimised in terms of 'logico-experimental method', the other rejected as pure irrationality (*NR* 511). Such an excluding dichotomy would make all action irrational, free choice not exercised according to the Cartesian *more geometrico* purely arbitrary and pointless. So they conclude that

> Only the existence of an argumentation that is neither compelling nor arbitrary can give meaning to human freedom, a state in which a reasonable choice can be exercised (ibid.).

Argumentation, as they have defined it, 'provides reasons, but not compelling reasons', since it refuses to see our lives as based on absolute and categorical truths. What it does do, however, is to provide 'the justification of the possibility of a human community in the sphere of action...' (*NR* 514). Their *Nouvelle Rhétorique*, it seems to me, more than justifies its claim to have revived ancient rhetoric and expanded its scope (*NR* 6). They have not just recovered rhetoric; they have re-animated and enlarged it.

V

My final point has been implicit in discussing Erasmus, Perelman and Olbrechts-Tyteca, namely that the proper recovery of rhetoric must be true to some essential aspect of the art of well-speaking. It can be purely stylistic, analysing or cataloguing expressive devices; it can consider modes of argument; it can insist on the moral duties of persuasion, abjuring violence and compulsion. Our sixteenth-century Dutchman and our twentieth-century Belgians were true to rhetoric in all those ways. The current revival of interest has seen comparable rediscoveries and reapplications of rhetoric: as a crucial feature in double-ledger book-keeping, in economics, law, historiography, science, and much else.[42] I welcome this expanding scope, and will follow its development with great interest.

But the corollary of a concern with true rhetoric must be the readiness to identify false rhetoric, and to attack it. I am thinking of the unscrupulous use of persuasive techniques designed to manipulate the purchasing decisions of consumers, often invoking a debased form of analogy or metonymy to associate themselves with virile, thickly-moustached young men who smoke Marlboro, generously-breasted women who wear a special kind of perfume, eat a particular brand of banana, use amazingly soft toilet paper, or whose little children owe their health and strength to eating tins of white beans in a reddish sauce. These are perhaps harmless instances, yet advertising has more sinister effects, such as the large agencies hired at enormous sums to sell a political candidate or party in a supposedly free election. The 1988 US Presidental campaign was marked, or stained, by the one-minute TV 'spot' which suggested that the Democratic candidate was a liberal, against handweapons, in favour of drug addicts, abortion, and the lenient treatment of criminals. The new rhetoric of Mrs Thatcher's Conservative party specialised in euphemism. To 'privatise' a national resource, we now know, was to sell to individual members of the public what the public as a community already owned. To apply the insight of Perelman and Olbrechts-Tyteca, such discourse makes use of 'couples philosophiques', paired categories in which two terms are juxtaposed, Term II embodying true values, of which Term I is a superficial imitation or perversion (*NR* 416-18). In Thatcherian rhetoric we find the following oppositions:

$$\text{Term I} \quad \frac{\text{Public ownership}}{\text{Privatisation}} = \frac{\text{State}}{\text{Individual}} = \frac{\text{Repression}}{\text{Freedom}}$$

Typically, one side of the pair is privileged, the other exhausted of all value. What the Thatcherite coupling does is to devalue any sense of society as an organism, a unity collectively responsible for the well-being of its citizens. As everyone in Britain during the 1980s connected with such 'non-essential service industries' as education, nursing, or social welfare knew, all that mattered to the Thatcherite was the strong individual or corporate enterprise making a profit. Intellectual activity and its centres committed to disinterested long-term research, the universities, could easily be sacrificed in favour of quick returns. We need to counter the Thatcherian formula with a different pair:

$$\frac{\text{Self}}{\text{Other}} = \frac{\text{Greed}}{\text{Charity}}$$

One last and ever-relevant advantage gained by the study of rhetoric is that it makes one highly sensitive to the use that others make of language and persuasive devices. Its study, then, is of more than personal benefit, for a properly sustained rhetorical analysis of the corruption of words and images by political and other manipulators can only help the health of our community. For, as Ben Jonson put it:

Wheresoever manners and fashions are corrupted, Language is. It imitates the publicke riot.[43]

Notes

1. The best survey of classical rhetoric for English readers is that by George Kennedy in a series of books: *The Art of Persuasion in Greece* (London: Routledge and Kegan Paul, 1963); *Quintilian* (New York: Twayne, 1969); *The Art of Persuasion in the Roman World (300 BC-AD 300)* (Princeton: Princeton University Press, 1972); *Classical Rhetoric and Its Christian and Secular Tradition from Ancient to Modern Times* (Chapel Hill: University of North Carolina Press, 1980); *Greek Rhetoric under Christian Emperors* (Princeton: Princeton University Press, 1983).
   I have drawn on these and other sources to give a concise outline of the classical period in my book *In Defence of Rhetoric* (Oxford: Oxford University Press, 1988) pp. 1-82. Page-references incorporated into the text, abbreviated as *IDR*.

2. *Satire* 15, lines 110-13, in *Juvenal: the Sixteen Satires,* trans. Peter Green (Harmondsworth: Penguin, 1967).

3. See J.J. Murphy, *Rhetoric in the Middle Ages* (Berkeley and Los Angeles: University of California Press, 1974) pp. 76-80 (abbreviated as *RMA*); and Calvin B. Kendall, 'Bede's *Historia ecclesiastica*: The Rhetoric of Faith', in J.J. Murphy (ed.), *Medieval Eloquence, Studies in the Theory and Practice of Medieval Rhetoric* (Berkeley and Los Angeles: University of California Press, 1978) pp. 145-72, which includes a useful discussion of Isidore, pp. 147-9. Bede's treatise *De schematibus et tropis* has been translated by G.H. Tannenhaus in *Quarterly Journal of Speech* 48 (1962) pp. 237-53, reprinted in J.M. Miller, M.H. Prosser, and T.W. Benson (eds), *Readings in Medieval Rhetoric* (Bloomington: Indiana University Press, 1973) pp. 96-122.

4. Ovid, *Metamorphoses* 5.572-641; Virgil, *Aeneid* 3.694-6. Milton invokes the myth in *Lycidas* (85-8, 132-3), drawing on the tradition going back to Theocritus in which the fountain of Arethusa became a symbol for Greek pastoral poetry. See A.S.P. Woodhouse and Douglas Bush (eds), *A Variorum Commentary on the Poems of John Milton*, vol. 2: *The Minor English Poems*, 3 vols (London: Routledge and Kegan Paul, 1972, and New York: Columbia University Press, 1972) pp. 2.666-7 and 706-7 (from which my quotation comes).

5. J.J. Murphy, *RMA* (op. cit., in note 3) provides useful information and analyses of Aelius Donatus (pp. 32-5), Isidore (pp. 72-6), and Cassiodorus (pp. 64-7). On the nature of education in this period it is still worth consulting Theodore Haarhoff, *Schools of Gaul. A Study of Pagan and Christian Education in the Last Century of the Western Empire* (Oxford: Oxford University Press, 1920), especially pp. 157-74 on 'The Persistence of Rhetoric' in Christian education. A broader study is Pierre Riché, *Education et culture dans l'Occident barbare, 6ᵉ – 8ᵉ siècles* (Paris, 1962), trans. by J.J. Contreni as *Education and Culture in the Barbarian West* (Columbia: University of South Carolina Press, 1976).

6. See W.S. Howell, translator and editor, *The Rhetoric of Alcuin and Charlemagne* (Princeton: Princeton University Press, 1941); Luitpold Wallach, *Alcuin and Charlemagne* (Ithaca: Cornell University Press, 1954).

7. Murphy, *RMA* 80-7.

8. Ward, John, 'From Antiquity to the Renaissance: Glosses and Commentaries on Cicero's *Rhetorica*', in J.J. Murphy (ed.), (1978) pp. 25-67, at p. 54, n. 74, and 'Renaissance Commentators on Ciceronian Rhetoric', in J.J. Murphy (ed.), *Renaissance Eloquence. Studies in the Theory and Practice of Renaissance Rhetoric* (Berkeley and Los Angeles: University of California Press, 1983) pp. 126-73, at p. 127. An exemplary edition of one of these commentaries is Karin Margareta Fredborg (ed.), *The Latin Rhetorical Commentaries by Thierry of Chartres* (Toronto: Pontifical Institute of Medieval Studies, 1988).

9. On St Augustine see Murphy, *RMA* 47-64, and the translation of *On Christian Doctrine* by D.W. Robertson, Jr, (Indianapolis, 1958).

10. For the history of medieval preaching the best starting point is Murphy, *RMA* 269-355; on Augustine's influence, pp. 285-90, 328-9, and *passim*.

11. See R.R. Bolgar, *The Classical Heritage and Its Beneficiaries. From the Carolingian Age to the End of the Renaissance* (Cambridge: Cambridge University Press, 1954; New York, 1964) pp. 69-70, 74-7. This also includes an excellent account of education in the Carolingian age (pp. 91-129). See also Bolgar's contribution, 'The Teaching of Rhetoric in the Middle Ages', in Brian Vickers (ed.), *Rhetoric Revalued* (Binghamton: Centre for Medieval and Early Renaissance Studies, 1982) pp. 79-86. On Byzantium a useful starting point is John Monfasani, 'The Byzantine Rhetorical Tradition and the Renaissance', in J.J. Murphy, *Renaissance Eloquence* (cit. in n. 8) pp. 174-87; with admirable documentation.

12. On Arabic rhetoric see S.A. Bonebakker, *Materials for the History of Arabic Rhetoric* (Naples: Istituto Orientali Napoli, 1975) and other literature cited in Vickers, *IDR* 473, n. 44.

13. I have argued this interpretation in detail in *IDR* 214-53.

14. See Murphy, *RMA* 135-93 (*ars poetriae*), 194-268 (*ars dictaminis*) and 269-355 (*ars praedicandi*). A fourth *ars*, as yet sparsely documented, is the *ars aregandi*, a form of public speaking which seems to have been restricted to a few Italian cities. See P.O. Kristeller, *Renaissance Thought and Its Sources*, M. Mooney (ed.) (New York: Columbia University Press, 1979) pp. 237-8, 320-1.

15. Letter to Jacopo Pizzinghe, in J.B. Ross and M.M. McLaughlin, translator and editor, *The Portable Renaissance Reader* (New York, 1953; Harmondsworth: Penguin, 1977) pp. 124-5.

16. Ibid., pp. 128-30.

17. The classic study of the recovery of ancient texts is Remigio Sabbadini, *Le scoperte dei codici latini e greci ne'secoli XIV e XV*, 2 vols (Florence, 1905-14; repr. Florence, 1967). An admirable study of the reintegration of rhetorical tradition is John Monfasani, 'Humanism and Rhetoric', in A. Rabil, Jr (ed.) *Renaissance Humanism: Foundations, Forms and Legacy*, 3 vols (Philadelphia: University of Pennsylvania Press, 1988) vol. 3, pp. 171- 270.

18. Bolgar (1954) op. cit., p. 250.

19. See *Le familiari*, V. Rossi and V. Bosco, (eds) 4 vols (Florence, 1933-42). I quote from the excellent translation by Aldo S. Bernardo (lacking, alas, any documentation), *Letters on Familiar Matters*, 3 vols (vol. 1: Albany, 1975; vols 2 and 3:

Baltimore, 1982 and 1985). References (included in the text) are to the book and epistle number, followed by the volume and page number of the translation, as (I.9; 1.47-50).

20. Hoskins, J., *Directions for Speech and Style* (ca. 1599), Hoyt H. Hudson (ed.) (Princeton: Princeton University Press, 1935) p. 2.

21. See index *s.v.* 'movere' 500 in B. Vickers *IDR* (1988).

22. See, for example, T.M. Greene, *The Light in Troy. Imitation and Discovery in Renaissance Poetry* (New Haven: Yale University Press, 1982).

23. As does J.E. Seigel, *Rhetoric and Philosophy in Renaissance Humanism* (Princeton: Princeton University Press, 1968) pp. 52ff.

24. There is no modern edition of the Latin text (a shameful reproach to the scholars involved for so many years in the 'Edizione Nazionale' of Petrarch). My quotations are from the lively translation by Thomas Twyne, *Phisicke against Fortune, as well prosperous, as adverse, conteyned in two Books* (London, 1579); page-references incorporated into the text. As the work is paginated by folios, 'a' and 'b' designate the left and right hand pages, respectively. On Petrarch's moral philosophy see Charles Trinkaus, *The Poet as Philosopher: Petrarch and the Formation of Renaissance Consciousness* (New Haven: Yale University Press, 1979), and Nicholas Mann, *Petrarch* (Oxford: Oxford University Press, 1984), in the 'Past Masters' series. See now the full translation by Conrad H. Rawski, *Petrarch's Remedies for Fortune Fair and Foul*, 5 vols (Bloomington: Indiana University Press, 1991).

25. *De oratore*, III.xvi.60-1: Socrates attacked the Sophists, who taught 'the liberal sciences' under the name of *philosophia*, and 'separated the science of wise thinking from that of elegant speaking, though in reality they are closely linked together.... This is the source from which has sprung the undoubtedly absurd and unprofitable and reprehensible severance between the tongue and the brain...'; trans. H. Rackham, Loeb edition (London, 1942).

26. See W.H. Woodward, *Vittorino da Feltre and other Humanist Educators* (Cambridge, 1912); R.R. Bolgar (ed.) (1954) op. cit.; E. Garin, *L'educazione in Europa 1400-1600. Problemi e programmi* (Bari: Laterza, 1957). The recent book by Anthony Grafton and Lisa Jardine, *From Humanism to the Humanities: Education and the Liberal Arts in Fifteenth- and Sixteenth-Century Europe* (London: Duckworth, 1986), challenges some features of this tradition, but with mixed success. On Erasmus' debts to Vittorino and other Italian educationalists see *Collected Works of Erasmus* vol. 25, xxix-xxxi (publication details in note 28).

27. See the admirable study, with generous translations, by Margaret Mann Phillips, *The 'Adages' of Erasmus* (Cambridge: Cambridge University Press, 1964).

28. Two great editions of Erasmus are under way at the present time, the *Opera omnia Desiderii Erasmi Roterodami* (Amsterdam, 1969-) and the *Collected Works of Erasmus*, in English translation (Toronto, 1974-). I have mostly used the latter, a mine of information and enlightened commentary.

29. The fullest study so far (nearly 1 200 pages, in effect) is Jacques Chomarat, *Grammaire et Rhétorique chez Erasme*, 2 vols (Paris: Les Belles Lettres, 1981); page-references incorporated into the text, abbreviated as *GRE*. See the index for copious documentation of Erasmus' debt to classical rhetoric.

30. See Vickers, *IDR* 1-3, 295-305, for the common argument that rhetorical figures and tropes are fundamental to everyday speech.

31. See ibid., pp. 242-3.

32. *La Nouvelle rhétorique: Traité de l'argumentation* (Paris, 1958; 3rd edn, Brussels, 1970); English trans. J. Wilkinson and P. Weaver, *The New Rhetoric. A Treatise on Argumentation* (Notre Dame: University of Notre Dame Press, 1969); page-references incorporated into the text, abbreviated as *NR*. A brief digest of their work was provided by Perelman in his *L'Empire Rhétorique: Rhétorique et Argumentation* (Paris, 1977), which I reviewed in *Quarterly Journal of Speech* 65 (1979) pp. 334-5.

33. See B. Vickers, *IDR* 6-8, 9-13, 214-93, 340-479.

34. See C. Perelman, *The New Rhetoric and the Humanities. Essays on Rhetoric and Its Applications* (Dordrecht: Reidel, 1979) p. 1, and J. Golden and J. Pilotta, *Practical Reasoning in Human Nature* (Dordrecht: Reidel, 1986) pp. 2-3.

35. On the work of Perelman and his collaborator see Sonja K. Foss, *et al.* (eds), *Contemporary Perspectives on Rhetoric* (Prospect Heights, IL: Waveland, 1985) pp. 28ff, limited to literature in English only. For the continental reception see the special number of *Revue Internationale de Philosophie* vol. 33, nos 127-8 (1979): 'La Nouvelle Rhétorique. The New Rhetoric. Essais en hommage à Chaïm Perelman', including a bibliography of his works, pp. 325-42; Michel Meyer (ed.), *De la Métaphysique à la Rhétorique. Essais à la mémoire de Chaïm Perelman avec un indit sur la logique* (Brussels: University of Brussels Press, 1986); Folker Siegert, 'Rhetorik und Philosophie in der *Neuen Rhetorik* Chaïm Perelmans', in H. Schanze and J. Kopperschmidt (eds), *Rhetorik und Philosophie* (Munich, 1989) pp. 217-29.

36. See G. Bateson, *Steps to an Ecology of Mind* (London: Paladin, 1973) pp. 261-2, 342-4, and A. Wilden, *System and Structure. Essays in Communication and Exchange* (London: Tavistock, 1972) pp. 24, 155-7, 161-3.

37. *Ad Herennium*, trans. H. Caplan, Loeb Library (London, 1954) p. 5.

38. Aristotle, *Rhetoric*, I.3: 1358a 36-1358b 6. Cf. Demosthenes, *On Organization*, para. 36, urging the Athenians to scrutinise the demagogues more closely: 'Your orators never make you either bad men or good, but you make them whichever you choose; for it is not you that aim at what they wish for, but they who aim at whatever they think you desire' (cit. *NR* 24).

39. See B. Vickers, *IDR* ch. 6, pp. 294-339.

40. Ibid., p. 209.

41. Ibid., pp. 86-7, 138-47.

42. See, for example, J.A. Aho, 'Rhetoric and the Invention of Double Entry Bookkeeping' *Rhetorica* 3 (1985) pp. 21-44 and D.N. McCloskey, *The Rhetoric of Economics* (Madison: University of Wisconsin Press, 1985), and a wide-ranging interdisciplinary collection by twenty-two scholars, J.J. Nelson, A. Megill, and D.N. McCloskey (eds), *The Rhetoric of the Human Sciences: Language and Argument in Scholarship and Public Affairs* (Madison: University of Wisconsin Press, 1987).

43. From *Discoveries,* in Ben Jonson, *Works*, E. Herford and P. Simpson (eds), 11 vols (Oxford, 1925-52) vol. 8, p. 593.

2

Commonplace-Rhetoric and Thought-Patterns in Early Modern Culture

Ann Moss (University of Durham)

The logocentric cultural models of Early Modern Europe, constituted to a large extent by written and spoken commentary on canonical texts faithfully reproduced and multiplied by typographic process, generated varieties of discourse with a common dynamic: the manipulation of words in order to persuade; or, to translate that into the terminology of the time, rhetoric. As the zeal of fifteenth-century Italian humanists was carried through Northern Europe in the first 30 or 40 years of the sixteenth century, the curricula of all schools and universities were reformed so as to give to the arts of verbal expression a prestige as foreign to the purposes of late medieval logic and theology as it is now to the concerns of modern science or economic enterprise.[1] But the humanist philologists' enthusiasm for words not only produced the linguistic expertise from which great literature was born in the sixteenth and seventeenth centuries. It also produced an élite of readers imprinted with certain stereotyped approaches to inquiry in all intellectual disciplines, educated to admire verbal dexterity and display, and also sharpened by their own practice in rhetorical composition to recognise rhetoric at work, in speech and writing, for good or ill.

The recognition and conscious manipulation of rhetorical devices is a mark of education. In the sixteenth century all Western Europe was obsessed with the processes of education. If we take the Early Modern period as a whole, there probably never was an era, apart from some moments in antiquity, in which skills in critical reading and in composition were given so high a value at such an early and formative stage of the school-curriculum; nor was there one in which there was so general an agreement about what those skills were and how they could best be taught. One of the main reasons why this consensus was secured was that, for the greater part of the period in question, every schoolboy in Western Europe had one major thing in common: the language of his education was Latin. Educated language was a foreign language for everyone. The first thing that had to be learnt by every Western

European schoolboy was Latin, and this meant that, in the minds of theorists and practitioners alike, language was necessarily and emphatically prior to knowledge.[2] Competence in language was taught through three disciplines: grammar, rhetoric and dialectic. Grammar described and inculcated the correct use of Latin language, exemplified by the usage of a canonical list of 'good authors', representative of what was considered to be the best Latinity, i.e., that in use in the written language of a particular historical period of antiquity. The discipline of grammar also included the exposition of the (mainly literary) texts in which this ideal state of the language was to be found. However, in the Early Modern classroom, reading without production was always considered an incomplete process. One learnt to read in order to speak and to write. Linguistic performance was the province of rhetoric and dialectic. Rhetoric dealt in ways of finding, manipulating and expressing arguments in order to induce belief in the probability or plausibility of propositions advanced; dialectic dealt in logically tenable relationships which ensure conviction. Rhetoric was taught by the analysis and genesis of texts. These were not separate, but complementary procedures, or, as Melanchthon, the schoolmaster of Germany says, introducing his Rhetoric:

> We shall put rhetoric to this purpose, namely to help the young in their reading of good authors, who cannot be understood except by this method.... Then, having understood those authors, they will find no difficulty in imitating them.... For no-one can become a successful author without imitating, yet no imitation is feasible without knowledge of the necessary precepts of rhetoric.[3]

In practice, grammar, rhetoric and dialectic overlapped. Firstly, all three arts of language put the analysis of a particular canon of Latin literary texts at the core of the curriculum, and performance in all three areas was taught by exercises in close imitation of selected passages of those texts. Between rhetoric and grammar the particular area of overlap was the 'improper' use of language: that is to say figurative language (tropes, figures of thought and figures of diction), denoted by the grammarian and manipulated by the rhetorician for the purposes of amplification, ornamentation and expressivity proper to his discipline. The area of overlap between rhetoric and dialectic was place-theory, a method of generating discourse by putting one's initial theme through a recognised series of questions ('places' or 'tropics'): how? when? why? to what effect? and so on. The development of any argument or the exposition of any subject could be read (or written) as an ordered sequence of answers to implied questions about its origins, antecedents, purpose, attendant circumstances and so on.[4]

So, the main thrust of rhetoric was the generation of cogent discourse, in which it overlapped with dialectic; and the proliferation of figures of speech, in which it overlapped with grammar. What, then, was specific to rhetoric? Its field was the probable, the plausible, the truth-like; its aim, not certainty beyond rational doubt, but the agreement of the listener or reader to believe in the case presented. In its purest form, removed from the practicalities of council-chamber and court-room, rhetoric could be seen as the maker of credible fictions. Now, according to another cultural model inherited from antiquity, fiction-making was also considered to be the proper office of the poet. However, poetic composition was not at this period thought to be radically different from prose rhetoric, only different in degree, in that poetry operates under stricter metrical constraints and is freer to explore the resources of language in terms of vocabulary and figures. Rhetoric as actually practised in the Early Modern period, be it for serious teaching purposes, as in sermons or for pleasure, as in fiction-making (and that, as it happens, means primarily poetry), was almost always of a specific kind, defined in rhetorical theory as epideictic or demonstrative rhetoric. This kind of rhetoric was not used to promote policies or argue judicial cases, but to manoeuvre language in such a way as to persuade the reader to a belief, to an emotional response, and to a moral judgement involving praise or blame. In other words, rhetorically articulated language, language which persuades to belief or to an emotional reaction, was also deemed to shape a concommitant moral response. Epideictic rhetoric in all its fields of application was as much an exercise in moral judgement as in words.

Here we are moving away from prescriptions for writing towards the question which dominated most Renaissance attempts at theory: what is the relationship between fictive writing (or, more generally, rhetoric itself) and truth? Words beautifully woven may be a deceptive lure, a travesty of the truth, an enticement to false judgement and immoral action: can language itself guarantee its own truth? Contemporary rhetorical theorists, in their pursuit of strategies for persuasive argument and verbal contortions for emotional effect, usually side-step any debate about the truth-value of the fictions rhetoric has it in its power to create. But rhetoric, with its stress on the reader as reproducer of texts, did in fact coexist, often uneasily, during the greater part of the sixteenth century with an equally forceful, non-rhetorical concept of the reader as interpreter of texts. Here attention turns directly to the referential aspect of language.

The reader as interpreter, rather than potential producer, regarded the text as a code to be deciphered. There were keys to decipherment, recognised ways of reading texts, which, for example, would allow any mythological fiction to be a veiled account either of historical events or of the behaviour of natural phenomena, like elements and planets, or a demonstration of moral truisms or of religious truth. This interpretative schema had been elaborated in its most complex form in the fourteenth century, but it was reactivated in the Renaissance by the excitement of rediscovered Platonic texts in which fables were claimed to be divinely inspired allegories of arcane truths.[5] Allegorical interpretation, as such schemata were known, works by unpicking and reconstituting texts. It is reader-centred and very little concerned with the author and his intentions. The reader-interpreter works from similitudes. He searches his text for words and references to objects and events which have a likeness to words, objects and events in other types of discourse – historical, scientific, moral, and religious. He then makes appropriate substitutions for both signifiers and things signified. Thus he demonstrates his ingenuity as a reader of fiction by coming up with a coherent translation of his text into another code, whose reference is to the 'truth', whereas the original text, in a naive reading, referred only to a fiction, a non-truth. The story of Acteon, for example, as Ovid tells it in Book III of the *Metamorphoses* (lines 138-252), recounts how a hunter who met the virgin goddess Diana bathing naked in a wood, was turned by her into a stag, and, in this guise, was then hunted by his servants and killed by his own dogs. This may usefully be read, in the religious code, as an account of Christ, who, surveying the wood of this world and there encountering the Blessed Virgin clean-washed in the fountain of purity, changed his nature (from God to man), and was in his new form unrecognised and unknown by his own people and hounded to death by his own dogs (the Jews). This is merely a possible reading. The number of possible readings was theoretically open-ended. In the medieval tradition readings were judged as to whether they were more or less ingenious, more or less profitable equations to a known truth, not as right or wrong; in the Renaissance, under the influence of standards set by historical and philological criticism, adequacy of inter-pretation became more of an issue. But the reference of all such reading is always to a truth extrinsic to the text itself. In fact, this sort of reading is not tied to any specific text. It can operate as well with a paraphrase as with the original text. Even non-verbal signifiers may be read in this way: the Book of Nature and all its phenomena are signs, to be interpreted by readers who can perceive similitudes. Some historians have claimed that the whole sixteenth-century *episteme* was con-stituted in this way.[6] However, the reality is more complex. There was also rhetoric, at least as potent a creator of mind-sets as allegorical interpretation and imprinted far more forcibly on the intellects (and bottoms) of Early Modern schoolboys than interpretative speculations. The reading required by rhetoric is virtually incom-patible with allegorical interpretation. Rhetoric is concerned with combinations of words which acquire meaning and expressivity from their interrelations with each other within a particular spoken or written passage. Therefore, rhetorical analysis comments on, but does not change the text. It is not angled towards re-reading, but towards response and reproduction; and in rhetoric, symptomatically, similitude and allegory are but two out of a great number of figures of speech and are not privi-leged as keys to understanding. Melanchthon, for example, in his *Rhetoric* defines allegory as a mutilated enthymeme (a simile expressed eliptically, with referent occluded), and he digresses from his main theme precisely to take issue with the principles and procedures of allegorical interpretation indiscriminately applied:

> If figurative expressions are encountered in a text, it is not to open the way to a plurality of senses, but, as in ordinary language, to express a single, specific meaning which fits in with the rest of the text.[7]

Sixteenth-century literary texts in particular are often marked (and excitingly so) by tensions between rhetorical performance on the one hand and the retention of potential for allegorical interpretation on the other. Renaissance rhetoric encourages amplification, exuberance, and a sense that meaning is controlled by verbal colloca-tion; allegorical interpretation asserts a cognitive, extrinsically referential function for narrated fictions.[8] However, by the beginning of the seventeenth century alle-gorical interpretation, though still surviving and nurtured by plenty of new works, survives by and large as a curiosity on the margins of the intellectual mainstream, a fascinating and very pretty backwater. An irreversible paradigm-shift had been put into operation by other forces activated by other currents of humanist scholarship: historical criticism, which, by placing texts in a historical context, made the essentially unhistorical claims of allegorical interpretation untenable; and the domination of theory by Aristotle's *Poetics*, for which the 'truth' of fiction was constituted in terms of 'universal truths', actions and words conceived as probable and necessary in a given situation rather than as material for translation into other discourse. Meanwhile, from the beginning of the sixteenth century, school-rhetoric had established a method of reading which was to produce a way of thinking about the nature of things as well as procedures for manipulating words.

In every schoolroom in the sixteenth century, and in most of the seventeenth, pupils were instructed to equip themselves with a blank notebook divided into headed sections. The purpose of keeping these notebooks, called 'commonplace' books, was to extrapolate short passages from books studied in class or at home and to enter them under appropriate headings in the notebook. The headings would cover a multitude of topics, though the more usual prescriptions were for topics with some sort of moral import. These headings were the 'places' into which collected quotations sharing a 'common' theme were stored for use. The arrangement of the headings, or places, varied considerably. Most often they came in alphabetical order, at other times in a more or less complicated scheme of related subjects and sub-divisions of subjects, or arranged in patterns of similars and opposites, not because similitude itself was significant, but simply for the sake of easy memorising. The advice given by Erasmus is typical:

> Prepare for yourself a sufficient number of headings and arrange them as you please, subdivide them into the appropriate sections, and under each section add your commonplace and maxims; and then whatever you come across in any author, particularly if it is rather striking, you will be able to note down immediately in the proper place, be it an anecdote or a fable or an illustrative example or a strange incident or a maxim or a witty remark or a remark notable for some other quality or a proverb or a metaphor or a simile. This has the double advantage of fixing what you have read more firmly in your mind, and getting you into the habit of using the riches supplied by your reading.[9]

Whatever the arrangement, the purpose of commonplace books was the same: they were a way of sifting and categorising the matter of texts studied, and they were an information retrieval system. As we have seen, analysis and genesis were inseparable in rhetoric, and the commonplace book was the point of juncture between them. The pupil was expected to draw on the matter stored in his commonplace book in order to produce his own compositions. And it was a treasure-house not only of matter, but of words, for the commonplace book was a fine array of quotations, an anthology of aphorisms, examples, parallels, synonyms, epithets, and figures of all sorts, to be inserted into one's own work in order to dilate and vary it and make it 'a magnificent and impressive thing, surging along like a golden river, with thoughts and words pouring out in rich abundance'.[10] The writers privileged for entry into the commonplace book were, of course, by and large the same canon as was studied in the rhetoric class. The collected quotations were employed in an essentially rhetorical way, with stress laid on using language rather than on reference. Yet, the commonplace book does perhaps make rhetoric's most cogent claim to be considered an adequate representation of the true nature of things. Some, if not all proponents of commonplace books contended that the places, or heads, into which the books were divided were not at all arbitrary or conventional, but did indeed represent the 'forms and rules of things deep-seated in nature'.[11] So, the headings of the commonplace book – fortune, wealth, honour, life, death, virtue, prudence, justice, generosity, temperance, and all their subdivisions – could be held to reflect certain norms in nature. At the same time, promoters of commonplace books were adamant that the quotations extrapolated and listed together in groups under these heads were to be as diverse as possible, and in their very diversity they were again taken to be an apt representation of nature, for 'nature above all delights in variety; in all this huge concourse of things she has left nothing anywhere unpainted by her wonderful technique of variety'.[12] Here the emphasis is put on the ramifying diversity and multiplicity of nature, which it is rhetoric's peculiar virtue to reproduce by the art of verbal technique. This is a very different concept of nature's plurality from the criss-cross patternings of similitudes and analogies presupposed by the model of nature as a Book of Signs. Yet it is precisely this commonplace-book view of nature, as both normative and different (différant), which informs the final state of thinking of the most influential writers of Early Modern Europe. In the last chapter of Montaigne's *Essais*, all things are said to hold together by some degree of similitude, but no one thing is an exact likeness of another: 'La ressemblance ne faict pas tant un que la difference faict autre.'[13]

The commonplace-book method permeated every intellectual discipline in Western Europe. Not only did the educated person keep one for his private use, but there were countless printed versions functioning as aids to memory and composition, and books in every scholastic discipline were indexed by topics, or 'digested into commonplaces', as the publicity jargon of the day had it. There were speciality commonplace books, such as collections of epithets, adages, and aphorisms. Law and medicine had their commonplace books. Whole encyclopaedias were modelled on commonplace-book taxonomy. More important still, the commonplace-book method of extrapolation under heads was recommended by Erasmus, among others, as the paradigm for reading Scripture. In this way, difficult passages on similar topics could be juxtaposed and could illuminate each other, reinforcing the principle that Scripture is always the authority on Scripture.[14] Here the commonplace book takes us into the arena of religious controversy, where it undoubtedly helped to establish the centrality of the text, the Word, in Reformist theology, and to place the Word within the competence of the layman educated in rhetoric, not theology. From 1521, under the influence of Melanchthon, the method of the *Loci communes*, the method of drawing up heads, or articles of religion, derived from and articulated in quotations from Scripture, was established as the new dogmatics of the new religion; for, the doctrine of the Church, as Melanchthon put it, 'is not derived from demonstrations, but from sayings'.[15] This became the ground on which debates with the Catholics were conducted. As Montaigne was to say about the religious troubles of his time, again in *De l'Expérience*: 'Notre contestation est verbale'.

The wider history of the influence of commonplace-book method has yet to be written. However, although its origins lay in classroom rhetoric, its nearest affiliation was to literature, from which the rhetoric manuals took their examples of good practice. For teachers and pupils in the Early Modern classroom, the rhetorical analysis of pre-existing texts led as a matter of course to the generation of new ones. Commonplace books made the assumption that the reader is a potential writer, and they proposed themselves as mediators between the old texts they harvested and the new ones they held in germ. The headings under which excerpts were classified (and which tended to become standardised in printed commonplace books in the later sixteenth century) were overwhelmingly moral in scope. This moral cast was partly imposed by editors of printed versions seeking to underscore the moral content of their largely pagan material in a sales bid to schools (which always advertised the moral training they gave to their pupils). It was partly a by-product of the equation of literature with epideictic rhetoric, whose function, as we have already noted, was to praise and blame. It was also partly a reflection of thought-patterns actually discernible in ancient literature and consciously adopted. But the effect of thinking about texts in this way of adjusting them to such headings, is a uniform belief that there is a universe of (primarily moral) ideas proper to literature, to which all literary writing can and should refer, and to which Greek and, more especially, Latin writing has given privileged and paradigmatic expression. Yet, at the same time as the subjects of literature seem invariable, the production of language is seen as variety itself, with open-ended lists of juxtaposed quotations stimulating the pursuit of abundance, versatility and inventiveness. Variation on a theme or 'commonplace' is the hallmark of Renaissance poetry, as of much literary prose, and so also is the manipulation of allusions to ancient texts, juxtaposed with each other and with the new text to produce new meanings.

Rhetoric promoted the imitation of ancient authors as the best way of writing, whether in Latin or in the vernacular; the habit of memorising and juxtaposing quotations produced the intertextuality characteristic of most Renaissance poetry. For, if Renaissance literature, like the commonplace book, does in a remote sense imitate nature, it is even more obviously a self-referring universe, juxtaposing poem with poem and setting up an interplay of literary allusions and an array of linguistic reminiscences and significant differences. Literary fiction becomes above all self-referential, and thereby states a claim to autonomy. It is not obliged to be a sign for something outside itself. A poem signifies by reference to other poems, is true by virtue of its relationship to literary commonplaces and literary models, poetic because it takes its material from a repertory of literary fictions and employs distinctive and recognised idioms of speech, and has entirely within its own linguistic resources the power to produce aesthetic ecstasy. But literature becomes a fully signifying universe in this sense, only if writer and reader share a common memory bank. What most theorists looked for in the imitating poet was the dexterity with which tracer-marks of other poems were left within the text so as to alert and delight the reader with the shock of recognition. And it was precisely by being made to memorise the contents of their commonplace books, that pupils were trained in memory, which was, in any case, one of the five constituent parts of the art of rhetoric formulated by ancient authors.

The commonplace-book mentality had at least two major effects on literature. One was that it kept the notion of literature as a code, though a very different sort of code from the one unlocked by allegorical interpretation. This 'rhetorical' code was a code of references and allusions understood only by an educated élite. The critical reader was a knowledgeable reader, but, more pertinently still, a reader who could make informed comparisons between texts. Indeed the commonplace-book may be said to have invented the critical reader, in a modern sense. It was by bringing together analogous excerpts from different poets under common heads that Julius Caesar Scaliger, in the most influential theory of poetry produced in the Early Modern period (his *Poetice* of 1561), provided the apparatus for detailed critical comparisons in which we recognise an activity we would call literary criticism.

The second major effect of the commonplace-book formula for writing was that, like the theory of literary imitation generally, it made new writing intensely problematic. It might seem at first sight that all theories of literary production based on the imitation of model authors must be inhibiting. Yet, paradoxically, they lead to a heightened self-consciousness in the new writer, the unique individual, who at this period, almost always describes himself in the commonplace image of a honey-producing bee roaming through anthologies culled from ancient authors.[16] The choice of an author to imitate involves an analysis of differences in outlook and style; the imitation of a single author prompts self-promoting emulation; the combining of passages from different authors entails the assertion of editorial decision; specificities of the vernacular language and of the personal and historical moment are realised more acutely in the attempt to recover and revivify a dead culture and an artificially-preserved language. The French poet, Pierre de Ronsard, one of the most imitative and most self-conscious of Renaissance poets, saw the commonplace-book as a prototype for a solution to the imitator's 'anxiety of influence', enabling him to run through his books collecting, sorting, selecting all the finest materials to paint a picture in a hundred colours, of which he alone was master. It was precisely his arrangement of intertextual references which enabled him to dominate them and speak with his own voice.[17] Slightly later, we have the *Essais* of Montaigne, which, with their accretions of Latin quotations inserted into the French text, superficially resemble a commonplace-book. Here we come to a literary enterprise rooted in the imitation of classical antiquity, but self-referring, self-reflexive in every sense of the word. By essaying/assaying himself against his quotations, it is himself that Montaigne tries out and tests. He invents the self as subject; discovers personal memory as well as cultural memory; and creates a reader who, if he can keep up with Montaigne's game of hide-and-seek-me round his quotations, will recognise both commonplaces and private places in the *Essais*.[18]

In the seventeenth century, commonplace-books remain an important factor in the European mentality. Detractors there were in plenty, but their attacks bear witness to the entrenched position of the commonplace-book in the schools where they had learnt the rudiments of eloquence. However, the very fact of the extraordinary success and lengthy survival of commonplace-books in the education system raises questions which contemporaries did not directly ask, but which need answering. Is their popularity within an education system serving a power élite (and serving it very ably) to be explained by the fact that they could be made to inhibit new thought? This was, perhaps, because they implied that every new text, every new discovery had to find a place in the corpus of received wisdom, so that, in effect, they contained the consensus, and even possibly connived with the *doxae* of the dominant political and social power structure. Certainly in the schools of the Jesuits, who were the most influential educationalists in the seventeenth century, commonplace-books were used as a way of controlling reading by selection and censorship. Yet, though commonplace-books can be used to imprint norms, it is of the very nature of the commonplace-book that the quotations it gathers tend to pull away from the norms to which they are attached. The very function of the 'places' as ever expanding receptacles of multiple quotations is to add, not to foreclose, perhaps to invite, self-contradictions and the scepticism that goes with them. This was certainly what happened with Montaigne. And by the turn of the century there does seem to have been a marked increase in collections of political aphorisms reflecting very diverse opinions and proposed in a positive spirit as issues for open debate. Francis Bacon had a characteristically ambivalent attitude to the commonplace-book (as to rhetoric in general). He recognised that the commonplace book could be an instrument of discovery, unlike other forms of rhetorical analysis, which must always remain parasitic on pre-existing texts and, at best, generate strategies for insinuating truths already known:

The delivery of knowledge in distinct and disjointed aphorisms doth leave the wit of man more free to turn and toss, and to make use of that which is so delivered to more several purposes and applications.[19]

As far as rhetoric itself is concerned, both prose and verse composition continue for some time to show the effects of the commonplace-book, whether it be in the concatenation of the aphorisms in which so many commonplace-books specialised or in the pursuit of linguistic connections more admired for their virtuosity than for their referentiality. Certainly the publishing houses continued a brisk trade in commonplace-books well into the seventeenth century and even beyond. But, just as certainly, taste was changing. 'Taste' is the right word, and it is not a word typical of the sixteenth century. But in the seventeenth century, good taste was the mark of the educated man, now grown into the gentleman or 'honnête homme', and gentlemen of good taste fastidiously eschew pedantry and ostentation (which were certainly social solecisms of which the commonplace-book was guilty). Other factors also tended to ensure that the commonplace-book was kept well out of sight, if not out of mind. Montaigne had engaged in self-exploration through a continual reflecting and refracting of himself in the Latin quotations which he incorporated in his essays; and Montaigne had explored the potential of his vernacular by pitting it against what he claimed to be the more flexible and more vigorous Latin language of his authors. In the later seventeenth century, and especially in France, representation of the self aimed at clarity and distinction; authors claimed implicitly to be masters of their own discourse; unities replaced variety; the vernacular was no longer in *statu pupillari*; and the proof of authorial control and pure vernacular style was that, whatever diverse foreign ingredients went into the confection of a text, they should be undetectable to readers of taste. As for the commonplace-book's more ambitious claim, that it was rhetoric's Book of Nature, that book was being written now in quite another language, the language of mathematics. Even so, commonplaces were still there and still open to receive new matter when Giambattista Vico came to rewrite rhetoric as *New Science*.[20]

Notes

1. For the most up-to-date (and critical) account of humanist schooling, see A. Grafton and L. Jardine, *From Humanism to the Humanities. Education and the Liberal Arts in Fifteenth- and Sixteenth-century Europe* (London: Duckworth, 1986).

2. The writings of Erasmus on education are the best key to understanding the Renaissance theory of education, for example, *De Ratione studii ac legendi interpretandique auctores* (1512): 'In principle, knowledge as a whole seems to be of two kinds, of things and of words [a sophisticated, philosophical distinction, derived from Plato and Aristotle, imported into rhetorical theory by Quintilian and others, and a commonplace in the Renaissance]. Knowledge of words comes earlier.... But some, the uninitiated, while they hurry on to learn about things, neglect a concern for language and, striving after a false economy, incur a very heavy loss. For since things are learnt only by the sounds we attach to them, a person who is not skilled in the force of language is, of necessity, short-sighted, deluded, and unbalanced in his judgement of things as well' (*On the Method of Study*, trans. B. McGregor, *Collected Works of Erasmus*, XXIV [Toronto, Buffalo and London: University of Toronto Press, 1978] p. 666).

3. *Elementorum rhetorices libri duo* (first published 1531), in *Philippi Melanthonis Opera*, C.G. Bretschneider (ed.), *Corpus Reformatorum* XIII (Halle, 1846) col. 418.

4. Sources for all these ideas are to be found in the ancient authorities from whom the humanist educators derived their precepts, primarily in Aristotle, Cicero and Quintilian. They were extrapolated, codified, simplified and disseminated in hundreds of pedagogic manuals. The most characteristic twist which humanist education gave to the tradition was its move away from the more philosophical issues of logic and its concentration on dialectic, narrowed down so as to become, in effect, little more than the more rigorous branch of the rhetorical analysis of the cogency of extended discourse.

5. The most general histories of allegorical interpretation as practised in the Renaissance are: J. Seznec, *The Survival of the Pagan Gods. The Mythological Tradition and its Place in Renaissance Humanism and Art*, trans. B.F. Sessions (New York: Pantheon, 1953); D.C. Allen, *Mysteriously Meant. The Rediscovery of Pagan Symbolism and Allegorical Interpretation in the Renaissance* (Baltimore:

John Hopkins University Press, 1970); and, most recent, L. Barkan, *The Gods made Flesh. Metamorphosis and the Pursuit of Paganism* (New Haven and London: Yale University Press, 1986).

6. Notably M. Foucault, in his chapter on the Renaissance in *Les Mots et les choses* (Paris: Gallimard, 1966).

7. *Elementa rhetorices*, ed. cit., col. 468. Melanchthon is here primarily, but not exclusively dealing with the reading of Scripture. For an account of different reading-strategies, rhetorical and allegorical, applied in the Renaissance to the *Metamorphoses* of Ovid, the paradigm of all fiction, see A. Moss, *Ovid in Renaissance France. A Survey of the Latin Editions of Ovid and Commentaries printed in France before 1600* (London: Warburg Institute, 1982).

8. For a stimulating discussion of related issues, see R. Waswo, *Language and Meaning in the Renaissance* (Princeton: Princeton University Press, 1987). The disarray of modern critics trying to net the centrifugal tendencies of Renaissance literature was anticipated by the response of contemporary theorists. Among the relatively few who tried to grapple with the task of accommodating allegorical interpretation to rhetorical reproduction was Alessandro Lionardi in his *Dialoghi dell'Invenzione poetica* (Venice, 1554), hardly a giant among critics, but, perhaps significantly, the only poetic theorist writing in Italian who was translated almost immediately into French, and that at a period when the tensions I have just referred to were at their most productive in French poetry.

9. Erasmus, *De deplici copia verborum ac rerum* (1512), trans. B.I. Knott, *Collected Works of Erasmus*, ed. cit., XXIV, p. 638.

10. The opening sentence of Erasmus, *De Copia*, ed. cit., p. 295.

11. See Melanchthon, *De Locis communibus ratio*, in *Opera*, ed. cit.,p. XX, cols 695-8.

12. Erasmus, *De Copia*, ed. cit., p. 302.

13. De l'Expérience, in *Essais*, A Thibaudet (ed.) (Paris: Gallimard, 1950) p. 1195.

14. Erasmus, *Ratio seu methodus compendio perveniendi ad veram theologiam*, in *Opera omnia*, J. Clericus (ed.), 11 vols (Leyden, 1703-6) V, cols 130-1. The cross-reference Erasmus makes to his description of commonplace-books in his *De Copia* (from which we have quoted) makes it clear that Erasmus is here adapting his favourite tool of secular rhetoric to sacred texts.

15. From Melanchthon's preface to the 1543 edition of his *Loci communes*, in *Opera*, ed. cit., p. XXI, col. 604.

16. For a short, but comprehensive survey of attitudes to literary imitation, developed out of a commentary on the 'bee' similitude, see G.W. Pigman, 'Versions of Imitation in the Renaissance', *Renaissance Quarterly* 33 (1980) p. 1-32.

17. For a self-conscious glimpse into his practice, see the end of his *Hylas*, lines 417-26, in *Oeuvres complètes*, P. Laumonier, 9th edn), 20 vols (Paris, 1914-75) XV, p. 252.

18. Among the many books which touch on Montaigne's use of quotations, see M.B. McKinley, *Words in a Corner. Studies in Montaigne's Latin Quotations* (Lexington: French Forum, 1981).

19. Bacon, Francis, *Works*, J. Spedding, R.L. Ellis, and D.D. Heath (eds), 14 vols (London, 1857-74) VII, p. 321.

20. The history of commonplace books and their influence has yet to be written. The following are some of the contributions so far: B.L. Ullman, Joseph Lang and his anthologies in *Middle Ages, Reformation, Volkskunde. Festschrift for John G. Kunstmann* (Chapel Hill: University of North Carolina Press 1959) pp. 186-200; M.J. Lechner, *Renaissance Concepts of the Commonplaces* (New York: Pageant Press, 1962); A. Buck, *Die humanistische Tradition in der Romania* (Bad Homburg: Gehlen, 1968) pp. 133-50; W.J. Ong, *Rhetoric, Romance and Technology* (Ithaca: Cornell University Press, 1971); E. Mertner, 'Topos und Commonplace', in *Toposforschung, Eine Dokumentation*, P. Jehn (ed.) (Frankfurt a. M.: Athenäum, 1972) pp. 20-68; B. Beugnot, 'Floriléges et *Polyanthea*. Diffusion et statut du lieu commun l'époque classique' in *Le Lieu commun*, R. Melanon (ed.), *Etudes françaises* 13 (1977) pp. 119-41; A. Compagnon, *La Seconde main, ou le travail de la citation* (Paris: Editions du Seuil, 1979); C. Balavoine, 'Bouquets de fleurs et colliers de perles: sur les recueils de formes brèves au XVIe siècle', in *Les Formes brèves de la prose et le discours discontinu (XVIe-XVIIe siècles)*, J. Lafond (ed.) (Paris: Urin, 1984) pp. 51-71.

3

The Rhetoric of Rhetoric:
Six Tropes of Disciplinary Self-Constitution

Michael Cahn (University of Konstanz)

This discovery was so great and overwhelming that all the steps by which I had been
progressively led it to were obliterated, and I beheld only the result.[1]

Introduction

Rhetoric has always been more than merely the art of persuasion. It also implied a
theory of speaking and of language, and it represented certain philosophical assumptions about the nature of man. It also becomes increasingly apparent that rhetoric
offers a number of powerful tools for an analysis of discourse which places special
emphasis on the institutional background of utterances. This potential of rhetoric
seems particularly important for an analysis of the discourse of science. The words
of science are always embedded in a highly elaborate institutional frame. But at the
same time, science, claiming to speak the truth, negates the importance of its institutional background. Science conceives of truth as something that is seen rather than
said, and it tends to think of language as a tool that would in no way affect what is
being said with its help. To insist, against these notions, on the discursive nature of
scientific disciplines, has become a common procedure in the history of science. It
alone allows us to analyse sciences rhetorically. The principal gesture of this analysis is that it asks how a given discipline established itself as a source of authority
and reliability. The normative differentiation between arts and sciences, between
science and pseudo-science, or between craft and science, do in this perspective lose
the authority they enjoyed within a philosophical theory of science. They give way
to an attempt to envision the production of knowledge as a linguistic enterprise, in
which the classical differences between forms and degrees of knowledge no longer
function as pure epistemological concepts, but are understood as terms of strategic
ennoblement.

While the rhetorical approach in the history of science itself is new, rhetoric has
traditionally been close to the theory of knowledge. The Aristotelian theory of the

61

different degrees of belief (*pistis*), the description of metaphor as an instrument in the production of knowledge, but also Chaïm Perelman's and Stephen Toulmin's reconstruction of rhetoric as a theory of argumentation are all examples of the proximity of rhetoric and epistemology. The rhetorical tendency to analyse a discourse in terms of the interests of its speakers constitutes perhaps the principal value of this approach. On the other hand, this reference to the speakers of a discourse has obvious shortcomings for the sciences. To reduce the sciences to the personal interests of those engaged in them would indeed be rather reductive. What is needed, then, is an analysis that would attempt to circumscribe those rhetorical effects within the sphere of knowledge which are not reducible to a single identifiable speaker and their possibly malicious intent.

Rhetorical effects occur not only when individuals speak. They are no less present in the utterances of institutions, in which the person of the speaker is no longer identifiable. The most important of such institutional effects take place in the domain of the sciences (*Wissenschaften*). An investigation of these rhetorical effects within the sciences (disciplines) will here be undertaken in order to argue for the analytical power of rhetoric in the context of the history of science. I would like to try to carry this out upon an example which may seem confusing at first sight, but which should prove to be especially interesting. I will argue for the centrality and importance of rhetoric today by means of an analysis of the rhetoric of rhetoric. It is the goal of this essay to describe some of the argumentative strategies (tropes) through which the ancient discipline called rhetoric, proposed and instituted by the Sophists, presented itself, and indeed, constituted itself. The argumentative strategies with which rhetoric faces its critics and its customers are never external ornaments. Rather, they pertain to the very possibility of the discipline of rhetoric. These strategies are the source of power that enables any discipline to establish itself at all.

I am here calling rhetoric a discipline in order to indicate that it surely cannot satisfy the current criteria applicable to a rigorous science. The term discipline designates a science as an institutional entity, without prejudging its truth or objectivity. The character of rhetoric as discipline results, first of all, from the process of professionalisation it underwent in ancient Greece. Its elements were logography, paid lessons, and textbooks.[2] The textbooks of rhetoric are particularly important for our purposes, because we will have to anchor our analysis of the rhetorical constitution of the discourse of rhetoric in these texts. Using rhetoric as our example to demonstrate the value of a rhetorical analysis does not imply that the results of this analysis could be representative for other disciplines. To be sure, the difficulty of defining its own subject matter made rhetoric a disciplinary anomaly. Therefore, strategies of disciplinary self-affirmation are particularly well developed in the case of rhetoric. It is precisely in this sense that our example qualifies for present purposes.

The concept of discipline indicates the institutional dimension of science. It expresses the fact that rhetoric has taken that wondrous step from inspiration to knowledge, that it is more than merely the private affair of an underemployed sophist, wandering from town to town with his bizarre offerings. Rhetoric itself represents the effective power of speech regardless of the truth of what is being said. This makes us suspect that the constitution of rhetoric as a discipline was in turn independent of the truth implicit in its propositions. But how then was rhetoric possible? How did rhetoric constitute itself as a discipline? To this question classical rhetoric responded with histories of its inventors.[3] Empedocles, (Diog. Laert, VIII. 57; Quint. III.1.8) Corax, and sometimes even the Homeric heroes appear as the first rhetoricians. The inadequacy of these fabulous accounts of the origins of rhetoric is today generally recognised. Instead, modern research favours the conception that disciplines grow through a slow and gradual process, in which the place of single inventors is of minimal importance. Yet the mysterious bridge between the practice of good speaking and its theory remains unexplained in this evolutionary account. It neglects the revolutionary character of the invention of rhetoric to which the vehemence of Plato's critique bears witness. Accounts of the birth of rhetoric either in terms of the intervention of heroic inventors or through an evolutionary process, which fail to appreciate the spectacular nature of the origin of rhetoric, shall here be confronted with a different approach. Through an examination of the tropes of the rhetorical self-presentation of rhetoric, we can represent the abrupt invention of rhetoric. But rather than ascribing the constitution of rhetoric to a single inventor, we will argue that the possibility of its invention and of its continued existence can best be understood as depending on the strategic use of a few peculiar argumentative tropes. Often, the origins of rhetorical knowledge have been traced back to social and political conditions in ancient Greece, but these reconstructions remain distant from the traumatic rupture that attends every becoming of knowledge.

Rhetoric itself has made us aware of the performative power of texts. The theory of language implicit in rhetoric includes the recognition that the interests of the speaker inevitably find expression in every utterance. Using this rhetorical insight as our starting point, rhetoric's own statements concerning its status as art and the circumstances of persuasion should not be taken naively at face value, but rather should be considered with regard to their role in the constitution and 'survival' of the discipline. The only way in which a discipline can establish itself is through rhetorical self-affirmation, and rhetoric itself is no exception. Even the occasional alarmingly systematic representation of the figures of rhetoric is more than a mere formalisation of the rules of persuasion; in addition, it is always an attempt to ensure its existence as a discipline.

The term rhetoric of rhetoric is a device that can be used to designate the tendency of the art of persuasion to assure itself rhetorically of its own disciplinary status. Unfortunately, scholarship in the history of rhetoric has largely lost a sense of urgency in tackling this question. It has not been widely recognised that when the question of the disciplinary status of the discipline arose, 'the bread and the butter of many a [...] rhetorician was at stake'.[4] Instead, the struggle over the status of rhetoric as an art has generally been perceived as pointless and unprofitable.[5] Historians of rhetoric have often found it more important to trace the genealogy of specific theorems than to address Plato's preoccupation with the scientific authority of the art.[6] Perhaps it was the philosophical nature of the latter question that has deterred historians of rhetoric from approaching the subject in depth. Looked at more closely, the self-presentation of rhetoric, the question as to whether rhetoric is an art, concerns the very conditions of the possibility of rhetoric. Operating with the tacit assumption which we can no longer share, classical scholars long held that the existence of rhetoric as a discipline was simply unproblematic. The disappearance of rhetoric as a subject of formal instruction over the course of the last two centuries reinforced the diminishing awareness of its intrinsically problematic character. Thus here we attempt to trace how rhetoric itself overcame its own improbability and how it was able to constitute itself in discourse as more than mere words, in fact as a discipline.

Rhetoric itself has left behind the best tools for an analysis of its own self-affirmation. It distinguished three kinds of speech (deliberative, juridical, encomiastic) in which, according to Aristotle, the listener appears variously as judging the future, the past, or the present (Aristotle, *Rhet.* I.3).[7] Rhetoric itself, however, could not situate its own discourse as a discipline in this schema. Other than in the traditional *genera dicendi*, its addressee is by definition excluded from judging these lessons. It is only when we introduce, as in Renaissance rhetoric, the discourse of teaching as a fourth rhetorical genre, that the gates of rhetoric open, and, so to speak, allow its own discourse to be bathed in its own light. However, the discourse of teaching constitutes a genre of a peculiar character. Its speaker, either as teacher or as author of a rhetorical handbook, is always more than a private individual. He is rather the representative of a discipline.

In the following analysis we examine the ways in which rhetoric initially defined itself as a discipline and how it thus accomplished something fundamental in every discipline: the securing of its continued existence, even perhaps its apparent timeless quality. Its status was traditionally debated in terms of the question as to whether rhetoric is a *techne* or an art.[8] Here we shall not attempt to decide if rhetoric is an art or not. Instead, we attempt to find the basis of this question by way of a rhetorical analysis. This approach aims at the rhetorical tropes of the self-affirmation of rhetoric which always served to lend plausibility to rhetoric's claim to artistic standing. They are presented under the following headings: the artist, the language, *kairos*, *techne*, nature, and *ars est artem celare*.

The Artist

Throughout the rhetorical tradition, rhetoric has almost exclusively been conceived of with reference to the practitioners of the art.[9] The art of rhetoric defined itself constantly through the masterly personal performance of the orator. It made its very existence dependent upon the occurrence of a natural rhetorical mastery which somehow managed to transform itself, so it was always thought, into theoretical knowledge. Thus, for example, a reference to the artist informs the biographical structure of Cicero's *Brutus* and the same tendency is evident in his ridiculing of those who compose arts of rhetoric: '*per ridiculos qui artis rhetoricas exponunt*' (*De or.* III.75). Cicero has Crassus say that rhetoric consists not in such handbooks, but in what the orator is capable of: '*quid orator possit*' (*idem.*). By means of this derivation the rhetorical art finds its root and its paradigm in the performance of an exceptional speaker whose acumen need no further justification. This personalising account is basically inductive and secures the crucial step from practice to theory. Such an account does not recognise, however, that for every masterly performance a theoretical framework is essential which allows the rhetorical performance to become the object of perception and to be evaluated.

The definition of the discipline through its agents is rhetorical because these very agents are only able to define themselves by means of the discipline. Rhetoric as such, that is the fragile connection of rhetorical insights, is always more than the sum of the personal performances of its representatives; it is the framework within which these performances first become possible, visible, and criticisable as rhetorical performances. This is why rhetoric has never ceased to exist, although scarcely a single practitioner has ever fulfilled its highest claims. Nevertheless, rhetoric itself has always tended to identify the art with the artist. It has made its disciplinary status dependent upon the ideal performances of its heroes (for example, Pericles, Demosthenes and Cicero), or justified itself with reference to the imagined perfection in rhetorical achievement, embodied in the notion of the *orator perfectus*.[10] This personalising tendency has in turn led theoreticians of rhetoric to affirm that the role of the rhetorician is not a (part-time) professional role, but one that defines the whole personality of the rhetor.[11]

A second rhetorical content of this personalising conception of knowledge is the result of a certain ambiguity which is liable to appear in any discussion of quality or artistic skill. The meaning of the 'good' comprises both a technical and a moral sense. In the Stoic definition of rhetoric the discipline's dependence on the moral position of the speaker is firmly established: '*vir bonus dicendi peritus.*'[12] Importing the goodness of the speaker into the definition of rhetoric made it possible to evade the popular reproach that rhetoric represented an amoral form of knowledge. But such a reconstruction of the discipline of rhetoric by reference to the morality of its respective practitioners will always be a very precarious way in which to guarantee its status as a discipline. Human behaviour is certainly not a very reliable basis upon which to secure a discipline. On the other hand, the historical success of rhetoric as a humanistic discipline indicates that such a weak, personalising legitimation of a discipline can unfold a distinctive power.

First and foremost among the figures or tropes of disciplinary self-affirmation is the blurring of the difference between art and artist. This identification functions as a strategy of authorisation which is addressed to the student and requires his acknowledgement. Whenever a *techne* or *ars* is identified with the human dimension of its practitioners, and whenever the history of science adopts a biographical approach, the institutional aspect of knowledge may be neglected. This very neglect of the institutional nature of rhetorical instruction paradoxically tends to yield a real benefit for that teaching. This personalisation is evident in Isocrates, who presents his instruction as a training discipline interpreting it as personal interaction between teacher and student. On the other hand, the fact that Socrates took no payment for his discussions is strong evidence that he too considered teaching to be a 'private' activity without an institutional background. The value of rhetoric's artist-centred mode of self-presentation consists in passing over the institutional nature of rhetoric. What still remains to be understood is how and why rhetoric is able to become a discipline (which is by definition always more than the sum total of individual persons), though denying its disciplinarity. In other words, how can rhetoric expect to secure its existence as a discipline by making itself dependent upon the performance of the artist or the student?

Language

So far we have tried to understand the rhetorical value of the strategy of personalisation. A further strategy used by the discourse of rhetoric in order to authorise itself is closely related to its subject-matter: language. The 'finest and most invisible' (Gorg. *Hel.* 8) materiality of language does not permit work upon it to objectify itself in the same way as construction of a city-wall (*Gorg.* 455bf.) or the composition of an elaborate meal. Rhetoric understood in this way, is at a disadvantage compared with those disciplines which are able to show off what they have created and can recognise themselves in their productions. Even though it has been called a producer of persuasion *(peithous demiourgos, Gorg.* 453a), it does in fact never produce a concrete, material result. In language or in what has been written down, rhetoric possesses no 'manual product' (Plato *Gorg.* 450b), but at most a medium. It is for two reasons unable to show off its work, the speech, and the persuasion produced. Firstly, it is unable to do so because its work (the speech) possesses only an elusive materiality in which it would be able to recognise its achievement, and secondly, it is not permitted to do so because then it would, like a self-conscious advertisement, refer to itself instead of presenting its case. The smell of the midnight oil emanating from the orator's study has always been detrimental to his cause: the orator had to purge all traces of exertion and difficulty from his product. Due to this double deficiency of self-confirmation, rhetoric has always been highly motivated in its struggle to secure a disciplinary anchoring. In asserting itself as the art of all arts it wants to make us forget that the proof of its existence, its product, is threadbare indeed.

Plato argued that rhetoric could not be a *techne* because it could not be constituted from the product of its activities. It is indeterminate; it is about everything. Plato's treatment of rhetoric assumes that a discipline, like a word, must have a specific and well-defined object and can only lay claim to a status as *techne* in reference to it. While Plato held that rhetoric's lack of such an object was an argument against its artistic status, here it would seem as if rhetoric, which performs its work in the fleeting medium of language, must for this reason be particularly desirous of having its pretensions to artistic standing acknowledged. The difficulty rhetoric has recognising itself in its works as a result of the 'instantaneous effect' (Lausberg, para. 10) of language is further aggravated by the postulate that the artistic skill of its work should be rigorously concealed in accordance with the first basic principle of rhetorical success, to wit, the addressee ought not to know of the rhetorical nature of the discourse to which he is being exposed (cf. later section *ars est artem celare*).

Rhetoric lacks the tangible evidence of its linguistically constituted product. The same deficiency has led the art of poetry to call itself by a name (*poiein*) which, while signifying art of producing, was meant to hide inability to produce anything else but mere words. For the artistic standing of rhetoric, however, the peculiar materiality of language is not only a problem. The distance from the atmosphere of craft could also result in a gain in dignity which, precisely in view of the classical disdain for craftsmanship, should not be neglected.

Language, moreover, can even become a source of authorisation for the art of rhetoric. As *logos* it can be invoked as the 'mighty sovereign' (Gorg. *Hel.* 8), which affords protection for the project of rhetoric. This authorising function of language is clearly traceable to Gorgias' *Helena*, the earliest and theoretically most interesting self-presentation of sophistic rhetoric, which, to be sure, does not yet acknowledge the title rhetoric.[13] The discipline of rhetoric which brilliantly announces itself in this text, does not, on this occasion, formulate its claims directly in relation to the personality of the teacher, but asserts its claims of its subject-matter: language. Gorgias develops the praise of the discipline and its authorisation as the praise of language – not least out of rhetorical considerations.[14] The rhetorical discipline glories in the power which it first ascribed to language itself. Through deliberate ambiguity Gorgias praises language as a way of praising its own project. Even though the *Helena* concludes by referring to itself as a plaything (*painion*), this is not to be understood as a declaration of its non-seriousness, but once more as evidence of speech's power over men, a skill which Gorgias masterfully demonstrates, and which he attempts to transfer to his new discipline.

As regards the discourse of rhetoric it can thus be maintained that the teacher, as the spokesman of rhetoric, always appears as the representative of something impersonal, protected by the authority of an anonymous abstraction: rhetoric. Just as the discipline of rhetoric articulates language, so the teacher is spokesman for the discipline. Later on, when, due to its own history, rhetoric could take for granted with less pain and struggle its own existence, the discipline itself began to displace this camouflage function of language. In this situation it becomes true that rhetoric could exist merely because it has existed before.

It is in the fundamental relation between the teacher and the anonymity of the discipline that the teacher first can lay claim to his name as rhetor and possess the authority to teach students. He must constantly reaffirm the disciplinary status of his discipline because it is only on this basis that his voice can claim authority. Only the strategy, itself rhetorical, of speaking as the spokesman of the discipline (*prosopopoeia*) lends credibility to the founding presumption of the rhetorical instruction: that it is possible to improve that which everybody already thinks he knows how to do, that is, to speak. Indeed, such strategies have especially to be reckoned with, since the marketing of rhetorical instruction was in no way institutionally secure.[15] Even after a market for such instruction had been created, its trustworthiness (which could never be acquired simply through the personality of the teacher) had to be demonstrated over and over again.

Kairos

Kairos, understood as the ability to cope with the contingency of the moment, belongs to the second generation of strategies that serve to authorise rhetorical knowledge.[16] In opposition to each and every technical or methodological reconstruction of rhetoric, *kairos* designates the magic of timing, of catching the right moment. It is the anti-disciplinary principle of rhetoric; it represents an unanalysable capacity for success. Pope called it 'a grace beyond the reach of art.' It opposes the idea of a methodical rhetoric as presented in Plato's *Phaedrus* (271d). *Kairos* outdoes the rigour and appeal of the formal scientific approach (*techne*) by emphasising the difficulty of hitting upon the right word at the right moment. The art of rhetoric would be easy, and for that very reason insignificant, if it were limited to the mastery of rules.[17] Its dignity came to depend upon the difficulty of mastering the moment, an ability which is not obtainable by means of rules.

We possess evidence that Gorgias had composed a work on *kairos* which is now lost. It must have been a strange treatise that tried to grasp what lies beyond the reach of methodological reconstruction, written by the first writer to link his teachings to the term *techne*. In the speech *On the Sophists*, his student Isocrates outlined an art of rhetoric which is strongly kairotic in its orientation and thus waives every claim to scientific sovereignty. He acknowledged the elusive nature of *kairos* by recognising the paramount importance of the personality of each individual student. His competitors, who thought they could sell rhetorical skill like shoes (Aristotle, *Soph. El.* 34.183b 26), or teach it as they would teach the art of writing, assumed, according to Isocrates, a conception of rhetoric determined by an untenable analogy with the art of writing and its fixed (orthographical) rules (Isoc. XIII.12f). According to Isocrates, the real insight of the discipline did not reside in strict rules of correlation of linguistic form and persuasive function (*Phaedr.* 217d), but in the recognition that the rhetorical rules of persuasion resist systematisation. In opposition to a scientific conception of rhetoric analogous to orthography, for his school he only formulated claims referring to his own person. Thus the authority of his instruction is not objectively, but subjectively warranted and that is why his personal apologia in the *Antidosis* occupies an important place in his system of rhetoric.

Isocrates' kairotic rhetoric crystallises around the personality of the teacher and can therefore also take into account the personality and talent of his students. That, in turn, has a paradoxical consequence for the existence of the discipline of rhetoric. *Kairos* brings the discipline which always strove for the autonomy of *techne*, to the verge of its dissolution as an independent authority. In Isocrates, as in Cicero later on, art engages in a vehement, self-undermining polemic against the codification of art. It was therefore only logical that Isocrates wrote no handbook of rhetoric.[18] His stress upon situational necessities did of course do justice to aspects of speaking, but it was primarily an important rhetorical strategy for promoting public acceptance of his discipline. In Isocrates, rhetoric acquires its status by presenting itself as ignorant, thereby following a model which the Socrates of the Platonic dialogues realised

68

as irony. Isocrates' rhetoric implied that rules are quite irrelevant for rhetorical success and that only the student's grasp of the moment could produce persuasion. Surpassing the rule-oriented rhetoric, which first established the discipline, the emphasis on *kairos* is a paradoxical strategy of disciplinary self-affirmation.

The sophistic competitors of Isocrates claimed rhetoric was a 'super-art' in which the highest pretensions for the effectiveness of the art of persuasion were combined with the impression that this art could be readily acquired in return for the payment of a reasonable fee. This type of sophistic rhetoric, which could be called 'hard rhetoric', maintained an unrestricted disciplinary self-confidence. This can be glimpsed in Polus' praise of rhetoric (*Gorg.* 448c), and it can be reconstructed, despite obvious gaps in the tradition, from the polemics in the writings of Isocrates and Plato.[19] Rhetoric is still held by Plato's Gorgias to be a super-knowledge, namely the art of utilising other people for one's own ends (*Gorg.* 452d f. cf. Rhet. ad Alex.). Isocrates, on the other hand, designed a program which, as 'soft rhetoric' based on *kairos*, breaks with the strong promises of the sophists in order thereby to acquire – albeit paradoxically – a new credibility. The fact that it promises virtually nothing makes it all the more trustworthy. The elements of the 'softness' of the Isocratic system are as follows: the length of the period of training (several years instead of an 'intensive course'); the taking into account of natural aptitudes; and the presentation of the discipline as lacking the knowledge implied by fixed rules of orthography and by a handbook. These aspects converge in the concept of *kairos*, that intuitive and unsystematisable delicacy of feeling which itself can never be part of any art. Isocrates' model of a 'soft rhetoric' consistently negates all the claims that have been made for the art as an independent authority. His rhetoric is not an autonomous aggregate of knowledge for which the teacher makes himself the spokesman, but is rather located in the unsystematic personal relationship that exists between student and teacher.

Historically speaking, Isocrates' program was a sensational success. Since that time two contradictory strategies for providing disciplinary authority have counterbalanced each other in the history of rhetoric. The affirmation of rigorous technical rules (*techne*) constantly finds its counterpart in the emphasis on the limits of art (*kairos*). These tendencies have often been conceived as mutually interdependent. Accordingly, the rhetorical knowledge of rules would have to be supplemented by a delicacy of feeling (*kairos*) which defies technical reconstruction and which can be considered as a gift of nature.[20] Hence, the rules of persuasion would be incomplete without the (kairotic) knowledge (itself never contained in those rules) of when they are to be applied. In practice, this resolution of the opposition of 'hard' and 'soft' rhetoric is certainly indisputable. Nevertheless, this apparent resolution neglects the fact that *techne* and *kairos* pursue mutually incompatible rhetorical strategies in the self-presentation of rhetoric. If *kairos* were to become the supplement of *techne* in the self-presentation of rhetoric, then it would inevitably dissolve the pretensions of rhetoric to knowledge. Without the strong claims of its technical system, rhetoric evaporates into ephemeral and momentary insight or mere 'gut-feeling.' The self-presentation of rhetorical instruction is thus not only rhetorical when it formulates grand claims to disciplinary dignity, but also paradoxical when it sets itself against such claims, and, in negating the knowledge it embodies, arrives at the (imaginary) point of disciplinary self-dissolution.

Techne

Three of the tropes of self-affirmation through which rhetorical knowledge grants itself disciplinary status have been presented so far. The presentation of rhetoric in terms of the person of the rhetor; the reference to the power of language and the corresponding difficulty of recognising oneself as productive in language; and thirdly the emphasis on *kairos*, that aspect of rhetorical knowledge which lies beyond any system. All three are *indirect* tropes of the rhetoric of rhetoric insofar as they avoid asserting directly the authority of the discipline. We now turn to the *direct* strategy of rhetorical self-affirmation which asserts the scientific character of rhetoric as discipline.

The true scandal of rhetoric in Athens derived not from its moral indifference, but from its pretension to disciplinary autonomy,[21] comprised in the impudent assertion of its claim to be a *techne*. This claim is already implicit in the titles of the rhetorical textbooks (*téchnai*, Phaedr. 261b), and it is against such pretensions to disciplinary authority that Plato deployed his polemical powers. As in the case of the 'good' speaker, here too it is a conceptual ambiguity, that of the term *techne*, that allows rhetoric to enter the well-protected domain of knowledge. The bibliographical meaning of *techne* as handbook was even thought to confirm the technical or scientific dignity of their undertaking (Quint. II.17.2). The momentous objections raised by Plato are directed precisely against the sophistic claim of autonomy for the technique of persuasion. How was rhetoric able to sustain this claim? But it is only when we reverse this question that it reveals its centrality: why was rhetoric obliged to make this claim? Why could it absolutely not avoid making this claim?

Rhetoric is always more than the nameless practice of the odd foreigner dressed in colourful robes. What such foreigners practised in the marketplaces of Greece has always already presented itself under the name of a universal – the discipline of rhetoric. It is not important whether this discipline is called rhetoric, eristic, sophistic, or *techne ton logon*: the decisive factor is the pragmatic effect of the title itself.[22] The ascription of any such title rhetorically yields a status that goes well beyond what a personal action could ever be. I call the effectiveness of this designation rhetorical.

In terms of the history of science, the concept of *techne* confers upon a discipline a certain professional quality, an honorific degree of knowledge, and a superior rank in the scale of knowledge as a whole. Its opposite is not poor individual performance as such, but pseudo-art and sham knowledge.[23] *Techne* and *ars* must be understood primarily as concepts within the theory of science. These stand in contradistinction to the dimension of action which focuses on the speech of the *vir bonus* and that of which the speaker is capable of (*quid orator possit*), which cumulates in the '*orator perfectus*'. By presenting itself as *techne*, the enterprise of rhetoric places itself in the context of comparable disciplines. In rhetoric, *techne* never means a naive or natural ability. Rather *techne* always relates this ability to its disciplinary setting. Gorgias draws upon magic[24] and medicine as disciplinary prototypes (model disciplines); Plato calls upon a large number of such *techne*, including medicine, shoemaking, music, weaving, geometry, sculpture, military strategy, beautification, seafaring, and cookery. In Plato's polemic we recognise the urgency of attributing a disciplinary constitution to the new discipline of rhetoric. He attempts to identify rhetoric, and to determine its place in the universe of knowledge. In comparing rhetoric with other disciplines he argues that rhetoric does not fulfil the conditions of disciplinarity. The teachers of rhetoric engaged in the same attempt to define the place of rhetoric. They too compared it with other disciplines, but here in this instance, an identical strategy of disciplinary comparison served to authorise their instruction in the eyes of potential students. The tendency to reinforce the disciplinary status of rhetoric by means of the comparison with other disciplines was from then on both a timeless topic of rhetorical self-affirmation *and* its critique.

The comparison of rhetoric with other *technai* is itself rhetorical because it always ignores the fact that rhetoric differed fundamentally from disciplines like medicine and magic. According to all we know about them, these other disciplines provided for no general or commercial access to their respective forms of knowledge, but instead bound their students firmly to their discipline by means of initiation procedures and other social regulations (guilds). The scientific novelty of rhetoric, affirmed by Gorgias as its universality, consists precisely in its being able to address itself to everyone. Since its relation to its students could then no longer be conceived of as a lifelong initiation, this relation was conducted as sales promotion. The rhetoric of rhetoric, the assertion of the 'technical' aspect of this discipline, compensates for the absence of other mechanisms for controlling the dissemination of knowledge.

From this point on, disciplinary comparison was part and parcel of the standard equipment of the rhetoric of rhetoric. In rhetoric's self-comparison with medicine, cookery, cosmetics, dialectics, helmsmanship, or gymnastics,[25] it laid a rhetorical claim to disciplinary status without entering into the terminological qualifications of *techne*. The comparison with the 'established' disciplines of medicine or magic (in many languages the principal paradigms of disciplinarity)[26] functioned as an authorisation of the discourse of rhetoric in the sense of inserting it into the sphere of knowledge. It therefore participated in the discursive mechanisms which were already serving not only to protect the (occult) sciences from unauthorised access, but also to safeguard the authority of their spokesmen.[27] The publication of knowledge characteristic of the Greek enlightenment in the fifth century BC could not, in principle, detach itself from those strategies for ensuring power which were already typical for the guilds and for occult knowledge.[28] The teacher of rhetoric would never offer his wares as his personal property and as his private invention, but as the product of that anonymous discipline that he called rhetoric, the reality of which had still to be proven.

Techne designates first of all a craft,[29] but in a broader sense it also applied to the rhetorical handbook. For Plato the concept referred to the codification of an activity, which, 'with a specific teachable method, is directed towards a specific end, and thus left neither to mere natural endowment nor to uncontrollable inspiration.'[30] In the strict use of the term, it designates the ability of a form of knowledge success-fully to direct action, the ability to master it through the formulation of rules. Therefore *techne* is fundamentally ambivalent. It belongs to two domains at once: to both method and action. *Techne* promises the knowledge of first principles to suc-cess and effectiveness in the fabrication of a product. This double promise is what makes the title of *techne* so desirable for the rhetorician. The rhetorical value of this concept is, however, grounded in an irresolvable ambiguity between acting and knowing.

In the framework of the unity of knowledge and action which the concept of *techne* envisions, two aspects of its rhetorical impact can be distinguished. The concept can refer to the pedagogical effectiveness of knowledge itself, primarily the capacity of making students of rhetoric into better speakers (action). Not to be confused with the former is a second, more rigorous scientific dimension, which involves the tendency of rhetoric to develop a great number of conceptual distinc-tions with which it underscores its authority and unassailability (knowledge). The first aspect may be called pedagogical effectiveness; the second 'system-mania.' The second aspect which involves an increase of internal complexity cannot simply be subordinated to the pedagogical utility of its rhetorical insights. The complexity of its rules never guarantees the effectiveness of rhetorical training.

Methodological control over the subject-matter of rhetoric needs to manifest itself in coherent written form in the disciplinary representation of the handbook. Only thus can the handbook authorise the discipline. However this rhetorical insight can never be directly translated into the practical abilities of the student. In rhetoric, theory and practice are divided rather than united, and this is shown in Aristotle's rhetoric by the discrepancy in it between high scientific rigour and low pedagogical effectiveness. This bifurcation is also evident in the program of Isocrates, where by contrast he was apparently able to dispense with almost all manner of theoretical elaboration. The successful training of orators can evidently not be guaranteed simply by means of the scientific penetration of the subject-matter or by speculative hypotheses concerning the principles of persuasion. While rhetorical theory as such cannot guarantee success, an emphasis on its proper 'scientificity' can provide an important, though hidden, pedagogical service: it awakens the student's confidence in the existence of the discipline and, in return, this confidence will also positively influence his subsequent performance.

The praise of rhetoric as the noblest of sciences (*techne*, *Gorg.* 448c) is a rhetori-cal strategy directly aimed at the student. When Polus, travelling with Gorgias, employed it, he ascribes to the teacher the diffuse authority of an institution. Simi-larly, Isocrates tried to replace systematisable rhetorical knowledge by a personal relationship into which he drew his student for the duration of his study. He ac-cepted his client as a fallible human being, and did not attempt to reduce him to the executor of established rhetorical rules. The alternative strategy involved the cre-ation of a theoretically controlled science of rhetoric whose primary orientation was towards the abstract domain of knowledge (Aristotle). Rather than addressing the individual student, by means of this strategy the discipline asserts its high scientific individual student, by means of this strategy the discipline asserts its high scientific and theoretical status before an imaginary assembly of all scientists. The rhetorical difference between these strategies of disciplinary authorisation is evident. It is especially interesting that most of the earliest documents of rhetorical knowledge we possess do not address the student, but concern themselves with establishing the abstract scientific status of the discipline.

Instead of deriving its self-image and its disciplinary confidence from the fact that its students did frequently become better speakers, rhetoric concentrated upon its internal coherence or tried to find its place in the universe of comparable disciplines. Perhaps because oratorical practice was never again to acquire the social importance it had enjoyed in the Greek city states and also because its contribution to the education of its students could never be rigorously proved, that disciplinary status was pursued, above all, through an internal increase in complexity (as, for example, is the notoriously complex doctrines of Hermagoras [Quint, III.11.12]).

There are, in fact, several ways in which rhetoric asserted its scientific complexity. Since Aristotle, rhetoric has ordered its insights according to the notion of time. The schema of the rhetorical genres (political: decisions concerning the future; juridical: decisions about the past; epideictic: decisions about the present) and the sequential differentiation of the parts of a speech (introduction, middle, conclusion, etc.) are based on the logic of time. Solmsen[31] has shown that the ordering of rhetoric according to the parts of a speech was opposed to a second, likewise temporal, intra-rhetorical organisation, which, as the five-part sequence of the *officia oratoris (inventio, dispositio, elocutio, actio, memoria)*, structured rhetoric according to an idealised process of speech preparation. Both models, as an analysis of their rhetorical implications would reveal, afforded in their pure form a very high degree of internal organisation, but they were not oriented toward the specific needs of the students. Quintilian repeatedly complained about this separation of rhetorical science from pedagogical needs (II.15.37; III.1.7). He did, however, fail to recognise that rhetoric's tendency to assure itself of its embattled scientific status was unavoidable, even if it entailed little immediate use to students.

The assertion of the status of rhetoric as art (*techne*), the simple affirmation of its scientific nature, created authority and built trust, but in the end it also contributed to the self-confidence of those students who fancied themselves to be in good hands. Yet, is not such self-confidence precisely the psychological factor most likely to produce successful speakers? If this were true, then the difference between effective teaching and disciplinary coherence, between pedagogy and science would be paradoxically overcome. The obsessive concern with scientific status would not necessarily distance rhetoric from its students, and it could be to their advantage as they gained an increased self-confidence.

It is, however, not only through the claim of scientific status that rhetoric endeavours to obtain recognition as a discipline. A topic is always fully reversible: both its positive and its negative expression can work as strategies of disciplinary self-constitution. Negating the scientific nature of rhetoric can therefore also function as a strategy of ennoblement. I have already shown that the emphasis on *kairos* and Isocrates' stressing of the teacher/student relationship functioned this way. Cicero's presentation of his text not as a handbook but as an *aide-mémoire* for a colleague, show how rhetoric also seeks to affirm itself by means of the critique of rigorous science. That these, too, were rhetorical strategies (the technical term would be *paralipsis*) is a fact that rhetoricians are often fond of ignoring. The entry of Iso-cratic rhetoric into the mainstream of Western educational humanism is proof that these negative strategies of disciplinary authorisation were frequently more effective and more powerful than the straightforward claim to the status of rigorous science. It is precisely because these anti-technical strategies can give the appearance of free-dom from rhetoric that they could realise their rhetorical power.

Natura

We have so far examined the following tropes of the self-affirmation of rhetoric: the tendency of rhetoric to personalise its project; its attempt to establish itself in the protective shadow of the power of language; the reference to the unsystematisable 'art' of the appropriate moment (*kairos*), and lastly the rhetoric of hard science (*techne*). In each case these often ambivalent tropes accomplished a two-fold objec-tive: they allowed rhetoric to assure itself of its own disciplinary possibility and at the same time enabled it to advertise its services. This connection between the epistemological and pragmatic aspects can also be extended to the concept of nature.

Nature enters into rhetoric as the material into which rhetoric, like a craft, ex-pands its energy. Rhetoric improves the natural ability of speaking persuasively. The relation between art and nature, however, is more multi-levelled than the Aristote-lian notion of art as complement or as imitation of nature would lead one to expect.[32] Rhetoric is, of course, also a supplement to its students' natural faculty of speech, but it must be more than this if it is to establish itself as a discipline. Just as medicine promises the healing of bodily affliction, so rhetoric promises to make better speakers out of its students. This promise is, so to speak, rhetoric's birth certificate. It is, one is tempted to say, 'at the same time its death sentence' since it is, as we all know, quite impossible to make every student into a successful speaker. As a result, rhetoric must protect itself from its failures and from the uncertainties of life which call into question its disciplinary standing. It must emphasise its success and hide its failures.

Aristotle provides a good example of how this protection can be accomplished through a strategic use of the concept of nature.[33] Remarking on the similarity between medicine and rhetoric which both promise their clients the restoration or an improvement of their nature, Aristotle underscored the right of both disciplines to disregard the actual outcome of their treatment when assessing the technical dignity of their respective forms of knowledge. Since medicine has never ceased to be an art even if a patient dies, so rhetoric, too, should not be denied its status as a *techne*, despite being occasionally unable to make a student into a better speaker (Aristotle *Rhet.* I.1.14). This leads to a remarkable resilience in disciplinary knowledge which devolves onto rhetoric. Unlike any other human expression, it disposes of the un-canny ability to be right in the end. Only when rhetoric has immunised itself against the criticism of its clients is it strictly speaking a discipline: it denies its customers the right to pass judgement upon the quality of its achievements.[34] Rhetoric remains an art even if the customer testifies to its being a fraud. The improvement of speaking by rhetoric is an activity which, because being mediated through a discipline, is thereby able to rise above the simple opposition of success and failure characteristic of the activities of pleading, wooing, or campaigning. As a discipline, rhetoric disposes of the marvellous, at times almost miraculous power of not allowing its pedagogical failures to unsettle its own self-esteem. The assertions of rhetoric, in particular the claim to teach the power of persuasion, can never be as easily rebutted as the words of the man on the street. Being the utterances of a discipline, they remain immune to the criticism of any single client, and can perhaps only be disproven by a rival discipline. Given this power of the rhetoric of rhetoric, the fate of the student and the outcome of the cultivation of his natural abilities appear almost as an accidental outcome of the discipline. The right of the student to criticise the art is controlled by the art itself. This is the core of Aristotle's exoneration of rhetoric from charges of incompetence. The fact that Aristotle carries out this immunisation, not in order to help a rhetorician friend in difficulties, but in order to establish the epistemological status of this discipline as *techne*, further raises the value of his defence as testimony to the events attending the constitution of rhetoric.

After Aristotle had taken the sting out of the failure of rhetorical training, he proceeded to uncouple rhetoric from the sensational promises of power acquisition made by the Sophists. Instead he tried to guarantee the standing of rhetoric through an articulation of its theoretical coherence. The Aristotelian re-invention of rhetoric is, contrary to what he himself implied, not a mere systematisation or an advancement of the rhetoric that proceeded him. In his hands, rhetoric totally changes its orientation: apprenticeship in persuasion is transformed into theoretical knowledge.

Such 'scientification' does not place itself at the disposal of rhetorical training. On the contrary, it would appear to replace this training. In Aristotle's scientific rhetoric, the fate of the student is nothing compared with the fate of the art itself, which at this point begins its philosophical development as a theory of knowledge. What is true today was true then: it is not the students who control their training, but their teachers. As a logical consequence, rhetoric increasingly withdrew itself from a preoccupation with the natural dispositions of students and was subsumed by philosophy. Thus the rhetorical force of the concept of nature is quite unsettling. It reminds rhetoric of what it had promised to improve, but was in fact unable to improve systematically or all the time. Instead of avoiding the concept, rhetoric assigns 'nature' a new conceptual role and in that way attempts to lessen its destructive potential. Thus the concept of nature no longer served as a reminder of the vulnerability of the discipline, but came to designate, on the contrary, the privileged status of this form of knowledge. For this, too, Aristotle offers the following proof.

In the first sentence of his *Rhetoric* Aristotle formulates the thesis that rhetoric is not a private matter. All men have a share in it:

> Rhetoric is the counterpart of dialectic, since both are concerned with things of which the cognizance is, in a manner, common to all men and belongs to no definite science.

Hence all men in a manner use both, for all men to some extent make the effort of examining and submitting to inquiry, of defending or accusing.[35]

In what way can the assertion that all men have a share in rhetoric, the sense that it 'belongs' to everyone, increase the legitimacy of the discipline of rhetoric and support its disciplinary survival? The benefit gained from this assumption consists precisely in the fact that, by means of its declared universality rhetoric is released from the particularity of its disciplinary interest. In analogy with the universality of language, the discipline of rhetoric designates itself a natural property possessed by the general public. What the teacher of rhetoric then represents is not his own property, for which he personally could be held responsible and for which he re-ceives payment, but only a systematisation of that which everybody, inasmuch as he can speak, is acquainted with and has already partially mastered. A logical conse-quence of this universalising view is that rhetoric makes its way towards becoming the master-teacher of humanity. Rhetoric thus presents itself as a natural ability. The concept of nature is thus transformed from being a point of vulnerability to being a source of disciplinary security. Art, as it seemed at first, primarily acts upon nature. Here, however, rhetoric furnishes all of its utterances with the indication that they are not the words of a single individual, of this or that particular teacher of the art; rather, in its discourse humanity itself speaks.[36] This trope, through which the disci-pline offers merely a systematisation of something in which all human beings participate, runs like a red thread through the entire history of rhetoric.[37] According to this trope, the rhetorician is not a solitary inventor. He is superior to his students only by degrees. The distance between teacher and student, which the authorisation of the discipline had by all means tried to establish, is thus seriously jeopardised. Thus rhetoric begins by saying that it is reporting what everybody already knows, that it is summarising the existing 'rhetorical' knowledge of mankind, and not speaking on behalf of any new knowledge of its own. It constitutes itself by denying its having been constituted and by referring to its previous existence in the common consciousness of all men. We can now see that the concept of nature is of strategic importance for the constitution of rhetoric. It allows the rhetorician to pass off his words as the utterance of nature itself.

The centrality of the concept of nature in rhetoric is also reinforced by a number of well-known anti-rhetorical arguments. The discipline of rhetoric was repeatedly called into question because rhetorical achievements were apparently possible with-out any kind of technical training (Quint. II.17.7-9; *De* or. I.91). There were convincing speeches before there was rhetoric, and untaught orators could some-times attain their rhetorical aims better than those who had been trained (Alcidamas *Soph.* 12).[38] Yet it is precisely these arguments, which threaten to render the disci-pline superfluous, which were deprived of their power to invalidate rhetoric by rhetoric's self-representation as a representative of nature. When rhetoric takes its place on the side of nature, then it is no longer vulnerable to the charge that its services do not exceed what nature itself offers.

Also relevant in this context is, of course, reference to the 'natural' qualifications that the student has to bring with him to the teacher. The triad of nature, art and exercise,[39] that is, *doctrina, imitatio* and *exercitatio*, which since the *Auctor Ad Her.* (I.2.3) comprises the components of successful rhetorical training, was able to confront very effectively the discontent arising from student failure. If the outcome was not as desired, it was now always possible to blame the student himself for the unsatisfactory result. In addition to acquiring its technical aspects (*doctrina, epistéme*), rhetoric had acknowledged in this triad two equally important schooling methods. The rhetorical value of this acknowledgement consisted in explaining the deficiencies in rhetorical teaching while simultaneously absolving the art itself from all responsibility. Emphasising the central role of nature, exercise, or imitation in rhetorical training had, on the one hand, to detract from the prestige of the discipline; on the other hand, however, the tripartite discipline thereby entered upon the royal highway leading towards irrefutability. When rhetoric declared that it depended upon exercise, imitation, or a certain natural talent, it found for itself a grand argument with which it could preserve its disciplinary status even if no student ever became a better speaker.

Natural ability, imitation, and exercise, are strictly unsystematisable activities. That is, no technical criteria can be given for their correct application. Exercise can be systematic in that it has to be repeated every day, but no technical or methodological account can be given of its efficacy. Rhetorical theory admitted these non-technical methods of schooling, but since it could not govern them, the acknowledgement of natural predispositions to a successful instruction always already amounted to a limitation of its own claims. The Sophists taught, or rather sold as a 'commodity' the ability to speak persuasively. But in the subsequent history of rhetoric the separation of powers (*doctrina, imitatio* and *exercitatio*) leads to a disappearance of the commercial character of this discipline. Due to the increasing stress on exercise and imitation, rhetorical knowledge became something that the student could only teach himself. In this way rhetoric cancelled itself out. The defensive gesture with which the art, in the context of *imitatio* (Isocr. XIII.12; XV. 187; IV.10) and *exercitatio*, placed itself in the shadow of nature (Cicero, *De Or.* I. 18.80ff., 25.113ff.) nevertheless served the project of disciplinary self-preservation, that is as an excuse for its failure.

Failure to educate is not a late danger in rhetoric, but stands godfather at rhetoric's cradle. Rhetoric was inaugurated with a malpractice suit. Only today, in the twilight of educational humanism, has 'failure to educate' once again become the legal category it was in the fifth century BC. Its importance can be seen in the anecdote of Corax and Tisias which stands at the very origin of rhetoric:

> [Tisias], seized with a desire for rhetoric went to [Corax] and promised that he would pay him the fee he would charge, if he would win his first case. And when the compact was made, and the youth was now displaying sufficient skill, Corax demanded his fee, but [Tisias] said 'No.' Both then repaired to the court and had the case tried; and then, it was said, Corax used an argument of this kind, – that whether he won the case or lost it he ought to receive the fee; if he won, because he had won, and if he lost, in accordance with the terms of the compact. [...] [Tisias] in turn began his speech, and used the same argument, altering nothing: 'Whether I win,' he says, 'or whether I am beaten, I am not bound to pay Corax the fee; if I win, because I have won, and if I lose,

in accordance with the terms of the compact, for I promised to pay the fee if I should win my first case, but if I should lose, I shall not pay.' The judges [...] drove them both out of the court.[40]

The anecdote thematises more than the tricks of probabilistic argumentation:[41] it dramatises the institutional relationship, unceasingly rich in tensions, between teacher and student in the framework of which economic and epistemological aspects are fused. In view of this fraud at the source of rhetoric, the relationship between teacher and student is never innocent like one of friendship, love or trust. Since Corax, no teacher has offered his lessons without first exploring possible excuses with which he might protect himself from refund demands in the event of failure. This is the condition under which knowledge can enter the sphere of economic exchange. It is the nature of the student that afforded rhetoric an excuse with which it could not so much constitute itself as avoid its own abolition. Today an insurance policy may perform a similar function.[42]

As I have emphasised, the imponderabilities of any education are more than merely an external aspect of knowledge. Rhetoric does not exist without its promise of improving persuasive speaking. The relationship with the student circumscribes the discursive zone in which rhetoric has first to come to itself as a discipline. It constitutes itself not as knowledge, but as knowledge *for* the student, that is, more exactly, as purchasable knowledge. When Aristotle asserts that there is no science of the 'individual' (*Rhet.* I.2.11), he tries to make us forget that, in the marketplace of knowledge, rhetoric was always meant to be a science for that 'individual' who paid for it. And indeed, if one follows J.-F. Lyotard, then teaching appears as both an economic and an epistemological necessity for any form of knowledge. Competence and quality of disciplinary insight must repeatedly be proved to one's peers: 'one must therefore train one's equals.'[43] The pains taken to train a younger generation, according to Lyotard's reconstruction, are revealed as a side-effect of the overriding concern for the scientific character of a discipline which, without competent acknowledgement, could not lay claim that status. Analogous to the secondary pedagogical effects of disciplinary dignity seen in the increased self-confidence of the student, we now realise that the training of its students seems to be a mere by-product of rhetoric's attempt to assert itself as an art.

The constitution of rhetoric confronts a two-fold difficulty. Rhetoric must first defend itself from the threat of natural endowment: it has to be more than nature. At the same time, it must be more than the dubious invention of the individual teacher; it must assert that its knowledge is a systematising of nature. It was exceedingly unlikely that rhetoric, in the face of this contradictory constellation, would be capable of assuming its place as a discipline. Only because of its rhetorical power was rhetoric able to avoid turning into an example of disciplinary failure, comparable with cookery, cosmetics, the science of parasitology (Lucian), and the art of murder (de Quincey), to name only a few cases of failed institutionalisation (*átechnia*). Yet once having set out on the course of its history as a *techne*, rhetoric encountered a new difficulty. As it entered into competition with other schools, the teacher of rhetoric no longer struggled against the impossibility of his project, but had to convince his students of the specific superiority of his own program over that of his competitors. Rhetorical teaching thus comprised far more than insight into the correlation between linguistic structure and psychological effects (*Phaedr.* 271d). It had to win the hearts of its students, who, after Corax, have never ceased to fear being swindled. At the same time, rhetoric must set itself apart from competing schools. This need to distinguish itself led to interesting forms of 'soft' rhetoric which neglected their own scientific status in order to emphasise their difference from their competitors. Rhetoric then once more begins to contradict itself. One example is found in Isocrates, whose rhetoric denies its superiority over the student, discredits its own rules, and is perhaps nothing more than the sustained call to dedicate attention to language. Only in this way can Isocrates set himself apart from the promises of his competitors. Here rhetoric becomes a framework within which the student develops a capacity for self-criticism. Its character as art, which depends on superior knowledge expressible in rules, thereby turns progressively into a fiction. The art constitutes itself as a non-art.

Ars est artem celare

The tendency of rhetoric to constitute itself as the agent of a pre-existent nature has found, within rhetoric itself an epistemological formulation which has often been misunderstood as a mere stylistic[44] or psychological formula. The naturalising motto *ars est artem celare* says that the highest art consists in the concealment of its artfulness. It thus raises the trope of rhetorical modesty to the level of a theory which presents the discipline as cancelling itself out.

One of the peculiarities of language is that the claim to truthfulness is incompatible with any elaboration and artistic sophistication. Of all the comparable arts and métiers in the history of science (medicine, cookery, gymnastics, military science, architecture, shoemaking) against which rhetoric has been measured in its history, none has had to live with the requirement of concealing its achievement in order to attain recognition. The instruction that the students should not show their training[45] is not a late weakening of the rhetorical project. Rather, this rule occupies the very heart of rhetoric. Rhetoric does not primarily consist in a knowledge of the secret gateway to rhetorical deception, which would afterwards have to be concealed. Rather, the postulate that art conceal itself is a unique insight of rhetoric because it refers to rhetoric's existence as a discipline. This requirement marks the site on which rhetoric confronts its disciplinary constitution, but only in order to negate it. In the mannerist forms of rhetoric alone,[46] where the pride of the artist is not felt to contradict the effectiveness of his persuasion, do other constellations appear.

The connection between art and artificiality in rhetoric is a particularly close one. Rhetoric rationalises a domain in which any suspicion of artificiality will evoke especially vehement reactions. At the same time rhetoric always confronts a singular need to insure itself of its disciplinary status, not to dissolve itself in nature. Two contradictory demands are imposed on every rhetoric: it must hold firm to its disciplinary character, but simultaneously it can never be permitted to appear publicly as the proud producer of its artful works. Rhetoric is never allowed to reveal its identity as the representative of the power of the word. From the point of view of the theory of science, the rule that art conceal its artfulness translates directly into the demand that rhetoric give up its disciplinary status and its authority as rule-giver.

Cato's vision of an artless rhetoric according to this principle of *rem tene verba sequentur*[47] and the assertion of Quintilian that the rules of the art should always assume a secondary importance to that which the given case itself 'teaches,'[48] subvert the authority of rules, which was the primary domain of rhetorical knowledge in its confrontation with its students. As rhetoric moved away from the scene of instruction, it becomes apparent to us that rhetoric turned into a cultural self-awareness, primarily concerned with the uses of language. When rhetoric finally took on this course in the eighteenth century, as it promoted the art of reading rather than the art of persuading, then it could do so only because it had found in the universities an institutional setting which, in a way more powerful than any rhetoric of rhetoric, guaranteed its existence by means of officially instituted professorships.

The strategies with which rhetoric affirms itself as discipline or avoids its nullification – the rhetoric of rhetoric – are never simple. The following tropes circumscribe the conditions of the possibility of the discipline of rhetoric: the reduction of a discipline to its spokespersons; presenting the art of rhetoric under the protection of the might of language; insisting on the impossibility of teaching *kairos* or presenting rhetoric as a system of technical insights (*techne*); introducing the knowledge of rhetoric as a natural gift or as an artless achievement.[49] While it remains true that rhetoric could only turn into a cultural reality in the context of democratic structures of ancient Greece, these political conditions were never sufficient to explain the establishment of rhetoric as a discipline. Focussing on the discursive strategies of self-affirmation has perhaps allowed us to get a little closer to the moment at which rhetorical insight transformed itself into a discipline. However, the becoming of knowledge has not lost its enigmatic character.

Almost every one of the rhetorical strategies discussed above has two sides and serves more than one interest. As in every rhetorical argument, they possess implications which neither are known to their speakers nor further their purposes. The force of these tropes, which have made rhetoric possible as a discipline and have postponed its abolition, should at all events guarantee them a place of honour in the history of science.

A rhetorical analysis of the history of science attempts to understand the polemical value of the discourse of a given discipline. It will analyse the assertions and theories of a discipline for the value they possess in the making of that discipline.[50] This kind of analysis no longer accepts as a natural given the claim to autonomy, which institutions of knowledge tend to posit. Disciplines secure their status by negating the interactions that they too, by necessity, maintain with what surrounds them. By asserting their independence from those who are to accept, use or to buy their insights, disciplines gain a degree of authority, to which no single speaker can ever lay claim. Through these strategies, as I have explored them above, rhetoric constitutes itself as a discipline and simultaneously makes us forget the rhetorical ever lay claim. Through these strategies, as I have explored them above, rhetoric constitutes itself as a discipline and simultaneously makes us forget the rhetorical conditions of its disciplinary existence. The early history of rhetoric affords a rare view of a discipline in the state of incomplete closure. At the same time, it seems that the rhetorical analysis employed in this attempt has proven that rhetoric still has a great future among the analytic tools of the history of science. But no doubt, the use of rhetorical analysis in the history of science will necessitate some changes within this historical discipline. To delineate them will be the scope of another essay.

Notes

1. Shelley, Mary, *Frankenstein, Or, The Modern Prometheus* (New York: Signet, 1965) pp. 51.

2. Lloyd, Geoffrey, *Magic, Reason and Experience. Studies in the Origin and Development of Greek Science* (Cambridge: Cambridge University Press, 1979), esp. pp. 79-86.

3. Kleingnther, Adolf, *Protos Euretes* (Philologus supp. xxvi, 1; Leipzig: Dieterich, 1933).

4. Hubbell, H.M., *The Rhetorica of Philodemus* (*Transactions of the Connecticut Academy of Science*, 1920) vol. 23, p. 368. Important: Robert Hariman, 'Status, Marginality, and Rhetorical Theory' *Quarterly Journal of Speech* 72 (1989) pp. 38-54.

5. Kennedy, George, *The Art of Persuasion in Greece* (Princeton: Princeton University Press, 1963) vol. 325; but cf. pp. 123f. and pp. 322f.

6. Roochnik, David, 'Socrate's Use of the Techne-Analogy' *Journal of the History of Philosophy* 24 (1986) pp. 295-310.

7. Cf. Romain Laufer, 'Systéme de légitimité, marketing et sophistique' in Barbara Cassin (ed.), *Le Plaisir de Parler* (Paris: Minuit, 1986) pp. 209-36.

8. Most recently Jonathan Barnes, 'Is Rhetoric an Art?', in *darg Newsletter* (Discourse Analysis Research Group, University of Calgary, Fall 1986) p. 2, no. 2-22.

9. Shorey, Paul, 'physis, melete, epistéme', in *American Philogical Ass., Transactions and Proceedings* 40 (1909) pp. 185-201; Clark, D.L., 'The Requirements of a Poet', in *Modern Philology* 16 (1918) pp. 413ff. See also 'L'ideologia della retorica' *Helikon* (1990); forthcoming Pierre Bourdieu has discussed this complex in terms of the 'ideology of giftedness', in Pierre Bourdieu and Jean-Claude Passeron, *Reproduction in Education, Society and Cultures* (London: Sage, 1977).

10. Barwick, Karl, *Das rednerische Bildungsideal Ciceros* (Berlin: Akademieverlag, 1963; Abhandlungen der Sächsischen Akademie der Wissenschaften zu Leipzig, Philologisch-historische Klasse) vol. 54, no. 3. Quadlbauer, Franz, 'Optimus Orator/Perfecte Eloquens: Zu Ciceros formalem Rednerideal und seiner Nachwirkung' *Rhetorica* 2 (1984) pp. 102-20.

11. Aristides, K.II (=D.XLV) pp. 249, 376, 430.

12. Quint. I, pr. 9; XII.1.2; cf. II.15.1.34.

13. VS 82 B11; Cf. also the new edition by Thomas Buchheim, *Gorgias von Leontinoi, Reden, Fragmente und Testimonien* (Hamburg: Meiner, 1989).

14. Isoc. XV.254; Plato *Gorg.* 448 c; *Hel.* 8; Cic. *De inv.* I.4.5.

15. Tenbruck, Friedrich, 'Zur Soziologie der Sophistik', in *Neue Hefte für Philosophie* 10 (1976) pp. 51-77.

16. Pohlenz, Max, 'prepon. Ein Beitrag zur Geschichte des griechischen Geistes', in *Nachrichten der Gesellschaft der Wissenschaften zu Göttingen, phil.-hist. Klasse* I, 16 (1933) pp. 53-92; Kinneavy, James, '*Kairos*: A Neglected Concept in Classical Rhetoric', in Jean Dietz Moss (ed.), *Rhetoric and Practice* (Washington, DC: Catholic University of America, 1985) pp. 79-105; White, Eric, *Kaironomia. On the Will to Invent* (Ithaca: Cornell University Press, 1987).

17. Quint. II.13.2, Cic. *De or.* I.5.19; *De off.* 135; Seneca, *Controv. praef.* 10.

18. Cahn, Michael, 'Reading Rhetoric Rhetorically. Isocrates and the Marketing of Insight' *Rhetorica* 7 (1989) pp. 121-44.

19. The value of the Platonic polemics against rhetoric for such a reconstruction has often been questioned. In a certain sense his presentation of rhetoric, even if it is malicious and historically unreliable, testifies to the existence of a certain impression of rhetoric, that, even if it was never correct, was nevertheless a cultural and consequently disciplinary reality.

20. Auct. ad. Alex 1436a12; Auct. ad Her. III.9.16; 10.17; Horaz: *Ars Poetica*, 408 ff. Heinrich Lausberg (*Handbuch der literarischen Rhetorik*) is quite right when he called it 'harmonising' when *natura* is considered as a source of *ars*. This marks the point where an analysis of the ideological implications of rhetoric could take place. That there always already was something called practical rhetoric is irrelevant for the analysis of the constitution of rhetoric. Precisely this gesture of naturalising the art of rhetoric is here analysed as a rhetorical strategy.

21. Cf. Carnes Lord, 'The Intention of Aristotle's Rhetoric', in *Hermes* (1981) pp. 109, 326-39.

22. Schiappa, Edward, 'Did Plato Coin *Retorike*?' *American Journal of Philology* 111 (1990).

23. *átechnia*, Arist. EN 6.4; 1140a 20; *kakotechnia*, Quint. II.15.2; 20.2; *ars fallendi*, Quint. II.15.23.

24. Gorg. *Hel.* 10.14. Cf. Jacqueline de Romilly, *Magic and Rhetoric in Ancient Greece* (Cambridge, MA: Harvard University Press, 1975); George Walsh, *The Varieties of Enchantment* (Chapel Hill: University of North Carolina Press, 1984); John Ward, 'Magic and Rhetoric from Antiquity to the Renaissance', in *Rhetorica* 6 (1988) pp. 57-118; Carlo Viano, 'Rhetorica, magia e natura in Platone', in *Rivista di Filosofia* 56 (1965) pp. 411-53.

25. Medicine: Arist. *Rhet.* I.1.14, 1355b 12; Quint. I.10.6; II.17.9; III.2.3; 6.64; IV.2.84; VI.4.19; Cic. *De inv.* 1.6; *De or.* 2.44.186; Cookery: *Gorg.* 463b, 518b; H. Dohm, *Mageiros. Die Rolle Des Kochs in der griechisch-römishcen Komödie* (München, 1964); Cosmetics: Plato *Gorg.* 465b; Petron *Sat.* 2.6; Dio. Halik. Iso. 3; Dialectics: Arist. *Rhet.* init; Quint. II.20.7; Helmsmanship: Plato *Gorg.* 511d ff.; Gymnastics: Isocr. XV.181 ff.; Plato *Gorg.* 465b.

27. Foucault, Michael, *L'ordre du discours* (Paris, 1970).

28. Gigon, Olof, 'Philosophie und Wissenschaft bei den Griechen', in *Griechische Literatur*, Ernst Vogt (ed.), *Neues Handbuch der Literaturwissenschaft* 2 (1981) p. 244; Lloyd, Geoffrey, *Science, Folklore and Ideology. Studies in the Life Sciences in Ancient Greece* (Cambridge: Cambridge University Press, 1983) pp. 201-17.

29. Kube, Jörg, *téchne und arete. Sophistisches und platonisches Tugendwissen* (Berlin: De Gruyter, 1969) pp. 31f.

30. Gigon, op. cit., p. 197; cf. Antje Hellwig, *Untersuchungen zur Theorie der Rhetorik bei Platon und Aristoteles* (Göttingen: Vandenhoeck & Ruprecht, 1973) pp. 39, 45; Wolfgang Schadewaldt, 'Die Begriffe Natur und Technik bei den Griechen', in *Hellas und Hesperien. Gesammelte Schriften* (Zürich: Artemis, 1970) II, pp. 512-25.

31. Solmsen, Friedrich, 'The Aristotelian Tradition in Ancient Rhetoric', in *American Journal of Philology* 62 (1941) pp. 35-50; 169-180. Cf. Michael Leff, 'Genre and Paradigm in the Second Book of *De Oratore*', in *Southern Speech Communication Journal* 51 (1986) pp. 308-25.

32. Blumenberg, Hans, 'Nachahmung der Natur. Zur Vorgeschichte der Idee des schöpferischen Menschen', *Wirklichkeiten in denen wir Leben* (Stuttgart: Reclam, 1981) pp. 55-103.

33. In rhetorical studies, Aristotle often figures as the authority on what can count as a science, and how theoretical sciences should be distinguished from practical sciences. While this essay does not propose to analyse the important disciplinary value of these apparently purely philosophical distinctions, the necessity of such a reconstruction is evident.

34. Cahn, Michael, *Kunst der Überlistung. Studien zur Wissenschaftsgeschichte der Rhetorik* (München: Fink, 1986) p. 34.

35. Aristotle, *Aristotle's Rhetoric*, trans. Richard Jebb, J.E. Sandys (ed.) (Cambridge: Cambridge University Press, 1909) p. 1.

36. Being a philosopher and not a rhetorician, why does Aristotle champion rhetoric to this extraordinary extent? Why does he conceive of such a strong legitimation for the art of his competitors? The only possible answer to this question seems to be that for Aristotle philosophy does not exclude rhetoric.

37. *De Or.* I.146. I have called this the theory of 'secondarity' in *Kunst der Überlistung*, 23, 41 etc.

38. Kennedy, George, *The Art of Persuasion in Greece* (Princeton: Princeton University Press, 1963) p. 323.

39. Shorey, Paul, 'Physis, Melete, Epistéme' *American Philological Association, Transactions and Proceedings* 40 (1909) pp. 185-201.

40. Sextus Empiricus, *Against the Professors* II.97f.; R.G. Bury (ed.) (London: Heinemann, 1961) pp. 253f. Cf. Walz IV, 11, 14f.; Blaß: Attische Beredsamkeit I. 20; Durrell Amundsen, 'The Liability of the Physician in Classical Greek Legal Theory and Practice,' in *Journal of the History of Medicine and Allied Sciences* 32 (1977) pp. 172-203. The anecdote has also been told about Protagoras (DK 80 A1).

41. Hinks, D.A., 'Tisias and Corax and the Invention of Rhetoric', in *Classical Quarterly* 34 (1940) pp. 61-9.

42. 'Educators Professional-Liability Insurance' *MLA Newsletter* 21, no. 3 (Fall 1989) p. 2.

43. Lyotard, J.-F., *La condition postmoderne. Rapport sur le savoir* (Paris: Minuit, 1979) p. 45.

44. Quint. II.12.1; Lausberg para. 41, Arthur Lovejoy, George Boas, *A Documentary History of Primitivism and Related Ideas* (Baltimore: John Hopkins University Press, 1935).

45. Arist. *Rhet.* III.2; III.7; Ps.-Long. *De subl.* 17.1; 18.2; 22.1; 38.2f.; Auct. *ad Her.* I.10.17; II.30. 47; IV.7.10; Quint. I.11.3; II.5.7; IV.1.8f.; IV.1.54-59; IV.2.126; IX.4.120.144.147; XI.2.47; Cic. *Brut.* 37.139; Cic. *De inv.* I.28.25; 52.98; Cic. *Or.* 12.38; Cic. *De orat.* II.37.156.

46. Cf. William Covino, *The Art of Wondering. A Revisionist Return to the History of Rhetoric* (Portsmouth: Boynton, 1988) p. 31.

47. Cato fr. 15, Halm (1863) p. 374.

48. 'causae docebunt', Quint. II.13.5.

49. In my article 'Ars', *Historisches Wörterbuch der Rhetorik*, Gerg Ueding, Walter Jens (eds) (in press), I have tried to reduce these tropes of rhetorical self-constitution into two major classes: those which assert rhetoric to be an art (*techne*), and those which assert it not to be an art (*kairos*).

50. Latour, Bruno, *Science in Action* (Cambridge, MA: Harvard University Press, 1987) pp. 13ff.

PART II

The Disciplinary Turn: Rhetoric and the Emergence of the Human Sciences

Whilst it was not possible to represent exhaustively the historical evolution of rhetoric in this volume, the first section has provided insights into the processes involved. It is, however, with the emergence of disciplines in the human sciences that the disciplinary and pedagogic status of rhetoric was challenged, seemingly to its detractors, to irreversible and mortal effect. Walter Rüegg and Philippe-Joseph Salazar explore the German and French contexts in which this crisis took place, providing what amount to 'archaeologies' of rhetoric's own going-to-ground in the course of the nineteenth century. It becomes obvious that no simple occlusion (or *occultation*') of rhetoric comes about, but a far more complex and interesting process takes place which illustrates, in reverse as it were, Cahn's thesis. Thus the latter's assertion that the self-constitution of a discipline invariably involves rhetorical strategies, applies even when such an emergent discipline explicitly disavows *all* rhetorical antecedents or affinities. So it is that Rüegg and Salazar explore the dialectics of rhetorical concealment and the renewed exploitation of rhetorical techniques in what publicly purported to be a post-rhetorical era.

Walter Rüegg begins his contribution with some autobiographical remarks which recall his experience at the Sorbonne immediately before the Second World War. At that time the cultural hegemony of Germany in the humanities was still recognised, a hegemony which has now, according to Rüegg, passed to the United States. The origin of Germany's potent and self-conscious cultural mission lay in the rise to prominence of classical studies and Rüegg shows how *Altertumswissenschaft* played a constitutive role in the construction of the cultural identity of a unifying and increasingly powerful nation, and its own rhetorical self-projection. In this context of nascent national identity, the problem of how the differentiation of the emergent human sciences (*Geisteswissenschaften*) ought to be understood and managed gave rise to a contemporary analogate to the ancestral problem of the relation of rhetoric and dialectic. In the face of the growing fragmentation in the *Geisteswissenschaften* implied by the differentiation of the human sciences, rhetorical means were indispensable in the cultivation of national identity and cultural integrity (and indeed in the whole political culture). Rüegg's account of the crisis goes some way to explain the later societal plausibility of post-war West German intellectual and social strategies of conflict resolution through 'communicative action', characteristic, for example, of Jürgen Habermas.

Philippe-Joseph Salazar is a representative of the multi-disciplinary, post-Marxian, *'sociologie de l'imaginaire'* (predominantly francophone) school which lays particular emphasis upon the micro-sociological analysis of everyday life, the *'quotidien'*. Two tendencies in contemporary rhetorical work, the historical and the general (that is the theoretical), oppose each other, yet when they are understood together they can be seen to threaten the legacies of both structuralism and post-structuralist deconstruction. The 'new rhetoricians' value the conceptions of *'tradition'* and *'permanence'* and re-infuse ethical content into a more broadly drawn category of *'littérature'*. This 'recovery of rhetoric' entails, it would seem, a far-reaching re-integration of the disciplines of the human sciences, a task currently being attempted by the members of the Groupe de l'Imaginaire, among others.[1] Salazar's approach here involves a fusion of anthropological and sociological methods and the adoption of a rhetorical stance over against the 'scientistic' tendencies of Durkheim; thus the 'sociologus like the orator expresses and fashions culture, representing what is best and most striking in it'. In consequence, the task of sociology entails the careful rediscovery and recovery of a form of wisdom.

Both Salazar and Rüegg confront a similar conflict in different contexts, that is the struggle between rhetoric and anti-rhetoric in the emergence of the human sciences. Where the latter are true to tradition they reflect the ideals of *humanitas*. When they too rashly embody the yearning for a 'hard' socio-scientific configuration, they then tend to slide into a deceptive and ultimately self-stultifying repression of precisely those rhetorical dimensions that are essential to the successful communication of the polyvalence of the 'human condition' to humanity itself.

Note

1. The publications of M. Maffesoli, G. Duand, P. Tacussel, and Ph.-J. Salazar are by their range and polymathic mastery indicative. The aims and methods of this school are expounded in the review, *Cahiers de l'Imaginaire* (Paris: Editions Privat, 1988ff).

4

Rhetoric and Anti-Rhetoric in the Nineteenth- and Twentieth-Century Human Sciences in Germany

Walter Rüegg (University of Berne)

In 1938, when I was studying at the Sorbonne,[1] participants in philosophical and philological seminars used to be asked whether they could read German books. Without a knowledge of German it was thought impossible to pursue true scholarship in these areas, for not only were the most important reference works, but also the most significant research monographs of German origin. The German humanities were indeed still living off the reputation which they had gained before the First World War. At that time, would-be students with scientific ambitions from throughout the world made their academic pilgrimage to Berlin, Bonn, Göttingen and Heidelberg. Moreover, in 1930 Abraham Flexner argued in his comparison of American, English and German universities that it was only from 1876 onwards, when the Johns Hopkins University set up a research-oriented Graduate School according to the German model, that one could speak of *universities* in America.[2]

In one of the many speeches made in celebration of the turn of the century, the Marburg classical philologist Th. Birt emphatically underlined the pioneering achievements of Germany when he cited the following examples, for it was: 'not an Englishman, but a Delius in Bonn who first securely established the text of Shakespeare', and, 'Sybel was the first to recount to the French the history of their great Revolution on the basis of their own documents'. Birt even went so far as to assert that: 'the German *Wissenschaft* (science) of our century signifies the triumph of the German *Geist* (spirit) over every foreign country; this science is our title of honour and its workshops are the German universities'.[3]

In a more discriminating way, but no less unambiguously, on the 13th of January 1900 the well-known philologist U. von Wilamowitz-Moellendorff emphasised the surpassing significance of German science:

> What will undoubtedly remain forever in the memory of man as the greatest event of the nineteenth century is the rise of Germany to the status of a world power, not just in the political sphere but in the unmeasurably great attainments made by the hand and

brain of German labour, both for us and on behalf of the whole of humanity.

By means of this achievement, Germany 'would have paid back its debt of gratitude to the peoples of older cultures for their centuries of enlightenment and education'. In the twentieth century, this role would be taken over by America:

> If now, however, we joyfully and readily greet the rise and strengthening of other peoples as a gain for humanity as a whole, and if, moreover, we are happy to concede that an event of foreign fame will define the twentieth century, we have nonetheless the right on this festive occasion to claim that the most precious gain won by humanity in the nineteenth century bears the stamp of German origin.[4]

We are still separated by some years from the turn of the century, but we are already in a position to confirm that Wilamovitz was not erroneous in his prediction. In order now to attain academic heights, one must be able to read English and not German. North America (i.e., the United States) has taken over from Germany as the Mecca of the rising scientific generation. How should we now evaluate what the German mind achieved for humanity in the nineteenth century? Allan Bloom regards this achievement as a Trojan horse. By contrast, Anthony Grafton detects a wide and haunted empty space at the centre of the intellectual landscape of the Germany of that time. Classical philology which is known to have been of fundamental importance both for the development of the *Geisteswissenschaften* (the human sciences) and for the education of the intellectual and political élites of Germany seemed to him inadequately researched. As Grafton puts it:

> The internal history of scholarship remains, even in the best modern works, a series of brilliant sub-histories of individual fields and approaches; and the relation between these sub-histories and the political and institutional context is even more obscure than their connections to one another.

Grafton threw new light on this situation when he investigated the methods, institutional presuppositions and patterns of innovation, besides the context of philology, examining it in relation to its goals and social functions during the period 1780 to 1850. This, however, brought him to the conclusion, expressed earlier by many others before him, that the increasing splitting apart and loss of connection between research and teaching ran increasingly counter to the goal first established by the professional class of philologists; this was originally directed towards the attainment of education through science. Grafton remarks furthermore that, 'In the years after 1850 the great creation of Humboldt and Wolf looked very much like a self-consuming artifact.'[5] Grafton also edited the reprint in 1986 of Ludwig Hatvany's *Die Wissenschaft des Nicht Wissenswerten* (*The Science of the Not-Worth- Knowing*) of 1908[6] in which the latter mocked the instruction provided by such renowned philologists as Diels and Wilamowitz. Despite his intelligent and appreciative introduction to this satirical text, Grafton does not answer the question as to how it came about that the philologists lapsed from their original goal.

In this chapter I would like to look into one aspect of this problem, the fundamental significance of which is scarcely acknowledged, and which has until now gone unnoticed in the 'sub-histories': we refer to the relationship of the German humanities to rhetoric. This is a matter neither of the general decline in rhetorical technique (which has been dealt with by more competent colleagues like Brian Vickers[7]), nor is it concerned with rhetorical instruction in the German grammar school. Although in comparison with France and Belgium, formal instruction in rhetoric declined significantly earlier in Germany, it did so in locally varying degrees. For example, in Bavaria, Baden and Württemberg rhetoric continued to be taught in German lessons; in Prussia, instruction in rhetoric was neither prescribed nor forbidden; such instruction was abolished in the *Fürstenschulen* (Prince's schools) in Saxony in 1819 and in Austria in 1849; and it was generally viewed in negative terms where it persisted as a special taught subject.[8]

Rather than investigate this decline, I would like to develop some arguments for the following thesis. My contention is that both *Altertumswissenschaft* (the scientific study of the ancient world) and the *Geisteswissenschaften* (the human sciences which developed later in the nineteenth century in forms modelled upon the earlier method) can be seen to emerge from a fundamentally different understanding of humankind and its associated cultural forms and modes of action from that of the rhetorical tradition of the *studia humanitatis*. From the fifteenth century onwards the latter had determined higher education in the whole of Europe. I hope to be able to make this paradigm shift from the rhetorical conception of human self-understanding to that of the human sciences appear at least sufficiently plausible for it to be taken up in future research. For, as Walter Jens states in his lexicon article on 'Rhetoric' in the nineteenth century, 'Here a great field awaits cultivation'.[9]

It is well-known that attacks upon rhetoric, and its representative Cicero, were never so vehemently delivered as in nineteenth century Germany.[10] Attempts made so far to explain this contempt for rhetoric fail to convince. Neither can the decline of rhetoric be attributed to the claim that the German bourgeoisie had constructed for itself a world of illusion out of the arts and the realm of ideas as a surrogate for its political impotence. Indeed these factors were more marked during the period of absolutism and in the court circles of the sixteenth and seventeenth centuries when rhetoric as *regina artium* ruled *belles lettres*,[11] literature and the education of the bourgeois elites. Nor, moreover, is the obvious explanation satisfactory – that with the abolition of Latin as the language of scholarship, so Latin drilling became superfluous.[12] In the other cities of Western Europe where Latin had already been displaced by the vernacular, rhetoric retreated significantly more slowly, and, as already mentioned, in South Germany rhetoric remained a subject in German school instruction.

The very violence of the German attacks upon rhetoric lend weight to the conjecture that the assailants had in their sights not only Latin instruction but a greater enemy, namely the rhetorical character of the Latin tradition itself. In 1901 the Swiss writer Carl Spitteler (who later was to receive the 1919 Nobel Prize for Literature for his *Olympischer Frühling*) expressed the general disparagement of rhetorically-cast Latin literature in the German humanities that characterised his (and indeed, my own) time as an undergraduate. Thus in his essay, '*Professor*

Glauberecht Goethefest Dunkel von Weisenstein über Weltliteratur' (renderable as 'Professor Right-think Goethe-firm Self-conceit of Sage's Stone on the Subject of World Literature'), Spitteler articulated this dissatisfaction as follows: 'the Romans were basically an arch-prosaic nation: hollow rhetoric, imitation without imagination, sober prudence'.[13]

This specifically German abuse of the Latin tradition can be found as early as 1767 in Herder's first work:

> The refined Greek taste in language, science and the arts had first to pale under the Roman sky and exhale its perfume: truth and beauty, half-withered, grieve like wilted flowers – and now northern hordes come and completely trample these blooms into the ground. Decayed Roman literature mingles itself with the crude conceptions of its conquerers.

Charlemagne, so Herder claimed, did not cure this. On the contrary, he brought the papist idolatry of Latin religion to the Germans, suffocated their intellect with Latin literature and with the Latin language drew eternal barbarism in German culture:

> And this Flood had to stand there through many centuries in a stagnant calm until it had soaked into the very marrow of literature, poisoned the spirit of the Nation and left behind everlasting and indelible impressions upon scholarship and the language, and upon the external conditions which are the form of culture.

How fortunate it would be for the German national character should Germany have been a Brittanic island. What an advantage it would be for a way of thinking and for taste 'if Europe had been a slave of Greek Constantinople rather than of Latin Rome'.[14] Later on certainly, Herder expressed himself more moderately, even positively, on the subject of the Latin culture of antiquity and the Middle Ages. Nevertheless, like many other contemporaries, he remained convinced that only with the help of the Greeks could the Germans recover the originality suppressed by the Latin-French tradition.

Johann Winckelmann, often regarded as the first German scholar in the modern sense of the word and founder of the German *Geschichtswissenschaft* (science of history),[15] had already given expression in 1755 to the feeling of oppression of German taste through Latin Baroque and Rococo art. He himself took refuge from this in the noble simplicity and calm grandeur of Greek works of art. Winckelmann's first work provided the programme for an entire generation in which he urged his readers to search for the originality of the divine beauty of youth found in Greek antiquity and there to find their spiritual home. Herder expanded this new perspective into the *'schönen Wissenschaften'*, *belles lettres*, in which 'the ideal of their works and beautiful nature almost compose a picture in themselves'. The works of the Greeks should be read with the intention 'that we not only unfold this tender seed of humanity in a sophisticated way, but also implant it in ourselves and in the hearts of our youth. We do not desire to possess Greek art, rather that it should possess us'.[16]

This last sentence, taken from the *Briefe Zur Beförderung der Humanität* of

1793, contains a programme for the human sciences *in nuce*: the task of science is to grasp the idea of humanity in its essence and to represent it in its historical configuration in such a way that as this image takes possession of the student so it forms and instructs him. Before we pursue further this fundamental paradigm shift in the conceptions of scholarship and education, the significance of the year 1793 obliges us to take a look at the contemporary political setting. It is generally recognised today that the experience of the French Revolution and the Napoleonic Wars was instrumental in the development of the German human sciences, but the role of rhetoric in this, so far as I can judge, is scarcely considered at all.

During the French Revolution, republican Rome became the great prototype for forensic and political debate. '*Ainsi faisaient les Romains*' was the stock phrase used in meetings and clubs. The popularity of Cicero was seldom greater. In his *Cicero im Wandel der Jahrhunderte*, Zielinski provided such a multiplicity of examples of the direct appropriation of republican conceptions, arguments and even of whole institutions from Ciceronic writings, to the extent that Cicero could be called 'the great hero of the French Revolution'.[17]

As statesman of the Republic and as philosophical authority on republican virtues, but above all as rhetorician, Cicero was revered, read and imitated down to the smallest details in political pamphlets and speeches, as well as in prosecution and defence speeches by all parties. The fact that he owed his political career to advocacy was not regarded as a deficiency but as a positive advantage in the eyes of the Third Estate. Even Cicero's failure and death at the hands of the executioner provided the victims of the *terreur* with a comforting example. It was because of the political and social importance of rhetoric during the Revolution that its continued influence in nineteenth-century French culture made it appear all the more questionable to the German observer. That is once the enthusiasm for the liberating power of the word had given way to revulsion in face of the bloody consequences of demagogy. This was even more valid in the case of Napoleon's rule, which commanded all the instruments of classical rhetoric but took its inspiration rather from Caesar, Justinian and Charlemagne. Thus for Germans such rhetoric incorporated the Latin powers of order and oppression that had already been denounced by Herder.[18]

It is not hereby claimed that the German human sciences came into existence simply as a reaction to the rhetoric of the French Revolution and Napoleonic rule. But there is no doubt that contemporary events, and in particular the wars of independence, gave a national dimension to the generally acknowledged bias of German classicism towards the Greek ideal of humanity. Certainly it was not feasible for the Greek *polis* to offer a direct model for the German kingdoms and princedoms in the way republican Rome had served for the French Revolution. However, shattered German self-consciousness needed what Hegel called the 'plastic, morally unambiguous virtue and love of the Fatherland'[19] besides other ideals which could serve as the shining examples that since Wincklemann had been drawn from Greek art and culture. This was the more so since such ideals could be attributed to the spiritual affinity between Greeks and Germans, who were both regarded as young, creative, poetic and philosophical nations, as distinct from the ageing, superficial and rhetorical Latin cultures. In 1807, Wilhelm von Humboldt attested[20] in his fragments on the

'Theme of the Greek National Character' that the German in his striving after ideality and political eloquence was more similar to the Greek than to the Frenchman, who 'could never raise himself above imitation of the Romans'. The Greek and the German embodied both the general and the particular in a way which distinguishes powerful individuality in its pure and original form. Thus it was for both von Humboldt and Goethe that the science of classical studies (*Altertumswissenschaft*), a discipline founded by their mutual friend Friedrich August Wolf through his discernment in the Greeks of that embodiment of ideals in the totality of their conditions and realisations, sought equally to promote the education of the Germans into humanity. After 1809 the study of Greek as a means of German *Nationalerziehung* (national education and training) was propagated along with the francophobe fervour of the wars of liberation.[21]

It was thus that the German *Altertumswissenschaft* found its fetish in the culture of the Greeks, but also its taboo in the rhetorically-stamped Latin tradition. Before the First World War this tendency became politically virulent in different ways, but eventually it had negative repercussions for German science as a whole as the archeologist Ludwig Curtius was to confirm in 1926. Outstanding scholars from Italy and England had indicated to him that the political and intellectual isolation of Germany after 1918 could be attributed to the far-reaching equation of the Greek mind with that of Germany and to the deprecation of Latin culture by German scholarship: Germany had thereby been itself excluded from the European tradition.[22]

It is well known that the term '*Geisteswissenschaften*' is only with difficulty translatable. In English it is rendered by 'human sciences' or 'human studies' and in French by '*sciences humaines*' or '*sciences de l'homme*'. What does this semantic difference and the paradigm shift it expresses signify? The second part of this chapter is devoted to this question.

August Boeckh, who was responsible for turning the new paradigm of *Altertumswissenschaft* into a philosophically-based system couched in terms of historically-oriented philology criticised the study of the humanities and previous philology for its lack of scientific qualities. In his lectures on *Enzyklopädie* and *Methodologie* of the philological sciences (which he repeated twenty-six times between 1809 and 1865) Boeckh maintained that these sciences had neither philosophically nor historically advanced the *Erkennens des Erkannten* ('knowledge of the known') which should be the task of the human sciences.[23]

The great Dutch philologists had as it were passed through the landscape of antiquity as though marching on an isolated highroad and as a result only collected external facts. Boeckh could have applied the same image to the rhetorico-humanistic cultural movement. Thus when Fénélon's Télémaque or Wieland's Agathon are introduced into the world of antiquity, they are supposed, like the young nobleman on the Grand Tour, to be educated through encountering foreigners and their customs, and, as the *Agathon* has it, to experience what *virtus et sapientia* are capable of. 'Such a procedure', Boeckh maintained, 'does not lead to the essence of things. The only correct method is cyclical, in which one refers everything back to a single point and from there proceeds to all points on the periphery.'[24]

This centre of scientific research and culture is to be found in what Boeckh called the 'principle of a people or an epoch', the 'innermost kernel of its whole struc-ture',[25] in what Herder had called 'the tender seed of humanity', and Hegel characterised as the *Wesen des Geistes* ('true universal being of the mind'). For Hegel, the departure-point of culture is the 'centrifugal drive of the soul'. The latter alienates man from his natural being and establishes the necessity 'of having to posit a distant, strange world in the young mind'. This strange world is to be found in the language and world of the ancients:

> It separates ourselves from ourselves, yet at the same time it contains all starting-points and all the threads that enable us to return to ourselves; it thus has the capacity to establish our friendship with it and the regaining of our selves, but of the self regained in accordance with the true universal being of the spirit.[26]

Of the ancient peoples, it is the Greeks who stand closest to the Germans as a philosophical nation and with whom 'we instantly feel at home'. For

> Greece offers us a happy glimpse of the youthful freshness of the intellectual life. It is here first of all that the spirit grows up and where the contents of its will and knowledge are constituted, but it does so in such a way that the state, family, law and religion are equally goals of individuality, and are only realised through the goals of each individual.[27]

It is not man in the fullness of his personality who is the subject of his volition and action but the mind of a whole people; it is in the latter, the spirit (*Geist*), that individuality is defined and humanity finds its origin and completion. One of Wolf's pupils imagined the Greek world as a 'beautifully formed body organised down to the smallest detail in which everything individual reflects the spirit (*Geist*) of the whole'.[28]

Accordingly, historical and social phenomena, including language and literary works, are no longer simply to be understood as the consequences of human will and action but as objectifications of the *Weltgeist* (world mind) as objects of scientific research and the starting-point of human education. Moreover, since the world spirit manifests itself in its purest and most original form in the spirit of the ancient Greeks, then *Altertumswissenschaft*, and in particular critical philology (which re-stores texts to their original form), become the prototype for the other humanities. The first professors of German studies (*Germanistik*) were classical philogists (e.g., Beneke, Göttingen, 1805; Lachmann, Berlin, 1825).[29]

Romance, and then similarly English, Slav and oriental philology, as well as general linguistics, the scientific study of the Bible, and modern historical science all arose and developed as the intelligent but often rebellious daughters of the historical–critical *Altertumswissenschaft*. In all of them, however, is to be found the typical paradigm shift from the person to the idea as the subject of scientific investi-gation and education. In order to illustrate this let us take three examples. First, David Friedrich Strauss, the founder of historical–critical study of the Bible, saw the novelty of his approach in 'positing instead of an individual an idea (but a real one) as subject of the predicates which are attributed to Christ by the Church'.[30] Gervinus applied Boeckh's cyclical method to the German *Literaturwissenschaft* (literary studies) and he demanded in 1833 that:

> Anyone wishing to proceed in a descriptive manner must first have found the idea which is to guide him in examining his subject; and the more it pervades his subject down to its smallest details, so the more likely it is that he has hit upon the one fundamental idea which runs through just this series of events he has chosen as his theme, which comes to appear in them and relates them to world events.[31]

Ranke, too, although he opposed the method of classical studies, wanted to

> gaze upon and sense the intellectual, life-producing, creative powers in their interrelatedness and differential sequence, in their life and passing away, in their return to life in which greater fullness, higher meaning, and wider range it comprehends and the sympathy it engenders with its being.[32]

This paradigm shift which could similarly be demonstrated in linguistics and the scientific study of mythology, is illustrated by the *neue Metaphorik* also expressed in the earlier quotations. The latter would deserve examination in a separate study, but I here confine myself to the *topos* of intellectual nourishment mediated by literature. In the Middle Ages it was compared to the honey sucked with bee-like industry from the flowers of Christian and Pagan writings. For humanists of the Renaissance the written word was no longer the ephemeral husk surrounding the divine essence but the work of human beings which became available as friends open to questions and whose answers furnished intellectual nourishment in appetising form. Hegel begins with these images but changes them fundamentally. His starting-point is the collapse of Prussia, which he attributes to the utilitarian ideas of the Enlightenment that had instrumentalised the intellect and in so doing had neglected the spiritual background: 'The works of the ancients contain the most precious nutrient in its noblest form – golden apples in silver bowls'. This striking image illustrates the *pathos* that inspired the new human sciences, but also the pathology of their claim to educate into *Bildung* (culture).

The golden apples of the Hesperides are a symbol of youthful immortality embodying the Greek mind in their golden substance; whereas the silver bowls represent the shining and less valuable Roman surface. Attainable in the Hercules myth by cunning or by force, they can be grasped and appropriated by the human sciences through hermeneutics and critique – that is by advancing cyclically from the centre to the whole structure. As a means of nourishment, albeit intellectual, golden apples are difficult to digest. Indeed, as objects of possession, in contrast to the mediaeval divine gift of honey and the humanist's intellectual sustenance provided by as it were a friend, the apples are a gift of Midas.

Hegel, then, lays foundations for the study of Greek literature with images which correspond with the objectivity of the golden apples, which, as subjects of culture and science, do not reveal man but antiquity itself:

> The consummation and majesty of these masterful works must be the intellectual

immersion, the profane baptism, which gives to the soul its first unforgettable infusion of taste and science. For this initiation, a general and superficial acquaintance with the ancients is insufficient [as it was apparently conveyed by the former *studia humanitatis*], but we must give ourselves to them in the way we eat and how we live in order to be infused with the air they breathed, their ideas, their customs, even if you wish, with their errors and prejudices, and thus become inhabitants of that world – the most beautiful that there has ever been. If the first paradise was the paradise of human nature then this second, higher one, is the paradise of the human mind (*Menschengeistes*), a mind which in its beautiful naturalness, freedom, depth and serenity ventures forth like the bride from her chamber.[33]

This hymn-like metaphorical passage from an otherwise rather dry philosopher is characteristic of the almost religious fervour with which science sought to comprehend the mind as origin and goal of world events. But thereby the 'mind', the 'idea', the 'essence of things' are themselves put in question and demythologised. As early as 1818, in his *Staatshaushaltung der Athener*, a masterpiece of the new historical–critical science, Boeckh came to the sobering conclusion that: 'The Hellenes, in the splendour of their art and the prime of their independence, were more unhappy than most would believe, they carried the seed of destruction in themselves and the tree had to be felled when it turned rotten'.[34]

It was not only the science of *Altertumswissenschaft* which was destroyed by the ensuing disclosure of the ideality of its subject matter. At the same time the other sciences of literature and history also searched for, and lost through their probings, the meaning-giving unity expressed in the progress of the world spirit (*Weltgeist*) through history. They replaced it with other constructs drawn from the philosophy of history, like dialectical materialism, or restricted themselves to a positivistic examination and classification of things deprived of their ideality; thus they attempted, as it were, to determine and utilise the gold contained in the apples of the Hesperides.

Where is rhetoric to be found in this development of the human sciences? Boeckh's *Enzklopädie* includes rhetoric in the chapter on the empirical human sciences and understands it as a theory of stylistic speech form, which, as 'technology' had been an ingenious, though unscientific art in the time of the Sophists, Antiphon and Isocrates.[35] According to Boeckh, through Plato (who derived rhetoric from dialectics) and Aristotle (who regarded it as dialectics applied to politics) rhetoric became a philosophical science. It was to find its technical completion as an independent empirical science in the schools of rhetoric but it then finally relapsed into insubstantial and affected verbosity. In the modern period, however, the theory of rhetoric made no progress, indeed it had been neglected and almost forgotten 'because attention is directed more towards intellectual substance than to form'.[36]

Boeckh's statement indicates the three-fold aspects of the 'anti-rhetoric' apparent in the human sciences. First, form is considered as external, as something imposed upon the intellectual content; second, rhetoric is devalued as an unphilosophical artistic skill; and, third, as a persuasive art it is subordinated to the dialectical theory of knowledge.

Viewed positively, these factors form the basis of the *studia humanitatis* and in the twentieth-century they have also rehabilitated rhetoric in the human sciences. The attempt to understand the logic of discourse from the linguistic understanding of the author led, from Valla onwards, to a fruitful relationship between rhetoric and dialectic, and this is now once more being taken seriously in contemporary hermeneutics. Chaïm Perelman's thesis 'that philosophical proof is of a rhetorical nature and that philosophical argumentation insofar as it relies on appropriate premisses, proceeds from what is generally recognised, that is from ordinary principles, concepts and commonplaces'[37] is in accordance with views held by the humanists of the fifteenth to eighteenth centuries. The significance of the linguistic form for the constitution of social reality, the development of attitudes and values, and the dialogical structuring of the open experiential horizon of humankind (which is stressed by phenomenological philosophy and the social sciences) refers back to the 'pre-theoretical cognitive formation' in the rhetorical humanist tradition from Isocrates and Cicero to the *studia humanitatis*. In the light of these considerations I would therefore finally like to indicate briefly the ways in which rhetoric has sought its rehabilitation in the modern humanities, and, in so doing, to remind us of some of the achievements which the 'new rhetoric' owes to the *studia humanitatis*.

Within the science of *Altertumswissenschaft* this change in the study of human-kind occured when it dispensed with the normative role of Hellenism, with which all other cultures had been compared, and extended itself to include the ancient Orient. At the same time, Roman literature was recognised, even if hesitantly, for its own worth. In relation to this, Momigliano made the interesting discovery that four Jewish philologists, Ludwig Friedlander, Traube, Leo and Norden had first introduced a change in attitude.[38] The rehabilitation of Roman literature was most obvious as regards the assessment of Cicero, who, as orator and stylist, had been the target of German anti-rhetoricism. In his epoch-making work *Die antike Kunstprosa* (1896), Eduard Norden demonstrated the difference between the methods of the human sciences and those of the humanities with respect to research into Cicero. The former had opened up the thought-content of many of Cicero's speeches about law and history and had also recognised many of the rules of Cicero's diction better than had, for example, Lorenzo Valla. But the humanists of the Renaissance should have known how to listen to Cicero, in other words, how to comprehend his speeches as the expression of a living personality. Norden held that the modern researcher must therefore try to understand Cicero as orator and stylist from within his own time on the basis of factual material, compare his rhetorical theories with his practice, and, above all, consider the reception of his work by contemporaries and future generations.[39] Thus, it is no longer the 'spirit' (*Geist*) or other principles of an epoch or a nation that stand centre-stage but the forms used by people in a definite historical–social situation to express their knowledge and intentions about the ways in which they thereby influenced others.

In a similar way, rhetoric was understood in relation to its actual origins with the Sophists and Isocrates and no longer assessed and condemned exclusively according to Platonic categories; it was taken seriously in terms of its self-understanding as an educational programme for the new political elites. This is how it was seen by Dilthey in his *Einleitung in die Geisteswissenschaften* written in 1883.[40] This work brought the *Geisteswissenschaften* to a turning-point at which they became more recognisable as moral and human sciences and open to a new understanding of rhetoric. What Dilthey lists as the aims of the *Geisteswissenschaften* applies to rhetoric as well: 'to grasp the singular, individual element of historical social reality, to discern the uniformity at work in its formation and to establish the goals and rules of its continual development'(p. 27). Thus, by means of the 'interrelation of single individuals, their passions, their vanities, their interests observable in cultural systems'(p. 59f) and forms of social organisation 'the necessary and interconnected purpose of the history of mankind is realised' (p. 64f). Consequently, Dilthey rejected historico-philosophical methods which attempted to sum up the course of world history in 'colourless abstractions' like *Geist* or *Vernunft* (p. 104), and he was the first to acknowledge the world-historical significance of Cicero's writings for the cultivation and diffusion of the European ideas of common sense and to give special attention to its mediation through the rhetorically-influenced philosophy of the humanists.[41]

Since Dilthey's reorientation of the human sciences, central concerns of the humanist rhetorical tradition have been taken up and rigorously pursued in historico-critical research. Coluccio Salutati circumscribed the task of the *studia humanitatis* at the beginning of the fifteenth-century with the pithy sentence they should '*ad recte scribendum quandam ianuam aperire quo per te possis in alia diviniora et magis ardua penetrare*'[42] (i.e., open a door to correct writing so that one might penetrate, by one's own power into other, more divine and less easily accessible regions of knowledge). The place of the *studia humanitatis* is in the outer court of the sanctuary of the one truth, in the forum where people of various origins, tendencies and convictions must interact, communicate, and co-operate with one another, and where they must do so by means of the right use of language. In anthropological terms, the humanists accepted the sophistic conception (further developed by Isocrates and Cicero) of humankind as creatures who by means of language create social and political order and establish values.

The *studia humanitatis* therefore made rhetoric the basis of education: human beings cultivate their humanity and grow into a linguistically-convincing, morally-responsible people by studying the written evidence of the communicated self-expression of others and by practising correct formulations for the communication of their own self-expression.

For that reason the *studia humanitatis* was equated with *eruditio moralis*, and history understood primarily as the arena of political and moral decisions. This was based on the attempt to learn to understand people as persons in all the complexities of their feelings, desires, thoughts, actions and experiences, in order thereby to gain greater self-understanding and better to express one's own feelings, desires, thoughts and experiences.

Cassirer's definition of man as an *animal symbolicum* extended that of the *homo loquens*: it is only as a meaning-creating being, guided by significant memories, that man (sic) is able to endow the particular with the significance of the universal and in this way to turn individual self-interpretation into general patterns of action. Because of this, the humanistic way to humanity leads not from the ideal to its plastic form,[43] but from historically-situated individual instances of every-day life through affective literary stylisation and the dramatic and powerful cooperation of the reading public to a general concatenation of meaning, the *sensus communis*.

Style impresses itself upon a person's individuality, but it also shapes the person in the public context of a shared cultural background. In the effort to attain the linguistic power to convince, a person acquires competence in social action and learns to realise him/herself as a social being, and thereby becomes more human. As I have remarked elsewhere, the establishment of rhetoric by the Renaissance humanists anticipates insights in the modern human and social sciences.[44] The latter proceed from the primacy of personal experience in everyday life and they grant decisive significance to persuasive speech and its ability to produce a *sensus communis* achieved through symbolic interaction, dialogical communication, the formation of a common *habitus*, and a market-like exchange of other forms of social behaviour, which conversely issue in an interpretation of social behaviour as text. Through this it can be said that rhetoric has won back an authoritative if not leading position in the *Geisteswissenschaften* of the twentieth-century. The strengthening of this position should be seen as not be the least important objective of this book.

Notes

1. This lecture was given on 26 July 1989 at the opening plenary meeting of the seventh biennial conference of the International Society for the History of Rhetoric in the Aula of the Georg-August University, Göttingen. The text has been revised for publication. The translation is by Gesine Leo and Richard Roberts.

2. Flexner, A., *Universities: American, English, German* (Oxford, 1930) p. 342.

3. Birt, Th., *'Deutsche Wissenschaft im 19. Jahrhundert, Eine Rede zur Jahrhundertwende'*, delivered in Marburg (9 January 1900) pp. 8, 13.

4. von Wilamowitz-Moellendorff, U. (New Year 1900), *Rede zur Feier des Jahrhundertwechsels*, official speech delivered at the University of Berlin on 13 January 1900; *Reden und Vortrage* vol. 2 (Berlin 1926) pp. 41f. Compare this with the dedication he sent with the speech to an American colleague: '*Hunc saecularem fiximus clavem Iovi/Germania inquit. Saeculum vigesimum/Americana terminato gloria', Errinnerungen*, (Leipzig, 1928) p. 246.

5. Grafton, A., 'Polyhistor into Philolog: Notes on the Transformation of German Classical Scholarship, 1780-1850' *History of Universities* 3 (1983) pp. 159-192, citations pp. 159, 162, 184.

6. Grafton, A. (ed.), *Die Wissenschaft des Nichtswissenwerten, ein Kollegienheft von Ludwig Hatvany* (Oxford: Oxford University Press, 1986).

7. For example see ch. 1.

8. Dietrich, 'Rhetorik', in K.A. Schmidt, *Encyklopädie des gesammten Erziehungs- und Unterrichtswesens* (Gotha, 1869) vol. 7, pp. 143, 155.

9. Jens, W., 'Rhetorik', in P. Merker and W. Stammler, *Reallexikon der deutschen Literaturgeschichte* (Berlin: de Gruyter, 1972) vol. 3, p. 443.

10. See M. Fuhrmann, Rhetorik und öffentliche Rede, *Über die Ursachen des*

Verfalls der Rhetorik im ausgehenden 18, Jahrhundert, Konstanzer Universitäts-reden 147 (Konstanz, 1983) pp. 16ff.

11. We use the rather outmoded term *'belles lettres'* to render *'die schönen Wissenschaften'*. The obsolescence of this term is indicated by the renaming of the Regius Chairs of 'Rhetoric and Belles Lettres' in Edinburgh and Glasgow as Chairs of English Literature. Likewise in the previous sentence 'arts' is a rather lacklustre, but inevitable translation of *'die schönen Kunste'*.

12. Fuhrmann, M., 'Die Tradition der Rhetorik-Verachtung und das deutsche Bild vom "Advokaten" Cicero' *Ciceronia* 6 (1988) pp. 24ff.

13. Spitteler, C., *Aesthetische Schriften, Lächende Wahrheiten in erweiterter Folge, Gesammelte Schriften* (Zurich, 1947) vol. 7, p. 684.

14. von Herder, J.G., *Fragmente zur deutschen Literatur*, zweite und dritte Sammlung, Hyne (ed.), *Sammtliche Werke; Zur schonen Literatur und Kunst* (Stuttgart and Tübingen, 1827) Zweiter Theil, pp. 137-43.

15. See L. Curtius, 'Die Antike Kunst und der moderne Humanismus' (1927), in H. Oppermann (ed.), *Humanismus, Wege der Forschung* XVII (Darmstadt, 1970) p. 5.

16. Paulsen, F., *Geschichte des gelehrten Unterrichts auf den deutschen Schulen und Universitäten vom Ausgang des Mittelalters bis zur Gegenwart; Mit besonderer Rucksicht auf den klassischen Unterricht* (Berlin, 3rd edn, 1921) vol 2, p. 199.

17. See Th. Zielinski, *Cicero im Wandel der Jahrhunderte* (Leipzig/Berlin, 4th edn, 1929) pp. 257-72; F. Schnabel, *Deutsche Geschichte im 19. Jahrhundert* (Freiburg im Breisgau, 1947) vol. 1, p. 170.

18. Schnabel, F., *Deutsche Geschichte im neunzehnten Jahrhundert* (Freiburg im Breisgau, 3rd edn, 1947) vol. 7, pp. 172-4.

19. *Gymnasiel-Rede* on the 29 September 1809, *Werke* (Berlin, 1834) vol. 16, p. 141. Professor Rüegg comments as follows upon 'plastisch':

>...in German this use is quite unusual. But it expresses in an excellent way the new world view. That Hegel characterized Greek virtue as *plastisch* indicates that he considered the idea of virtue materialized by the Greeks as a sculpture-like and therefore 'unambiguous' corporeality or totality, like gold in the form of the golden apples of the ideal of youth and beauty in a Greek sculpture. [This 'plastic' ideal corresponds to the new cyclical approach of the *Geisteswissenschaften* which, as he argues in his paper – RHR]...refers everything back to a single (i.e., central) point and from there proceeds to all points on the periphery.

20. In his fragments on the *Thema des griechischen Nationalcharakters*.

21. See W. Rüegg, 'Die Antike als Begrundung des deutschen Nationalbewusst-sein', in W. Schuller (ed.), *Antike in der Moderne* (Konstanz, 1985) pp. 275ff.

22. L. Curtius, op. cit., p. 51.

23. Boeckh, A., *Encyklopädie und Methodologie der philologischen Wissen-schaften*, E. von Bratuschek (Leipzig, 1877) pp. 3-14.

24. Boeckh, A., op. cit., p. 47.

25. Boeckh, A., op.cit., p. 56.

26. Hegel, G.W.F., *Gymnasial-Rede*, op. cit. (n.19 supra) p. 144.

27. Hegel, G.W.F., *Vorlesungen über die Philosophie der Geschichte,*

Werkausgabe (Frankfurt a. M.: Suhrkamp, 1970) vol. 12, p. 275.

28. Ast, F., *Über den Geist des Altertums und dessen Bedeutung für unser Zeitalter*, in R. von Joerden (ed.), *Dokumente des Neuhumanismus* (Weinheim, 2nd edn, 1962) vol. I, p. 16.

29. Christmann, H.H., *Romanistik und Anglistik an der deutschen Universität im 19. Jahrhundert. Ihre Herausbildung als Fächer im Verhaltnis zu Germanistik und klassischer Philologie, Abhandlungen der geistes-und sozialwissenschaftlichen Klasse, Akademie der Wissenschaften und der Literatur, Mainz* no. 1 (Stuttgart, 1985) p. 13.

30. Strauss, D.F., *Das Leben Jesu, kritisch bearbeitet* I (1835) VII; II, 736, cited by W. Kummel, *Das neue Testament, Geschichte der Forschung seiner Probleme* (Freiburg-München, 1948) p. 148.

31. Gervinus, G.G.F., *Schriften zur Literatur* (Berlin, 1982), cited by B. Huppauf, *Literaturgeschichte zwischen Revolution und Reaktion, Aus den Anfängen der Germanistik 1830-1870* (Frankfurt, 1972) p. 10.

32. Ranke, F., 'Die Grossen Mächte', *Hist. polit. Zeitschrift* I (1832) p. 345, cited according to F. Wagner, *Geschichtswissenschaft* (Freiburg-München, 1951) p. 195.

33. Hegel, *Werke* (Berlin, 1834) vol. 16, p. 139

34. Boeckh, A., *Die Staatshaushaltung der Athener* (Berlin, 1863) vol. I, p. 711.

35. Boeckh, A., *Enzyklopädie*, pp. 600f.

36. Boeckh, A., *Enzyklopädie*, loc. cit.

37. Perelman, Chaïm, *Philosophie, Rhetorik, Gemeinplatze*, in H. G. Gadamer (ed.), *Seminar: Die Hermeneutik und die Wissenschaft* (Frankfurt a. M.: Suhrkamp, 1978) p. 381.

38. *Les Études classiques aux XIXème et XXème siécles: Leur place dans l'histoire des ideés. Entretiens sur l'Antiquité Classique* (Vandoeuvres-Geneva, 1980) vol. XXVI, p. 120.

39. Norden, E., *Antike Kunstprosa* (Darmstadt, 5th edn, 1958) vol. I, pp. 212-6.

40. Dilthey, W., *Einleitung in die Geisteswissenschaften, Versuch einer Grundlegung fur das Studium der Gesellschaft und der Geschichte, Gesammelte Schriften*, vol. I (Leipzig/Berlin, 2nd edn, 1923) vol. I.

41. Dilthey, W., *Weltanschauung und Analyse des Menschen seit Renaissance und Reformation, Gesammelte Schriften* (Leipzig/Berlin, 1914) vol. 2, pp. 499; 19ff.

42. Coluccio Salutati, *Epistolario* vol. 3, F. Novati (ed.) (Rome, 1896) p. 614.

43. For comment on 'plastisch' see note 19 above.

44. Rüegg, W., *'Soziologie als humanistische Wissenschaft'* (1977) in W. Rüegg, *Bedrohte Lebensordnung, Studien zur humanistischen Soziologie* (Zürich-München, 1978) pp. 48-56.

5

The Unspeakable Origin:
Rhetoric and the Social Sciences.
A Re-Assessment of the French Tradition

Philippe-Joseph Salazar (University of Capetown)

In memoriam Roland Barthes

Recent developments in French sociology are attracting the attention of historiographers of the discipline away from ideological debates to the emergence of a new problematic. Practioners suddenly find themselves confronted with the emergence of new approaches, and more decisively of a style of tackling theoretical as well as empirical issues that smacks of 'literature' as such. For instance, the rise of the *sociologie de l'imaginaire* has signalled the end of the French sociological establishment of neo-marxist or neo-positivist observance.[1] Although a 'retour à Durkheim' is noticeable, it is the social micro-analyst who is attracting the new generation more than the positivist philosopher. Vilfredo Pareto and Georg Simmel, valued for their finely-tuned understanding of political psychology, and Gabriel Tarde and Frédéric Le Play, thanks to their anti-positivist stance, are now finding favour in sociological debates.[2] A new vocabulary is emerging which disturbs semantics stamped with either systematic or marxist scientism and adopts the new interpretive tools: 'forme', 'fluidité', 'quotidien', 'style', 'esthétique', 'empathie'; all these signal that French sociology and, to some extent, social anthropology are on the point of reassessment.

At the same time, it is noticeable that specialists in literary theory are increasingly aware of the drawbacks of a scientific approach to literature based solely upon structural linguistics and that they are thus proceeding towards an *aggiornamento*. There are two notable features in this changing situation. First, one finds a steadily growing interest in 'orality', the oral as opposed to the written transmission of culture, which was until recently the exclusive domain of some ethnologists and medievalists who were, in fact, working in the wake of the Anglo-American school of orality. Second, rhetoric has already made a forceful and somewhat ambiguous

101

return. Since Roland Barthes' allusive and somewhat ambiguous recourse to what he called 'Ancient Rhetoric', a lively debate has developed between the champions of a 'rhétorique générale', in essence a semiotics of figures of speech and discourse, and the more historically-oriented school of rhetorical studies led by Marc Fumaroli at the Collège de France. The combination of the former tends to undermine the two scientific tenets upon which a 'scientific' approach to literature was based, and this is currently contributing to the reshaping of French literary theory at a distance from positivism. First, in consequence, the Saussurian theory of the sign, which had been drawn upon to sustain the priority of the printed text against oral discourse, is losing credibility, and this undermines the strongest basis of modern French criticism. Second, the undue emphasis laid on the signifier in literary analyses no longer holds firm. The French 'new rhetoricians' stress notions such as 'tradition', 'permanence', 'ideal', while they aim at restoring the ethical content of a reborn 'literature'.[3]

Now, it is apparent that these developments in the social sciences as well as in literary theory are joining forces to restore France's intellectual idiom. In this context, the 'recovery of rhetoric' affects the entire field of inquiry in the humanities and is helping slowly but decisively to shape its renewed coherence.

Undoubtedly, in the social sciences, this 'retour à la rhétorique' is not taking place without creating some confusion, since its conceptual vocabulary is no longer familiar to the practitioners of these disciplines. Sociology, however, is now having to re-evaluate its own tradition and thus come to terms both with its own mythology and with the realisation that before it had itself acquired the rôle of binding agent between all the human sciences, this prestigious and authoritive function had been performed by rhetoric. In consequence, the question which comes to the fore is not merely that of the rhetorical grounding of the human sciences as a whole in a rhetorical past the memory and original concepts of which have undergone occultation, but also the requirement that the conditions of the emergence of the human sciences be defined.

Concerning imitation

Durkheim, in an article entitled 'la sociologia e il suo dominio scientifico' (1900), exposed the epistemological myth at the heart of the French sociological tradition:

> Sociology originated in the shadow of these sciences [i.e., the natural sciences] and as a result it maintained a close connection with the latter while drawing into its sphere of activity all the particular social sciences originally comprised by it, which have now been pervaded by a new spirit.... Under the influence of the ideas summed up by this term, the various fields of study which had thus far sprung from literature or scholarship, began to demonstrate that their true affinities lay elsewhere.... Instead of stopping short at merely reflecting upon the surface events of social life, the need was felt to study the most obscure underlying points, the intimate causes, and the impersonal and hidden forces which drive both the individual and collective society to action. This tendency has already manifested itself amongst certain historians, but the onus is on sociology to arouse a greater consciousness and to clarify and develop this tendency.[4]

Durkheim's historiographical analysis turns upon the problematic term 'literature': sociology, the science of clarification, has to escape from the literary path. The string of metaphors spun out by Durkheim speaks for itself: the humanities are a 'source', the sciences 'overshadow', and history is 'superficial' yet it manages to glimpse those 'depths' which are sociology's own preferred domain. At the same time, Durkheim specifies a process of sequential development, leading from the most extreme superficiality to the most solemn profundity, from literary erudition – traditional *'belles lettres'* – to sociological rationality, and this by way of two borrowed outlooks according to which sociology derives its inspiration from the life sciences or from history, respectively. However, by reading this text blindfold so to speak, we risk missing its unspoken purpose. For Durkheim's literature is not what we understand by the term – in short the novel – but rather that body of critical texts inspired by the tradition of eloquence which links humanist culture to scholarly creation achieved through education. In terms of Durkheim's own culture, the most pertinent examples would be *La cité antique* by Fustel de Coulanges and *L'histoire de Port-Royal* by Sainte-Beuve. In the guise of asserting the originality of sociology against the ascendency of the exact sciences whilst simultaneously having recourse to the latter as a model to be emulated, Durkheim in fact resorts to a methodological concept which lies at the heart of rhetoric: imitation.

In this text, which is a paradigm of discourse on the foundation of the social sciences, Durkheim in reality erected a barrier between two empirical fields of study, history and sociology, both of which are capable of conveying the meaning of the social (*le sens social*). In order to achieve this, he opened up a debate that still continues between two types of rationality. Sociology is conceived as a discipline that aims to prove the existence of social beings or social facts by a form of demonstration (*administration de la preuve*), whereas history, a fundamentally mimetic discipline, is seen to rest on imitating the 'natural' narrative of facts. Now this distinction corresponds in turn with a line of rupture between rhetoric and poetics, and whilst these are both imitative techniques, poetics lacks one aspect of rhetoric: that is the latter's crucial goal of establishing facts and demonstrating their reality.[5] It was at such a juncture that Tarde and Durkheim confronted each other in a dispute concerning the nature of imitation which has ever since dictated the terms underlying certain sociological attitudes held in France.[6]

It is recognised that Tarde located imitation at the root of social diffusion: social facts are considered to be the result of a duplicating action. This view was derided by Durkheim as 'mechanical', 'unintelligible' and 'blind' precisely because he understood imitation as a self-propagating energy, as distinct from any moral 'utility'. Durkheim reproached Tarde with having as a result placed 'the irrational and the miraculous at the base of life' and with thus having banished any hope of developing a mode of sociological description capable of explaining the facts upon which imitation is grounded. Durkheim remains the prisoner of a bias, a *'prénotion'* or preconception which he inherits from a rhetorical culture that held that imitation pertains to *poiesis*. Indeed, Durkheim's attack on Tarde strongly resembles that of the classical rhetorician who (imbued with 'truth') directed this weapon against the poet, as Cicero does in the *Orator*.[7] In short, Durkheim accused Tarde of lacking

103

'wisdom'. It is possible to interpret this polemic against *Les lois de l'imitation* as an attack directed against a sociology which places emphasis upon a social poetics in ways that bring to life an old perspective. This is the stance adapted by Aristotle[8] and the rhetorical-poetic tradition, save for the fact that the *mimesis* fundamentally related to political conditions, here serves to bring the *dramata* and the social actors to the forefront by inserting them into a sort of *'fable'*, a *logos* which nevertheless operates through representation. The law of imitation is a privilege granted to the poetic chain linking, as Michel Maffesoli would rightly put it, the individuals of a social 'tribe' to one another. With Aristotle,[9] moreoever, this *mimesis* procures pleasure, and in Tarde's vocabulary it imposes an *intermentale* or intersubjective imprint on social relations. It is thus evident that Durkheim's sociology concerns itself more with instruction than with emotion. In terms of the three tasks assigned by Cicero to the orator (to teach/instruct, to please and to move) it is apparent that the sociology of Durkheim is more concerned with instruction than with the evocation of feeling. This is notwithstanding, Durkheim is fully aware of the priorities in persuasive discourse: '*Docere debitum est, delectare honorarium, permovere necessarium*'.[10]

That social mimesis could serve as a source of pleasure is a sociological issue left in abeyance until the appearance of Maffesoli's recent works. Similarly, I also consider that Roland Barthes re-invented the notion of 'textual pleasure' (*plaisir du texte*) in the shadow of Aristotle, and thereby sketched out a sociology of reading, poles apart from the aesthetics of reception which has evinced, by contrast, a strong Durkheimian flavour.[11] All of this revolves around imitation and its justification, and it was just this which positivist asceticism was determined to thwart in the name of all that was dignified and serious in sociology. The consequent stress laid upon *'administration de la preuve'* is inherited from the rigorist concept of rhetoric formulated by Quintilian. Through this appropriation sociology reinvented the techniques of the rhetorical *probatio* (as opposed to dialectics) the arguments of which are thought to relate solely to rational beings.[12] Simmel, a third participant in the Durkheim-Tarde debates, denied the scientific status of historical discourse in his *Problems of Philosophy of History* and favoured an aesthetic or artistic conception of the exploits of the historian who organises mimetically a reality atomised by the passage of time.[13] In this instance, it is the historian who, posing the question: 'How does one understand the other?', contents himself with the role of imitator, thus reproducing life (the *Nachbildung*) at the cost of uncertainty.

The bitter disputes between Durkheim, Tarde and Simmel can be seen as a struggle between the new Sorbonne, the traditional Collège de France and the nascent spirit of German Expressionism. Contemporary debates on structure and function in anthropology, besides the critical reproaches directed at sociologists of *l'imaginaire* by their neo-positivist colleagues, all relate to the question as to the nature of proof in sociology and then, *volens nolens*, add further embellishment to the canvas first woven by Durkheim in *The Rules of Sociological Method*.[14] These 'rules' included: belief in the value of concomitant variations supported by statistics, a conviction that the persuasiveness of any sociological or anthropological investigation must be measured by its rigour and independence; and a felt conviction that the investigator is executing an original inquiry that is self-consciously somewhat disdainful towards the findings of history or metaphysics.[15] Sociological hypotheses are based on induction, and even though the sociologist is unable to test them as in the applied sciences, Durkheim stipulates that:

All that it [i.e., sociology] asks is that the principle of causality be applied to social phenomena. Again, this principle is enunciated for sociology not as a rational necessity but only as an empirical postulate, produced by legitimate induction. Since the law of causality has been verified in the other realms of nature, and since it has progressively extended its authority from the physico-chemical world to the biological, and from the latter to the psychological, we are justified in claiming that it is equally true of the social world: and it is possible to add today that the researches undertaken on the basis of this postulate tend to confirm it.[16]

Nevertheless, this inductive method, exemplified in ethnographic questionnaires and in the programme outlined by Marcel Mauss in his *Manuel d'ethnographie*,[17] does not lack persuasive bias, despite its endorsement of John Stuart Mill's *A System of Logic*.[18] If the aim of this method is indeed to secure intellectual commitment, and if it channels persuasive energy even more urgently because of sociology's reliance on the authority of natural science as justification or validation of its recourse to a whole logical arsenal, and, moreover, if sociological discourse possesses a pathetic ('*pathos*') dimension and appeals to feeling, then all this is so because the inductive method itself pays tribute to rhetoric.

In reality the induction practised in deliberative and forensic eloquence (as contrasted with the set-piece encomium)[19] consists in a persuasive method which purports to establish and demonstrate facts in a way similar to that of Durkheim or Mauss as they approached and tried to give form to social facts. In the *Institutia Oratoria*,[20] Quintilian presents a canonical exposition of the theory of rhetorical *probatio*. The Aristotelian 'artificial proofs',[21] which derive from the demonstrative technique themselves (what Durkheim calls '*l'administration de la preuve*') are divided into three categories: examples, signs and enthymemes. They relate the latter together as follows: the example or 'paradigm' is an analogical induction based on the frequency of facts; the enthymeme is likewise an induction derived from the repetition of similar facts, that takes the form of an incomplete syllogism; and, finally, the sign links a particular fact to a general one. Without dwelling on this at length, it should be stressed that the existence of the fact which constitutes the 'cause' or topic of a speech relies entirely on these three categories of proof. The aim is not to base these facts on universal truth – that being the role or domain of the dialectician – but on a relative *probability*. Above all, any rhetorical demonstration attaches importance to having the audience *feel* the significance of the subject of debate, through a tangible and vivid rendition of the fact enacted in the energetic pursuit of the *probatio*. This process is, in Simmelian terms, a *Nachbildung*.

Sociological topics

The important things to note here are not only the stylistic dimensions of induction, which allow for reading the canonic sociological and anthropological texts in a different light, but also the intellectual foundations of rhetorical proof itself. Rhetorical or sociological induction is not sufficient in itself: persuasion cannot be reduced to proof as such. The effectiveness or *enargeia* of a demonstration was a rhetorical concept before it became a scientific term and it necessarily implies recourse to *topoi* or commonplaces. In rhetoric, the example, sign and argument are empty forms which are nourished by such *topoi*, through a method that affects the audience and creates in them an impression of reality. This theory of commonplaces comprises the point of reference, which allows the orator to extrapolate and exemplify his argument and mental images in the sense summarised by Frances Yates in her *Art of Memory*. Commonplaces thus map the possibilities latent in reality and provide discourse with an objective setting and a concreteness in which the facts to be proved actually *take shape*. These commonplaces are real things in an external and objectivisable form.

Thus it becomes apparent that sociology frequents the space abandoned by rhetoric. Moreover, Durkheim's formulation of social types through the inductive method and Max Weber's theory of ideal types can also be seen as modern reformulations of the topical method.[22] Both methods invite us to establish a sociological *topic* and we may thus ask if this is not in fact a reconstitution of the social fact in a preconceived setting, as Mauss' *Manuel* (a direct disclosure of Durkheim's thought on this matter) would appear to indicate. As the commonplace in poetics was one way of investing the *'fable'*[23] with general significance, so Weber's appeal to the type can be understood as an act of construction which permitted historical interpretation to take place.[24]

Mauss' conception of the morphological mapping undertaken by the ethnologist is in effect a transformation of the *topoi* method into a mode of interrogation (the *questionnaire*).[25] The very term *form*, that was so much part of the emergent sociological vocabulary is a translation of the Greek *kharakter*, a word equally capable of being rendered *type*. This exposes the seeming innocence of the semantics associated with sociological method. It is interesting, however, to discern yet another rhetorical resurgence characterising the persuasive element in sociological induction. Both the orator and the rhetorician knew that apart from the realistic effect created by demonstration of the proof, their technique was eminently social if not downright political.[26] The proof always has an affective or emphathetic dimension and relies upon the stimulation of feeling. The exploitation of feeling represents a hidden aspect of the social sciences, which sociologists have not, generally-speaking, learned to master, except possibly in some societies where they are forced to play a more direct role as social agents and to grant practice an advantage over mere theory.[27] We do, however, find an example of a sociological approach which explicitly recognises the role of *pathos* in the work of Vilfredo Pareto.[28] In his theory of

106

residues and derivations in the *Trattato di sociologia generale*, Pareto distinguished between the constant and variable elements in different cultures and argued that social action was, in consequence, indistinct as it was inevitably an agglomeration of such contingent materials. Contrary to a positivist approach that forcefully distinguishes between the fixed and the changing elements, the Paretan theory (which is close to Saussure's linguistics and its reliance on structured signs),[29] leads to the formulation of sociological 'topics' in terms of the passions and thus attributes what it labels as the logic and illogicality of human acts to commonplaces of the real. These latter, in turn, enable the sociologist to deal exhaustively with all classes of behaviour, and in the course of his enthusiastic efforts at persuasion, to draw the reader who is himself a social actor (and in accordance with Pareto's political tendencies, an eminently dramatic, historical actor) back into a system of the passions.

Pareto's system gives rise to both a realistic effect (the 'fictional reality' or verisimilitude advocated originally by Quintilian)[30] and to an empathic effect in the reader. An examination of the six types of residues and four types of derivations reveals the extent to which the residues fashion a commonplace of social facts not unlike that proposed by Aristotle,[31] and, furthermore, it shows how the derivations reproduce the traditional stages of rhetorical proof. The logic that justifies action on the basis of which the derivations accumulate, this apparent 'need for logical developments',[32] proceeds to confirm itself in reports that take on the allure of 'experimental facts'. This logic is the rhetorical paradigm through which appeals are made to diverse forms of authority. In the art of oratory this is the tried and tested technique of the enthymeme, the rhetorical syllogism, which transforms a motive of personal interest into something which represents the public good. At its deepest level, this logical technique takes on its most effective form in Pareto's 'verbal derivations' which are in effect a small treatise on the rhetoric of social use which can be used to expose the logical power of the figures of rhetoric that function in currently fashionable (i.e., 'trendy') words and, more generally, in the language of the mass media.[33] In short, the derivations are a 'social sophistic', a rhetorical usage intended to deceive and, in consequence, it is apparent that here we no longer operate upon the level of sociological proof and its form of demonstration but upon that of the real social bond. Thus when it is said, with a view to his exclusion, that Pareto was too 'cultured' to be a good sociologist, I would reply that he is too good an inheritor of four centuries of the Italian rhetorical tradition. Laying to one side the question of the sophistic, which could divert us from the major issue,[34] it is possible on the basis of a model similar to that of Pareto to understand the Weberian types of behaviour ('*zweckrational, wertrational, affektuell, traditionel*')[35] in terms of a set of *topoi* which provide an outline recollection of social acts rather than a crude contrast of rationality with irrationality.[36]

To summarise: the social facts which the sociologist attempts to extract and to explain from the indistinctness of phenomena (whether it be through Paretan 'indistinctness', Durkheimian 'energy', Malinowski's organic totality[37] or Lévi-Strauss' concept of communication)[38] and the facts which the orator strains to evoke in the consciousness of his audience are part of the same theoretical impetus: they both approximate to the possible and seek to render its verisimilitude. In short, the sociologist proceeds to an 'inter-pretation': in Latin, an *'inter-pretatio'* denotes an act of interposition which gives its value (*'pretium'*) to the exchange.

The difficulty of knowing

One can appreciate Durkheim's horror at this inopportune return of a rhetoric of the possible in the newly born science of sociology. In accusing Simmel of subservience to the 'quirks of inspiration' and of indulging in 'meditations',[39] Durkheim in effect denounced the 'fullness' of a theory which had reduced the scientific division of labour and the alleged imperative of specialisation in the social sciences to the manipulation of rhetorical topics:

> To create such a kind of privileged speculation where demonstrations need not be as rigorous as possible, where things are *told as they are seen* and where the personal feelings and the imagination of the author have the last word, is to bastardize sociology and reduce it to a genre in which reality is necessarily expressed in subjective terms as in Art, albeit here abstracted as in Science. [40]

In this passage Durkheim is commenting upon Simmel's treatment of the topic of money in the *Philosophy of Money*.[41] It is obvious that the author of the *Rules* cannot accept a sociological proof based upon 'subjective' discourse and social agents. In short, the issue turns on the position of the sociologist with respect to the nature of knowledge.

In order to extend this debate further, we may refer to works of ethnology or social anthropology, since these disciplines shed a merciless light on the 'estrangement' of the thinker from his object. Bronislav Malinowski and A.R. Radcliffe-Brown's patiently pursued functionalism, as seen in the former's belief in the total coherence of facts and in the latter's analysis of the concreteness of social links,[42] scarcely disguises their impatience when faced with the difficulty of comprehending a primitive or radically different mentality. Radcliffe-Brown finds his way forward by formulating a distinction between ideographic inquiry[43] (history and ethnography) and nomothetic enquiry (sociology and social anthropology). The anthropologist is thus torn between two forms of inquiry. On the one hand there is intensive research which is exemplified by Mauss' remark that 'A professional ethnographer, working hard, can proceed on his own to complete a near exhaustive study of a tribe within three or four years'[44] and, on the other, more synchronic forms of investigation. Time and again the anthropologist immerses herself in social facts, only then to detach herself from them.

This two-fold approach to research into the primitive *logos* is not unlike the two phases of Platonic dialectics: that is first the *sunagoge* which envisages the multiple and serialises it, and secondly the *diairesis*, which only theorises about ideal facts.[45] Another key word of positivist social sciences, observation, retains its strongest sense of 'keeping an eye on' social facts, and this, in a tradition which no longer bewilders us, refers back to the Platonic metaphor of dialectics as it 'pulls the soul's eye out of the mire'.[46] The problematic epistemological status of a comprehensive sociology, as in the Weberian '*verstehen*', resides in this:[47] how may it conceive of of the other and in turn make this understandable to others. Both the anthropologist and the sociologist have surreptitiously assumed the role of the orator. Traditional rhetoric insists that the orator's essentially probatory discourse is a *fiction* which lodges the reality of facts in, as it were, the mouth of the orator who thus feigns reality by means of a technically skilled demonstration. Quintilian never stops reminding his readers that the orator is a *persona*, only the mask through which evidence may take shape. It is this that makes rhetoric a *theoria*, a vision of things.[48]

Thus we conclude that the sociologist should consciously assume the role of a modern rhetorician. Instead of forbidding herself from making approximations of social facts or from asserting claims to social control she should accept her duty to acknowledge these 'facts' as necessary fictions. Furthermore, the anthropologist's identification with the 'savage' implies commitment to a realistic deception. Lévi-Strauss sees this as a gesture of 'confirmation', for:

> Anthropology consists in inventing for one's own purpose an object that is simultaneously both objectively estranged and subjectively concrete, and the causal explanation of which is based upon a mode of comprehension which is for me a *supplementary type of proof.*[49]

Neither Quintilian, Cicero nor Aristotle could more aptly describe this 'supplement' to the rhetorical proof necessary to persuasion, and it is this which gives the rhetor-sociologist an almost Shamanic role as interpreter of society.

Three concepts in the sociological persona

The main aspects of the *persona* of the sociologist, the teller of social facts, can be better understood by dwelling for a moment on the three concepts which give it its coherence: analogy, *fable*, and the ideal. Let us bear in mind that Durkheim's admiration for the *Kathedar-Soziologen*, the initiators of German sociology, was fuelled by his reflection on the nature of analogy.[50] According to Durkheim, reasoning by analogy bestows richness and scientific dignity on social description. Analogy consecrates the position of sociology as the latest arrival of the positive or logico-experimental sciences. It metamorphoses the methods of the latter and transforms epistemological paradigms inherited and drawn from biology (as found in Durkheim and Malinowski), physics (as in Pareto) and phonology (as in Lévi-Strauss). Analogy draws upon theories of humankind as biological being and harmonises them with those of humankind as social being where, according to Durkheim, reality really lies. Sociology therefore functions as a *mousike*, in short, as a unification of scientific knowledge dedicated to the benefit of society. In the context of the sciences, sociology attempts to restore to humanity a harmonious completeness. Just as rhetoric co-ordinated all branches of knowledge, so also should sociology restore unity to the differentiated knowledge of humankind bequeathed by scientific experimentation. Thus by way of the manipulation of analogies, sociology should be understood as *amnemosune*, the first Muse.[51]

Moreover, analogy is endowed with a virtue familiar to rhetoric, as much of the inductive and probatory value of exemplification is drawn from its resort to analogy. The orator constructs games in discourse which in turn evoke analogical resonances and relations in the auditor. Their energy and power of representation, that is the *enargeia*[52] of oratory itself, confirms the logic of the mental images clustered together by analogy. If homology, the application of the analogical process to social diffusion, has such a strong bearing on sociological description, then this can be attributed to the fact that all social links and all forms of solidarity call upon an analogical chain of images: 'ordinary knowledge' can only be analogical.[53]

Now, the *imaginative* energy of analogy rests on a dynamic motor – the *fable*. In the tradition of eloquence, the analogical appeal in fact pertains to *fable* or story, the function of which is to relate events with one another, and in consequence the *fable* allows for the uncovering of hidden links which are not of a circumstantial or historical nature.[54] Correspondingly, in Aristotle's *Poetics* a line is drawn between 'fabulous' and 'historical' knowledge.

> The distinction between historian and poet is not in the one writing prose and the other verse.... It consists really in this, that the one describes the thing that has been, and the other a kind of being that might be. Hence poetry is something more philosophic and of graver import than history, since its statements are of the nature of the universals, whereas those of history are singular.[55]

When rhetoric draws support from analogy it most frequently operates within the fable, a general if not a universal narrative; whereas historical narrative is obliged to remain ensconced within the confines of the event. The dispute between the social and historical sciences which is intimately associated with the development of these disciplines[56] finds immediate accurate expression at this juncture. Sociology, the science of the social fable, does not draw upon the historicist illusion of an 'internalised' and 'intelligible' reality, that is 'the illusion of a provisional interiority' as Lévi-Strauss maintains in *La pensée sauvage*.[57] The Aristotelian individual then takes on the form of an 'absolute contingency'.[58] Paradoxical as this may seem, sociology is a science of the general, and 'nomothetic' to the extent that it is a suitable fabulation, an analogical narrative of reality. This proposal is at the foundation of Gilbert Durand's *Structures anthropologiques de l'imaginaire*.[59] Its most incisive function is to aid reflection upon the images which contribute to the formation of the social bond, to draw up a poetics and to derive a rhetoric from the latter. So far as I am concerned, the destiny of anthropology will remain problematic to the extent that it fails to elucidate the fable proper to this type of exercise, which, in a word, is termed 'idolatry' (*l'idolâtrie*). There is not sufficient space here to expand upon the anthropological discourse of the rhetoricians of the seventeenth century who, in extrapolating the fable, called it *idololatria*.[60]

A secondary aspect of the 'fable' concerns style. If the social sciences are understood as narratives of representation, an assertion Durkheim would not have denied, then it is striking to note that the sociological 'art' makes use of a style in which recourse to fable is ever present. There is an intimate relation between social representations generalised through discourse and the way in which this discourse is presented, that is itself a social act. This relation is otherwise more complex than one would suspect from simply resorting to the concept of 'enunciation'. It is indeed impossible to write one line of sociology without 'making images' or engaging in 'idolatry'. Thus, mathematical models,[61] the use of diagrams and graphs, and statistical tables, are more than merely signs of recognition shared by professionals: they are also signs of a particular 'fable' and of sociology's figures of speech. These are only instruments of the sociological *elocutio* and proof of its rhetorical heritage. Accordingly, it would be possible to elaborate a stylistics of sociological and ethnological discourses based upon an examination of their 'figures' and forms of elocution. Far from diminishing their scientific range, such a study could demonstrate how the social sciences have become integrated into a universe of images. It is interesting, furthermore, to compare, for instance, Cicero's description of the combinative power of elocution in the *Orator* with Lévi-Strauss' *Structural Anthropology*.[62] What, after all, is a stylistic figure (the basis of the *elocutio*) if it is not a method of earnest insistence? According to Cicero it consists in having the reader 'adhere to facts, thanks to the images'.[63]

The power of images lies in their adherence to and being drawn towards social facts. It is this process which gives sociology its energy, with the result that social science is naturally mass-media oriented. It would be desirable when expounding Durkheim's foundational concept of social density (which he terms 'dynamic density' as opposed to a simple material density),[64] to pinpoint the rhetorical theme of the *enargeia*, transposed from the description to the object being described. According to Durkheim, the 'principal effort' of the sociologist should be directed at the clarification of the different social energies which shape representation and which ultimately mould social communication. Rhetoric should thereby restore to sociology sound analytical instruments and help validate, *ipso facto*, the fascination social science has for social facts.[65] In spite of the acknowledged difficulty encountered by Mauss in cataloguing aesthetic facts, it must be noted, furthermore, that he opens the chapter on aesthetics in the *Manuel* with a reference to the Aristotelian *theoria* and also stresses the necessity for the study of the syllogism, metaphor and rhetoric, advice which has in the event been little heeded.[66]

Indeed, the aims of a Mauss or a Durkheim have a bearing upon the training of the social scientist. The *Rules*, the *Manuel*, and, especially, Durkheim's works on education, all exemplify a distinct ideal taught at the Sorbonne in a very precise fashion as 'science of education' and not sociology.[67] Durkheim's public lectures on education suggest that the educational field is a microcosm of the totality of society and *analogous* to it.[68] Moreover, in these lectures Durkheim presents the school as the scene of the very experimentation which sociology so unjustly lacks in comparison with the applied natural sciences:

Sociology alone can both help us to understand it [i.e., the goal of education], by relating it to the social conditions upon which it depends and which it expresses; it can also help us to discover it when the public consciousness, disturbed and uncertain, no longer knows what it should be.[69]

The sociologist thus sees himself as carrying out a fundamental task which affects the object of his study as much as his own role. For the discerning reader who can link these lectures to the final pages of the *Rules of Sociological Method*, it is impossible not to detect the Ciceronian doctrine concerning the mission of the *orator*: here we find a true peroration in defense of a 'culture' both 'esoteric', 'dignified', 'authoritative' and derived from a 'preliminary initiation', that is simultaneously put at the service of social education.

The *sociologus* like the *orator* expresses and fashions culture, representing what is best and most lively in it. Durkheim's continual reticence towards Tarde and the contemporary neo-positivist sarcasm directed against Lévi-Strauss' phonological anthropology, only re-enact, in my view, the debate between a rhetoric supposedly pursued in the service of the *polis* or the *civitas* on the one hand and a sophistics which is otherwise seen as boosting the prestige of the individual who had mastered the art of speech. In a way unconfessed and unexpressed by the sociological enterprise itself, the sociologist actually desires to incarnate a human *ideal*. A counter-traditional historiography of the social sciences could well be written which would demonstrate how the canonical debate between rhetoric and sophistics has left a profound yet seemingly inadmissable imprint upon the development of these disciplines.[70] The conception propounded by Simmel,[71] that sociology is the only mimetic knowledge appropriate to a mass culture, exposes the rhetorical heritage reminiscent of another tradition in which the speech of the orator represented a political civilisation, and more specifically, thrived on the democratic idea itself. The statement of defeat which concludes Pseudo-Longinus' treatise *On the Sublime*, that rhetoric can only survive as the art of praise in a society deprived of political freedom, corresponds to the refusal or inability of neo-positivist sociology to envisage modernity other than through ideology, the contemporary form of praise. Alternatively, to use a distinction made by Cicero, the debate delineated by Pseudo-Longinus may serve as a solemn warning to contemporary sociology:[72] from beyond the limits of their limited memory of their own uncritical tradition and through a profound *anamnesis* of its origins and stages of development, social scientists must retrieve a sense of virtue and wisdom.

Notes

1. Gilbert Durand and Michel Maffesoli, together with Africanist Louis-Vincent Thomas and Edgar Morin, lead the *Centre de Recherche sur l'Imaginaire* (CRI), a research institute affiliated to the *Centre National de la Recherche Scientifique*. The CRI convenes regular international symposia on the '*imaginaire*'. An ad hoc group on the '*sociologie du quotidien et de l'imaginaire social*' functions within the International Sociological Association as well as being represented in the *Association*

Internationale des Sociologues de Langue Française. M. Maffesoli recently edited an issue of *Current Sociology* on the 'quotidien' (37, no.1, Spring 1989) while another issue is scheduled for 1991 on the 'imaginaire'.

2. The journal *Sociétés* (soon to be replaced by a more voluminous *Revue d'Histoire de la Sociologie*) the *Cahiers de l'Imaginaire*, and Méridiens-Klincksieck Publishers are the main channels through which the '*sociologie de l'imaginaire*' publicises its views.

3. See, in particular, Marc Fumaroli, *L'âge de l'Éloquence* (Paris/Geneva: Champion/Droz, 1980). Also the Special Review Essay: 'Some Perspectives on Rhetoric, Science and History' by Carolyn R. Miller, *Rhetorica* 7, 1 (Winter, 1989) pp. 101-14. A recent volume of collected essays, *Rhetoric in the Human Sciences* (Herbert W. Simons [ed.], London: Sage, 1989) bears witness to the disquieting lack of familiarity of theoreticians of sociology when it comes to understanding and utilising concepts and debates of the rhetorical tradition. Nevertheless this is an interesting attempt, inasmuch as it reveals a growing discontent among some American sociologists with regard to their own methodological tradition. In a different light, the work of Swiss sociologist Blaise Galland is noteworthy: he resorts to 'rhetoric' to illuminate the issue of sociological empathy in fieldwork (Blaise Galland, '*Art sociologique: le critre esthtique dans la recherche en sciences humaines*' 1 [1988] pp. 129-45). Lastly, it is another sign of the 'recovery of rhetoric' that the German sociologist Alois Hahn, whose position is often close to Maffesoli's, has recently published a contribution to a collection of essays on rhetorical '*actio*' (Volker Kapp [ed.],'*Religiöse Dimension der Leiblichkeit*', in *Die Sprache der Zeichen und Bilder, Ars Rhetorica* 1 [Marburg: W. Hitzeroth, 1990, pp. 130-41]). At the time of writing I had not seen volume 3.2, June 1990 of the journal *History of the Human Sciences*, on the topic 'Rhetoric and Science'.

4. Durkheim, Emile, article in *Textes*, 2 vols (Paris: Minuit, 1975) I, pp. 34-5.

5. Quintilian, *Institutio oratoria* (hereafter: *IO*) I, pp. 14-21, II, pp. 1-5.

6. Durkheim, Emile, '*L'état actuel des études sociologiques en France*' (1895) pp. 83-9; '*La sociologie*' (1905) pp. 115 ff; extract of a debate with Tarde in the *Revue Internationale de Sociologie* (1904) pp. 160 ff, in *Textes* I (1904); extract from a debate in the *Revue Int. de Soc.*, ibid., pp. 160 ff. See Gabriel Tarde, *Les lois de l'imitation* (Paris: Alcan, 1892).

7. Cicero, *Orator* (hereafter: *O*) 20, 21, 24-5.

8. Aristotle, *Rhetoric*, trans. W. Rhys Roberts and *On Poetics*, trans. Ingram Bywater (Chicago: University of Chicago/Encyclopaedia Britannica, 1952).

9. Ibid., IV, p. 433.

10. Cicero, *Du meilleur genre d'orateurs*, in *O*, I, 3, 110.

11. I refer to H.R. Jauss and the Konstanz School.

12. *R*, I.3.1359a, pp. 10-15.

13. See Raymond Aron, *La philosophie critique de l'histoire* (Paris: Seuil, 1970) ch. 3 on Simmel. Aron analyses the *Problème der Geschichtsphilosophie* (1892). See *The Problems of the Philosophy of History*, trans. G. Wakes (New York: Free Press, 1977).

14. Durkheim, Emile, *The Rules of Sociological Method* (1st edn, 1895) trans.

S.A. Solovay and J.H. Mueller (Glencoe, Illinois: Free Press, 1938) p. 140.

15. Ibid., p. 146.

16. Ibid., p. 141.

17. Mauss, Marcel, *Manuel d'ethnographie* (Paris: Payot, 1947).

18. Durkheim often mentions him, as if he played the rôle of modern Aristotle.

19. The tripartition between the judiciary, the deliberative (political) and demonstrative or epideictic (praise, panegyric, invective) genres is here in fact brought back to the opposition, from a civic point of view, between encomiastic eloquence and eloquence of true causes.

20. *IO*, V.8-12.

21. R, I.2: on the *pisteis entekhnoi*.

22. Weber, Max, *The theory of social and economic organization* (1st edn, 1960) trans. A.M. Henderson and Talcott Parsons (New York: Free Press, 1974). Yates, Frances B., *The Art of Memory* (Chicago: University of Chicago Press, 1974).

23. *P*, 9.1451b.

24. Aron, R., op. cit., pp. 251-2.

25. Mauss, Marcel, op. cit., III.

26. See *IO*, II.16.

27. Salazar, Philippe-Joseph, *L'intrigue raciale* (Paris: Méridiens-Klincsieck, 1989) where I attempt such an analysis.

28. Pareto, Vilfredo, *The Mind and Society (Trattato di Sociologia generale)*, A. Livingstone (ed.), trans. A. Bongiorno and A. Livingstone (London: Jonathan Cape, 1935) 4 vols; in particular vol. 3, chs IX-X, *Theory of Derivations*.

29. See Julien Freund, *Pareto* (Paris: Seghers, 1974) p. 84.

30. *IO*, VI.2.

31. *R*, II.6-10.

32. Freund, J., op. cit., p. 101.

33. Ibid., p. 109.

34. Salazar, Philippe-Joseph, 'Rhetoric or sophistic: the place of sociology', forthcoming in *Current Sociology* (1991), special issue on '*sociologie de l'imaginaire*'.

35. Weber, M., op. cit.

36. Aron, R., op. cit., p. 253.

37. Malinowski, Bronislav, *A Scientific Theory of Culture* (Chapel Hill: University of North Carolina Press, 1944) ch. 5 in particular.

38 Lévi-Strauss, Claude, *Structural anthropology* (New York: Basic Books, 1st edn, 1958; 2nd edn, 1963).

39. Durkheim, Emile, and Fauconnet, Paul, '*Sociologie et sciences sociales*' (1901) in *Textes*, p. 138.

40. Durkheim, Emile, 'Review' (1901) in *Textes*, p. 181 (own translation).

41. See Patrick Watier (ed.), *Georg Simmel, la sociologie et l'exprience du monde moderne* (Paris: Méridiens-Klincksieck, 1986): a series of papers which presents a vivid depiction of Simmelian studies in France. Also: Georg Simmel, *The Philosophy of Money*, trans. T. Bottomore and D. Frisby (London: Routledge and Kegan Paul, 1978).

42. Radcliffe-Brown, A.R., *Structure and Function in Primitive Society* (1st edn,

1952; London: Cohen and West, 1968). Introduction. See the tightly argumented work by P. Descola (ed.), *Les idées de l'anthropologie* (Paris: Armand Colin, 1988).

43. Radcliffe-Brown, A.R., op. cit., pp. 57-8.

44. Mauss, M., op. cit., p. 9.

45. Plato, *Republic*, VI.511b and *Phaedrus*, 245d.

46. Plato, *Republic*, VII.533 cd.

47. Aron, R., op. cit., p. 239.

48. *IO*, II.18.

49. Lévi-Strauss, Claude, *Anthropologie structurale II* (Paris: Plon, 1973) p. 17 (own translation).

50. Durkheim, Emile, *Textes*, pp. 245-407.

51. On the complex issue of 'musical science' I refer to the reader E. Havelock's well-known works on orality, especially *The Muse Learns to Write* (New Haven and London: Yale University Press, 1986).

52. See B.M. Stafford, *Voyage into substance: Art, Science, Nature* (Cambridge, MA: MIT Press, 1984) an innovative essay viewing the narrative of the pre-anthropological voyage as a form imbued with *enargeia*: a work essential to the study of ethnological 'imaginaire'.

53. I refer back to the title of Michel Maffesoli's, *La connaissance ordinaire* (Paris: Méridiens-Klincksieck, 1986).

54. *R*, II.20.1393a-1394a.

55. *P*, 19.1451b.4-5.

56. See Raymond Aron, op. cit., and P. Descola, op. cit.

57. Lévi-Strauss, Claude, *La pensée sauvage* (Paris: Plon, 1962) pp. 340-1.

58. As pointed out by P. Descola, op. cit., p. 182.

59. Durand, Gilbert, *Les structures anthropologiques de l'imaginaire* (Paris: Bordas, 1969).

60. I refer the reader to my forthcoming book (*Naissances inavouables: sociologie et littérature*) where I devote a chapter to the question of *idololatria* from the Late Renaissance to the early Enlightment and to my forthcoming article on 'Fable' in the *Revue d'Histoire Littéraire de la France*.

61. *Anthropologie et calcul* (Paris: UGE, 1971). See also the cognate and incisive study by Philip Mirowski, 'How Not to Do Things with Metaphors: Paul Samuelson and the Science of Neo-Classical Economics' *Studies in the History and Philosophy of Science* 20, 2 (June 1989) pp. 175-91.

62. I would like to mention a line of investigation into the concept of structure and its diagrammatic formalisation as apparent with Lévi-Strauss (see his '*L'analyse structurale en linguistique et en anthropologie*', in *Anthropologie structurale*). Ramus introduced the usage of graphs to represent the places of argumentation. Thus detached from the body of rhetoric, the *dispositio* tended to function as a collation of all relations between elements, so that their logical relations were immediately evident. In the Ramist conception, rhetoric is an exact image of the world, a true 'mapping'. It remains to be asked in the wake of W. Ong's seminal works, whether the Ramist heritage, usually studied in the context of the English or German traditions did not in fact survive far more strongly than it is usually believed, into French nineteenth-century rhetorical and scientific trainings where it reappeared in French positivism. See my forthcoming *Naissances inavouables* and, in contradistinction, my article '*Modernité de Ballanche*', *Cahiers de l'Imaginaire* 3 (1989) pp. 49-53.

63. *O*, 48.

64. Durkheim, Emile, *Rules*, pp. 113-14.

65. This fact did not escape the notice of Maffesoli. See *La conquête du présent* (Paris: PUF, 1979) p. 184.

66. Mauss, M., op. cit., pp. 98-9.

67. Durkheim, Emile, *Education and sociology*, (1st edn, 1925) trans. S.D. Fox (Glencoe, Illinois: Free Press of Glencoe, 1956).

68. Ibid., p. 131.

69. Ibid., p. 129.

70. See Marc Fumaroli, op. cit. and, for a contemporary debate, Brigitte Cassin (ed.), *Le plaisir de parler* (Paris: Minuit, 1986) and my forthcoming article (note 34).

71. See Raymond Aron, op. cit., p. 201.

72. *O*, XXXVI.45-6.

PART III

Rhetoric and Disciplinarity: Case Studies

This third part of *The Recovery of Rhetoric* contains four case studies which illustrate in contrasting ways the vitality of rhetorical analysis in contemporary disciplinary discourse. In the current era of differentiated human sciences rhetorical analysis does not expose a simple uniformity of response. Nevertheless, each contributor uses rhetorical analysis to indicate how their respective disciplines both promote approved practices and proscribe or exclude others. In this way they reveal the concealed operation of disciplinary authority embodied in the discourse and practices of the discipline itself. The rhetorical analyses in this section can also be seen as promoting disciplinary reflexivity.

In his consideration of the relationship of rhetoric and psychology, Michael Billig responds critically to the common assumption on the part of the practitioners of modern physical sciences (and especially technology) that ancient science is of merely antiquarian value. The position of modern psychology is, however, more ambiguous, for in the case of memory, for example, the inferiority of the ancient is in no way proven, rather the reverse. The 'postmodern revival of rhetoric' offers important insights into the nature of thought itself, which Billig proceeds to characterise as both dialogic and rhetorical. Traditional accounts of the monologic categorisation of information and the argumentative emergence of dialogical commonplaces are contrasted. Billig's argument is a forceful defence of the distinctiveness of the socially-constituted nature of human thought and language, which he illustrates by reference to British attitudes to the royal family. The rhetorical approach can reach parts of psychology that the contemporary cognitive psychologist fails to attain. Indeed we might gloss Billig's argument with the remark that real psychology is the social psychology revealed at least in part through the rhetorical mode and in the 'commonplaces' of everyday life. Furthermore, this paper has implications for the discipline of psychology as a whole.

Herbert W. Simons engages in the critical exposure and deconstruction of the rhetorical strategies concealed in a seemingly 'hard' scientific paper. Despite an apparently factual and unemotive style, the latter may embody a set of values, the successful transmission of which may affect significant financial expenditure and life-chances. In his paper Simons thus explores the limits and practices of medical research as a discipline.

Donald McCloskey, an active and prominent exponent of the 'rhetoric of inquiry', provides in his chapter a sequel to his influential and provocative book, *The Rhetoric of Economics*. In this book McCloskey argued for a radical new look at the role of language in the formulation and presentation of economic theory and at the consequences of the ever more pervasive mathematisation of economics as a discipline. McCloskey's informal style should not deceive the reader. His depiction of the 'Rhetorical Tetrad' comprising the 'scientific' pairing of fact and logic and the 'humanistic' coupling of metaphor and story, crystallises in a distinctive way a fundamental problem in Anglo-American culture: the arbitrary and distortive privileging of paradigms drawn from physical and biological science and their enforcement in areas ill-suited to their reception. McCloskey's exemplification of the transformatory power of 'capital' implies the necessity of a critical juxtaposition of metaphor and story. It here that 'rhetoric', understood in McCloskey's sense of 'discourse on the use of discourse', comes into its own as it creates space for the interrogation of the metaphors that economists, capitalists (and others) live by, and in terms of which they construe their stories. This is a theme to which Roberts will later return.

John S. Nelson, likewise one of the founder members of the *Project on Rhetoric of Inquiry* (POROI) at the University of Iowa, provides us with a case history of his efforts to transform his own discipline by the injection of the rhetoric of inquiry into political science. This paper draws upon extended interdisciplinary experience. Nelson's case for the rhetoric of inquiry extends well beyond the claim that it merely effects improvements within a discipline. The extension of 'political science' over many disciplines necessitates the articulation of the epistemologies and presuppositions of the latter, with the result that these exercises in comparative and self-critical epistemology come together as the 'rhetoric of inquiry'. In contrast to foundationalism, Nelson argues that the rhetoric of inquiry subverts authoritarian discourse, encourages reflexivity and challenges arcane obscurity. Yet, in Nelson's view, rhetoric should never seek to become a subject (or discipline) in itself over and above its role within any given research project or cluster of such projects. Here questions raised in our introductory chapter and by Michael Cahn once more come to the fore. Nelson has touched upon the difficult question as to how far the rhetoric of inquiry should render autonomous its own distinctive body of perspectives, principles and practices (and thus become a 'discipline'); or how far it should preserve an unbroken incognito and remain as the Scarlet Pimpernel of the realm of the critical intellect. In conclusion, Nelson present us with a challenging sevenfold agenda of problematics for the rhetoric of inquiry that implies far more than merely stylistic or procedural engagement with the deficencies of residual positivism.

6

Psychology, Rhetoric And Cognition

Michael Billig (Loughborough University)

It is easy for those who work in psychology to accept uncritically the notion of scientific progress, for a belief in progress seems to be built into the very routines of being an academic psychologist. The researcher is expected to be aware of the current research programmes in laboratories across the world. The latest issues of journals should be read. And the articles in these issues will themselves quote recent studies; even better, they will dangle in front of the reader information on studies about to be published in the near future. In short, nothing recent should be over-looked, since it is professionally damaging for the academic to be unaware of the very latest developments. These practices of professional reading and publishing would seem to be an enactment of the assumption that today's knowledge is better than yesterday's and that tomorrow's will be better still. Within psychology, this habit of mind can be accompanied by a condescension towards past psychologies, especially those from the distant past. Textbooks of psychology, which fill their pages with information about recent discoveries sometimes will quote an old name. The tone is likely to be patronising with words to the effect: 'Although Aristotle lived over two thousand years ago, he had some interesting things to say about persuasion' or about interpersonal attraction, or whatever. It is as if the ancient figure is to be given a beta-plus for effort; the alphas can be awarded only to those who have taken courses in experimental methodology and can handle the latest computer-run statistical packages.

When the applications of modern physical sciences are compared to those of ancient sciences, the condescending attitude towards the science of the past is not difficult to hold. The performances of computers, sports cars and F1-11 bombers so obviously outstrip those of abacuses, chariots and vats of boiling oil. In all these instances, and in many others, the technologies of modern science can achieve similar objectives to those of the ancients but with greater accuracy and on an obviously vaster scale. If it is so evident that the technological achievements of the modern physical sciences outstrip those of the ancient sciences, one can ask whether

119

the same unbalanced comparison can be made between the technologies of ancient and modern psychologies. For instance, one might wonder whether Antiphon, who set up a sorrow-assuaging shop near the market-place of Corinth, was less successful in his aims of cheering the grief-stricken than are modern psychotherapists who treat the depressed. However, in the case of psychology, the answer to the question is not as immediately obvious as it was when comparing the physical sciences. Perhaps Antiphon was inferior – we cannot know. Yet, there are few reasons for supposing that his inferiority, when compared to the moderns, is so self-evident as to be in the ratio of the abacus to the computer.

In fact, in one area of psychological endeavour, namely the study of memory, there are reasons for suspecting the superiority of the ancient technologies. In the days before plentiful supplies of paper, pencils and autocues, a developed memory was a vital skill for the orator. Ancient rhetorical theorists, devised systems for improving their memories, and notable feats were achieved by such rhetoricians as Hippias and Seneca the Elder. The latter, it was claimed, could repeat up to two thousand words verbatim.[1] For all the experimental studies of memory, and for all the expensively-funded research projects on the topic, there is no evidence that professional psychologists have been able to better such ancient achievements. In the psychological Grand Prix, there is not the certainty that the chariot would lag distantly behind the latest Ferrari. That being so, one should not assume that ancient psychological ideas can be dismissed as so much useless phlogiston.

Thinking and Conversation

The recent renewal of interest in the rhetorical tradition indicates the extent to which a number of critical social scientists, uneasy with the facile assumptions of scientific progress, are turning to older ways of viewing the social world.[2] The modern, or rather postmodern, revival of rhetoric raises a whole series of fundamental issues about the nature of social inquiry and about the claims of the scientific method to provide a certain foundation for knowledge. Habermas,[3] in criticising the whole postmodernist project, describes it as a challenge by rhetoric to the supremacy of logic. Although the revival of rhetoric provokes, and is provoked by, such fundamental issues, here a much more limited question will be asked. This refers to the specific study of psychology: can ancient rhetoric provide insights which are generally lacking in contemporary modern psychology? In answer to this, it will be suggested that the rhetorical tradition offers an important perspective on the psychology of thinking. By characterising thinking as an essentially rhetorical process, the rhetorical perspective offers a very different view of thinking from that which is typically found in cognitive psychology today.

The rhetorical insight can be summarised in the comment by the Eleatic Stranger in Plato's dialogue *The Sophist*:

> Thought and speech are the same: only, the former, which is a silent inner conversation of the soul with itself, has been given the special name of thought.[4]

If one leaves aside the metaphysical implications of the word 'soul', there are two immediate points of contact between this formula and critical trends within contemporary psychology. In the first place, the Eleatic Stranger's comment, with its claim that conversation and thinking do not qualitatively differ from each other, seems to accept the dialogic nature of thought. Thinking is not a process locked within the individual brain, and taking place in Cartesian isolation. Just as conversation is socially produced as dialogue, so thinking is inherently dialogic. This is an assumption which features prominently in the works of the social constructionist movement. Drawing upon psychological ideas from Russia, especially Bakhtin[5] and Vygotsky,[6] social constructionists have been exploring the implications of considering thinking to be a dialogic process.[7] The second implication is as much a methodological one as a theoretical one. If conversation and thinking are similar, then those who wish to study psychological processes should pay attention to the details of conversational interaction. Thus, Potter and Wetherell[8] advocate that social psychology should adopt the methodology of discourse analysis. They suggest that conversation analysts, who have demonstrated the complexities of even the most casual of conversational encounters, are analysing the subject-matter of social psychology. If the comment of the Eleatic Stranger is taken seriously, then such analysts, in revealing the intricacy of conversational manoeuvres, are studying directly the processes of practical thinking.[9]

However, there is a third implication in the Eliatic Stranger's comment, and this implication goes beyond stating the general dialogic and discursive nature of thinking. The ancient study of rhetoric points to the importance of a specific type of dialogue or discourse. The Eleatic Stranger need not be understood to be equating thinking with any sort of conversation – certainly not with the inconsequential greetings and dinner invitations so often studied by conversation analysts. Given that the Eleatic Stranger is almost certainly intended to be the sophist Zeno, and given the philosophical context of the remark in *The Sophist*, then that remark takes on a particular force if thinking is compared with the sort of conversations in which the sophists excelled. In brief, these were arguments. Therefore, the Eleatic Stranger's statement can be read to suggest that there is an intrinsic connection between thinking and arguing. Thinking is not merely the silent argument of the soul with itself, but, even more frequently, it is the noisier argument of one individual with another. And rhetoric, as the traditional study and practice of argumentation, provides an entry to an understanding of thinking.[10]

Argumentative nature of rhetoric

At first sight, the ancient study of rhetoric does not seem to offer dialogic skills, since it was typically presented as the art of the monologue. Aristotle defined the art of rhetorical analysis as 'to discover the available means of persuasion in each case'.[11] As such, rhetoric could be seen to be providing orators with the requisite skills so that their monologues would be irresistibly convincing. The traditional divisions of rhetoric can be understood in this light: the student needed to master the stages of inventing arguments, then arranging, adorning, memorising, and finally delivering them. Once these skills had been acquired, the students would be able to stand up and produce speeches which so perfectly drew upon the available means of persuasion in their construction and enunciation, that persuasive success was bound to follow.

Certainly, some rhetorical teachers advertised their courses with the boast that students would be able to win over any audience. It was claimed that once students had mastered the various divisions of oratory, and in particular that of delivery, they would possess the powers of *logos*. As Cicero wrote in *Brutus*, teachers, such as Protagoras, Gorgias, and Hippias, used to claim

> ...not without arrogance, to be sure, to teach how by the force of eloquence the worse (as they called it) could be made the better cause.[12]

It was, of course, such claims which down the ages provoked the hostility from those who feared the hidden powers of rhetoric.[13] The image of rhetoric, expressed in its champions' boasts and its opponents' fears, is essentially monologic. There is one speaker, the skilled orator, who delivers the powerful words. The audience, captured by these words, has no speech to make, but reacts with tears, cheers, and helpless admiration. As such there is no dialogic argument, for the message passes unstoppably from the speaker's lips into the audience's brain.

If this monologic image of rhetoric is inserted into the Eleatic Stranger's formula, then the result is somewhat curious. Thinking is then seen as a monologic process, as the soul silently convinces itself. It is as if the mind of the thinker is divided into two parts: one which speaks and the other which listens in order to applaud. Thus the speaking part, armed with all the rhetorical skills of invention and delivery, would be able to charm persuasively the listening part, which could only lie back in ecstatic pleasure at the brilliance of it all. Such internal monologues may very well take place, as we persuade ourselves of what we want to hear and do not argue with the internal voice to which we wish to listen. However, it might be a mistake to consider such occurrences as being the prototypical occasions of thinking. If anything, they are occasions when thought is avoided, for they are occasions when we display what existentialists called *mauvais fois*.

However, this image of thinking may be inappropriate because it is based upon a false image of rhetoric. Despite the self-serving claims of some rhetoricians, the practice of rhetoric has been dialogic rather than monologic. To be persuasive the orator could not operate in a rhetorical vacuum, but had to win arguments. Above all, this entailed defeating the counter-arguments of opponents, for the context of rhetoric was inherently argumentative. This can be seen in relation to the three main contexts of rhetoric, as outlined by Aristotle in the *Rhetoric*: forensic, deliberative, and epideictic oratory. The forensic oratory, which was the oratory of the court-room, was clearly argumentative in a dialogic sense. The lawyer needed to do more than charm the jury or judge with an eloquent performance: the arguments of the other side must be defeated. Thus, prosecution and defence would be locked in an argumentative confrontation, and each position had to be justified in relation to criticisms from the opponent. A similar situation obtains with deliberative, or political, oratory. A speaker does not advocate a policy in isolation from the possibility of counter-policies being advocated. The speaker, proposing that the state should go to war, is arguing against the counter-policy of peace. Thus, if persuasion takes place, it does so in a context of controversy.

The one branch of oratory which prima facie seems to be monologic, rather than dialogic, is epideictic oratory. Primarily this branch covered the funeral speech of praise. The orator delivering praise of the departed did not expect interruption, nor to be followed by another speaker, begging to differ and wishing to point out the faults of the recently dead. However, the funeral orations can be considered to be implicitly argumentative, as the speaker constructs the most favourable account possible of the person's life. This construction is made in the knowledge that other more critical accounts have been made in the past and will be made in the future. If the public argument ceases during the actual moments of grief, nevertheless what is said during these periods can be seen as an argument against the past and future criticisms, as the dead person's character and achievements are justified. That being so, even epideictic oratory can be seen to fit the patterns of justification and criticism, which, according to Perelman and Olbrechts-Tyteca,[14] characterise the very nature of rhetoric. And if rhetorical speech is marked by the dialectic between justification and criticism, then it is inherently argumentative, for argumentation is based upon the activities of criticising and justifying.

Argumentation and thought

The Eleatic Stranger's formula can be interpreted to imply that thinking is the silent argument of the soul with itself. When we think, we argue with ourselves, silently playing the parts of both sides, prosecutor and defender, justifier and critic. Thus the model of thinking is dialogic rather than monologic. Or, at least, it should be. It might be suggested that these silent arguments all too rarely occur, for individuals frequently avoid thinking by refusing to act as their own internal critics. As such, the model is as much a prescriptive one as it is descriptive. Cicero in *De Inventione*[15] gave hints to the orator for inventing arguments. The process of invention might be considered to be the silent process of cognition, taking place individually before the public display of speech. One might assume that invention involves cognitive acts, which are qualitatively different from the publicly observable argumentative dialogue. These internal acts would represent the sorts of phenomena which cognitive psychologists wish to study, but whose silence and internality makes them so mysterious and inaccessible. However, Cicero advised the orator to practise the skills of invention by imagining the debate in advance: one should think of one's own arguments by imagining those of the opponent and by seeking to counter them. The debate should be enacted in advance in the silence of the soul's inner debating chamber, as justifications and criticisms are pitted against each other. A silent monologue, in which the speaker imagines an unchallenged voice and the cheers of the crowd, would not be conducive to invention. What this suggests is that the mental events, which should occur before the display of oratory, should not be qualitatively different from the publicly observable argument. Instead, the internal conversation should be modelled upon publicly observable conversation.

The theoretical point is that cognitive processes are not simply anterior to argumentation, but, as anticipations of arguments, they are themselves constituted by socially observable arguments. In this sense, as the social constructivists emphasise, human thinking is socially constituted. There is also the point emphasised by Cicero, which is pedagogic rather than strictly empirical: thinking *should* be modelled upon argumentation. The rhetoricians, in teaching their pupils the skills of debate, were also teaching the skills of thinking. Thinking is not a mysterious process which unfolds ineluctably within the brain and which is not amenable to alteration. Instead, it is something which can be taught and learnt. In pointing to debates of high quality, in which inventive justifications and criticisms meet in dialectical opposition, teachers provided their pupils not only with models for speech, but also with models for thought.

Implications for cognitive psychology

The rhetorical perspective has a number of implications for the study of cognition. In fact, the perspective itself can be taken as an argument against certain trends in cognitive psychology. In particular, it can be argued that cognitive psychologists have tended to study forms of thinking in which rhetorical aspects are minimal. For example, there has been a tendency to equate 'thinking' with 'problem-solving' and then to study the ways that experimental subjects deal with mathematical or logical problems.[16] These problems tend to have defined right and wrong answers, such that the problem disappears when its solution has been uncovered.

However, the traditional problems of rhetoric have been of a very different order. These are problems of everyday life, such as those of ethics, politics, judging character, etc. These are not problems which admit of clearly defined right and wrong answers in a 'logical' or 'mathematical' sense. Instead, opposing sides may both produce reasoned and reasonable 'answers' which are in direct opposition to each other.[17] It is not a matter of uncovering which solution is wrong in a 'mathematical' or 'logical' sense, but of choosing between opposing sets of reasonableness, which might be themselves irreconcilable. The opposing sides might argue their cases with equal logical consistency, for the differences between them will not have arisen because one side has been seduced by an error of logic. Disagreements about ethics and politics are more basic than that. Diogenes Laertius recounts that a young Athenian was in doubt whether to marry or not. He approached Socrates for advice. The great philosopher shrugged and replied: 'Whichever you do, you will repent it'.[18] Such dilemmas are not to be resolved easily. The pros and cons of the debate cannot be arranged in such a way that logic will demonstrate with neutral certainty the right answer. Instead, there will always be the possibility of further debate and potentially endless argument.

These sorts of dilemma are constituted in language, because without the relevant

124

discourses, such as those of morality, there could be no dilemmas. Yet the argumentative nature of such dilemmas draws attention to a vital aspect of language which perhaps has not received due attention from psychologists. The ability to negate is a universal property of human language and is a feature which distinguishes human language from systems of animal communication. However, much work in the psychology of language, and in cognitive social psychology, has proceeded from the assumption that one of the prime functions of language is to name. For example, in cognitive social psychology the importance of categorisation has been stressed by theorists.[19] It is asserted that the stimulus world needs to be divided up into units, which are to be named by category-labels.[20] Since animals are presumed to divide up their perceptual worlds into analogous manageable units, then human and animal processes of cognition are not seen to differ in qualitative terms: it is as if human language merely added labels to top off those basic cognitive processes of information reduction, which are shared by all species to a greater or lesser degree.

This stress upon the role of categorisation can be said to lead to a rather unflattering view of the thinker. If the categorisation of information is the basic cognitive process, then the thinker is seen as an organism which goes around, automatically applying pre-set categorisations and labels to incoming information in order to reduce stimulus uncertainty. It is a bureaucratic model of thinking, as thinking is seen to be the pigeon-holing of the outside world.[21] Labels, schemata, and even whole ideologies are the filing systems into which the world must be placed, in order to render it safe and familiar. The paradoxical result is that this image of the thinker concentrates upon what is done unthinkingly, in order to alleviate the soul from the need to converse with itself or with anybody else.

However, human beings do more than merely categorise the stimulus world. Alone among the animal world, we can reflexively examine and dispute such categorisations. And for this the ability to negate is crucial. Significantly it has been shown that chimpanzees, trained in the sign language of the deaf, might be able to apply categories of stimuli-objects, but even the star-pupils were unable to handle negations or to criticise the categorisations of others.[22] Human beings, possessed of natural languages, do not merely have a determined way of describing, or categorising, the world. We can say 'X is Y', categorising the particular X along with other Ys. But we can also particularise X, instead of categorising it, stating that 'X is unique', thereby negating the categorisation. As Aristotle showed in his *Topica*,[23] for every propositional type there is a contrary type of proposition: categorisations, or propositions of quantity, can be opposed by particularisations, or propositions of quality. The stimulus object can be categorised and particularised, and, most importantly, there can be an argument, either loudly public or silently internal, as to whether the categorisation or the particularisation is most suitable. In doing this, we are arguing, and thereby thinking, about the meaning of our categorisations, rather than applying them unthinkingly.

In fact, many rhetorical arguments often seem to involve arguments about words. In classical and medieval times, pupils were encouraged to enact the classic rhetorical debates. One famous case, beloved of rhetorical teachers, was that of Epaminondas, who led the Thebans to a great victory over the Lacedaemonians. In so doing, he had neglected to observe the Theban law that forbade any citizen to retain supreme military power for more than a month. On his return to Thebes Epaminondas was arrested, and forced to stand trial on a charge of treason. The problem, to be repeated in the schools of rhetoric during the subsequent ages, was whether he should be properly categorised as a hero, the saviour of the Thebans, or as a traitor, whose actions undermined the state. As orators and oratorical students debated the question, they argued not merely about Epaminondas himself, but about the meaning of treason, heroism, and observance of the law. In other words, the categories themselves became the objects of dispute. For this to occur, people must be able to do more with their categories than merely apply them to the stimulus world. One must be able to negate – to say X is not a Y – and to negate the justifications of others with criticisms, and to negate their criticisms with justifications. Bees might be able to wiggle their stomachs in such a way as to communicate where pollen is to be found, but neither bees, nor instructed chimpanzees, can reflexively use words to argue about the meaning of words.

Commonplaces and the contents of argumentation

When rhetoricians argued about such a case as that of Epaminondas, they did not merely use the grammatical syntax of negation to oppose the counter-view. They may have used the identifiable proposition forms of negation – counterposing propositions of quantity to those of quality – but their arguments would have contained content as well as form. They argued about ideas, values, and character, as they discussed over and over again what it meant to be a hero or a criminal, and whether Epaminondas' character was such that a special case should be made for him. The important point, stressed by the textbooks of rhetoric, was that speakers might have to invent the particular arguments to be used on the rhetorical occasion, but they did not invent the basic materials from which these speeches were constructed. Thus the individual speaker does not invent the values (perhaps of heroism or of obedience to the law) to which an appeal is to be made. Instead the speaker draws upon the value-laden vocabularies which are shared with the audience. To use the old rhetorical term, the speaker will use 'commonplaces' in a discourse. In so doing, the speaker appeals to, and speaks within, the *sensus communis*, or the sense which is commonly shared.

There is an application from this rhetorical perspective concerning the nature of common sense or ideology. The basic oratorical situation is one in which two opposing speakers are making opposite cases, while attempting to appeal to the same audience. If both speakers are drawing upon the same common sense, or *sensus communis*, which is shared by the audience, then this common sense itself must contain contrary themes, or contrary commonplaces. In this way, the rhetorical perspective suggests that common sense or ideology is not, as is supposed in some sociological accounts, a unitary block, rather like a giant schema, which is imposed on the stimulus world and which acts to prevent thought. Instead, common sense will be dilemmatic, in that it contains contrary themes and commonplaces, and these

126

will ensure that members of the community have the resources to think and argue about their social worlds.[24]

The rhetorical textbooks illustrated this dilemmatic quality of common sense, when they provided lists of commonplaces to help the unimaginative orator. For example, *Rhetorica Ad Herennium*, the Roman textbook which was so popular during the Middle Ages, provided the sort of stock phrases which might be used to add colour to speeches. The point is that commonplaces could be provided for both sides: the prosecutor could be provided with commonplaces about justice, while the defence was offered those concerning mercy. The fact that the audience would be expected to approve in the mercy, ensures that there would be much to argue about if speakers could bring these commonplaces into rhetorical collision. Francis Bacon included in his *Of the Dignity and Advancement of Learning*[25] a list of proverbs, arranged to show that for each proverb an opposing one could be found. In the nineteenth century, Bacon's list was reproduced by Bishop Whately[26] as an appendix to his textbook Elements of Rhetoric. In modern times the maxims of common sense likewise can be shown to have this antithetical character: 'Many hands make light work' can be contrasted with 'Too many cooks spoil the broth'; 'Look before you leap' with 'Nothing ventured nothing gained', etc. Moreover, the same people will accept the reasonableness of such competing maxims, without feeling impelled by some internal dissonance-reducing force to choose between the many hands or the few cooks.[27] Social psychology textbooks sometimes cite these opposing pairs in their introductory chapters to show the 'confusions' of common sense and to hold out the hope that the experimental methodology will settle once and for all the competing truths of the many hands lightening the work or the multiplicity of cooks spoiling the broth.[28] However, from the rhetorical perspective, such contradictions are not considered to be matters in desperate need of resolution, but are part of the resources which enable common sense thinking. Moreover, such thinking would not be possible if common sense did not possess a dilemmatic, potentially argumentative structure, and it is this which permits the existence of what Moscovici[29] refers to as 'the thinking society'.

Discourse about the British Monarchy

Some of the assumptions of the rhetorical approach can be illustrated by examples from discourse about the British Monarchy. The examples are taken from a project, whose main focus is upon the way that British families talk about that extraordinary family which sits upon the throne of the land. In a number of respects the topic of monarchy offers an opportune topic for studying contemporary common sense. The royal family is universally well known in Britain, with its doings appearing virtually daily in every newspaper and on practically every news broadcast. Its members are familiar to the nation as a whole, whereas film stars, pop singers, and football players tend to have more restricted circles of fame. Public interest in the topic of royalty provides an opportunity for examining the dilemmatic aspects of contemporary common sense. The royal family would not be commonsensically interesting if it provoked a popular reaction only of silent reverence, as the British public bowed wordlessly towards the ground whenever the image of royalty appeared on television screen or in newsprint. Instead, the Family is interesting because it provides the public with matters for thought and discussion. Constantly there is discussion about the behaviour of this or that royal; the figures for criticism or praise may change and the behaviour in question may alter, but what is constant is that there is a matter for controversy.[30]

Although the topic has tended to be ignored by British social scientists, it is not an ideologically insignificant one.[31] In fact, the discourse relating to monarchy could hardly fail to contain ideologically significant themes; how could all the interested talk, both solicitous and critical, about the richest family in the land – and moreover, a family which is held to be the symbolic personification of the nation itself – not be ideological? As people talk or write about this family, they also raise topics of major ideological significance: for example, about privilege, family, gender, equality, responsibility, etc. In fact, the assumption that royalty may be a trivial topic for social scientific research, when put beside other 'serious' topics, such as attitudes to welfare, crime, and the sexual morality of the young, may itself be ideological. This suspicion grows if ideology is seen to function in a way that makes the symbols of state and privilege appear so 'natural'. Then social scientists, who think that monarchy in Britain does not merit a second critical glance, may be reflecting ideological assumption, rather than basing their reactions upon a thought-out position about the significance of inherited monarchy in an avowedly democratic culture.

The present study of discourse about the royal family is based upon unstructured tape-recorded discussions by families. There was an interviewer present, and she encouraged the family members to talk among themselves as far as possible, rather than herself directing the conversation. Often, as the family members discussed and argued about the royal family, they were talking about themselves and their own family. As such, the resulting discourse was rich in argumentative, ideological, and personal themes.[32] By and large the members interviewed expressed support for the monarchy as an institution, and their responses match the pattern to be found in public opinion surveys indicating widespread approval for monarchy and virtually no support for republicism.[33] However, if there is general agreement in public opinion about the broad desirability of monarchy over republicanism for Britain, this does not imply that the discourse about monarchy is based upon nothing but mutual agreement, with no hint of argumentation whenever the royal family is raised as a topic. In fact, the discourse itself revealed the contrary or dilemmatic aspects of common sense, as these ordinary speakers delivered their argumentative rhetoric in the comfort of their own homes.

The use of contrary themes by the same person was common in the discourse. A brief example can be given from an interview with a mother and father and their teenage son and daughter.[34] The interviewer had asked whether the existence of the royal family tended to heighten differences between rich and poor. The father, who at other times had expressed traditionalist support for monarchy and the individual members of the royal family, began his answer with an egalitarian statement: 'We should all be on the same level'. Then he started to criticise the ceremonial aspects of monarchy as a waste of money, but paused to criticise his criticism:

> But having said that, I suppose really the waste is paying other people, keeping other people in work.

But then this criticism is qualified: the money spent in making paper flags and bunting could be better spent and more productive jobs could be created. This was not the end of his dialectic of criticism:

> But having said that, people have got to make them, so it's giving people work in that respect, so it's a vicious circle anyway.

His wife, at that point, added the comment: 'You'll never get everybody on the same level.'

There are several points which can be noted about such discursive interchanges and their rhetorical features. In the first place, the speakers were not inventing new themes, but were expressing commonplace, or commonsensical, notions. The father's economic arguments were not original, nor were they claimed to be: he was voicing common-sense economics, whose good sense was being presented as if it were familiar to speaker and auditor. The discourse represented a form of collective remembering, as speakers were recalling all that needs to be taken into account, when discussing the matter. This form of memorising is not experienced as such, for the participants were talking about royalty, rather than recalling their own past. As Moscovici has written, 'Social and intellectual activity is, after all, a rehearsal or recital, yet most social psychologists treat it as if it were amnesic'.[35] Nor is this memorising an individual process, but, like so many other acts of recall, it is collectively achieved.[36] In this case the mother and father were collaborating in a joint conversation to rehearse the relevant, commonly held sense.

From a rhetorical perspective what is particularly interesting is the nature of the common sense which is recalled. In this example, as in so many others, it was a succession of contrary, or dilemmatic, themes, which were produced:[37] we should be equal/we can't be equal; pageantry is a waste of money/pageantry produces jobs; monarchy must be justified economically/monarchy is more valuable than mere money; and so on. Thus these everyday rhetoricians, in producing their homely rhetoric, were reproducing the dilemmas of common sense, just as the classic theorists of oratory recalled the contradictions of commonplaces in their famous textbooks. The example illustrates a further point. The contradictions of common sense are shared by participants. It is not the case that speakers must inevitably divide up into opposing camps – into prosecutors and defendants – for discussion to take place, since the dilemmatic aspects are commonly shared. Thus mother and father shared the same dilemmatic themes; sometimes one would take the more egalitarian theme and then be countered by the spouse. And sometimes the roles of justifier and critic would be reversed. In the quoted example, the father takes both sides and, in rehearsing the common sense economics of the monarchy, he recalls themes which have an argumentative structure. He makes a statement and then criticises it: the contrary point must be put. His successive statements could have been divided into two opposing rhetorical camps, as if they had been spoken by opponents, each arguing for a different rhetorical brief. However, both sides are spoken by the single speaker: in its form his discourse is the noisy conversation of the soul with itself.

Variability in discourse

If common sense and ideologies are seen to contain contrary themes, then this would account for one feature of discourse, which analysts have claimed is so damaging to the presuppositions of traditional attitude theorists. It has been claimed that people in their discourse show great variability in their views, using contrasting discursive themes at different times.[38] As Potter and Wetherell[39] suggest, people have recourse to differing 'interpretative repertoires' for differing rhetorical and conversational purposes.[40] As the ancient authors of rhetorical textbooks would have recognised, sometimes the accuser needs the rhetoric of defence, and vice versa. It is a poor rhetorician who has but a single speech, or a single set of commonplaces with which to adorn all discourse. In ordinary discourse, everyday rhetoricians, arguing and discussing their worlds, are usually not so monotonically limited.

The topic of monarchy, as a topic of continuing fascination for the British public, contains a network of contrary, or dilemmatic, themes. Billig[41] suggests that there may be two commonsensically reasonable, but opposing, accounts of national history, which are part and parcel of the discourse about royalty. On the one hand, there is the theme of the unbroken tradition of monarchy, stretching back into the distant national past, uniting the nation with itself and with its history. On the other hand, there is a story of popular struggle, as the people battle against unreasonable kingly power, in order to establish the rights of parliament. These two competing histories may figure in rhetorically different discourses today. For example, in the interview described above, the father used the first historical account in an argument that modern life misses the authenticity and sense of community which characterised the nation in unspecified 'past' times, but then praised the royal family for their relaxed, 'modern' standards of behaviour. The mother at times criticised these standards, urging a return to earlier, more authoritarian codes of behaviour, even to the extent of advocating more political power for the monarch. Yet, at other times she used the history of progress to celebrate the better and freer lives which ordinary people like themselves had today, as compared to those dark days when the family would have been mere serfs of the aristocracy.

Similar variability in the use of historical repertoires can be seen in the printed rhetoric of the mass media. Billig[42] has analysed the accounts of history used by the best-selling newspaper in Britain, the *Sun*. In celebrating the birth of a grandchild to the Queen, the *Sun* published a special history, which drew upon themes of tradition and national unity: the struggles between the people and the crown were absent from this account. However, as part of the *Sun*'s celebration of the happy royal birth, it published a private photograph:

> Wide-eyed Princess Beatrice is the Queen Bea as four generations of royals get together for a fabulous family picture. [13 October 1988]

When Buckingham Palace objected so strongly to the newspaper's printing of the photograph that it called the police to investigate, the paper switched immediately from panegyric to criticism. And in articulating its criticism, it employed another tale of history. This other rhetoric appeared four days after the publication of the photograph, and while the special *The Sun Souvenir Royal Album*, detailing the history of 'our illustrious Royal Family', was still on sale. In this rhetoric, designed to counter the criticisms from the Palace, a tale was told in which the rich historically opposed the people and its government, and still continue to do so in the present:

> We have today a society in which the Government is dedicated to bringing democratic power to the people...but one thing has not changed in 300 years: The power of the richest families.

In this discourse, no longer is the royal family fabulously royal; it is merely 'rich' and 'privileged', as a switch is made to a different discourse of interpretation with its own set of commonplace assumptions and its own recognisable account of history.

It might be objected that the variability shown by the *Sun* newspaper has few implications for traditional attitude theory, for what is revealed is primarily a lack of attitudes rather than anything else. For example, it could be objected that the *Sun* holds few attitudes as such, except a forceful opportunism which leads it to pursue the day's case with the most extreme and simplified rhetoric possible. The traditional attitude theorist might claim that variability is not to be found in cases where people genuinely hold 'strong views'. However, some of the discourse data from the royal family project indicates that this may be an over-simplification. Billig[43] writes of the case in which a father was recognised by the rest of his family to have 'strong views' about monarchy. He would regularly read the royal items in the newspapers, and would watch the televised news for snippets of regal information, so that he could launch into the critical denunciations, which were so familiar to the rest of the family. Here was a man who was socially recognised as having strong attitudes.

There were a number of points about the family discussions involving the father with these strong views critical of monarchy.[44] In the discussions, the individual members did not merely give their own individual positions regarding a series of issues: i.e., 'I strongly feel that the Queen should smile more', 'I tend to feel that Charles will make a good king', etc. The discussions did not resemble a series of answers to attitude questionnaires. Instead, from beginning to end, there was argumentation. As the father gave his strong views, he did so in relation to those of the other family members, and vice versa. The argument was without hostility or rancour, but it was clear that the holding of strong views was taking place in a context of rhetorical controversy. Moreover, the arguments were not merely about the monarchy and the behaviour of members of the royal family. The arguments were about the views of each other, and whether the family members' respective views were reasonable or not. Thus the mother would downgrade the father's views with the claim that he said what he did only to try to stir things up. The father, by way of reply, asserted the reasonableness of attacking the monarchy. In this way, what are often called 'attitudes' are not merely rhetorical stances about the social world, but they are stances in relation to other stances: they are arguments about counter-arguments and about what are reasonable positions to take about matters of controversy.

In addition, the rhetorical stances, even of somebody presumed to hold strong views about a particular hobby-horse, are not necessarily fixed unvariably. The father modified his rhetoric at different times of the interview. At one point, he had been speaking in a radical way about 'we, the people' having been exploited by the rich, including the royal family. His son, supporting the traditions of the nation but not those of his own father, suddenly accused his father of being a communist. The father rejected the label, and then justified himself. His rhetoric changed in the course of his justification, although he claimed to be clarifying his earlier point. No longer was the image one of a divided society, with the people fighting their historic battle against the privileged. Instead, he used an image of harmony: 'we' need 'our' rich people, 'our' business men. Even kings and queens could have their place in this non-communist harmony: if only, he mused, there were good kings and queens who cared about the poor.

This switch from the rhetoric of egalitarian republicanism to that of a royalist utopia occurred in a brief moment and was achieved by a man recognised to have strong views. This sort of switch is not surprising if one assumes that the common sense ideology, with which the speaker operated and which he broadly shared with his argumentative disputants, contains the contrary themes which permit noisy, dialogic thinking.

Thoughts and arguments

Even people recognised to have strong views do not repeat themselves in a fully determined way. The conversation may return to the same topic, but it does not return in precisely the same terms. Exactly what is said is not entirely predictable, and the strong views are not themselves fully determinate. Indeed, there can be new rhetorical reactions to new rhetorical contexts. This sort of variability does not indicate that the speaker has not thought about the issue in question. Nor is it a sign that the speaker does not care what is said. Instead, the more that the speaker thinks about the issue and the more that the speaker cares about challenging the views of others, the more there is to be said. As such, there is more to think about every time the issue is publicly raised. In consequence, the speaker with strong views may be someone who continues to think about the issue in question and who can be observed publicly thinking when the arguments get going.

More generally, it might be suggested that analysts can observe thinking in action in the course of argumentative discourse. The thrust of comment and counter-comment unfolds too quickly for the words to be thoughtful representations of inner cognitive processes of a qualitatively different nature. Instead the dialogue, with its immediate interruptions and contradictions, can be seen as the process of thinking. There would not be such observable thinking if all members of a discussion merely voiced their agreement with one another, for it is the criticisms and the negations which provide the thoughtful, argumentative context. Therefore, thinking can be seen as a social, argumentative process, rather than a monologic, individual one.

In this respect, the rhetorical approach focuses upon those aspects and types of thinking which tend to be overlooked by contemporary cognitive psychology. Moreover, the linkage with ancient rhetoric does not only connect modern psychological notions with ancient ones, in a way that cautions against contemporary theoretical hubris. It also can connect the contemporary subjects of psychological research with their ancient forebears. The families, discussing the monarchy of Britain, are arguing about their political and ethical worlds. And as they use common sense themes to argue dilemmatically, so they continue to think about the world. In doing this, they are heirs to Socrates and his fellow philosophers arguing in the streets of Athens about the nature of virtue and about the duty of citizens. For the most part, the Platonic dialogues end in a state of *aporia*, as the participants realise there is always more to speak about. Similarly, the modern families talking about the perplexities of modern monarchy and the modern state have more to say. It is not that they have failed to think, but that as they argue rhetorically so they continue to think noisily.[45]

Notes

1. See Philostratus, *Lives of the Sophists* (London: Loeb Classical Library, 1956); and Seneca the Elder, *Controversiae* (London: Loeb Classical Library, 1974).

2. See M. Billig, *Arguing and Thinking: A Rhetorical Approach to Social Psychology* (Cambridge: Cambridge University Press, 1987) and 'The rhetoric of social psychology', in I. Parker and J. Shotter (eds), *Deconstructing Social Psychology* (London: Routledge, 1990). Also M. Gane, 'Rhetoric' *Economy and Society* vol. 18 (1989) pp. 127-31; D.N. McCloskey, *The Rhetoric of Economics* (Brighton: Harvester, 1986); J.S. Nelson, A. Megill, and D.N. McCloskey, *The Rhetoric of the Human Sciences* (Madison: University of Wisconsin Press, 1987); J. Shotter, 'A sense of place: Vico and the social production of social identies' *British Journal of Social Psychology* 25 (1986) pp. 199-211, and 'Rhetoric and the recovery of civil society' *Economy and Society* vol. 18 (1989) pp. 132-48; H.W. Simon (ed.), *Rhetoric in the Human Sciences* (London: Sage, 1989), and 'Rhetoric of inquiry as an intellectual movement', in H.W. Simons (ed.), *The Rhetorical Turn* (Chicago: University of Chicago Press, 1990).

3. Habermas, J., *The Philosophical Discourse of Modernity* (Cambridge: Polity Press, 1987).

4. Plato, *The Sophist* (London: Loeb Classical Library, 1948) p. 263e.

5. Bakhtin, M.M., *The Dialogic Imagination* (Austin: University of Texas Press, 1981).

6. Vygotsky, B., *Thought and Language* (Cambridge, MA: MIT Press, 1962).

7. See J. Wertsch, *Culture, Communication and Cognition* (Cambridge: Cambridge University Press, 1985); J. Shotter, *Social Accountability and Selfhood* (Oxford: Blackwell, 1984), and 'Vygotsky's psychology: joint activity in the developmental zone' *New Ideas in Psychology* 7 (1989) pp. 185-204; K.J. Gergen, *Towards Transformation in Social Knowledge* (New York: Springer-Verlag, 1982) and 'The social constructionist movement in social psychology' *American Psychologist* 40 (1985) pp. 266-75; J. Shotter and K.J. Gergen, *Texts of Identity* (London: Sage, 1989); and J. Valsiner, 'Ontogeny of co-construction of culture within socially organised settings' in J. Valsiner (ed.), *Child Development Within Culturally Structured Environments* (Norwood: Ablex, 1988).

8. Potter, J., and Wetherell, M., *Discourse and Social Psychology* (London: Sage, 1987).

9. See also M. Wetherell and J. Potter, 'Discourse analysis and the identification of interpretative repertoires', in C. Antaki (ed.), *Analysing Everyday Explanation* (London: Sage, 1988).

10. See M. Billig (1987); as in note 2.

11. Aristotle, *Rhetoric* (Cambridge: Cambridge University Press, 1909) I.i.14.

12. Cicero, *Brutus* (London: Loeb Classical Library, 1971) p. 30.

13. See B. Vickers, *In Defence of Rhetoric* (Oxford: Clarendon Press, 1988).

14. Perelman, C., and Olbrechts-Tyteca, L., *The New Rhetoric* (Notre Dame: University of Notre Dame Press, 1971).

15. Cicero, *De Inventione* (London: Loeb Classical Library, 1959).

16. See, for example, the influential work of P.N. Johnson-Laird, 'Mental models in cognitive science', in D.A. Norman (ed.), *Perspectives on Cognitive Science* (Hilldale: Erlbaum, 1981), and *Mental Models* (Cambridge: Cambridge University Press, 1983).

17. See C. Perelman, *The New Rhetoric and the Humanities* (Dordrecht: Reidel, 1979); and M. Billig (1987); as in note 2.

18. Diogenes Laertius, *Lives of Eminent Philosophers* (London: Loeb Classical Library, 1972) p. 163.

19. Billig, M., 'Prejudice, categorisation and particularisation: from a perceptual to a rhetorical approach' *European Journal of Social Psychology* 15 (1985) pp. 79-103, and Billig (1987) ch. 6 for critiques. (See note 2.)

20. For example, E. Rosch, 'Principles of categorisation', in E. Rosch and B. Lloyd (eds), *Cognition and Categorisation* (Hillsdale: Erlbaum, 1978); and C.B. Mervis and E. Rosch, 'Categorisation of natural objects' *Annual Review of Psychology* 32 (1981) pp. 89-115.

21. See M. Billig (1985); as in note 19.

22. See T.A. Seboek and J. Umiker-Seboek, *Speaking of Apes* (New York: Plenum Press, 1980).

23. Aristotle, *Topica* (Cambridge: Loeb Classical Library, 1976).

24. See M. Billig, S. Condor, D. Edwards, M. Gane, D. Middleton, and A.R. Radley, *Ideological Dilemmas* (London: Sage, 1988).

25. Bacon, F., *Of the Dignity and Advancement of Learning* (London: Longman, 1905).

26. Whately, R., *Elements of Rhetoric* (Carbondale: Southern Illinois University Press, 1846).

27. See M. Billig, *et al.* (1988); as in note 24.

28. See M. Billig (in press).

29. Moscovici, S., 'The phenomenon of social representations', in R. Farr and S. Moscovici (eds), *Social Representations* (Cambridge: Cambridge University Press, 1983).

30. See M. Billig, 'Common-places of the British royal family: a rhetorical analysis of plain and argumentative sense' *Text* 8 (1988) pp. 91-110, and 'Rhetorical and historical attitudes: the case of the British Monarchy' *Philosophical Psychology* 1 (1986) pp. 83-104.

31. For an extended discussion of the role of royalty in the construction of English nationalism, see T. Nairn, *The Enchanted Glass: Britain and its Monarch* (London: Radius, 1988); and also D. Cannadine, 'The context, performance and meaning of ritual: the British monarchy and the "invention of tradition" ', in E. Hobsbaum and T. Ranger (eds), *Invention of Tradition* (Cambridge: Cambridge University Press, 1983).

32. See M. Billig, 'Collective memory, ideology and the British Royal Family', in D. Middleton and D. Edwards (eds), *Collective Remembering* (London: Sage; in press), and 'The argumentative nature of holding strong views: a case study' *European Journal of Social Psychology* vol. 19 (1989) pp. 203-23.

33. See National Opinion Polls, 'The Royal Family' *Political, Social Economic Review* 59 (1986) pp. 12-15; R. Rose and D. Kavanagh, 'The monarchy in contemporary culture' *Comparative Politics* 8 (1976) pp. 548-76; and P. Ziegler, *Crown and People* (London: Collins, 1977).

34. The example is discussed in greater detail in M. Billig (London: Sage); as in note 32.

35. See S. Moscovici (1983) p. 10; as in note 29.

36. See D. Edwards and D. Middleton, 'Joint remembering: constructing an account of shared experience through conversational discourse' *Discourse Processes* 9 (1986) pp. 423-59; and 'Conversational remembering and family relationships: how children learn to remember' *Journal of Social and Personal Relationships* 5 (1988) pp. 3-25; and J. Potter and D. Edwards, 'Nigel Lawson's tent: factual rhetoric and political hot water', paper given at Conversation, Discourse and Conflict Conference (Dublin, 1989).

37. See M. Billig, *et al.* (1988); as in note 24.

38. See J. Potter and M. Wetherell (1987); as in note 8, and 'Accomplishing attitudes' *Text* 8 (1988) pp. 51-68; E. Frazer, 'Teenage girls talking about class' *Sociology* 22 (1988) pp. 343-59; M. Wetherell and J. Potter (1988); as in note 9; and M. Wetherell, H. Stiven, and J. Potter, 'Unequal egalitarianism: a preliminary study of discourses concerning gender and unemployment opportunities' *British Journal of Social Psychology* 26 (1987) pp. 59-71.

39. See J. Potter and M. Wetherell (1987); as in note 8.

40. See also G.N. Gilbert and M. Mulkay, *Opening Pandora's Box* (Cambridge: Cambridge University Press, 1984).

41. Billig, M. (London: Sage); as in note 32, and 'Stacking the cards of ideology: the history of the *Sun's Royal Souvenir Album' Discourse and Society* vol. 1 (1990) pp. 17-37.

42. Billig, M. ('Stacking the cards...'); as in note 41.

43. Billig, M. ('The argumentative nature...'); as in note 32.

44. Refer to notes 32 and 43.

45. This paper is based upon a talk given to the British Psychological Society Conference, St Andrews, 1989. The empirical research reported in the paper was funded by an ESRC grant investigating 'Family discourse: socio-psychological aspects'. The author is grateful to Marie Kennedy for conducting the interviews.

7

The Rhetoric of Economic Expertise

Donald N. McCloskey[1] (University of Iowa)

In one of his last books the San Francisco dock worker and sage, Eric Hoffer, wrote that 'The harm done by self-appointed experts in human affairs is usually a product of *a priori* logic.... The logic of events may draw from man's actions consequences which *a priori* logic cannot foresee'.[2] Hoffer was no logician or experimenter, and was not using the words '*a priori*' and 'the logic of events' in senses that a philosopher of science would recognise. He meant only to distinguish what an economist would call a model from what a historian would call a story.

Hoffer was making, in other words, the distinction between metaphor and narrative, the synchronic and the diachronic, cross-section and time series, the differential equation and the solution (to run the gamut of the available jargon). One can look at trade negotiations between America and Russia as part of a game or as part of a relationship, as something timelessly similar to chess and cricket or as something timefully similar to marriage and destiny. The way one looks at it will matter. Hoffer was surely right that the '*a priori* logic' – the metaphor – can do harm even when it comes with the authority of expertise. The expert recommends a gaming approach to the trade negotiation, the metaphor gets pushed too far, and the *a priori* leads us to World War Three. The expert's fanaticism about his models provides a plot for an international thriller.

I wish to add merely that the case is symmetric: that expert history also can do harm. The story of evolution was made over into the story of racial destiny, with damage to us all. The generation young in 1938 has never forgotten Munich, and has imposed the logic of those events on each post-war crisis from Greece to Cambodia. Hoffer was wrong to suggest that the *a priori* metaphor is the only dangerous tool in the hands of experts. The logic of events, which is to say the story imposed on events, has its own dangers.

The problem comes as a pair, the problem of the misuse by experts of both models and stories. A model such as game theory or a story such as national destiny can be used with open eyes and yet still be misused, if the expert does not give a damn. People with careers to make will misuse whatever rhetorical tool is put into

137

their hands. Most experts, though, are not characters from *Yes, Minister*. Commonly they do not realise that they are misusing a story – they think they are simply taking history as their guide. They would be startled to be told that they are using, much less misusing, metaphors – they think that they are simply taking science as their guide.

Consider economics. Economists will tell you that they rely strictly on fact and logic. When pressed they will give an account of fact and logic derived from British empiricism and French rationalism long ago, the common if dusty heritage of Western intellectual life. A fact is the unit of things seen and a logic is the unit of links postulated. Economic science would seem straightforward, then, although the economic scientist can give no credible explanation of why a straightforward procedure of 'looking at' the facts and 'checking' the logic would so often lead to disagreement. It is not, by the way, the unscientific character of economics that causes the disagreement: paleontologists and biochemists disagree just as much, asserting stoutly that fact and logic stand on their side.

Disagreement in science shows that fact and logic are not enough. This is so even if 'science' is defined in the peculiar English-language sense, as 'fields of study that look like what non-physicists a century ago thought physics was'. English speakers since the early nineteenth century have used the word 'science' in a peculiar way: as in the British academic usage of 'arts and sciences' where the 'arts' of literature and philosophy are set against the 'sciences' of chemistry and geology. A historical geologist in English is a scientist; a political historian is not. The English usage would puzzle an Italian mother boasting of her studious son, *mio scienziato*, my learned one. Like Italian, other languages use the science word to mean simply 'systematic inquiry' (for example, French, German, Dutch, Spanish, Swedish, Polish, Hungarian, Turkish, Korean, Tamil, Hindi). Only English, and only the English of the past century, has made physical and biological science (sense 5b in the old *Oxford English Dictionary*) into, as the *Supplement* (1982; compare OED, 2nd edn 1989) describes it, 'the dominant sense in ordinary use'.

Economics looks like such a science. But in the manner of physics (and geology and history and philology) it uses daily the humanistic tropes of metaphor and story. Depend on it, fact and logic are admirable. Economics certainly makes ample use of them. But an economist or physicist confined to fact and logic would have nothing to say. Sciences require humanism, such as literary methods, right in the middle of their sciences; and likewise the humanities require fact and logic. Newton used logic and metaphors; Darwin used facts and stories. Science is literary, requiring metaphors and stories in its daily work, and literature is scientific.

Fact and logic, with metaphor and story, make up what might be called the Rhetorical Tetrad. Economists, like other experts, must use the whole tetrad if they are going to make sense. The supposedly scientific half of the tetrad, the fact-and-logic, does not suffice for a science of economics or even for a science of rocks or stars. Nor does the allegedly humanistic half, by itself. Scientists and scholars had better be factual and logical. But (and this is the point here) they had also better be literary, devising good metaphors and telling good stories about the first three minutes of the universe or the last three months of the American economy. A scientist with only half the culture will do bad science.

The assertion is that an expert in economic science is like a poet in using metaphors and like a novelist in using stories – using them not for ornament or teaching alone but for the very science. The dependence on metaphor is the easiest to demonstrate. Economists, who talk incessantly of their models, are even aware of it. Once they have recovered from the insult of using so literary a word they can see that the models are metaphors, as they are in physics.[3]

During 1946 the agricultural economist Theodore Schultz, later to win a Nobel prize for the work, spent a term based at Auburn University interviewing Alabama farmers.[4] One day he interviewed an old and poor farm couple and was struck by how contented they seemed. Why are you so contented, he asked, though very poor? They answered: You're wrong, Professor. We're not poor. We used up the farm to educate our four children through university, remaking fertile land and well-stocked pens into knowledge of law and Latin. We get pleasure from this different wealth in educated children. We are rich.

The parents had told Schultz that the *physical* capital (which economists think they understand) is in some sense just like the *human* capital of education. The children now embodied it. Formerly it had been rail fences, hog pens and mules. Now it lay in the children's brains and in the parents' hearts, this 'human capital'. The farm couple was indeed rich.

The average economist in later years was willing to accept the simple but profound discovery of human capital as soon as he understood it. It was an argument in a metaphor (or if you like in an analogy, a simile, a model). A hog pen, Schultz would say to another economist, is 'just like' Latin 101. The other economist would have to admit right away that there was something to it. Both the hog pen and the Latin course are paid for by saving. Both are valuable assets for earning income, understanding 'income' to mean, as economists put it, 'a stream of satisfaction', pouring bits of happiness out year after year like an oil well. Both the hog pen and the Latin course last a long time but finally wear out. And the one piece of 'capital' can be made into the other. An educated farmer, because of his degree in Agriculture from Auburn, can get a bank loan to build a hog pen; when he raises his own children he can sell off part of the farm with the hog pen to pay for another term for the children up at Auburn.

Calling education 'human capital' might cause offence. The phrase takes the shaping of the human mind as something similar to the shaping of fences and concrete. So long as the economist knows that the metaphor of human capital is a human device and not a Truth – so long, that is, as he/she has learned somehow the chief humanistic truth – no harm is done. Such a metaphor makes thinking possible. It is not a luxury. Speaking of education as equivalent to investment in farm buildings allows an economist to ask sharply whether enough education has been purchased relative to farm buildings. Or it allows him/her to stress the high returns (relative to alternative investments) of teaching people how to read.

Economists go on this way, dancing among their metaphors half aware. When economists look at a phenomenon like 'childcare' they think of markets. 'Childcare' – which to other people looks like a piece of political control or a set of rooms or a problem in social work – looks to economists like a stock certificate traded on the London exchange, a 'market'. The economists are led by their choice of metaphor to identify a demand curve, a supply curve, and a price. If the economists are of the usual 'neoclassical' kind they will see also what they are pleased to call rationality in such a market. If they are Marxist, institutionalist or Austrian economists, to name a few of the alternatives, they will see something different, though still see it through their version of the market metaphor.

A rhetorician will note that the market is 'just' a figure of speech. It is, as we say, a commonplace. The economist uses his commonplace of the market over and over again. To be reflexive about it, I am now using the metaphor of 'literature' as a rhetorical commonplace for the language game of economists. The game is not trivial or stupid merely for being a game. Economics is not demeaned by being compared with the games of Homer, Shakespeare and Tolstoy, or even with those of W.G. Grace and Babe Ruth.

The metaphor, and the economic poetry that goes with it, is not 'true' in a simple way. 'France is hexagonal' is neither true nor false in the way a statement in arithmetic is true or false.[5] It is right, in a certain way of speaking, which is to say, useful for some purpose (though one could say that rightness, not Truth, is also what we find useful about statements in arithmetic). The methodology of Science that economists and other scientists believe they employ gives no way to evaluate the rightness of metaphors. The assertion of likeness, so important in biology and physics, involves standards that can only be human and cultural. How similar *is* the smooth pea to the wrinkled, the planetary orbit to an ellipse, Latin 101 to a hog pen? These are questions about our present use of language, constrained by the universe sitting out there, to be sure, but human decisions about human use.

That is where 'rhetoric' comes in, the discourse on the use of discourse. Only our rhetoric can provide standards of likeness. Paul Fussell notes 'It has been said that what makes the world so hard to understand is that there's nothing to compare it with. But that's not right: there's literature to compare it with',[6] which is to say our words in practice. How smooth is the pea? It depends on how you want to argue with other people. If they are persuaded by simple proportions, then you will want to assign the peas in a way that makes the proportions come out simply (as Gregor Mendel did).[7] How close is a planetary orbit to an ellipse? It depends on the accuracy that observations have attained, which is again a matter of human arguing, such as Tycho Brahe's argument for greater precision of celestial observation than was once thought worth the trouble. It is fruitless to argue for a complicated shape like an ellipse when the figures of argument are not accurate enough to distinguish a nearly circular ellipse from a circle. How close is a hog pen to a college degree? It depends on how deep in capitalism we are, and how plausible it is therefore to lump one kind of 'capital' with another.

We economists, or audiences for economists – not God – decide how useful a scientific metaphor is. It's our little scientific drama, not written in the stars alone. And we decide, too, in every part of the rhetorical tetrad, deciding by our scientific conversations what is a fact,[8] what is a logic,[9] and what is a story.[10]

Talking this way about the social construction of economics or other sciences does not commit one to dreaded Relativism. The Johnsonians among philosophers need not commence kicking rocks and pounding tables to show that the world is more than socially constructed. The world is still there. But we nonetheless construct it. The situation is like fishing. The fish are there by God's command; but still the humans make the nets. To catch fish we need both. It is unhelpful to argue that the caught fish are 'really' or 'ultimately' either social or objective. They had better be both, or we are not going to eat on Friday.

So an economist is a poet but doesn't know it. He/she is also a storyteller, who lives happily ever after. It is not hard to come upon economists, as good scientists, in the act of using stories for their science. Outsiders will find it easier to see the stories than will the economists themselves, because the economists are trained to think of themselves not as storytellers but as metaphor-makers, builders of models.

Economists spend a good deal of time retelling stories that non-economists tell about the economy, such as: once upon a time the economy seemed to be doing fine but had a secret monetary illness, then the illness broke out, and therefore everyone became poor. And economists have their own stories that they tell to each other: once upon a time there was a hog market out of equilibrium, then the sellers lowered the price, and as a result the market got back into equilibrium. Once upon a time the government cleverly reckoned it would drop taxes to achieve full employment, but the public had already discounted the move, and as a result the government ended up with egg on its face. Once upon a time a third-world country was poor, then it studied hard, saved a lot, and borrowed money and ideas from the first world, and therefore became rich. These are not going to dry up the market for *King Lear* or *Pride and Prejudice*, but anyway they are the stories that economists tell.

Not gods but people tell the stories. The stories are not facts made by nature. That does not make them arbitrary, merely various. A geologist is constrained by what in fact happened on the earth, and by what he thinks are relevant logics and metaphors; but nonetheless with the same facts he can tell the story in varied ways, as gradualist or catastrophist, for example. The same is true in economics. Not all the ways of telling a story are equally good. To criticise them, though, you have to know that they are being told.

Tale-telling in economics follows the usual constraints of fiction. The most important is the sense of an ending. One must go all the way to the third act. Gerald Prince used some ingenious mental experiments with stories and non-stories to formulate a definition of the 'minimal story', which has:

> three conjoined events. The first and third events are stative [such as 'John was poor'], the second is active [such as 'then John found a pot of gold']. Furthermore, the third event is the inverse of the first [such as 'John was rich'.... The three events are conjoined by conjunctive features in such a way that (a) the first event precedes the second in time and the second precedes the third, and (b) the second event causes the third.[11]

One can use Prince's examples to construct stories and non- stories in economics. Test the pattern:

Poland was poor, then it adopted capitalism, then as a result it became rich.

The money supply increased this year, then, as a result, productivity last year rose and the business cycle that began three decades ago peaked.

A few firms existed in chemicals, then they merged, and then only one firm existed.

Britain in the late nineteenth century was capitalistic and rich and powerful.

The pattern is story/non-story/story/non-story.

Many of the disagreements inside economics turn on this sense of an ending. To an eclectic Keynesian, raised on picaresque tales of economic surprise, the story idea 'Oil prices went up, which caused inflation' is full of meaning, having the merits that stories are supposed to have. But to a monetarist, raised on the classical unities of money, it seems incomplete, no story at all, a flop. As the economist A.C. Harberger likes to say, it doesn't make the economics 'sing'. It ends too soon, half-way through the second act. As the jargon has it, a rise in oil prices without some corresponding fall elsewhere is 'not an equilibrium'.

From the other side, the criticism of monetarism by Keynesians is likewise a criticism of the plot line, complaining of an ill-motivated beginning rather than a premature ending: where on earth does the money you monetarists think is so important *come* from, and why? The jargon word is 'exogenous': if you start the story in the middle the money will be treated as though it is unrelated to, exogenous to, the rest of the action, even though it is not.

Stories, then, are used by everybody, even by the economic expert. The second point is that the stories can be bad if they are used in ignorance of the other figure of argument, those models and metaphors. Bad stories yield snakeoil. The suckers gathered around the medicine wagon wish very much that the economist was an expert forecaster. They want him to sell them the simplest and most charming of stories: Once upon a time there was a newspaper reader who was poor; then she read a column by a very wise economist, who for some reason was making valuable advice available to her and two million other readers; and now as a result she is rich and happy. Or: Once upon a time there was a kingdom with people who did not like to study, preferring to sniff cocaine and watch rock videos on television; then the king hired a wonderfully expert social engineer who had done a great deal of studying; and then as a result the kingdom became miraculously prosperous, without having to study.

Economic snakeoil sells because the public wants it. The public wants it because of the fear that magicians and medicine men have always assuaged, and because the public does not know the limitations on economic storytelling. The economists, even the ones who do not plan a career in snakeoil, are disabled by their training from seeing how stories can go wrong. They do not know they are telling stories and therefore cannot distinguish good stories from bad.

A bad story of modern life, that is, has a final scene in which the expert, such as

142

the expert on the interest rate that will prevail next month, keeps us warm and happy. The analogy with physical engineering, which recently *has* in fact kept us warm and happy, is hard to resist. The social engineer promises to run the economy or the war or the culture with god-like expertise. But it is a naughty story, a wicked fairytale. Speaking about strategic bombing, Fussell notes the fairy tale of precision, which assumed 'that human beings could do without gross error anything they rationally proposed to do'.[12] Most social engineering is as impossible as bombing Uncle Harry's scullery in East London with intent.

The public and its experts would be happier (though not much richer) if they would grasp the silliness of relying on stories or metaphors alone. The way out of the muddle of over-specialisation in argument is to see that stories and metaphors can be used to criticise each other. Sir Arthur 'Bomber' Harris' story of precision bombing at night from six miles up can be criticised with the metaphor of Murphy's Law.

The stories that economists are asked to tell as advisers to governments or as social philosophers fit at best awkwardly and at worst disastrously with the metaphors they build elsewhere in their science. The metaphors, likewise, run up against the stories. Economic metaphors if pushed too far, as a 500-equation model of the American economy can be, produce silly stories. And stories, such as the story of America's tragic decline from Number One, contradict metaphors of maturity and of advantageous trade that we all know to be true. The badly used 500-equation metaphor can tempt us, as it did during the 1960s, into tricky policies rather than wise institutions. The bad story of America as Number One can tempt us, as it did the British a century ago, into figurative and then literal war with our 'competitors'.

Take the version of the Expert Story offered on some of the American cable TV stations, namely, 'You are now poor; but if you will send $50 to the address that appears now on your screen, you will as a result become rich'. The story is a story by Prince's definition: three conjoined events, the first and third being states of being (poor and then rich), the third the inverse of the first, the second event an action, such that the third event is its result. In optimistic America such stories are common. There is actually offered a computer program for $49.95 (available by mail order from Los Angeles) that calculates random numbers on which to place bets for the lottery. Europeans do not believe in such stories. Americans, by the millions, do.

Now consider the enrichment-by-advice story in the light of the economist's favourite metaphor, of people as calculating machines. The metaphor can be expressed as the Axiom of Modest Greed: if I throw a $20 bill on the floor, someone will pick it up. If $20 isn't enough, imagine a larger sum. True enough, we all stumble about in a fog, and often fail to see our interest. But $20 is enough to pierce most fogs (by actual experiment it has been found that Manhattanites will not stoop for a dime or a nickel, but a quarter gets them every time). The computing in the metaphor of *homo computans*, you see, does not have to be perfectly accurate or methodical.

It is a rigorous theorem from the Axiom of Modest Greed, therefore, that $20 bills will not lie around untaken on sidewalks. And there follows rigorously a corollary, the American Question: If you're so smart, why ain't you rich? If a computer company knows how to pick lottery numbers, why is it selling such Faustian wisdom to you? Why isn't it unlimitedly rich? Why doesn't it pick up the $20 bill itself? The offer to make you rich by sending in $50 to the TV huckster would appear to be a false story.

So a story in economics is being criticised by a metaphor in economics. An exercise in literary criticism is serving to warn off the suckers. It goes further. For one thing, the same criticism applies to all manner of economic predictions. A broker with a plausible manner who advises you on stocks is pretending to know something that would make both you and him rich. But if he's so smart, why ain't he rich? And the same American Question can be asked of the more official and scientific predictions of economists: the price of soybeans next spring; the interest rate in six months; the date of the next recession; what will happen to housing prices in Normandy when the Chunnel opens? If economists were so smart they would be rich.

This does not mean economists cannot predict anything. They can: they know a lot more about the economy than you do. I am not asserting that economists are dunces or charlatans. They cannot predict, however, an event for which it would be profitable to have foreknowledge. That covers a lot of ground. Economists work honestly at social history and social philosophy, giving an account of the past and imaginative possibilities for the future. But when the journalists demand social weather forecasting in detail, the wiser economists resist. If they were so smart they would be rich. They are not rich. Consequently, they are not so smart. The American Question demolishes the claims of social engineering. It does so by using economics to criticise economics. It criticises an economic story with an economic metaphor.

The coin of profit need not of course be monetary – it needs merely to be coveted. For instance, political scientists whose theories of voting imply that they could predict the outcome of elections run up against the American Question. If they're so smart, why ain't they powerful? Critics of art whose theories imply an ability to predict (as many do) run up against the American Question, too. The Question curbs the ambition of a human science. It criticises all expertise 'Whose deepness doth entice such forward wits/To practice more than heavenly power permits'.

Notice that the American Question does not draw on the usual humanistic criticisms of science. It does not come from outside the tropes of science, affirming bravely that humans are very different from gas molecules. In fact, the American Question is an application of the very trope of the gas molecules. It shows that certain classes of foretelling are perpetual motion machines that violate the first and second laws of thermodynamics.

Likewise the stories can criticise the metaphors. An example is the counterfactual – what would have happened in world history if Lenin had died of food poisoning before arriving at the Finland Station or what would have happened to American national income by 1890 had the railway not been invented? Economists view counterfactuals as quite ordinary and necessary. One can only agree. If you are going to assess the cause of anything you are going to be involved in bits of counterfactual speculation. You are going to have to imagine what would have happened without the alleged cause. The imagining will have to use a model, a metaphor that compares the actual economy of America in 1890 to a set of equations. One constructs the model of the American economy, then removes the railway and sees what happens. Whether the modelling is done explicitly or not, that is the reasoning involved. Counterfactuals are necessary for causal thinking, and the counterfactuals involve extrapolating a metaphor.

Too large a contemplated change, however, will result in *narrative* nonsense. The problem is that if an extrapolation reaches too far into the darkness it will inevitably produce contradictions of the actual history, the story we tell to ourselves about the past. In the railway counterfactual the trouble is that the world actually did invent the railway. In order to imagine an America without the railway in 1890 you have to imagine a Britain in 1825 failing for some reason to invent it. And then you have to imagine a world in 1760 that would lead to a world in 1825 that would not invent it. And then a world that would lead to that world, and then...and then...back to Creation. A world in which the railway would not have been available to Americans in 1890 might well have been a world in which the sea was boiling hot or in which pigs had wings, with different problems of transportation.

The more elaborated is the story into which, as Jon Elster put it, one tries to 'insert' the metaphor, the worse are going to be the contradictions.[13] In other words, there is a Basic Paradox of Metaphors and Stories. The more elaborate are the metaphors, the less well they will fit into a story of given complexity. That is, the more frequently will the metaphor of an American economy without the railway contradict the causes of the railway. But simple metaphors are often less richly persuasive than complex ones. A full 500-equation model of the American economy in 1890 will be more persuasive in detailing the effects of the absent railway. And yet (to return to the other side) in its very making the 500-equation model will more flatly contradict wider and wider stretches of actual, told history. Like most things, the selection of stories and metaphors about the same matter is subject to scarcity.

It is a pluralist's principle. Each part of the rhetorical tetrad places limits on the excesses of the others. If you are fanatical about stories alone or about metaphors alone (or logic or fact alone), you will start saying silly and dangerous things in the other realm. It is better to be moderately, reasonably committed to the observing of true facts, the following of true logic, the telling of true stories, and the constructing of true metaphors, which then can check each other's immoderation. Together they yield worthwhile scientific truth and sensible public policy (and, for that matter, prudent personal financial management).

Since the 1950s economics has believed itself narrowed down to the fact-and-logic half of the rhetorical tetrad. Economics shared then, belatedly, in the temporary narrowing of Western culture called 'positivism' or 'modernism'. Modernism has roots as deep as Plato and Descartes, but in full-blown form it suits its name. In the West around 1920 some philosophers came rather suddenly to believe that their whole subject could be narrowed to an artificial language; architects to believe their whole subject could be narrowed to a cube; painters to believe that their whole subject could be narrowed to a surface. Out of this narrowness was supposed to come insight and certitude.

Insight did come, if not certitude. In philosophy after modernism we know more about languages lacking human speakers; in architecture more about buildings lacking tops; in painting more about paintings lacking depth of field. When the news of modernism got out to economics it yielded some insight, too. In economics after modernism we know more about economic models lacking contact with the world.

On the whole, though, the narrowing did not work very well. The failure of modernism in economics and elsewhere in the culture does not imply that we should now abandon fact and logic, surface and cube, and surrender to the Celtic curve and the irrational. It suggests rather that we should turn back to the work at hand equipped with the full tetrad of fact, logic, metaphor, and story.

The modernist attempt to get along with fewer than all the resources of human reasoning puts one in mind of the Midwestern expression, 'a few bricks short of a load'. It means cracked, irrational. The modernist program of narrowing down our arguments in the name of rationality was a few bricks short of a load. To admit now that metaphor and story figure also in human reasoning is to become more, not less, rational, because of putting more of what persuades serious people under scrutiny. Modernism was rigorous about part of reasoning and angrily irrational about the rest. The modernist experts cannot reason with their opponents; on most matters they can only shout and sneer. We need now, after modernism, to become more rigorous and more reasonable, about all the arguments.

In 1979, after much horror imposed by the arrogance of expertise, Eric Hoffer remarked: 'Forty years ago the philosopher Alfred North Whitehead thought it self-evident that you would get a good government if you took power out of the hands of the acquisitive and gave it to the learned and cultivated. At present, a child in kindergarten knows better than that'.[14] The learned tend to specialise in one piece of the rhetorical tetrad. Perhaps the child knows something better than the philosopher: that in isolation the metaphor and the story, the fact and the logic, do mischief without end, in economics or in any field of expertise.

Notes

1. An elaborated version of the argument may be found in D.N. McCloskey, *If You're So Smart: The Narrative of Economic Expertise* (Chicago: University of Chicago Press, 1990), from which certain passages are taken.

2. Hoffer, E., *Before the Sabbath* (New York: Harper and Row, 1979) pp. 26, 28.

3. See D.N. McCloskey, *The Rhetoric of Economics* (Madison: University of Wisconsin Press, 1985); and M.B. Hesse, *Models and Analogies in Science* (London: Sheed and Ward, 1963).

4. Schultz, T., 'Are university scholars and scientists free agents?' *Southern Humanities Review* 22 (Summer, 1988) pp. 251-60.

5. See J.L. Austin, *How to do Things With Words* (Cambridge, MA: Harvard University Press, 1962).

6. Fussell, P. (1990) p. 154.

7. See R. Root-Bernstein, 'Mendel and Methodology' *History of Science* 21 (September, 1983) pp. 275-95.

8. See L. Fleck, *Genesis and Development of a Scientific Fact,* trans. F. Bradley and T.J. Trenn (Chicago: University of Chicago Press, 1979).

9. See I. Lakatos, *Proofs and Refutations: The Logic of Mathematical Discovery* (Cambridge: Cambridge University Press, 1976).

10. See S.J. Gould, *Time's Arrow, Time's Cycle: Myth and Metaphor in the Discovery of Geological Time* (Cambridge, MA: Harvard University Press, 1987).

11. Prince, G., *A Grammar of Stories* (The Hague/Paris: Moulton, 1973) p. 31.

12. Fussell, P., *Wartime: Understanding and Behavior in the Second World War* (New York: Oxford, 1989) p. 15. See also P. Fussell, *Poetic Meter and Poetic Form* (Revised edn, New York: Random House, 1979), and P. Fussell, *Thank God for the Atomic Bomb and Other Essays* (New York: Ballantine, 1988).

13. Elster, J., *Logic and Society: Contradictions and Possible Worlds* (New York: Wiley, 1978) p. 206.

14. Hoffer, E. (1979); as in note 2, p. 41.

8

The Rhetoric of the Scientific Research Report: 'Drug-pushing' in a Medical Journal Article

Herbert W. Simons (Temple University)

Acknowledgements

This essay has profited from comments on earlier drafts by audiences at Cooper Hospital Department of Medicine, University of Pennsylvania Medical School, Netherlands Institute of Advanced Study, Haifa and Hebrew Universities (Israel), University of Athens (Greece), University of Amsterdam (Holland), Loughborough and Durham Universities (UK), University of Jyvaskyla (Finland), University of Oslo (Norway), Temple University, UC David and UC Santa Barbara (United States). Special thanks for Joe Cappella, Mira Katz and Steve Gluckmann.

By way of introducing this essay's case study, I recently asked an audience of medical students whether the authors of the medical research articles that they read tended to put their collective 'best feet forward' or were inclined instead to 'tell it like it is.' A few thought the question unfair, as indeed it was, for it put the matter in overly dichotomous terms, requiring them to choose between appearing overly cynical and appearing naive. Still, they acknowledged that the question addresses a central tension in medical research writing, one that gets played out substantively and stylistically from beginning to end of the research report. A few students allowed that their profession's promulgation of the myth of 'telling it like it is' might in itself be a way of 'putting one's best foot forward.'

My own answer to the question is that reporters of every kind not only *do not* 'tell it like it is' but *cannot*. Moreover, even if they *could*, they would be under considerable institutional pressure *not to*. Hence, like the medical students I talked to, the researchers whose reports they read also confront serious dilemmas, for the norm of objective reporting is institutionally enshrined even as it is consistently (and inevitably) violated. A supreme test of the researcher is the capacity to *appear* to be 'telling it like it is' while at the same time putting his or her 'best foot' as far forward as a discriminating readership might be expected to allow.

This clearly is rhetoric in the traditional sense of attempted persuasion, but with one major difference. For, whereas such prototypical persuaders as editorialists, advertisers, and politicians explicitly or implicitly *announce* themselves as per-suaders, researchers typically *conceal* their rhetorical identities behind a mask of attempted objectivity.[1] There is good evidence that research communities know whereof I speak, even if they do not publicly advertise it,[2] and even if individual researchers still cling to the myth of objective reporting.

Of course one could distinguish between the different roles played by rhetoric in branches of science, types of task, or types of audience. One could insist, for example, that rhetorical factors weigh more heavily in the 'soft' sciences than in the 'hard' sciences, or in the interpretation of data rather than in the data itself, or in the discourse addressed to granting agencies, to the press or to one's students, rather than to one's peers. But, as I illustrate in this essay's case analysis of a medical research article, not even the 'hard' scientist addressing his or her peers can meet the requirements of accuracy, completeness and linguistic transparency that are entailed by the doctrine of 'telling it like it is'.

That this must be so should be apparent from an analysis of the very nature of the reportorial process. Consider first that the language used in reporting facts is necess-arily selective. In selecting some ways of putting things, we invariably neglect others. Moreover, because it is never possible to say everything about an object, we invariably deflect as we reflect, thus *functioning* rhetorically whether we intend to or not. Put more starkly, there can be no such thing as a true and complete description. Every representation is thus also in a certain sense a misrepresentation. In Nietz-schean terms it is a 'false arrest' of experience.[3]

An alternative conception of objective reporting to 'telling it like it is' is even-handedness or balance – a journalistic favourite that owes its popularity in large measure to the embarrassments of the 'telling it' criterion.[4] Particularly as regards controversial issues, it is difficult to imagine what 'telling it like it is' could possibly mean, or how it might be possible for the reporter to provide a neutral, transparent, value-free description of that external reality.[5] The reportorial problem is linked to the longstanding epistemological problem of erecting solid foundations for knowl-edge, a project that many philosophers now regard as futile.[6] The evenhandedness criterion presupposes, by contrast, a relativistic 'Mannheimian universe', requiring of the reporter a balanced presentation of multiple perspectives on an issue on the assumption that 'the truth lies somewhere in between'.[7]

In actual practice these opposed criteria manage to coexist – for example in newspapers whose editors somewhat arbitrarily decide what is to be considered controversial and what is to be treated as unquestionable fact. My point is not that one criterion of objectivity is necessarily better than another; rather, that there are no objective decision rules for choosing between them. The decision, meanwhile, can be highly consequential. If, to take an example from this essay's case study, foods high in lipid cholesterol were truly a menace to society, then we should probably not want our Mannheimian reporter evenhandedly saying as many good things as bad about them. If, indeed, these foods were as harmful as some scientists claim they are, the reporter who presented a balanced account could legitimately be accused of distorting 'the facts'. Not to consider opposing views, however, when scepticism is warranted, can be equally dangerous, and decisions of warrantability rest on judgements rather than certainties. The best one can do on this and a host of other issues is to advance informal arguments – as opposed to formal proofs and demonstrations – that salient audiences will find persuasive. But that takes us back again to rhetoric.

There is, then, no escape from rhetoric: no escape from informal argumentation, or from figures and tropes, or from the selective naming and framing of issues, or from appeals to communally-held values, or from the need to adapt arguments to ends, audiences, and circumstances. This is not to say that research reports should universally be dismissed as false to fact or unreasonable. Rather, it is to say that, as rhetorical documents, research reports are *extrafactual* and *extralogical*; they always rely on something more than hard fact and cold logic to accomplish their ends. That being so, it becomes a reasonable *hypothesis* that even the most objective-seeming report will, on closer inspection, reveal rhetorical colorations.[8]

Table 1 presents traditional distinctions between rhetoric and science. Rhetoricians of science entertain the hypothesis that, as applied to any given scientific discourse, at least some of the terms on the right might be usefully replaced by the equivalent terms on the left. Just how far the analyst should go in extending the claims of rhetoric is a matter of some controversy. For example, some rhetoricians focus exclusively on extra-factual, extra-logical factors, while others treat fact and logic themselves as rhetorical constructs, extending to the very ideas of the real and the rational. Representative of the first camp is Lyne[9] who maintains that 'rhetoric alone...cannot substitute for all the methods, plodding, tools, rationales, and (let us not forget) observables that the various sciences depend on'. Gross[10] argues, by contrast, that 'there is no empirical or theoretical core, no essential science that reveals itself all the more clearly after the rhetorically analysed components have been set aside'. Following Kuhn,[11] there seems little question but that rhetoric plays a pivotal role at the points of paradigm development and paradigm clash; but it is also the case, I think, that the rhetorical hypothesis can be applied profitably to so-called 'normal' science.[12]

Consider that the 'truths' of normal science are true in the Kuhnian sense only within the framework of a given paradigm; and furthermore, that if these truths are to be certified as such, they must be communicated convincingly to others. As Frye[13] has maintained, 'Anything which makes a functional use of words will always be involved in all of the technical problems of words, including rhetorical problems'. Frye is making reference here to a whole panoply of factors, some of them quite blatant, like the reification of theoretical constructs; other factors are quite subtle, like the ghost-like resonances of metaphorical concepts so familiar to us that we have long ceased to think of them as metaphors.[14] In the 'hard' sciences as well as the 'soft', all must contend with the influences of 'word' on the construction of 'world'[15] – with the need, for example, to create 'natural' categories, in recognition of the fact that they do not really exist 'in' nature but in people. Any category is, as one may put it, 'a set of differences which for a particular purpose, doesn't seem to make a difference'.

Table 1 Traditional distinctions between rhetoric and science	
Rhetoric	*Science*
Subjective, artistic	Objective, inartistic
Exploits 'resources of ambiguity' in language	Utilises an impersonal, unambiguous style
Extra-factual and extra-logical	Relies on facts and logic alone
Deals in matters of belief, judgement (*doxa*)	Deals in matters of certainty or near-certainty (*episteme*)
Audience-centered and ephemeral	Issue-centered and timeless
Utilised appeals to prejudice, authority, tradition, etc.	Rejects authority, prejudice, tradition, etc.
General lines of argument (commonplaces)	Specialised (technical) methods
Goals of advantage-seeking, effectiveness (e.g., what advertisers do)	Disinterested truth-seeking

My own analyses of research reports tend to focus on how discourse is adapted to ends, audiences, and circumstances.[16] In formulating hypotheses, interpreting data, deriving policy implications, and the like, scientists draw upon inventional resources of argumentation that are available in the general culture (called 'commonplaces') as well as technical lines of argument that may be distinctive to their own fields. In their roles as reporters, they also select from among what Burke[17] has called the 'resources of ambiguity' in language. These resources are called upon to perform all manner of reportorial functions – defining, illustrating, comparing, contrasting, typ- ifying, contextualising, emphasising, summarising, etc. – and they have enormous rhetorical potential. Any given language choice may serve to link or divide, make continuous or discontinuous, minimise or maximise, blur or sharpen, reveal or conceal, elevate or degrade. How a phenomenon is characterised may impact upon the core of an ideology: that is, on judgements as to what equals what, what leads to what, what opposes what, what is good and what is bad.[18]

In the process of 'picturing' the external world, reporters wittingly or unwittingly 'frame' their pictures by the manner in which they communicate about them.[19] Thus, there is not just rhetoric but rhetoric about rhetoric. Frequently at issue in discourses *about* scholarly discourses is the rhetorical status of a work. Moreover, researchers also 'go meta' to each other's discourse, commenting, for example, upon its form or style, or on its implicit motives, its latent meanings, its unexamined premises, or its performative functions.[20] This opens up additional avenues for persuasion. Not surprisingly, scholars often distance themselves from such negatively-valenced message classifications as 'rhetoric', 'propaganda', 'persuasion'. They prefer to cast their opponents' discourse in that persuasive light, while characterising their own opinions as facts, their arguments as demonstrations, their speculations as formal theories, and their ideological commitments as science.[21] Framing is also accomplished by nuances of style and self-presentation that present an image of the scholar as engaged, for example, in the 'doing' of science.[22]

I suggested earlier that even if researchers were personally inclined to 'tell it like it is', they would be under considerable institutional pressure not to. My general point here is that researchers are not free agents. Like all of us, they are subject to the influences of culture and history, but, more to the point of this essay, they are impelled and constrained by the conventions of their disciplines, by the norms and counternorms of their professions, and by political and economic pressures coming from the larger society. As Bazerman[23] says, the distinctive voice of the individual researcher is always in danger of being stifled by the institutional voice of his or her discipline or profession. In psychology, argues Bazerman, the conventions of reporting prescribed in the *American Psychological Association Manual* were increasingly geared to experimentalism, and until recently to behaviourism. As the style manual grew from seven pages in 1929 to 32 pages in 1944 to 61 pages in 1952 to 200 plus pages in 1974, it further restricted the psychologist's inventional resources, including the possibility of arranging the scholarly narrative to best suit the subject matter of the report. Not only in psychology, but in most research fields, the standard narrative structure encourages fragmented thinking, as Markus[24] has pointed out:

> The existence of the Abstract posits that it is possible to summarise its essential 'content', i.e., that the latter is independent from the exposition's literary form and argumentative context. The distinction between Introduction and Discussion, on the one hand, and Methods and Results on the other, implies the possibility to divorce 'interpretation' from 'description', while the division between Methods and Results indicates a similar possibility of separating the ways of investigation from its 'findings'.

In many respects, the social structure of science is exemplary, as Campbell[25] has argued. Surely Merton's[26] list of formal scientific norms of Universalism, Communality, Disinterestedness, and Originality, is quite appealing. But, as Prelli and Mulkay[27] have illustrated, for each of these formal norms there are operative counternorms which, in some contexts at least, can be equally functional for the promotion of the science. Thus, as Prelli and Mulkay have argued, the invocation of a norm or its opposite becomes, for the practising scientist, something of the order of a *rhetorical strategy*. Prelli notes that Merton himself came increasingly to acknowledge the influence of informal norms, at variance with the formal ones, such as those which sociologists of scientific knowledge have identified in their ethnographic studies of laboratory life.[28]

More disturbing, perhaps, are norms and practices that have intruded themselves into the sciences as a consequence of economic and political pressures, such as the need for tenure, promotion, and research grants. Scientists rarely commit outright lies in print, but they are not averse to milder forms of deception, including puffery and selective omission.[29]

But not all of the sins of research communities can be blamed on the political economy. The intense rivalries among scientists, the limited attention spans of most readers, the very human impulses to have one's work recognised and appreciated are all conducive to the widespread phenomenon of over-reporting of statistically significant findings, and under-reporting of non-significant ones. This, as Denton[30] has argued, is a collusive practice in which everyone's interests – the writer's, the journal referee's, and the reader's – are at least partially served.

The foregoing are among the kinds of considerations that have informed my own analyses of scholarly discourse. At this point I should like to illustrate how they might be applied to a given case.

'Drug Pushing' in a medical research article

In January 1984, the *Journal of the American Medical Association* (*JAMA*) was devoted exclusively to the problem of cholesterol. The report to be analysed here was of an exceptionally well-designed study: hence it cannot easily be dismissed as 'bad' science or 'pseudoscience'. Called 'The Lipid Research Clinics Coronary Primary Prevention Trial Results',[31] the study compared the effects on mortality and morbidity of a cholesterol-lowering drug known as cholestyramine with those of an inert placebo. Some 3 806 middle-aged males, selected over a three year period from a subject pool of 480 000 people, participated in this double-blind experiment. To be selected, the subjects had to be extremely high in blood cholesterol but not otherwise at special risk of heart disease from such factors as high blood pressure or diabetes. They also had to be willing to take the highly noxious placebo or the even more noxious experimental drug on a daily basis, and to be monitored frequently on a variety of health-related measures. Special care was taken in this study, in part because its findings were to figure in important policy decisions about a possible cholesterol-lowering campaign. In fact, its findings have been cited frequently as major justification for the National Cholesterol Education Program (NCEP), a mammoth campaign launched in 1986 that has had as one of its aims the *lifelong* treatment by diet and/or drugs for people with blood cholesterol levels of 240 deciliters or more.[32] Sponsored by the National Heart, Lung, and Blood Institute, the Lipid Study was conducted over a seven-and-a-half-year period at twelve cholesterol research centres in the United States. At a cost of over $142 million, it was, according to Moore,[33] the most expensive experiment of its kind ever conducted.

To be examined in this analysis are excerpts from the Lipid Study, as well as examples of recent commentaries on it.[34] The claims for rhetorical analysis to be defended here are fairly modest: first, that in 'de-centering' or 'de-familiarising' scholarly texts, such analysis can help us better to discern the devices by which our adherence is likely to be secured; second, that rhetorical analysis can help disputants advance consideration of the issues they confront, and perhaps even to resolve some of them.

Establishing the Genre

The first three sentences of the Lipid Study, excerpted from its Abstract, typify the familiar literary genre of the scientific research report.

> The Lipid Research Clinics Coronary Primary Prevention Trial (LRCCPPT), a multicenter, randomized, double-blind study, tested the efficacy of cholesterol lowering in reducing risk of coronary heart disease (CHD) in 3, 806 asymptomatic middle-aged men with primary hypercholesterolemia (type II hyperlipoproteinemia). The treatment group received the bile acid sequestrant cholestyramine resin and the control group received a placebo for an average of 7.4 years. Both groups followed a moderate cholesterol-lowering diet.[35]

Compare, too, the Lipid Report's long and technically precise title with the journal-istically-fetching title of an article in an opinion magazine – 'THE Cholesterol MYTH' – in which most letters in the word 'Cholesterol' are represented like fatty foods.[36] The title and author of the Lipid Report as well as the authority of the AMA journal itself, are conducive to the comforting feeling that reliable information is to be passed on, not mere opinion or speculation. These expectations are reinforced by headings that organise the report into conventional sections: Participants and Methods, Results, Comment, References. That the investigators are reporting on the doing of no-nonsense science is made manifest throughout by the report's 'style of non-style':[37] its use of the impersonal, third person, passive voice, and dry, technical vocabulary. The individual authors of the report are not named; instead we learn that it was prepared by the 'Lipid Research Clinics Program'. Presumably, then, this is a group-produced document, but, as is typically the case with such documents, all hints of any behind-the-scenes arguing or negotiating among authors about how to write the report are absent from the final, public document.

Establishing presumption

> This enormous toll has focused attention on the possible prevention of CHD....[38]

Although the dominant tone of the Lipid Report is that of detached, impersonal, objective science – of science untouched by human hands – the report nevertheless implicitly endorses a set of values in laying claim to the existence of a problem which motivates the study. The problem – never labelled as such – is that coronary heart disease (CHD), and, presumably, low-density lipoprotein cholesterol (LDLC), exert an 'enormous toll' on society in the form of deaths, disabilities, and attendant costs. Alongside the conventional structure of the research report, we have also a second, implicit structure: that of problem–cause–solution. Perhaps so as to mitigate the sense of personal involvement in the doing of detached scholarship, the problem is evidenced primarily in dollars and cents terms, culminating in the familiar generalisation: 'CHD costs the United States more than $60 billion a year'. This appeal to the 'bottom line' is presumed to be intrinsically compelling to the reader (who remains unnamed and unaddressed throughout) as reason enough to search in earnest for workable solutions. Thus, the article's essential narrative structure is set up, creating longings for a happy ending that will be psychologically as well as aesthetically satisfying. Although never stated as such, the 'enormous toll' on society of CHD also sets up a number of enthymematic (i.e., truncated, implicit) arguments as regards the article's burdens of proof and refutation. Presumably, the greater the problem, the more willing the reader should be to endorse costly solutions, or solutions that offer minimal benefit, or recommendations of unproven or inconclusive value. Considerations of burden of proof will figure importantly in discussions of statistical confidence levels, as we shall see. For now it is enough to recognise that a good deal of persuading has been going on in the guise of providing the reader with the introduction to a research report.

Contextualising findings

> The cholestyramine group experienced a 19% reduction in risk of the primary end point – definite CHD death and/or definite nonfatal myocardial infarction – reflecting a 24% reduction in definite CHD death and a 19% reduction in nonfatal myocardial infarction. The cumulative seven-year incidence of the primary end-point was 7% in the cholestyramine group vs 8.8% in the placebo group.[39]

Scholars persuade in part by the way they contextualise their results. The results of the Lipid experiment, quoted above, surely seem impressive. So, too, do the findings from another major study of drug therapy for hypocholesterolemia, the Helsinki Heart Study.[40] But, as Brett and Moore[41] have pointed out, these findings could be expressed in other – albeit, far less impressive – ways.

First, consider the differences, for example, between focusing only on problem cases in one's between-group comparisons vs. comparing proportions of problem cases in each group to the groups as a whole (including those who experienced neither morbidity nor mortality in the course of the Lipid experiment). In the Lipid Study, a mere 1.7% difference in proportions of placebo (187/1900) vs. treatment group (155/1906) subjects experiencing definite CHD death and/or definite nonfatal myocardial infarction is described as a 19% reduction in end-point differences (187 vs. 155). Here is a clear example of how the 'resources of ambiguity' in language may be used to minimise or maximise. The latter differences, while barely significant at the 0.05 level (one-tailed test), were surely of no real significance to the 90% or more of subjects in either group who had no measurable end-points.[42]

Second, from the perspective of proportionate risk, the findings translate into just a 1.6% improvement in the chances of experiencing a definite or suspect nonfatal heart attack for the Lipid treatment group – from 11.8 to 10.2%.

Third, by a bit of casuistic stretching (rationalised in a footnote) a difference of 38 definite CHD deaths in the placebo group vs. 30 in the treatment group is reported as a 24% reduction in risk, rather than a 21% reduction. This difference, while not reputed to be statistically significant by the authors, is even less significant when viewed in proportionate terms (2.0% vs. 1.6%).

Fourth, looked at from a cost-benefit perspective argues Moore, '[a] total of $23 million in drugs may have prevented thirty-six heart attacks. This works out to $647 205 per heart attack possibly forestalled'.[43] Brett[44] cites an estimate of $36 000 to over $1 million per life saved, depending on the patient's age, risk profile, and duration of therapy.

Fifth, taken together, says Brett,[45] the Lipid and Helsinki studies give a 30-year-old man reason to believe that if he continues to take the drug as recommended for the rest of his life, he may be expected to live an extra month in his 75th year.

Generalise first, qualify later

The risk of death from all causes was only slightly and not significantly reduced in the cholestyramine group. The magnitude of the decrease (7%) was less than for CHD end-points because of a greater number of violent and accidental deaths in the cholestyramine group.[46]

In the above extract from the Abstract of the Lipid Study, a post hoc causal inference is treated as fact (which, of course, is what most readers rely on exclusively) and only later is revealed to be the inference that it is. Whether the greater number of violent and accidental deaths in the treatment group (11) than the placebo group (4) was a 'chance' occurrence, as alleged by the authors, or was systematically related to membership in the treatment group in an as yet undetermined way is not at issue for me here. It is curious to note, however, that a similar trend occurred in the Helsinki study (four accidental or violent deaths in the placebo group; 10 in the treatment group). Admittedly, the investigators went to elaborate lengths (including autopsies and clinical studies) to rule out the more obvious causal connections, but the point is that any after-the-fact explanation of a disconfirming finding needs to be treated with some scepticism. It was not by the researchers, at least not in their Abstract. One wonders whether they would have conducted as strenuous a study to explain away hypothesis-confirming findings!

Playing down the negative

Diagnoses and procedures involving the gallbladder were scrutinised in view of the ability of certain lipid-lowering drugs to produce gallstones and gallbladder disease. A few more hospitalised participants in the cholestyramine group had, as their main diagnosis, gallstones (16 vs. 11) and more cholestyramine-treated participants had an operation involving the gallbladder (36 vs. 25), but the differences were not significant.[47]

The use of cholestyramine resin resulted in several GI side effects, although these were also common in the placebo group.... Of special interest is the absence of a significant increase in gallstones....[48]

Understandably, investigators cast the results of years of painstaking research in the most optimistic light, and this is certainly their prerogative.[49]

Brett is right in his above remark that investigators tend to cast their results optimistically. Whether it ought to be their prerogative to do so is a question for journal editors and ultimately for their scholarly communities. But puffery is commonplace across the academy, as I have argued. The task of the painstaking investigator is to be equally painstaking as a reporter of research in managing rhetorically the tension between the norms of advocacy and of scientific neutrality. Here let us note several ways that the authors play down potential gallbladder effects of cholestyramine:

First, the 'side effects' problem is nowhere mentioned in the Abstract.

Second, the first citation above speaks of '*the ability* of certain lipid-lowering drugs...'. Suppose it had said, instead, '*the danger that...*'?

Third, the first citation also counts *5 more* as '*a few more*'.

Fourth, by contrast with their reporting of results favourable to their investigation, the investigators choose not to report unfavourable differences in gallbladder side effects in percentage terms (e.g., 18% more gallstone diagnoses among hospitalised treatment group patients; 14% more gallbladder operations).

Fifth, more stringent (two-tailed) tests of the statistical significance of differences were used in comparing side-effects for the treatment and placebo groups than were used in comparing groups on primary end-points (one-tailed). The rationale for using one-tailed tests was the conventional one: that these effects had been hypothesised. But there was also prior evidence about the side-effects of lipid-lowering drugs.[50] Hence, the gallbladder effects found in this study could also have been hypothesised, and had a one-tailed test been used, the differences would have been statistically significant. The point is that the investigators were not consistent in their applications of statistical norms.

Sixth, the above citation from the 'Comment' section minimises further whatever sense one might have had of a gallbladder side-effects problem from reading the citation from the 'Results' section. Assuming a moderately ambitious reader, one who reads beyond the Abstract but skips past Methods and Results to get to the Comment, the lesson probably learned is that of the significant *absence* of a problem.

How far to generalise?

The consistency of the reductions...in this controlled trial leave little doubt of the benefit of cholestyramine therapy.... The trial's implications...could and should be extended to other age groups and women and, since cholesterol levels and CHD risk are continuous variables, to others with more modest elevations of cholesterol levels.[51]

However, a strongly interventionist perspective colours the published findings of the large trials of lipid-lowering drugs that have involved asymptomatic persons. Physicians must recognize this perspective before extrapolating from the clinical studies to office practice.[52]

In the remarks above, the Lipid investigators urge the reader to extend 'the benefit of cholestyramine therapy', whereas Brett urges physicians to exercise caution before extrapolating the trials' findings to their patients. Who is right?

One possibility is that both are right; after all, Brett is simply asking us to see things from another perspective. Usually rhetoricians resonate to that kind of talk, but in this case I suspect that Brett's talk of 'perspectives' is, in part at least, a diplomatic way of not criticising the report head-on while still being able to make his points.

As a nonspecialist, I am hardly in a position to pass final judgment on the worth of cholestyramine therapy. However, as was suggested earlier, rhetorical theory may be able to advance consideration of the question. Here it may be helpful to recognise that the argument put forth by the Lipid investigators for extending the range of the findings is based on a *commonplace*; it asserts the familiar theme of the similarity or continuity of things. But the study of rhetoric teaches us that for nearly every commonplace there is an *opposite* commonplace; one could speak with at least equal cogency of the dissimilarity of things, emphasising kind, rather than degree. Hence, before acceding to the logic of a generalisation, as Billig[53] suggests, we should try reversing the rule to see whether the reversal makes equal or even better sense in the particular context. Here it should be noted that other disciplines have been highly suspicious of generalisations to females from all male samples. For example, in the McHugh, Koeske, and Frieze[54] 'Guide for Researchers' such extrapolation is regarded as a form of sexism.

Conclusion

Having examined examples from the Lipid study we should now be in a better position to return to the general perspective on the rhetoric of the scientific report developed at the outset of this essay. Recall three of the central claims: (i) that scientific reporters *cannot* 'tell it like it is'; (ii) that they would be under institutional pressure *not to*, even if they could; (iii) that, instead, they strategically manage the *appearance* of 'telling it like it is' while functioning as persuaders. Brett says the following about the Lipid study: 'The tendency here is obvious. The language that frames results of uncertain significance is determined by whether those results support or detract from the investigators' hypotheses'.[55]

So it is. And the AMA's editors, apparently, did not insist that the study's findings be reframed so as to tell a more complete or evenhanded story. For example, they could have insisted, but did not, that the findings also be presented from the perspectives of these 90% or more subjects who had no deleterious endpoints. They could have required that proportionate differences be reported alongside relative end-point differences. And they could have mandated a consistent criterion for statistical significance where the direction of outcomes was predictable.

One wonders why they did not do so, and why, especially, they did not countermand the study's recommendation that the findings for a highly vulnerable group of middle-aged males should have been generalised so as to apply to all males and females. Perhaps the pressure to 'make good' on a study of this importance, involving so great an expenditure, and such a commitment of time and expertise, is what best explains this counternormative recommendation.[56]

I cannot say more on this. Rather than speculating further on the relationship between the rhetoric and the politics of science, I should like to turn to another key element of my rhetorical perspective: the notion that rhetorical argumentation does not necessarily make for 'bad' argumentation and should not be dismissed as such. In this, as in any study that does more than present raw data (if there be such), a number of judgements must be made – decisions that cannot possibly be reduced to a simple yes or no.[57] This extends, as Brett maintains, to the very question of when and how the researcher should function as a persuader:

> To some extent, this stance is appropriate; the findings of clinical trials are strengthened when they are supported by existing theories and other experimental evidence, regardless of statistical significance. Nevertheless, an experimental outcome that almost reaches significance should not necessarily lead to a widespread implementation in clinical practice because it makes biologic sense. Conversely, the lack of a rational biologic explanation for such an outcome is not a reason to dismiss it summarily. Furthermore, although one may legitimately speculate that further years of treatment could convert favourable trends into statistically significant ones, is it not conceivable that the same reasoning may hold for unfavourable trends such as gastrointestinal diseases and violent death?[58]

Brett provides here a number of examples of Billig's principle of reversal. These arguments are the stuff of good rhetoric; of reasoned judgements on issues for which there can be no formal proof. By definition, such issues resist full and final resolution; their adjudication must always be context-specific. Deciding what 'the particular context' is may also engender controversy; and there is likely to be no foolproof way of determining whether the rule of its reversal makes more sense, even assuming agreement on the context. Thus, the 'interventionists' whom Brett criticises could (and do) reasonably argue that the urgency of treatment for the cholesterol problem and the relative ineffectiveness of diet therapies at reducing the problem makes widespread drug therapy implementation imperative *in this case*, even if conventional 0.05 levels of significance aren't consistently reached.

On questions such as these, there is a need for talk about talk. Those engaged in the dispute over the cholestyramine research must be prepared to 'go meta' to their original arguments in the face of counterarguments.[59] However these disputes are fought out, it is a fair certainty that 'hard fact' and 'cold logic' will only carry the discussants so far. But saying this does not mean that their arguments will be false to fact or illogical. Of his own field of economics, McCloskey has argued that its so-called objectivity 'is exaggerated, and, what is more, overrated'. He adds:

> A rhetorical approach to economics is machine-building, not machine-breaking. It is not an invitation to irrationality in argument. Quite the contrary, it is an invitation to leave the irrationality of an artificially narrowed range of argument and to move to the rationality of arguing like human beings. It brings out into the open the arguing that

economists do anyway – in the dark, for they must do it somewhere, and the various official rhetorics leave them benighted.[60]

In that same spirit, I would agree with Clifford Geertz[61] that there is no need for all scientists to write in the same 'style of non-style'. That the style of a scholarly article may be influential in a given case need not invalidate its logic and may even enhance it. Quite the contrary, argues Geertz,[62] 'The strange idea that reality has an idiom in which it prefers to be described, that its very nature demands we talk about it without fuss', stems from a confusion, traceable to Plato, 'of the fictional with the false, making things out with making things up'.

What now of the place of the rhetorical analysis in the grand scheme of science? I suggested earlier that rhetoricians are themselves divided on this question, some of them concerned exclusively with the extra-factual and extra-logical, others concerned with what they regard as the 'rhetoric' of fact and logic. I would endorse the position eloquently expressed by Gusfield:

> It is not that Science is 'reduced' to rhetoric and thus rendered corrupt and useless. It is rather that the rhetorical component seems to be unavoidable if the work is to have a theoretical or policy relevance. Thus an analysis of scientific work should also include its rhetorical as well as its empirical component.[63]

In affirming Gusfield's view, however, I do not mean to suggest that statistical inference is outside the purview of rhetoric. On the contrary, this is another arena of judgement-making, the rhetorical character of which tends to be covered over in textbooks on the subject.[64] This extends to the suppression of controversy among experts about the very idea of reporting findings in terms of statistical confidence levels.[65] We have seen in this study how consequential the choice of a statistical comparison can be.

Gusfield[66] has himself acknowledged that one effect of his analysis of 'drunk driver' research reports has been to demonstrate that what gets called knowledge is rhetorically constructed.

Having argued for a rather broad view of the rhetoric of science, I recognise that I have opened myself up to attack from another direction: If rhetorical analysis extends to critiques of statistical judgements, then how separate are rhetorical analyses from the standard analyses offered by scientists themselves? Have I not relied to a great extent on Brett's expert critique of the Lipid study, a critique, it should be added, that was quite sensitive to the Lipid report's persuasive exploitation of the 'resources of ambiguity' in language?

Indeed I have. And I would grant that the Brett critique is not a solitary example of astute rhetorical analysis by a non-rhetorician. Those trained in rhetoric do not have an exclusive purchase on their craft; nor does training in rhetoric guarantee sensitive readings of scientific texts. All other things being equal, however, consciously rhetorical reading by persons sensitive to nuances of language and informal argument should assist in the analysis of scientific reports. Expertise in the subject matter should assist as well. And this has been one of the real virtues of the 'rhetorical turn', for it has exhibited, over a wide variety of disciplines, the advantages of combining rhetorical sensitivity with scholarly acumen.

Notes

1. See A. Weigart, 'The immortal rhetoric of scientific sociology' *American Psychologist* 5 (1970) pp. 111-19.
2. For example, see G.N. Gilbert and M. Mulkay, *Opening Pandora's Box: A Sociological Analysis of Scientists' Discourse* (Cambridge: Cambridge University Press, 1984).
3. See M. Shapiro, *The Politics of Representation* (Madison: University of Wisconsin Press, 1988) p. 14.
4. See R.A. Hackett, 'Decline of a paradigm: Bias and objectivity in news media studies' *Critical Studies in Mass Communication* 1 (1984) pp. 229-59.
5. See R.A. Hackett (1984); as in note 4.
6. See R. Rorty, *Philosophy and the Mirror of Nature* (Princeton: Princeton University Press, 1979); and R. Bernstein, *Beyond Objectivism and Relativism* (Philadelphia: Univerisity of Pennsylvania Press, 1983).
7. See R.A. Hackett (1984); as in note 4.
8. See A.G. Gross, 'The origin of species: Evolutionary taxonomy as an example of the rhetoric of science', in H.W. Simons (ed.), *The Rhetorical Turn* (Chicago: University of Chicago Press, 1990), and *The Rhetoric of Science* (Cambridge, MA: Harvard University Press, 1990); and L. Prelli, *A Rhetoric of Science: Inventing Scientific Discourse* (Columbia: University of South Carolina Press, 1989).
9. Lyne, J., 'Bio-rhetorics: moralising the life sciences', in H.W. Simons (ed.), *The Rhetorical Turn* (Chicago: University of Chicago Press, 1990).
10. Gross, A.G. ('The origin...'); as in note 8.
11. Kuhn, T., *The Structure of Scientific Revolutions* (Chicago: University of Chicago Press, 2nd edn, 1970).
12. See T. Kuhn (1970); as in note 11.
13. Frye, N., *Anatomy of Criticism* (Princeton: Princeton University Press, 1957).
14. See G. Lakoff and M. Johnson, *Metaphors We Live By* (Chicago: University of Chicago Press, 1980); and M. Johnson, *The Body in the Mind: The Bodily Basis of Reason and Imagination* (Chicago: University of Chicago Press, 1989).
15. See M. Mulkay, *The Word and the World* (London: Allen and Unwin, 1985).
16. For example, see H.W. Simons, *Rhetoric in the Human Sciences* (London: Sage, 1989), and *Persuasion: Understanding, Practice, and Analysis* (New York: Random House, 1986).
17. Burke, K., *A Grammar of Motives* (Berkeley: University of California Press, 1969).
18. See K. Burke (1969); as in note 17; H.W. Simons (1986); as in note 16.
19. See H.W. Simons (1986); as in note 16.
20. See H.W. Simons, ' "Going meta" in political confrontations', in B. Gronbeck (ed.), *Spheres of Argument* (Annandale: SCA, 1989).

21. See K. Burke (1989); as in note 17; M. Mulkay (1985); as in note 15; and M. Shapiro (1988); as in note 3.

22. See J. Gusfield, 'The literary rhetoric of science: comedy and pathos of drinking driver research' *American Sociological Review* (1976) pp. 16-33.

23. Bazerman, C., 'Codifying the social-scientific style: the APA Publication Manual as a behaviorist rhetoric', in J. Nelson, A. Megill, and D.N. McCloskey (eds), *The Rhetoric of the Human Sciences* (Madison, Wisconsin: University of Wisconsin Press, 1987).

24. Markus, G., 'Why is there no hermeneutics of natural sciences? Some preliminary theses' *Science in Context* 1 (1987) p. 12.

25. Campbell, D.C., 'Science's social system of validity-enhancing collective belief change and the problems of the social sciences', in D.W. Fiske and R.A Schweder (eds), *Metatheory in Social Science* (Chicago: University of Chicago Press, 1986).

26. Merton, R., 'Science and the social order' *Philosophy of Science* 5 (1938) pp. 321-7.

27. Prelli, L., (1989); as in note 8; and Mulkay, M. (1985); as in note 15.

28. For example, see B. Latour and S. Woolgar, 'Laboratory Life: the social construction of scientific facts' *Sage Library of Social Research* (Beverly Hills: Sage, 1979) vol. 80.

29. See G.N. Gilbert and M. Mulkay (1984); as in note 2.

30. Denton, F., 'The significance of significance: rhetorical aspects of statistical hypothesis testing in economics', in A.D. Klamer, D.N. McCloskey, and R. Solow (eds), *The Consequences of Rhetoric of Economics: A Conference* (Cambridge: Cambridge University Press, 1989).

31. Lipid Research Clinics Program, 'The Lipid Research Clinics Coronary Trial Results' *Journal of the American Medical Association* 251 (1984) pp. 351-64.

32. See T.J. Moore, 'The cholesterol myth' *Atlantic Monthly* (September, 1989) pp. 37-70.

33. Moore, T.J. (1989); as in note 32.

34. See A.S. Brett, 'Treating hypercholesterolemia: How should practicing physicians interpret the published data for patients?' *New England Journal of Medicine* 321 (1989) pp. 676-9; and T.J. Moore (1989); as in note 32.

35. Lipid Research Clinics Program (1984) 350; as in note 31.

36. See T.J. Moore (1989); as in note 32.

37. See J. Gusfield (1976); as in note 22.

38. Lipid Research Clinics Program (1984) 351; as in note 31.

39. As notes 31 and 38.

40. See M.H. Frick, 'Helsinki heart study: primary-prevention trial with gemfibrozil in middle-aged men with dyslipidemia' *New England Journal of Medicine* 317 (1987) p. 1237-45.

41. Brett, A.S. (1989); as in note 34; and Moore, T.J. (1989); as in note 32.

42. See A.S Brett (1989); as in note 34.

43. See T.J. Moore (1989); as in note 32.

44. Brett, A.S. (1989); as in note 34.

45. As notes 34 and 44.

46. Lipid Research Clinics Program (1984) p. 351; as in note 31.

47. Lipid Research Clinics Program (1984) p. 357; 'Results' section, as in note 31.

48. Lipid Research Clinics Program (1984) p. 358; 'Comment' section, as in note 31.

49. See A.S. Brett (1989) p. 677; as in note 34.

50. See T.J. Moore (1989); as in note 32.

51. Lipid Research Clinics Program (1984) p. 360; as in note 31.

52. See A.S. Brett (1989) p. 677; as in note 34.

53. Billig, M., *Arguing and Thinking: A Rhetorical Approach to Social Psychology* (Cambridge: Cambridge University Press, 1987).

54. McHugh, M.C., Koeske, R.D., and Frieze, I.H., 'Issues to consider in conducting nonsexist psychological research' *American Psychologist* 41 (1986) pp. 879-90.

55. See A.S Brett (1989) p. 678; as in note 34.

56. See T.J. Moore (1989); as in note 32.

57. See K. Burke (1969); as in note 17.

58. Brett, A.S. (1989) p. 678; as in note 34.

59. See H.W. Simons (' "Going meta"...'); as in note 20.

60. McCloskey, D.N., *The Rhetoric of Economics* (Madison: University of Wisconsin Press, 1985) p. 36.

61. Geertz, C., *Works and Lives: The Anthropologist as Author* (Palo Alto: Stanford University Press, 1988).

62. Geertz, C. (1988) p. 140; as in note 61.

63. Gusfield, J. (1976) p. 31; as in note 22.

64. See F. Denton (1989); as in note 30; D.N. McCloskey (1985); as in note 60; and P. Mirowski, 'The rhetoric of modern economic' *History of the Human Sciences* 3 (1990) pp. 243-58.

65. See V. Signorile, 'Review of the Empire of Chance' *History of the Human Sciences* 3 (1990) pp. 279-86.

66. Gusfield, J. (1976); as in note 22.

9

Approaches, Opportunities and Priorities in the Rhetoric of Political Inquiry: A Critical Synthesis

John S. Nelson (University of Iowa)

Rhetoric of political inquiry promises to improve studies of politics, especially within the discipline of political science. Most political scientists can benefit immensely from better attention to their own rhetoric and its roles in their inquiry. In ways and degrees far greater than logic of inquiry or philosophy of science alone, rhetoric of inquiry arises from and enters into the detailed conduct of research on an everyday basis. It seeks to provide any investigator with greater awareness of actual practices and diverse principles of science, and it emphasises the dependence of inquiry on considerations of community and communication. To reap its advantages, therefore, political scientists must become their own rhetoricians of inquiry – as well as attending to specialists in the subject. To explain and evidence these claims, let me explore some of what it may mean to practise rhetoric of inquiry within political science.

Throughout, my aim is to clarify approaches, opportunities, and priorities for this enterprise. I begin by tracing briefly the origins of the new field. Then I sketch several of its general concerns and purposes. The field has particular ties and importance to political inquiry, however, so I also examine its specifically political connections and dimensions. At the heart of the exploration, I summarise seven projects of real urgency for advancing inquiry into politics. My argument is that this initial agenda for rhetoric of inquiry within political science can make major and, at least in some cases, almost immediate improvements in the discipline. Moreover these projects permit and might eventually require contributions from every part of the discipline. They show how rhetoric of inquiry should be pursued, not only as an occasional focus for specialised research on the rhetoric of political scientists, but also as a continual aspect of the disciplined study of politics. Accordingly I point in conclusion toward additional approaches and opportunities for doing rhetoric of political inquiry.

Origins

> Many ideas grow better when transplanted into another mind than in the one where
> they sprang up.
>
> [Oliver Wendell Holmes, Jr]

For more than a decade, I have been helping to invent something of the order of a new field.[1] It is located within my home discipline of political science, but scarcely more there, than within any other organised domain of inquiry. Indeed it needs homes in all disciplines in order to flourish. Thus the new field is, and must remain at once within, but also across every discipline. It is an 'interdisciplinary' field in the deepest and best sense of the word.

I am educated in another oddly interdisciplinary field. Political theory self-consciously straddles the social sciences and humanities.[2] It encourages the graduate student to combine usual curricula in political science with those standard for philosophy, history, law, literature, economics, anthropology, sociology, and psychology. That circumstance plus unusual good fortune in teachers led me to recognise three peculiarities in these disciplines and their mutual relationships: none gives good accounts of its own inquiry, each does poorer inquiry because of that, and each thinks that its rules or procedures of inquiry come fundamentally from philosophy (and in some cases, secondarily from mathematics or statistics).

Seeing what I saw, others in political theory, political science, and the related disciplines argued with the rules then reigning in philosophical epistemology and treatments of science. So did I. Some of the others also sought to restructure actual research in political science or their individual disciplines. So did I. To a lesser and later degree, the same has occurred in disciplines and professions ordinarily even farther afield from political science. And by various routes, a growing group is arriving at the perspectives, principles, and practices which we want to weave into a new and interdisciplinary field of inquiry. The time seems opportune: for there are further arrivals virtually every day, and some of the finest talent around appears interested in this alternative to authoritarian epistemology and a priori philosophy of science.[3]

Along the way, I have called this endeavour by a host of names. I began by regarding it as a 'twilight zone' between detailed research design and abstract philosophy of inquiry.[4] Eventually this led me to look for an epistemology of everyday research in political science. But almost immediately, I ran into the rich variety of research practices already evident to me in that discipline alone. On one side, I started to explore the tropes which accounted for epistemological disparities among research practices apparently directed toward the same or closely related subjects.[5] On another, I plumbed anthropology and sociology for a better sense of how different situations and subjects of research produce inquiry.[6]

While thinking in terms of simultaneously epistemological and political theories of practice,[7] I continued to encounter still other domains and directions of research

165

not yet part of political science. That nudged me toward studying the many epistemologies immanent in these largely disconnected projects.[8] But it also made me aware of their need for mutual education. Sensitivity to other perspectives and incorporation of alien principles could make these diverse practices of research more accurate, beneficial, and self-critical. Hence I have come to endow my projects of comparative epistemology with an ethos of epistemology as comparison and self-criticism.[9] All of these projects and more are converging on what I now call *rhetoric of inquiry.*[10]

Purposes

> Few people even scratch the surface, much less exhaust the contemplation of their own experience.
>
> [Randolph Bourne]

Each field relies on distinctive methods of inquiry and modes of communication, but every field does its work through argument. Fields use various devices of speculation, assumption, definition, evidence, inference, testing, reporting, and criticism; yet all conduct inquiry through human persuasion. In a word, every field is rhetorical. Study of rhetorical dimensions in research can improve inquiry within disciplines, communication across them, and education beyond them. These are the purposes of emerging studies in the rhetoric of inquiry.[11]

Because inquiry depends on communication, rhetoric of inquiry studies how scholars communicate. In particular, it examines the reasoning of scholars in research communities. It rejects the notion that ironclad rules for inquiry can stand apart from actual practices. It seeks not to distil some single model of Reason, Logic, or Method, but to make the many styles of scholarship better aware of themselves and of one another. Working within projects of research, it makes their assumptions more intelligent and their operations more persuasive. Working across fields of inquiry, it increases the quality and quantity of collaboration. Inside and outside the academy, it explores how reason is rhetorical and how better recognition of rhetoric would alter inquiry.

Rhetoric of inquiry is interdisciplinary, stemming from the renewed emphasis on persuasion and expression evident throughout the humanities, sciences, arts, and professions.[12] As the name implies, its special virtue is an appreciation of the importance in research of rhetoric. Thus it concerns the quality of speaking and writing in our world, and it attends to interactions of media and messages. It seeks to enter the daily conduct of inquiries of every kind, in order that each may understand itself better and learn from related studies.

As an academic movement, rhetoric of inquiry arises in reaction against foundationalism – especially in epistemology and philosophy of science but also in aesthetics, metaethics, policy science, theology, or any other field conceiving itself to stand above and apart from practices of inquiry while thinking that it should nonetheless legislate for them in some absolute or at least authoritarian way. As an interdisciplinary field, rhetoric of inquiry arises in response to revivals of persuasive and expressive sensibility now discernible throughout the arts, humanities, professions, and sciences. It reflects a renewed concern for the quality of speaking and writing in academic disciplines, and it develops a postmodern interest in the interaction of media and messages. But mostly it tries to improve the actual conduct of inquiries – inside and outside the academy – by learning from the diversity of those practices of study which help to make our world what it is today.

The aim is not to replace logic of inquiry but to facilitate self-reflection in all studies. Rhetoric of inquiry achieves little if pursued a priori and apart from actual inquiries. Informally and intermittently, it is already part of many kinds of research. More systematic attention to it can improve projects individually and link them more effectively. In fact, rhetoric of inquiry thrives on comparison of projects, which contributes to its rationale as a continuing field of scholarship.

Rhetoric of inquiry also encourages and enables scholars to become more reflexive. It teaches them to examine with care the possible implications of their substantive arguments and conclusions for their methods of study and modes of inference. Thus it involves the practice and application of the sociology of sociology, the economics of economics, the history of historiography, the psychology of psychology, the anthropology of anthropology, the politics of political science, and the like.[13] Not only does rhetoric of inquiry emphasise such projects of reflection, but its approaches to the interaction of inquiry and communication provide especially effective paths for beginning and completing the projects well.

At the level of institutions, rhetoricians of inquiry explore rhetoric in virtually every aspect of scholarship. For example, they recognise many intellectual divisions among the human sciences as rhetorical divisions. Economists favour metaphors different from those of sociologists or psychologists. Political philosophers emphasise styles and topics of argument different from the ones favoured by political scientists or political historians. Rhetoricians raise questions about how scholars divide the world and how they reason toward claims of knowledge and recommendations of policy. Rhetoricians study disciplinary boundaries and methodologies as persuasions that alter the beliefs of those who operate professionally within them. Such persuasions come and go, as Thomas Kuhn has demonstrated. They serve purpose for their times; and then, with or without public and professional strife, they give way to new persuasions.[14]

In this respect, one aim of rhetoric of inquiry is to remind scientists of the diversity of argumentation in their research. It examines how good work arises apart from (and even in defiance of) pre-established procedures and textbook logics. Moreover it explores how scientists ignore abstract and supposedly universal standards of reason in favour of warrants and backings of particular arguments (to borrow the terminology of Stephen Toulmin).[15] It turns attention away from generalised methodologies and their applications towards particular situations of scholarly communication. Thus it emphasises the importance of *audiences* in research, since warrants and backings must be shared if arguments are to have force. Finally, it focuses on figurative and even mythic dimensions of inquiry, to study the common and often unarticulated characteristics of communities of inquiry.

167

At the level of individuals, rhetoricians of inquiry study the generation, communication, and reception of scholarship as argument. For instance, the quality of scholarly writing reflects the quality of scholarly research, since the processes which produce them are continuous and interactive. Accordingly, rhetoric of inquiry asks how scholars come to speak and write as they do, and how their styles influence the conduct and content of their research. It explores how to respond seriously to the recent worries that the professional discourse of academic disciplines in general, and of the social sciences in particular, have become too arcane for the good of inquiry or of society; they are too impersonal, condensed and unargued to foster strong science; yet too specialised, obscure and authoritarian to nurture wise policy or intelligent practice.[16]

But the main aim of rhetoric of inquiry is to become integrated into the normal business of scientists and scholars by sensitising them to good practices of rhetoric. Consequently, the interdisciplinary field considers in detail how substantive disciplines diverge from externally dictated norms and how researchers call on reasons specific to individual inquiries. Rhetoric of inquiry intends to replace philosophers of science with rhetoricians of science only insofar as the rhetoricians are the scientists themselves, within programs of substantive research. That is why rhetoric of inquiry arises throughout the social sciences and humanities. It is also why it proceeds through reports of researchers on the importance of rhetoric within their own disciplines, rather than outsiders telling practitioners in diverse fields to conform to some overarching norm.

Rhetoric of inquiry can never become an academic discipline in an ordinary sense. Therefore, it should never seek to become a subject unto itself or a subject for others only as master legislator. Instead it should serve other subjects as special parts of each, seeking to penetrate throughout and reach beyond any subject as practised. As immanent epistemology, rhetoric of inquiry cannot be severed from work within actual, substantive researches. As comparative epistemology, it cannot be divorced from work about and across disparate research projects as they continue to develop.

Thus rhetoric of inquiry addresses how, why, and with what effects inquiry is rhetorical. Rhetoricians of inquiry are already addressing many specific issues, and many more remain to emerge from future work. Even so, three sets of key questions indicate the field's domain:

1 What are the rhetorical practices of scientists and scholars? How do they differ from one field and time to another, why, and with what implications?
2 How do academic rhetorics relate to non-academic domains? What are the sources and results of these relationships, and where might they be improved?
3 How might increased awareness of rhetoric change inquiry and communication in the academy? Which changes should we cultivate, and when?

Although rhetoric of inquiry achieves little if pursued a priori and apart from actual inquiries, it thrives in terms of the pursuit of several studies at once. Moreover, it can and should cultivate a distinctive body of perspectives, principles and practices. Consequently it can and should be studied by some people as a distinct – if by no means utterly separate – field. Yet even contributions of that kind should strive to address and improve the substantive inquiries that supply its targets of research.

Thus far I have relied on ordinary understandings of 'rhetoric', 'politics' and 'inquiry'. If I am twisting these categories in any special way, it is mostly away from the highly charged evaluations that sometimes make the first two words express something evil or perverse and the third word something good or neutral. So let us begin with definitions both broad and diversified. For breadth, let us treat rhetoric as stylised communication, inquiry as systematic investigation, and politics as community participation. For diversity, we may approach inquiry as the purposeful exploration of what is, why it is, how it might be otherwise, and how we may know it. We may regard rhetoric as a pointed concern with what is communicated, how the communication is made, with what effect, and what the alternatives might have been. And we may approach politics as the central project of creating, comprehending, conserving and criticising communities.[17] These definitions suggest how closely connected 'rhetoric', 'politics', and 'inquiry' can, and almost must, become especially for rhetoric of political inquiry. By emphasising their interdependence, it encourages us to note, understand, and enhance as many ties as possible between these three terms.

Politics

A new science of Politics is needed for a new world.

[Alexis De Tocqueville]

Like all scholarship, political science is transacted through argument. In turn, argument is rhetorical, not in the cynical sense of empty or manipulative words, but in the artistic and political sense of styles or patterns of speech. Yet political scientists have been no more inclined than other scholars to recognise their own strategies of rhetoric. They sometimes act as though adherence to standard forms of reporting research enable them to avoid rhetoric altogether, and they often assume that their modes of argument do not affect their conduct of inquiry.

Thus the main resource neglected by political science and celebrated by rhetoric of inquiry is the capacity for persuasive argument.[18] As an internal need of the discipline, an ability to argue skilfully is the collective faculty for thinking well about problems of inquiry. As an external need of the discipline, persuasive argument provides the facility for learning from other projects and for teaching them what political scientists have discovered. Change in the world typically includes change in politics. This often mandates change in political inquiry, which in turn requires persistent reflection on the matters, methods, and meanings of political science. As it directs continual attention to the conditions of inquiry, and especially to the quality of argument in research, rhetoric of inquiry is a movement toward self-scrutiny and self-improvement on the part of all disciplines.

Political science stands at the centre of this movement for four reasons. The first form of political science simply was rhetoric, the earliest systematic study of politics on the part of the Sophists. Put the other way around, rhetoric began as political science and their close connection has held ever since. Speech, persuasion, deception, symbols, and other aspects of rhetoric are too important to politics for this tie to lapse or even loosen to any great degree. The same is true of the place of political processes and settings in the study of communication.

A second reason for the prominence of political science is that rhetoric of inquiry persistently comprehends academic disciplines as political systems. Thus it returns an epistemological dimension to questions about the significance of politics in the operations of science and scholarship. These considerations range from governmental policy for education and research to everyday politics of professions and university departments. So prominent are various kinds of politics in the conditions and conduct of systematic study that rhetoric of inquiry insistently reveals an inclination to become politics of inquiry. Hence the issues and methods of political science prove crucial for rhetoric of inquiry.

Appropriately, there are many times when rhetoric of inquiry for political scientists can and should become self-consciously a study of the politics of political inquiry. As I have already hinted through the above definitions, one potentially important effect on the discipline of such reflexivity is to challenge recent conceptions of politics – as well as of rhetoric and of inquiry. For example, an important point of rhetoric of inquiry as immanent and comparative epistemology is that each of these three activities intertwines its own study and practice so thoroughly that neither can be proceeded adequately without the other. 'Rhetoric' comprehends not only what is communicated, but the conditions, processes, effects, improvements, and comparative character of communications. Similarly 'politics' appears in a much broader guise than has become common in political science, opening the discipline more fully to important phenomena and issues long ignored.

Such perspectives encourage us to see social sciences as special projects of the humanities, and *vice versa*.[19] In this respect, rhetoric of inquiry is particularly attracted to fields which use both scientific and humanistic methods of study. Accordingly, a third reason that political science plays a major role in rhetoric of inquiry is the discipline's rich mixture of arguments, data, and techniques drawn from diverse humanities and social sciences. Its continuing questions of action, authority, community, law, legitimacy, and representation span the humanities and social sciences. Moreover many of its major programs of research combine methods of the humanities and social sciences.[20]

Examples abound. Formal modellers seek to reproduce processes of voting and legislation identified independently through humanistically 'thick' descriptions of decision-making by voters and legislators. Organisation theorists mesh data from surveys and social observation with depth interviews, archival research, and symbolical interpretations of work environments. Policy analysts inform normative evaluation with statistical studies of policy needs, effects, and processes. Students of public opinion and political ideology increasingly combine survey research and cognitive science with literary interpretation of texts and rhetorical analysis of communication, reasoning, and symbolism. Archival research on foreign policy interacts with computer simulations of decision processes. Analysis of aggregate data about refugees, trade, and flows of information reshape traditionally humanistic studies of human rights, distributive justice, and free speech. Comparative investigators of voting, regulations, and parties in various countries carry on a dialogue with conceptual analysts of authority, democracy, government, power, and rights. Such interactions of diverse issues, methods, and kinds of data make political science a natural laboratory for rhetoric of inquiry.

In this setting, it is not surprising that political scientists are leaders in the creation of rhetoric of inquiry as a discrete subject of research. This leadership is a fourth reason for the centrality of political inquiry in rhetoric of inquiry and is evidenced by the prominence of political scientists whose work pushes toward rhetoric of inquiry: Charles W. Anderson, G.R. Boynton, William E. Connolly, John G. Gunnell, Russell L. Hanson, Mary E. Hawkesworth, Paul F. Kress, Michael J. Shapiro, and Ira L. Strauber. These are only some of the central and self-conscious contributors so far. The list of less direct or intentional rhetoricians of inquiry among political scientists would be much longer, as would the roster of colleagues increasingly interested in the implications of the new field for research in the discipline. This situation reflects the special importance of politics for rhetoric, and thus of political science for rhetoric of inquiry. But it signals also that rhetoric of inquiry stands ready to become exceptionally significant for everyday research in political science.

In recognising how rhetoric is political, we can recover for every human science a neglected appreciation of politics and, therefore, political inquiry. In recognising how science is rhetorical, we can recover for political science a reflexive capacity to improve our inquiry – and in particular, our argument. To a considerable extent, rhetoric of political inquiry urges and helps political scientists to attend better to what they already know about conducting political inquiry. Rather than lessons from afar in the form of logic of inquiry, it identifies familiar objects of concern in concrete contexts of research. It seeks to learn from their recurrence and variance how to do better this time and next.

Problematics

> Men are much more apt to agree in what they do than in what they think.
>
> [Johann Wolfgang von Goethe]

In summarising rhetoric of inquiry, Ellen K. Coughlin has written that 'elements of rhetoric...are so thoroughly ingrained in scholarly research as to affect every step of the enterprise – how sources are used, how data are interpreted, how findings are communicated'.[21] By implication, almost no aspect of political inquiry remains irrelevant to rhetorical scrutiny. In order to develop rhetoric of political inquiry, then, priorities become all the more important. Seven problematics strike me as especially good places to begin: (1) approved versus underground rhetorics;

(2) standards of research; (3) stories of social science; (4) rhetorics of discovery; (5) humanities versus sciences; (6) prose for audiences; and (7) canons of knowledge.

Approved vs. underground rhetorics
Within political science as a discipline, the approved and quasi-official rhetorics of political research differ significantly from the informal and usually underground rhetoric of political inquiry. Thus the rhetorics that dominate mainstream journals and textbooks on research methods diverge widely from the rhetorics that surface in graduate seminars, collaborative inquiries, hallway conversations, and other secluded occasions for talking about how political scientists actually conduct their research. Many political scientists would concede this in general terms. But some would deny it altogether, and others would doubt whether it has implications important for the content or quality of political science.

Therefore one of the highest priorities for rhetoric of political inquiry must be to document contrasts between approved and underground rhetorics of inquiry within political science. This is probably the main way to release the discipline from continued domination by official slogans of inquiry imported from philosophy of science as a separate and supposedly authoritative study of the logical rules for conducting all rational inquiry. Thus rhetoric of political inquiry should examine the specifics and strategies characteristic of each set or level of rhetorics, both approved and underground. Simultaneously it should assess the comparative advantages of each, perhaps exploring their relationships to the actual conduct and content of the discipline. Further it should consider the repercussions of differences between approved and underground rhetorics for rhetoric of inquiry in general, conceived as epistemology both immanent within particular inquiries and comparative across diverse fields.

To characterise even the approved rhetorics of political science is a considerable challenge, because the discipline lacks overtly authoritative statements of the order of the manual of style promulgated by the American Psychological Association. In fact, the American Political Science Association is only now taking initial steps toward a manual of style for the discipline, and these on a scale far less ambitious (or presumptuous) than their predecessors in psychology. Nonetheless, textbooks on methods of political research provide specific examples and statements of the approved rhetorics that are: (1) widely taught; (2) mutually consistent; and (3) consonant with other quasi-official expressions of the approved rhetorics of political research. Working from such textbooks, rhetoricians of political inquiry can identify significant features of these approved rhetorics and examine their roles in the conduct of the discipline.

One major trouble in contrasting approved and underground rhetorics within political science is securing good examples and statements of the latter. Underground rhetorics are not countercultural or oppositional rhetorics that are proclaimed in manifestos and published in journals outside the mainstream. Instead they are largely private, and sometimes surprisingly diffuse rhetorics that complement and even correct the publicly accepted ways of thinking, speaking, and writing within and about disciplinary inquiries.

Possibly apocryphal stories and personal anecdotes have been the main kinds of evidence in support of recognising the underground rhetorics of political research. The resonance of such accounts in the everyday experience of political scientists makes these sorts of stories indispensable in explaining the character of underground rhetorics and in persuading political researchers to take them seriously. But such casual accounts cannot dispel nagging doubts that stem from the discipline's desire for more systematic data. Nor can anecdote provide texts detailed enough to sustain many kinds of analysis needed in contrasting underground with approved rhetorics of research. By themselves, these kinds of evidence offer enough for a decent start, but not for an adequate finish.

Surely underground rhetorics of research invite study by various forms of social-scientific inquiry: recording graduate seminars and hallway conversations for detailed study of their rhetorics, experimenting with situations for collaborative research disparate in their rhetorical needs or conditions, and so on. The resources required for such approaches will take time to generate, for I know of no one who has collected similar information adaptable to the study of underground rhetorics in political science or any other discipline.

Yet there does exist in political science, as in other social sciences, a scattered body of texts that offer usable, but not utterly direct, access to such underground rhetorics. In the short run, therefore, the main body of evidence about approved and underground rhetorics of political inquiry can come from the essays that a few political scientists have written about how their detailed conduct of inquiry carries through and (sometimes) departs from the discipline's usual assumptions and statements about methods of research.[22] By considering the rhetorical tensions explicit and implicit in these self-accounts of researchers, the rhetorician of political inquiry can transform them into case studies of the partial confessions of political scientists to having employed underground rhetorics of research that fail to surface in the discipline's generally approved talk about the conduct of science.

These texts are numerous enough to provide a focus for careful treatment of rhetorical details. But as far as I know, nobody has yet analysed these fascinating materials in any fashion, let alone with specific attention to issues in rhetoric of inquiry. The rhetorician should compare these special texts with the works by political scientists that promote the discipline's quasi-official rhetorics of research design and methodology. The rhetorician could also cast side glances toward similar texts in other social sciences, to ascertain how distinctive the underground rhetorics of political inquiry might now be.

Stories of social science

Another priority for rhetoric of political inquiry is the interplay of levels of story-telling in social science.[23] At least three levels deserve attention, and they are demarcated by different subjects: (1) the occurrence of phenomena; (2) the conduct of inquiry; and (3) the communication of research. But does the first level refer to the events as they really were, as observers would tell them, as participants conceived them, as the researchers (initially) perceived them or as the researchers (eventually) recounted them in print? Does the second purport to convey the steps of

173

research as they actually transpired, as observers might relate them, as the researchers experienced them in performance, or as the researchers traced them in publication? And does the third invoke the specific patterns of exposition, the general forms of literature, the basic purposes promoted, the precise audiences sought, the particular reactions received, or other standard referents of rhetoric?

As a topic, the 'storying' of research includes all these perspectives, plus issues of their distinction and interaction. From this broad topic, rhetoricians of political inquiry may carve particular projects, knowing that any one can cover only a small part of such a wide territory. These projects will be important precisely because study of the storying of research in political science (or perhaps any other discipline in the social sciences) may sound odd to its practitioners on at least three counts.

First, orthodox contrasts between social science and historiography lead to the opposing of general, theoretical sciences of society to particular, idiographic studies of history. The peculiar but unmistakable particularity of narratives accordingly associates them almost exclusively with the latter, or so the received view of social inquiry would have it. Actually some stories are exceedingly abstract, general, and formulaic – just as some generalisations are highly concrete, specific, and incipiently narrativistic. At any rate, official rhetorics of research currently encourage few political scientists to think of their 'findings' as stories about politics.[24]

This can pose a real difficulty to the inquiry recommended here, since an obvious result of such a lack of story-consciousness in research is that few political scientists explicitly relate their research as stories about politics. Instead they present their fruits of inquiry as descriptions, models, comparisons, theories, explanations of variance, and the like. Implicitly, though, they do 'story' many – if not all – their subjects. That is, political scientists endow their subjects with narrative sequence and significance. In this respect, an initial task for rhetoricians of political inquiry interested in narrative would be to show that political scientists do narrate events. Further tasks would include the exploration of how, why, with what implications, and to what effects political scientists in general or particular practitioners story their research.

Second, social scientists generally have encouraged themselves to believe that there is a decisive, standing difference between 'the context of discovery' and 'the context of justification'. Of course, we might say that there are two main contexts of justification, since there may be reason to distinguish what factors or standards (should) justify the researchers in believing their own conclusions and what (should) justify their colleagues in such belief. The former is more what I have intended here in writing of the actual conduct of inquiry. On this basis, it is easy (but not necessary) to regard most stories of the conduct of inquiry as irrelevant to methodical presentation of research results – and thus as inappropriate for research reports.

In their relevant respects, moreover, such stories are usually recounted in only a few standard forms. These are influenced as much by philosophies of what is supposed to happen in research, by practice of what others write about their studies, and by sensibilities about what others will find persuasive about the researchers' own investigations as by what actually occurs in the conduct of inquiry (either as observed by others or as experienced by the researchers themselves). Here again, then, some social scientists would have to be shown that narratives of the conduct of inquiry recur significantly in the reporting of research. But of course, rhetoricians of political inquiry would also want to consider what the standard narratives are, when they arise, and how they relate to political science as we have experienced and observed it. What might the stories of research tell us about what political inquiry can examine and how accounts of inquiry relate to accounts of (political) phenomena (purportedly) arising from that inquiry. Do some stories of research show a special affinity for some plots of politics? In what respects? Why might that be?

Third, even when social scientists concede there to be elements of art (rhetoric) in the communication of research to colleagues, the skills and principles involved are so poorly respected, studied, and (dare I say) practised that no ready recognition of their specific narrative choices – let alone of their various narrative effects – can be expected. To be sure, a few students of literature have ventured to teach and write in these terms about some products of social science. In programs of composition and school education, this sometimes occurs under the heading of 'writing across the curriculum'. But these forays into the literary criticism of social science have been few and confined for the most part to 'classic texts', which are seldom typical of the inquiry of their own periods, let alone of the research of more modern times. About current political science, we could ask: what are the overall narratives that express research? When, how, and why are they deployed? And with what effects on whom? How do political scientists try to quarantine this level of narrative from the other two? In what respects do they succeed? In what respects do they fail? And why?

Let me note also a further complication that cuts across all three of these levels. For even at the crudest cut, political science consists of three rhetorical communities rather than one. Although they interact continually and intensively, these communities remain importantly distinct. Perhaps their most common names among political scientists are: empirical theory, analytical theory, and normative theory. That each name fits its respective community poorly – if at all – is the kind of rhetorical convolution cum revelation that can be turned to the benefit of arguments by rhetoricians of political inquiry. But whatever the central level(s) and issue(s) of storying research chosen by rhetoricians of political inquiry, they will need, along the way, to give and take some account of the differences and dependences among these three communities of rhetoric in political science.[25]

On any and across all three levels of narrative in political science, and on any and across all three communities of political theory, rhetoricians of political inquiry should ask what the enhancement of specifically narrative or generally rhetorical self-consciousness might mean for political science.[26] To focus on narrative, rather than the whole array of rhetorical dimensions and projects in political science, offers the advantage of resisting the temptation to emphasise political features and principles of rhetoric in regard to the rest of the humanities and social sciences. It should enable rhetoricians of political inquiry to narrow their argumentative responsibilities to manageable amounts, especially at the outset.

Standards of research

Criteria for judging findings, arguments, and other aspects of political inquiry must be identified or selected, defended, and applied. This is the domain of political epistemology.[27] Due to the interdependence of rhetoric, politics, and inquiry, political theory must in some ways always be epistemological theory – and *vice versa*. I am inclined to think, moreover, that epistemology is an especially important part of politics in our times.[28] Exploring these claims and their implications for political science comprises for rhetoricians of political inquiry a set of issues about standards of research.

In order to defend a specifically rhetorical and political treatment of knowledge, rhetoricians of political inquiry must engage with recent controversies over the features and functions of epistemology. By explicating the rhetorical and political elements of epistemology in theorising about politics, they must study – and to some extent join – the struggles of style and perspective that permeate projects of inquiry in the humanities and social sciences alike. Thereby they must reveal compellingly for political scientists at least, some of the inadequacies of recent philosophies of science for informing political inquiry and action.

In particular, political epistemology examines how reflection on standards and methods of inquiry can and must be situating squarely within substantive research. By exploring the twilight zone between abstract philosophies of inquiry and specific patterns of argument in political theory, it draws detailed lessons for useful interactions between these realms – long related wrongly, when related at all. Thus does political epistemology show how rhetorical epistemology is importantly, *political* epistemology.

At least initially, rhetoricians of inquiry need to show in detail how substantive inquiries depart from externally dictated norms. They need to explain how scholars legitimately invoke different reasons which are persuasive in different contexts. And they need to study specifically how individual inquiries can improve their rhetorics and thus their results. Accordingly, political epistemologists should study political reasoning by analysing the rhetoric of actual political arguments – most of them by political theorists but also some by ordinary actors in politics. The aim is to reveal the rhetorical structures of good argument, in order to show how standards for good reasoning operate. These structures include the use of linguistic conventions to designate meaning and significance, the creation and application of standards for good reasoning, the invocation of symbols and more explicit comparisons to other entities or contexts, the projection of audiences, the reliance on tropes, and the other aspects of rhetoric identified by such theorists as Aristotle, Kenneth Burke, and Hayden White.[29]

The case for rhetorical and political epistemology rests in part on the manifest inadequacy of recent logics of inquiry. They are deficient for the practice not only of politics but also of political studies. To date, most so-called 'philosophies of political science' have been limited to adaptation of abstract principles of philosophy into very general rules for political inquiry. The focus has fallen on logical forms of description, explanation, prediction, and testing. Almost nothing has been said about specific subjects of political research. Very few implications actually follow from such philosophies of inquiry for detailed methods of political inquiry. This approach has been encouraged by borrowing from a family of philosophies of inquiry too broad to provide day-to-day guidance for studies within political theory and political science. That is why behaviouralism in political science must never be identified with – reduced to – logical positivisms and empiricisms, notwithstanding the many ties of behaviouralism to those epistemologies.

Part of the trouble has been that these philosophies are seriously misleading in their conceptions of inquiry, especially in the humanities and social sciences. But in practice, that has mattered much less than one might imagine. For the larger part of the problem has been that these epistemologies are simply too abstract to connect in any solid, reliable way with specific inquiry into politics. Within political theory and political science, such philosophies have had far less chance to produce perverse effects than critics typically assume. In fact, political theory and political science have of late developed in virtual isolation from any substantive, self-conscious theory of inquiry. As a result, their methods, research designs, and theories of political inquiry have suffered various and sometimes chronic defects.[30]

By contrast, political epistemology is predicated on the notion that apt principles of inquiry do not necessarily (or usually) come before practices of research. They are seldom so general that they span wide varieties of disciplines. Instead they come from specific programs of scholarship, through internal criticism and comparison with other projects. They are principles which express and direct the basic impulses, procedures, and perspectives of study – whether avowedly humanistic or scientific. Lacking substantive theories of inquiry, recent political inquiry has lacked precisely these principles of study.

Thus a distinctive feature of rhetoric is that its theoretical questions, categories, and methods are indivisible from its practical limits, tactics, and performances. Modern dichotomies between theory and practice are not central to rhetorical ways of addressing the world. Instead, rhetoric spans subject and object, epistemology and ontology, audience and action, academy and polity. It encourages a kind of 'practice theory' meant to keep inquiries aware of the contexts of events without sacrificing the capacity to criticise their conventions.

The mistake of most logics of inquiry has been to strive for fundamental separation from the contexts of concrete inquiry. Thus even the questions raised by such logics – let alone their answers – have been largely beside the point as regards scientific researches in particular fields. In this sense, many logics of inquiry have become caught up in pseudoquestions. The few scientists who attend much to them have been badly misled about priorities and techniques. Like their philosophical colleagues, they flounder in abstract problems which have no useful answers at the levels posed.[31]

Logics of inquiry must offer contexts through which scientists can (and will be encouraged to) criticise their own moves in theory and method. This does not rule out all divisions of labour between disciplinary scholars and philosophers of inquiry. But it does insist upon much greater overlap and interdependence than previous views have promoted. This means that epistemologies must stay in intimate touch with the substance of actual projects of inquiry. It also means that scholars –

humanistic or scientific – must in some degree remain within range of the principles and perspectives associated with (rhetorical) epistemology.

While this test is failed by logical positivisms, empiricisms, and the like, it is also failed by their contextualist critics. Such critics have couched their attacks upon philosophies of political inquiry at the same abstract plane originally appropriated by the philosophies criticised. Almost nowhere in this literature does the criticism lead into substantive reconstruction of actual, current projects of political research.[32]

Forays into specific examples of research must be the minimum requirement, and even then the main opportunity will be missed. Yet if research projects are to be rethought in the fundamental fashion produced by good philosophy of inquiry, this must not be done from above. The only saving grace of the imperial, dictatorial style of recent epistemologies has been the emptiness of their specific dictates. The needed reconstructions of research must be conducted from within particular programs of research. The would-be epistemologist must be informed by a reasonably full knowledge of the detailed studies of a given set of research disciplines.

It is equally important that the mirror mistake be avoided. Just as recent epistemologies have seldom condescended to the levels of theory and method, so have recent designs for substantive research refused to rise to the levels of epistemological and philosophical reflection. This is certainly not to say that there has been no criticism of political inquiry from within substantive fields. It is rather to notice that such scrutiny falls shy of thought about the basic assumptions out of which specific inquiries are generated. It is also to observe that such criticism is too little informed by careful comparisons among scholarly projects and across whole fields of inquiry. Indeed such reflection hardly has the language – not to mention the information – needed for a suitably searching attempt to comprehend and criticise its own research results. Finding little help in previous philosophies of inquiry, the average student of politics has learned to steer clear of such airy domains when trying to get on with day-to-day research.

That course offers some advantages, but it must fail in the end. In recent political inquiry, as in many of the humanities and social sciences, the result has been an abyss between theories and practices of inquiry. Neither side pays detailed attention to the other. Not even the critics, whose work seems to call for bridging this abyss, have done much to take up the crucial task themselves. Yet for the sake of political inquiry, as well as philosophy of inquiry, this is the task which now needs to be started. To do this is to sketch a loose conception of epistemology which would specify itself through interaction with substantive researches of all kinds. Thus rhetorical and political principles of epistemology can come into sharp focus only by fixing sights on actual research projects in political inquiry and elsewhere. In turn, that is why rhetoric of political inquiry moves from defending broad principles of inquiry to developing (not merely applying) them in concrete contexts of current political studies.

The attempt to shape a rhetorical and political epistemology will grow from at least five fairly distinct bodies of inquiry and argument: epistemology and philosophy of inquiry; philosophy of language; literary, rhetorical, and communications theory; political theory; and political science. A further way to evoke how political epistemology approaches standards in research is to note how these sources might figure in rhetoric of political inquiry.

Philosophical treatments of epistemology and inquiry serve primarily as targets of our criticism, since most have favoured the sorts of abstraction from substantive inquiry that rhetoric of political inquiry finds wanting. Nonetheless a small and provocative part of philosophical epistemologies bears some affinity for the rhetorical and political principles of the new field. The result is that the philosophical works of such scholars as Max Black, Stanley Cavell, Nelson Goodman, Paul Feyerabend, Thomas Kuhn, Hilary Putnam, Richard Rorty, Calvin Schrag, Wilfrid Sellars, and Stephen Toulmin should occupy a special part of the attention of political epistemologists. The point is less to repeat others' (typically trenchant) criticisms of abstractionist epistemology, however, than to co-ordinate and develop the rudiments of rhetorical and political epistemology scattered throughout their works. Writings of the people just mentioned are especially useful in accounting for the several substantive rationalities most evident within recent studies of society and politics. Of course, exploring recent rhetorics within these philosophies can also afford clues for correcting troubles that beset some recent theories of rhetoric as well.[33]

Sources from the philosophy of language, by contrast, provide more direct and detailed support for our rhetorical principles of epistemology. Increasingly, philosophers of language have tried to illuminate the figurative resources and limits of language. Their perspectives supplement the traditionally divergent approaches of literary and rhetorical theorists, although differences of topics and treatment have often been exaggerated by both sides. At any rate, such philosophers of language as Max Black, Richard Boyd, Ina Loewenberg, John Searle, and Paul Ziff have written a great deal which bears on our general conception of epistemology, its relationship to substantive inquiries and practices, and the particular principles according to which it may be presented.[34]

Currently a belated renaissance of rhetoric is under way in the domains of speech, communications, and literary theory. The names of useful sources are almost too numerous for a short sampling to suffice. But let me at least mention Wayne Booth, Kenneth Burke, Paul de Man, Jacques Derrida, Stanley Fish, Geoffrey Hartman, Michael Leff, and Hayden White. Over the last decade, journals of speech, communications and rhetoric have published article after article on aspect of the thesis that 'rhetoric is epistemic'. All these contribute to rhetoric of inquiry in general, and thus they provide the backdrop for political epistemology in particular.[35]

Because I am a political theorist by education and profession, I am especially sensitive to the rhetorical resources on which this fourth field relies. Since I am far from the only political theorist starting to see the promise of rhetorical and political epistemology, there is considerable aid in identifying and applying those resources. Richard Ashcraft, Terence Ball, Brian Barry, William Bluhm, Lance Bennett, William Connolly, John Gunnell, Russell Hanson, Paul Kress, Eugene Miller, Donald Moon, Hanna Pitkin, Glenn Tinder, Michael Walzer, and many others have written books and articles which contribute importantly to the principles at the heart of an epistemology which is importantly rhetorical and political. Partly this is symptomatic of the power of epistemological arguments to distract political theorists from politics. But more importantly, it is due to the special significance of the traditional and recent concerns of political theorists for shaping rhetorical and political epistemology. In both respects, this body of work by political theorists is salient to rhetoric of political inquiry.

Last let me mention the social-scientific projects of political science. They are important for political epistemology because reconstructing various research programs of political science has been one of its prime inspirations and promises to continue as one of its prime occasions. There is little point in an extensive list of political scientists of special importance in this regard, but a few should be mentioned: Hayward Alker, Charles Anderson, Robert Boynton, William Panning, and William Riker. The insistence on situating epistemology squarely within concrete contexts of research means that rhetoricians of political inquiry must attend alike to pathfinding and pathfollowing scientists, to both pioneering and problem-solving projects. Thus rhetoricians must try to explicate reasons for respecting and improving political researches as they actually occur.

Rhetorics of discovery
One of the received dichotomies undermined by rhetoric of inquiry is that between contexts of discovery and contexts of justification. Consequently a priority for rhetoric of political inquiry is to investigate the discovery of rhetoric in political science. These occur in many contexts and take many forms. Developing Abraham Kaplan's notion of 'logics in use',[36] rhetoric of inquiry insists both that there are multiple logics for initiating inquiry and that these play crucial roles in structuring later rhetorics of investigation and communication.

In political science, rhetorics of discovery involve 'Getting Started on Political Research'.[37] This concern relates directly to studies that rhetoricians of inquiry make of the twilight zone between abstract logics of science and concrete designs of research. Rhetorics of discovery also include the teaching rhetorics that introduce students, as beginning practitioners, to professional research in the discipline. Along these lines, a concern for rhetorics of inquiry intersects with a concern about approved versus underground rhetorics of political research. Similarly rhetorics of political discovery encompass our storied sensibility of proper and improper procedures of political inquiry. This can overlap at least one level of concern for stories of social science. And finally, rhetorics of discovery embrace the beginning beliefs and figures of speech that seldom become conscious for researchers, at least until after they have virtually finished their inquiry. This last interest engages with Stephen Pepper's 'world hypotheses' and 'root metaphors', Kenneth Burke's 'four master tropes', Northrop Frye's four master plots, and Hayden White's 'prefiguration of the phenomenal field' of inquiry by 'tropes of consciousness'.[38]

These aspects of rhetorics of discovery appear largely literary in the light of current categories, and this encourages rhetoricians of inquiry to assess how various projects in social science relate to disciplines in the humanities. By defending a rhetorical and political epistemology for the social sciences, rhetorics of inquiry may even be said to reveal themselves as research projects in the humanities, since rhetoric and political philosophy are among the oldest disciplines in the humanities. Accordingly, another priority for rhetoric of political inquiry is to investigate the historical and theoretical development of barriers between the social sciences and the humanities. This should include the reflexive project of addressing the current inclination of rhetoric of inquiry to lead beyond old divides between the two.

Humanities vs. sciences

The increased commonality between social sciences and humanities comes as a considerable surprise to veterans of old disputes between scientific and literary cultures. They remember well how each social science promised to supplant humanistic styles of inquiry into its subjects. For some contributors to the behavioural revolution in political science, the new conversations among traditionally humanistic and avowedly scientific projects might appear astonishing and, in some cases, even distressing. But the newly evident convergence does not reflect reduced dedication of social scientists to rigorous observation and testable theories of human behaviour. Instead it expresses an unanticipated tendency for scientific techniques to develop greater range and complexity in tandem with diverse methods still distinctive of the humanities. Hence many research programs in political science reveal intricate interrelationships among approaches previously segregated as scientific and humanistic.

This is more than a matter of preserving humanistic concerns in the field of political theory. For one thing, its projects of conceptual and institutional analysis, political ethics, epistemology, history, and imagination are slowly diffusing throughout the rest of the discipline – as theoretical projects in other fields interact more explicitly with those central to political theory as a field. For another, humanistic methods increasingly prove complementary to scientific techniques as students of politics argue through the meanings of their research. This surfaces in the two faces now presented by several fields of the discipline: judicial behaviour and public law, comparative politics and area studies, international relations and peace research, political socialisation and political education. It shows in the aim of policy analysis to meld empirical and normative studies. It appears in the proclivity of formal theories to elicit normative treatments of federalism, historical studies of parties, rhetorical analysis of movements such as environmentalism, and other humanistic inquiries.

One implication of the surprising interpenetration of political science and various humanities is that political scientists do far more humanistic research than they have recognised.[39] For rhetoric of inquiry, this raises fascinating issues about disparities between official rhetorics of research and actual practices or unofficial rhetorics of research. For political science, this also poses the intriguing possibility that resources available for research have gone unnoticed. These include humanistic disciplines with fields relevant substantively or methodologically to various projects in political science. The underused resources also include funding agencies interested in the sorts of humanistic studies in fact conducted by political scientists who nonetheless neglect the humanistic contents and techniques of their own research.

Also oriented toward the humanities is another lesson from rhetoric of inquiry:

the quality of scientific writing reflects the quality of scientific research, because the processes which produce them are so continuous and interactive as to defy distinction in most practices of inquiry. As Oliver Sacks recently argued in *Newsweek*, 'I'm not sure science can be, or even should be literature, but I'm very sure it should be prose. The professional journals are quite unreadable, the way the Dow Jones report is'. Accordingly, rhetoric of inquiry begins with issues of logic and method but extends beyond them to encompass as well, questions of expression, persuasion, and interpretation. More importantly, it explores the interdependence of these concerns. Thus it seeks improvements in the conception, conduct, and content of research throughout the human sciences. There emerges from these projects, therefore, a theme with immediate implications for political scientists: many recent projects in the social sciences and humanities share data, methods, and modes of analysis. That sharing is not bad for political science, and it can be made even better through rhetoric of political inquiry.

Prose for audiences

Rhetoric of inquiry emphasises *how* scholarly arguments do (or do not) persuade their audiences inside and outside the communities in which those arguments arise. Perhaps the most obvious priority for rhetoric of political inquiry is the rhetorical analysis of actual argumentation in political science. Field by field, project by project, book by book, article by article, page by page, sentence by sentence: how does argument in political science in fact proceed? What warrants and backings does it invoke? What assumptions, figures, images, symbols, and tropes does it deploy? How do these affect various audiences – and with what further effects?

The approaches available to such rhetorical analysis are as numerous and diverse as the field of rhetoric has made them. Eventually rhetoric of inquiry will surely contribute to developing new modes of rhetorical analysis: but for the time being, there are far more worthwhile strategies than rhetoricians of political inquiry have even begun to use. Political scientists have paid surprisingly little attention to detailed analysis of the arguments made by many of their behavioural and postbehavioural classics.

To see several ways in which rhetoricians of political inquiry might proceed to study the arguments of such texts, a fine example can be drawn from the discipline of economics. Donald McCloskey's *Rhetoric of Economics* scrutinises the persuasive appeals of a number of major works in the discipline. Chapter by chapter, the book brings different levels and strategies of rhetorical analysis to bear on the works selected, revealing their basic devices of argument in ways that allow more intelligent responses to the works. The same concerns and strategies surface also in the recent prominence of 'law and literature' and 'legal reasoning' as fields of legal studies.[40] Political science very much needs such rhetorical attention to be directed to its own works.

Canons of knowledge

Here my reference to 'canons of knowledge' is deliberately ambiguous as between three kinds of 'canons'. The first is a set of classic texts taken to encompass the

crucial, or at least the seminal knowledge of a field.[41] As repositories of organisational memory and sources of continuing inspiration, these canons of classics play
major roles in most of the dimensions already identified for rhetorics of inquiry. The
second is a set of conventions as rules or principles taken to constitute or regulate
the creation and dissemination of knowledge within and by a field.[42] As standards of
research, these conventions are studied by rhetoric of inquiry in its guise as political
epistemology. The third is a set of conventions as assumptions or beliefs taken to
express the basic convictions of a field.[43] As features of prose for audiences and
rhetorics of discovery, these latter conventions are studied through the strategies of
rhetorical analysis discussed earlier.

Rhetoric of inquiry studies all three canons of knowledge, but it especially explores their interdependence. In political science, the first kind is now the most
problematic. On the one hand, 'the traditional canon of Western classics of political
philosophy' is undergoing a sustained attack that will probably lead to a modest
restructuring and a thorough reconception.[44] On the other hand, anti-traditional
science since the Second World War has scarcely begun to produce its own canon of
key works. Even though the discipline's canon of classics ancient and modern must
surely comprise one of the richest traditions of rhetoric in all the social sciences, the
canons of knowledge in political science stand in special need of attention by
rhetoricians of political inquiry.

Ends

Watch your own speech, and notice how it is guided by your less conscious purposes.
[T.S. Eliot]

Recent students of rhetoric have begun an intriguing discussion of how rhetoric is
epistemic: that is, how it produces, displaces, and shapes knowledge. Their work
relates closely to the current criticism of foundationalism in philosophy of science.
Yet these endeavours repeatedly run up against at least two barriers to better appreciation and practice of rhetoric. One is a tendency to oppose rhetoric to
rationality, with the result that taking rhetoric seriously is mistaken for the endorsement of radical relativism. The other is a failure to examine rhetoric within contexts
of actual inquiry, with the prospect of turning rhetoric back into abstract dictates of
philosophy insensitive to real dynamics of research.

Rhetoric of political inquiry, in particular, can make contributions of special
value to addressing these two barriers, because various projects in political reasoning and belief systems have started to get beyond simplistic contrasts between
rationality and its utter absence.[45] Increasingly it investigates diverse rationalities as
reflected in distinct sets of beliefs, concepts, and symbols – that is to say – as
represented in different rhetorics. Political research on tolerance carries similar
implications for attempts to privilege any single perspective as an exclusive standard
of rationality.[46] Relatedly, studies of political communication, culture, and socialisation identify many aspects of political thinking which can be divorced from specific

occasions of learning, only at the cost of accurate understanding of their character and contents. This leads toward better appreciation of the political communication, culture, and socialisation of political scientists. It also enhances recognition of their many processes of inquiry within real situations of research.[47]

In the end, rhetoric of political inquiry strives to improve research by teaching political scientists to learn from their own studies that reason and inquiry are deeply rhetorical and political.

Notes

1. Over the years, I have worked with many excellent rhetoricians of inquiry, no doubt including some who would not want to be associated with the label. I hope that I have thanked in person most, if not all, of them for their help; and in any event, there is not room to list all of them here. Yet I must record special thanks to six of the best: G.R. Boynton, Jack Gunnell, Paul Kress, Don McCloskey, Bill Panning, and Ira Strauber.

2. See J.S. Nelson, 'Natures and future for political theory' *What Should Political Theory Be Now?* (Albany: State University of New York Press, 1983) pp. 3-24.

3. See F. Randall, 'Why scholars become storytellers' *New York Times Book Review* (29 January 1984) pp. 1, 31; A. Megill and J.S. Nelson, 'Academics meet to talk about making their talk understandable' *Des Moines Register* (25 March 1984), Op-Ed 3; E.K. Coughlin, 'Finding the message in the medium: the rhetoric of scholarly research' *Chronicle of Higher Education* (11 April 1984) pp. 1, 9; H.W. Simons, 'Chronicle and critique of a conference' *The Quarterly Journal of Speech* 71 (1985) pp. 52-64; J.R. Lyne, 'Rhetoric of inquiry' *The Quarterly Journal of Speech* 71 (1985) pp. 65-73; and K.J. Winkler, 'Questioning the science in social science, scholars signal a "Turn to Interpretation" ' *Chronicle of Higher Education* (26 June 1985) pp. 5-6.

4. My efforts directed toward the twilight zone between abstract philosophy of science and detailed design of research include: 'The ideological connection, I-II', *Theory and Society* 4 (1977) pp. 421-48 and 573-90; and 'Education for politics: rethinking research on political socialisation', in J.S. Nelson (1983) pp. 413-78; see note 2.

5. My studies of tropes in inquiry include: 'Review essay on *Metahistory* by Hayden White' *History and Theory* 14 (1975) pp. 74-91; 'Meaning and measurement across paradigms: metaphor and irony in political inquiry', paper for the Annual Meeting of the American Political Science Association, Washington, DC (1977); 'Tropical history and the social sciences' *History and Theory* 19 (1980) pp. 80-101; and 'Models, statistics, and other tropes of politics: or, whatever happened to argumentation in political science' *Argument in Transition*, D. Zarefsky, M.O. Sillars, and J. Rhodes (eds) (Annandale: Speech Communication Association, (1983) pp. 213-29.

6. See E. Mendelsohn and Y. Elkana (eds), *Sciences and Cultures* (Boston: Reidel, 1981).

7. See J.S. Nelson, 'Practice theory; what is is and why we need it', paper for the

Annual Meeting of the Midwest Political Science Association (Chicago, 1985).

   8. Nelson, J.S., 'Irony and autonomy: how and why to read John Gunnell' *Tradition, Interpretation, and Science* (Albany: State University of New York Press; in press); Strauber, I.L., and Nelson, J.S., 'Epistemology in political theory: the importance of rhetoric', unpublished paper.

   9. Nelson, J.S., 'Political theory as political rhetoric', in J.S. Nelson (1983) pp. 169-240; see note 2; and J.S. Nelson (1983) pp. 413-78; see note 4.

   10. See J.S. Nelson and A. Megill, 'Rhetoric of inquiry: projects and prospects' *Quarterly Journal of Speech* 72 (1986) pp. 20-37; J.S. Nelson, A. Megill and D.N. McCloskey (eds), *The Rhetoric of the Human Sciences* (Madison: University of Wisconsin Press, 1987).

   11. See J.S. Nelson, A. Megill, and D.N. McCloskey, 'Rhetoric of inquiry', in J.S. Nelson, *et al.* (1987); see note 10.

   12. In addition to works cited in notes 3 and 10, see W.J.T. Mitchell (ed.), 'The politics of interpretation' *Critical Inquiry* 9 (1982) pp. 1-278; D. Bell (ed.), 'New directions in modern thought' *Partisan Review* 51 (1984) pp. 215-300; R. Cohen (ed.), 'Interpretation and culture' *New Literary History* 17 (1986) pp. 183-390; R. Cohen (ed.), 'Philosophy of science and literary theory' *New Literary History* 17 (1985) pp. 1-171.

   13. On sociology, see R.W. Friedrichs, *A Sociology of Sociology* (New York: Free Press, 1970); and A.W. Gouldner, *The Coming Crisis of Western Sociology* (New York: Avon Books, 1970). On economics, see G.J. Stigler, *The Economist as Preacher* (Chicago: University of Chicago Press, 1982); and D.N. McCloskey, *The Rhetoric of Economics* (Madison: University of Wisconsin Press, 1985). On historiography, see J.H. Hexter, *On Historians* (Cambridge, MA.: Harvard University Press, 1979); D. LaCapra and S.L. Kaplan (eds), *Modern European Intellectual History* (Ithaca: Cornell University Press, 1982). On psychology, see R. Nisbet and L. Ross, *Human Inference* (Englewood Cliffs: Prentice-Hall, 1980); and D.E. Carlston, 'Turning psychology on itself: the rhetoric of psychology and the psychology of rhetoric', in J.S. Nelson, *et al.* (1987); see note 10. On anthropology, see D. Hymes (ed.), *Reinventing Anthropology* (New York: Random House, 1969); R. Rosaldo, 'Where objectivity lies: the rhetoric of anthropology', in J.S. Nelson, *et al.* (1987); see note 10. On political science, see D.M. Ricci, *The Tragedy of Political Science* (New Haven:Yale University Press, 1984); and J.G. Gunnell, *Between Philosophy and Politics* (Amherst: University of Massachusetts Press, 1986). On reflexive social science in general, see G. Morgan (ed.) *Beyond Method* (Beverly Hills: Sage, 1983).

   14. See J.S. Nelson (1977); see note 5; J.S. Nelson (1983) pp. 213-29; see note 5; and J.S. Nelson, *et al.* (1987); see note 10.

   15. See S. Toulmin, *The Uses of Argument* (New York: Cambridge University Press, 1964); and S. Toulmin, *Human Understanding* (Princeton: Princeton University Press, 1972).

   16. See J.S. Nelson, 'Toltechs, Aztechs, and the art of the possible: parenthetic comments on the political through language and aesthetics' *Polity* 8 (1975) pp. 80-116; and 'Seven rhetorics of inquiry: a provocation', in J.S. Nelson, *et al.* (1987);

see note 10.

17. See G. Tinder, *Community* (Baton Rouge: Louisiana State University Press, 1980); J.S. Nelson (1983) pp. 3-24; see note 2 and pp. 169-240; see note 9.

18. See J.S. Nelson (1983) pp. 213-29; see note 5 and pp. 169-240; see note 9.

19. See J.S. Nelson, 'Beyond an old divide: rediscovering humanities in political science' *Social Education* 49 (1985) pp. 433-34.

20. See W.T. Bluhm, M.G. Hermann, W.F. Murphy, J.S. Nelson, and L.W. Pye, 'Political science and the humanities: a report of the American Political Science Association' *PS* 18 (1985) pp. 247-59.

21. Coughlin, E.K., (1984) pp. 1-9; see note 3.

22. See W.P. Shively (ed.), *The Research Process in Political Science* (Itasca: F.E. Peacock, 1984); M.P. Golden (ed.), *The Research Experience* (Itasca: F.E. Peacock, 1976); E. Ostrom (ed.), *Strategies of Political Inquiry* (Beverly Hills: Sage, 1982); J.A. Gillespie, and D.A. Zinnes (eds), *Missing Elements in Political Inquiry* (Beverly Hills: Sage, 1982); A.W. Finifter (ed.), *Political Science* (Washington, DC: American Political Science Association, 1983); H.B. Asher, *et al.* (eds), *Theory-Building and Data Analysis in the Social Sciences* (Knoxville: University of Tennessee Press, 1984); and P.E. Hammond (ed.), *Sociologists at Work* (Garden City, NY: Doubleday, 1964).

23. See J.S. Nelson, 'Stories of science and politics: some rhetorics of political research', in J.S. Nelson, *et al.* (1987); see note 10.

24. Mitchell, W.J.T. (ed.), 'On narrative' *Critical Inquiry* (1980) pp. 5-236.

25. Nelson, J.S., 'Political argument in political science: a meditation on disappointments of political theory', paper for the Annual Meeting of the American Political Science Association (Chicago, 1983).

26. See M.C. McGee and J.S. Nelson, 'Narrative reason in public argument' *Journal of Communication* 35 (1985) pp. 139-55.

27. See I.L. Strauber and J.S. Nelson; see note 8.

28. See J.S. Nelson 'Political foundations for rhetoric of inquiry', paper for the Temple University Conference on Case Studies in the Rhetoric of the Human Sciences (Philadelphia, 1986).

29. See Aristotle, *Rhetoric and Poetics*, trans. W.R. Roberts and I. Bywater, F. Somlsen (ed.), (New York: Random House, 1954); K. Burke, *A Grammar of Motives* (Berkeley: University of California Press, 1945); K. Burke, *Language as Symbolic Action* (Berkeley: University of California Press, 1966); K. Burke, *The Philosophy of Literary Form* (Berkeley: University of California Press, 1941, 1967, 3rd edn 1973); K. Burke, *A Rhetoric of Motives* (Berkeley: University of California Press, 1950); W.C. Booth, *Modern Dogma and the Rhetoric of Assent* (Chicago: University of Chicago Press, 1974); W.C. Booth, *The Rhetoric of Fiction* (Chicago: University of Chicago Press, 1961); W.C. Booth, *A Rhetoric of Irony* (Chicago: University of Chicago Press, 1974); H. White, *Metahistory* (Baltimore: Johns Hopkins University Press, 1973); and H. White, *Tropics of Discourse* (Baltimore: Johns Hopkins University Press, 1978).

30. On the specific illness of fit between logical positivism and behaviouralism, see L.D. Smith, *Behaviorism and Logical Positivism: A Reassessment of the Al-*

liance (Palo Alto: Stanford University Press, 1986). On the general inadequacy of epistemology to political inquiry, see P.F. Kress, 'Against epistemology: apostate musings' *Journal of Politics* 41 (1979) pp. 526-42; D.R. Sabia, Jr, 'Comment on Paul Kress "Against epistemology" ' *Journal of Politics* 42 (1980) p. 1154; L.A. Scaff, 'Bringing politics back in' *Journal of Politics* 42 (1980) pp. 1155-9; E.F. Miller, 'Epistemology and political inquiry: comment on Kress' "Against epistemology" ' *Journal of Politics* 42 (1980) pp. 1160-67; P. Kress, 'Reply to commentaries on "Against epistemology" ' *Journal of Politics* 42 (1980) pp. 1168-69; J. Flax, 'Why epistemology matters: a reply to Kress' *Journal of Politics* 43 (1981) pp. 1006-24; and P. Kress, 'Rejoinder to Flax' *Journal of Politics* 43 (1981) pp. 1025-8. Also see many of the essays in J.S. Nelson (1983); see note 2.

31. See R. Ashcraft, 'On the problem of methodology and the nature of political theory' *Political Theory* 3 (1975) pp. 5-25; R. Ashcraft, 'Political theory and the problem of ideology' *Journal of Politics* 42 (1980) pp. 687-705; D.V.J. Bell, *Power, Influence, and Authority* (New York: Oxford University Press, 1975); R.J. Bernstein, *The Restructuring of Social and Political Theory* (Philadelphia: University of Pennsylvania Press, 1976); R.J. Bernstein, *Beyond Objectivism and Relativism* (Philadelphia: University of Pennsylvania Press, 1983); W.T. Bluhm, *Theories of the Political System* (Englewood Cliffs: Prentice-Hall, 1965); P. Bourdieu, *Outline of a Theory of Practice*, trans. R. Nice (Cambridge: Cambridge University Press, 1972, 1977); R.H. Brown, *A Poetic for Sociology* (New York: Cambridge University Press, 1977); W.E. Connolly, *The Terms of Political Discourse* (Lexington: D.C. Heath, 1974); W.E. Connolly, *Appearance and Reality* (Amherst: University of Massachusetts Press, 1981); J. Danford, *Wittgenstein and Political Philosophy* (Chicago: University of Chicago Press, 1978); M. Falco (ed.), *Through the Looking-Glass* (Washington, DC: University Press of America, 1979); P.K. Feyerabend, *Against Method* (Atlantic Highlands: Humanities Press, 1975); J. Habermas, *The Theory of Communicative Action*, trans. T. McCarthy (Boston: Beacon Press, 1981); T.S. Kuhn, *The Structure of Scientific Revolutions* (Chicago: University of Chicago Press, 2nd edn, 1970); H.D. Lasswell, *Politics* (New York: World, 1958); H.D. Lasswell and A.D. Kaplan, *Power and Society* (New Haven: Yale University Press, 1950); A. MacIntyre, *After Virtue* (Notre Dame: University of Notre Dame Press, 1981); E.F. Miller, 'The primary questions of political inquiry' *Review of Politics* 39 (1977) pp. 298-331; E.F. Miller, 'Metaphor and political knowledge' *American Politics Science Review* 73 (1979) pp. 155-70; E.F. Miller, 'Locke on the meaning of political language: the treaching of the Essay Concerning Human Understanding' *Political Science Reviewer* 9 (1979) pp. 163-93; R.M. Pirsig, *Zen and the Art of Motorcycle Maintenance* (New York: Bantam Books, 1974); H.F. Pitkin, *Wittgenstein and Justice* (Berkeley: University of California Press, 1972); P. Ricoeur, *The Rule of Metaphor*, trans. R. Czerny (Toronto: University of Toronto Press, 1977); S. Rosen, *Nihilism* (New Haven: Yale University Press, 1969); R.M. Unger, *Knowledge and Politics* (New York: Free Press, 1975); L. Wittgenstein, *Philosophical Investigations*, translator and editor, G.E.M. Anscombe (New York: Macmillan, 1953, 3rd edn, 1958); and E.M. Wood, *Mind and Politics* (Berkeley: University of California Press, 1972).

32. See J.G. Gunnell, *Philosophy, Science, and Political Inquiry* (Morristown:

32. See J.G. Gunnell, *Philosophy, Science, and Political Inquiry* (Morristown: General Learning Press, 1975); J.G. Gunnell, *Political Theory* (Cambridge, MA: Winthrop, 1979); J.G. Gunnell, 'Philosophy and political inquiry' *Government and Opposition* 14 (1979) pp. 198-216; J.G. Gunnell, 'Encounters of a third kind: the philosophical alienation of theory in American political science' *American Journal of Political Science* 25 (1981) pp. 440-61; J.G.A. Pocock, 'Political theory, history, and myth: a salute to John Gunnell' *Annals of Scholarship* I (1980) pp. 3-25; J.G. Gunnell, 'Method, methodology, and the search for traditions in the history of political theory: a reply to Pocock's salute' *Annals of Scholarship* I (1980) pp. 26-56; J.G.A. Pocock, 'Intentions, traditions and methods: some sounds on a foghorn' *Annals of Scholarship* I (1980) pp. 57-62.

33. See S. Cavell, *The Claim of Reason* (New York: Oxford University Press, 1979); A. MacIntyre (1981); see note 31; R. Nozick, *Philosophical Explanations* (Cambridge, MA: Harvard University Press, 1981); R. Rorty, *Philosophy and the Mirror of Nature* (Princeton: Princeton University Press, 1979).

34. See J. Culler, *Structuralist Poetics* (Ithaca: Cornell University Press, 1976); J. Derrida, *Of Grammatology*, trans. G.C. Spivak (Baltimore: Johns Hopkins University Press, 1976); J. Derrida, *Writing and Difference*, trans. A. Blass, (Chicago: University of Chicago Press, 1978); N. Frye, *Anatomy of Criticism* (Princeton: Princeton University Press, 1957); G.H. Hartman, *The Fate of Reading* (Chicago: University of Chicago Press, 1975); E.D. Hirsch, Jr., *Validity in Interpretation* (New Haven: Yale University Press, 1967); F. Jameson, *The Political Unconscious* (Ithaca: Cornell University Press, 1981); and E. Said, *Beginnings* (New York: Basic Books, 1975).

35. In addition to cited works in note 29, see P.N. Campbell, 'Poetic-Rhetorical, philosophical, and scientific discourse', *Philosophy and Rhetoric* 6 (1973) pp. 1-29; J. Benjamin, 'On symbolical hierarchies' *Philosophy and Rhetoric* 8 (1975) pp. 165-71; R.M. Weaver, *The Ethics of Rhetoric* (Chicago: Regnery, 1953). On the traditional contrast between rhetoric and either logic or philosophy, see J.E. Seigel, *Rhetoric and Philosophy in Renaissance Humanism* (Princeton: Princeton University Press, 1968); A.W. Levi, *Humanism and Politics* (Bloomington: Indiana University Press, 1969); N.S. Struever, *The Language of History in the Renaissance* (Princeton: Princeton University Press, 1974); L.G. Janik, 'Lorenzo Valla: the primacy of rhetoric and the demoralization of history' *History and Theory* 12 (1973) pp. 389-404; J. Stephens, 'Rhetorical problems in renaissance science' *Philosophy and Rhetoric* 8 (1975) pp. 213-29; L.J. Johnson, 'The "linguistic imperialism" of Lorenzo Valla and the renaissance humanists' *Interpretation* 7 (1978) pp. 29-49; R. Weiss, 'The humanist rediscovery of rhetoric as philosophy: Giovanni Viovano Pontano's Aegidius', trans. Y. Mundy, *Philosophy and Rhetoric* 13 (1980) pp. 25-42; E. Grassi, 'Can rhetoric provide a new basis for philosophizing? The humanist tradition, Parts I and II' *Philosophy and Rhetoric* 11 (1978) pp. 1-18; E. Grassi, 'Italian humanism and Heidegger's thesis of the end of philosophy', trans. J.M. Krois *Philosophy and Rhetoric* 13 (1980) pp. 79-98.

36. Kaplan, A., *The Conduct of Inquiry: Methodology of Behavioural Science* (San Francisco: Chandler, 1964).

37. See B.A. Most, 'Getting started on political research', paper for the Annual Meeting of the Midwest Political Association (Chicago, 1986).

38. See S.C. Pepper, *World Hypotheses* (Berkeley: University of California Press, 1942); K. Burke, 'Four master tropes', in K. Burke (1945) pp. 503-17; see note 20; A. White (1973); see note 29; W.J.T. Mitchell (ed.), 'Metaphor' *Critical Inquiry* 5 (1978) pp. 3-200; R. Cohen (ed.), 'Narrative analysis and interpretation' *New Literary History* 13 (1982) pp. 179-339; Nelson (1977); see note 5; J.S. Nelson [1975] pp. 74-91; see note 5; J.S. Nelson (1980) pp. 80-101; see note 5.

39. See W.T. Bluhm, *et al.* (1985) pp. 247-59; see note 20; J.S. Nelson (1985) pp. 433-4; see note 19.

40. See J.B. White, *The Legal Imagination* (Chicago: University of Chicago Press, 1973); J.B. White, *When Words Lose Their Meaning* (Chicago: University of Chicago Press, 1984); J.B. White, *Heracles' Bow* (Madison: University of Wisconsin Press, 1985).

41. See R. von Hallberg (ed.), 'Canons' *Critical Inquiry* 10 (1983) pp. iii-223; W.J.T. Mitchell (ed.), 'More on canons' *Critical Inquiry* 10 (1984) pp. 462-542.

42. See R. Cohen (ed.), 'On conventions: I' *New Literary History* 13 (1981) pp. 1-177.

43. See R. Cohen (ed.), 'On conventions: II' *New Literary History* 14 (1983) pp. 225-407.

44. See J.G. Gunnell, *Political Theory* (Lanham: University Press of America, 1979).

45. See J.S. Nelson (1977); see note 4.

46. See G. Tinder, *Tolerance* (Amherst: University of Massachusetts Press, 1975); J.L. Sullivan, J. Piereson, and G.E. Marcus, 'An alternative conceptualization of political tolerance: illusory increases 1950s-1970s' *American Political Science Review* 73 (1979) pp. 781-94.

47. See D.D. Nimmo and K.R. Sanders (eds), *Handbook of Political Communication* (Beverly Hills: Sage, 1981); and J.S. Nelson (1983) pp. 413-78; see note 4.

PART IV

Disciplines, Territorial Boundaries
and Rhetorics of Interdisciplinarity

We have placed three papers in the final part of this collection and have assembled them under the rubric of 'interdisciplinarity' because they address substantive cross-disciplinary issues as such, rather than the rhetorical analysis of single disciplines (however comprehensively conceived).

To begin with, David Cooper tackles the thorny relationship between philosophy and the post-structuralist deconstructive approach to the study of texts. This is an examination of a classic instance of the apparent transgression of disciplinary boundaries and the attempted absorption (or 'assimilation') of one disciplinary identity by another. Cooper proposes, and then attacks, an 'assimilationist thesis' which, under the inspiration of the deconstructive impulse, asserts the primacy of rhetoric and literature over philosophy. This is, of course, no entirely new phenomenon. As Cooper shows, Paul Valery's claim that 'philosophy is reduced to a rhetoric or poetics' is the countervailing proposal to those philosophers who, from Plato onwards, have objected to the intrusion of the literary and the rhetorical into philosophy. Having characterised the four main features of the assimilationist thesis, Cooper then asserts provocatively that 'Philosophy differs from literature only in the self-deception of its [literature's] practitioners' but that, in the final account, the affinities of philosophy do not imply or dictate its assimilation. The reader is perhaps tempted to ask if Cooper is taking seriously enough the challenge to philosophy from deconstruction. At root this challenge consists in making the move from the analysis of the form and content of texts to the consideration of the constitution of *textuality* itself. It is at this juncture that the affinity with (and ready acceptance of) rhetorical modes of thinking in postmodernity become apparent. Rhetorical analysis involves the diachronic inspection of all aspects of an act of persuasive communication, including elements of orality and the body, besides linguistic and literary factors, without the producer (the philosopher) or the product (her philosophy) being privileged.

The questions raised by the issue of gender run across the whole gamut of the sciences. They begin, as Hilary Rose recounts at the outset, with the male pronoun, the 'he' that influences through the rhetoric constitutive of influential discourse. Rose challenges the false collectivity of the involuntary inclusion of elided gender and the depersonalisation of the academic paper. This is the prelude to an examination of the feminine gender-casting of nature as the subject Other destined for violation. The battle ground of biology proves a rich source for examples of the rhetoric of sexist gender skew. On a more comprehensive level, Rose argues that the androcentric social study of science exposes the exclusion processes directed against scientific heterodoxy; but it does not, Rose claims, point up the contrast between the masculinist's dichotomy of the 'Either/Or' and the feminist's ability to work with 'Both/And'. Likewise the use of metaphors requires careful feminist re-reading in order to deconstruct the masculine appropriation and projection of the language of war and the market. Utopian options and the primacy of the body and experience can be regarded as central in the establishment of what we, as editors, designate a 'New Woman' Rhetoric of Inquiry that is both situated and political.

Richard Roberts provides a preliminary exploration of capitalism in terms of the portentous rhetoric of the 'enterprise culture' that has been central to the success of successive Conservative administrations in Britain during the period 1979-90. The power, universality and consequences of capitalism imply a global perspective which runs across the human sciences as a whole and whilst rhetorical analysis has a part to play in the investigation of this phenomenon, what is ultimately required is a socio-rhetorical methodology that combines discourse analysis with social theory. Rhetorical analysis is, however, indispensable, for it helps towards the provision of a post-Marxist (but non-exclusive) model for the interpretation of enforced political and social change in the era in which so-called Thatcherism held sway (1979-90). 'Capitalism', like 'feminism' denotes a complex and variegated construal and construction of reality that trancends the capacities of any one discipline to represent it. Faced with this incommensurability, many accounts of capitalism, and in particular the genre examined at length in this chapter, resort to the extended use of metonymy and metaphor, modes of indirectness that raise questions of interdisciplinarity in an acute way.

The final chapter of this section confronts directly the relationship between knowledge and academic disciplines. In this chapter, James Good exploits the dual heritage of social psychology to examine the politics of its disciplinary representation. Beginning from a consideration of some of the essential features of disciplines as such, he notes how two separate, but inextricably linked traditions of social psychology developed, each bearing some of the distinctive characteristics of its parent discipline, sociology or psychology. Good draws upon a wide variety of sources – introductory textbooks, disciplinary histories, handbooks and so on – to show how the two 'social psychologies' are rhetorically constituted. The long-standing quest for the development of an interdisciplinary social psychology is also examined rhetorically. Good draws attention to the tensions between social psychology's disciplinary and interdisciplinary rhetorics in terms of the disciplinary interests and anxieties of practitioners. The chapter ends with a rejection of the notion of an interdisciplinary social psychology and Good urges instead recourse to Serge Moscovici's proposal of 'flexible unions' in and between the human sciences.

10

Rhetoric, Literature and Philosophy

David E. Cooper (University of Durham)

This paper examines, mainly by way of diagnosis, a certain thesis about the relation-ship between philosophy, literature, and rhetoric. I label it 'the assimilation thesis', and refer to those who embrace it as 'assimilationists'. Let me begin by quoting three passages. Jacques Derrida writes:

> Philosophy is written.... A task is then prescribed: to study the philosophical text in its formal structure, in its rhetorical organization...its textual types...its *mises en scène*.... The task is to consider philosophy...as a 'particular literary genre', drawing on...a set of tropic resources older than philosophy itself.[1]

Paul de Man writes:

> The critical deconstruction that leads to the discovery of the literary, rhetorical nature of the philosophical claim to truth...cannot be refuted: literature turns out to be the main topic of philosophy and the model for the kind of truth to which it aspires.[2]

Finally, Jürgen Habermas summarises, without endorsing, the thesis as follows:

> Far from there being a genre distinction between philosophy and literature, philosophical texts can be rendered accessible in their essential contents by literary criticism.... The primacy of rhetoric over logic means the overall responsibility of rhetoric for the general qualities of an all-embracing context of texts, within which all genre distinctions are ultimately dissolved.[3]

Citation of these passages is my own rhetorical device for persuading you that there is indeed such an animal as the assimilation thesis, alive and kicking at the Sorbonne and Yale, and embraced or challenged by some of the most influential intellectuals of our times. From these passages, it emerges that the thesis comprises three elements. First, philosophy is to be assimilated to literature: and the study of philosophical writing to the examination of texts by literary critics. Second, this assimilation is not reciprocal, for while the concept of literature may require some adjustment, the radical adjustment is to our conception of philosophy. As de Man puts it, 'philosophy turns out to be an endless reflection on its own destruction at the hands of literature'.[4] Third, the main reason for the assimilation is that philosophy is imbued with what is already recognised as the distinctive feature of literature – rhetoricity. 'I would not hesitate', says de Man, 'to equate the rhetorical, figurative potentiality of language with literature itself.[5]

The assimilation thesis is not especially recent. Indeed it, or something similar, has been a staple in French intellectual circles for a good century. Paul Valéry, for example, held that 'philosophy as defined by its product, which is *in writing*, is...a branch of literature...we are forced to assign it a place not far from poetry'; or, more bluntly, 'philosophy is reduced to a rhetoric or poetics'.[6] What is very recent is the popularity and, in some places, the entrenchment of this thesis. Some of the reasons for this are doubtless ones of fashion, while others may reflect institutional rivalries within academia. Someone has described the thesis as the revenge taken by literary criticism for generations of subjection beneath the Queen of the Sciences. More interesting is the suggestion that deconstructors of metaphysical tradition, like Derrida, *need* the assimilation thesis in order to escape from the self-reflexive paradox which apparently faces those who wish to do away with metaphysics while still employing the traditional vocabulary and methods of argumentation. Habermas suggests that for Derrida this paradox disappears, since 'the deconstructive enterprise cannot be pinned down to the discursive obligations of philosophy'. If philosophy is assimilated to literature, if 'logic loses its conventional primacy over rhetoric', then the 'consistency requirements' which make paradoxes something to avoid 'lose their authority' and get 'subordinated to other demands – of an aesthetic nature, for example'.[7] It will then be no more appropriate to criticise Derrida for using the tools of philosophical tradition in order to dismantle it, than to complain at Cervantes for exploiting an earlier genre of the novel in the process of mocking it and replacing it by a very different genre.

Whatever the explanation for its popularity in some circles, the assimilation thesis has won predictably little favour among professional philosophers: though hostility has mainly taken the form of studied silence rather than published criticism. Derrida *et al.* are snubbed rather than smacked. Here one should recall the very long tradition, from Plato through Hobbes and Kant to Iris Murdoch, which complains at the intrusion into philosophy of the literary and rhetorical. Plato, indeed, complained at the unfortunate necessity for philosophy to be *written* at all. Writing is a *pharmakon*, in the dual sense of a remedy (for forgetfulness) and a poison (since the writer, unlike the speaker, is not around to cure the misunderstandings engendered by his words).

Derrida offers a tendentious explanation of this suspicion of writing and the literary. It manifests, he thinks, a 'phonocentric' prejudice which is an important ingredient in 'the metaphysics of *presence*' that has dominated Western thought. This metaphysics is the belief that there are certain items – Plato's forms, Descartes' clear and distinct ideas, Russell's sense-data, Husserl's essences, or whatever – which are directly and transparently open to, present to, consciousness or intuition.

194

This belief, argues Derrida, favours the spoken word, since the speaker, especially during inner monologue, can enjoy the sense, or illusion, of being in unmediated contact with items 'present' to his thought. The spoken word seems too ephemeral or gossamer-like to be a barrier between consciousness and reality. The written word, on the other hand, is too obviously an artifice, too grossly material, and too clearly dependent for its sense of belonging to a network of other signs, to be thought of as the mind's surrogate for something 'present' to it. Writing is a barrier between the philosopher and the 'presence' she would like to convey. As Richard Rorty puts it, 'writing is an unfortunate necessity; what is really wanted is to show...to make one's interlocutor stand and gaze before the world'.[8]

Perhaps there is something to this, but less tendentious explanations are available. Iris Murdoch refers to 'an ideal philosophical style which has a special unambiguous plainness...an austere unselfish candid style'. She continues:

> A philosopher must...avoid rhetoric and decoration...when [he] is as it were at the front line in relation to his problems I think he speaks with a certain cold clear recognizable voice.[9]

This reiterates, in part, the complaint of Hobbes and Locke that rhetoric, especially metaphor, gets in the way of clear, unambiguous thought. But it also recalls Kant's moral objection to rhetoric. Its persuasive devices secure people's verdicts before 'they have weighed the matter, and [so] rob the verdict of its freedom'. Rhetoric does not, therefore, do what philosophy ought: respect people's rational autonomy.[10]

Even when philosophers have been more willing than Kant to compare their writing with literary genres, the analogies have been with those where rhetoric should be kept at a minimum. Collingwood, for instance, says that the best philosophical writing has the form of the 'confession, a search by the mind for its own failings and an attempt to remedy them by recognizing them'. But, precisely for that reason, the 'style must be...plain and modest'; for this is the 'style proper to confession'.[11]

Assimilationists are not, of course, *recommending* that philosophers do what the ones just cited complain of – write in a florid, figurative manner, say. They are making the more alarming point that it is impossible for philosophical writing to free itself from rhetoric: that even books with the austere, unambiguous plainness admired by Murdoch are, when the surface is scratched, as rhetoric-ridden as those which wear their literary devices on the sleeve. The claim is not that philosophers should *try* to emulate those writings which everyone recognises as both literary and philosophical – Kierkegaard's 'aesthetic' works, say – but that they cannot avoid emulating them in some way or another. Derrida would no doubt enjoy pointing out, if only as a debating point, that the philosophers whose hostility towards the literary I have mentioned include Plato, the author of philosophical dramas; Hobbes, whose system revolves around the two metaphors of men as machines and the state of nature; and Iris Murdoch, the outstanding philosopher/novelist of our day.

When the assimilation thesis is presented in that stark form, can it be taken seriously? How could it be argued that *all* philosophical writing is as rhetorical as, say, Kierkegaard's *Either/Or*, with its pseudonymous authors, its cast of characters ('the seducer' etc.), its parables, ironies and floridity? Whether or not it can be taken seriously in the end, a rather obvious way of trying to dismiss the thesis turns out to be *too* quick. The obvious thought is this: *either* the assimilationist is using terms like 'literature' and 'rhetoric' in familiar ways, in which case his thesis is absurd; *or* he is simply redefining the terms in arbitrary fashion, in which case the thesis may be true, but is no longer the interesting one it sounded. The thesis is caught in the analytic philosopher's favourite fork: exciting but false, or true but trivial.

If the terms are being used ordinarily, then this must be compatible with such practices as dividing the books in one's library into separate shelves marked 'Philosophy' and 'Literature'. Admittedly I may hesitate where to place *Either/Or* or Sartre's *Nausea*, and may start a new shelf, 'Philosophical Fiction': but I shall have no hesitation when placing Kant's three *Critiques* or the collected poems of Wordsworth. Now what possible argument could show that my placing of them is without any grounds? Only, it seems, an arbitrary redefinition of the labels. And when we turn to Paul de Man's claims, this is exactly what we find. Having defined 'literature' as rhetoric, he then defines 'rhetoric' as any 'text...that allows for two incompatible mutually self-destructive points of view'. Since, in his opinion, philosophical texts suffer this same fate, they too are necessarily 'literary'.[12] Now hard-pressed students both of literature and of philosophy, especially those prescribed *Finnegan's Wake* or *The Phenomenology of Spirit*, may well conclude that the texts in their chosen discipline allow for two, or indeed twenty, incompatible points of view. But this would be a very poor reason for assimilating the texts or the disciplines: for the definitions of 'literary' and 'rhetorical' are little better than random.

Not all assimilationists, however, are as cavalier as de Man, and they might reasonably challenge the crude dichotomy on which the objection under discussion relies: 'literary' is *either* being used ordinarily *or* being arbitrarily redefined. The less extravagant assimilationist argues as follows: the 'ordinary' understanding of 'literary' is elastic, but to the extent that the word conjures up images of texts dominated by, inter alia, narrative structure, fictional episodes, intentional deployment of tropes, emotional expression, and attention to rhythm and prosody, then we assimilationists do not take the term in the ordinary way, nor claim that, when so taken, philosophy reduces to literature. But this traditional understanding has always been too loose for the purposes of literary criticism, and has become increasingly unsuitable in a century which has witnessed the development of genres that fit the old images badly: plotless novels, non-fictional narratives like *In Cold Blood*, introspective travel books by André Gide, and so on. From Schlegel onwards, literary critics have been concerned to dig beneath the relatively superficial features associated with 'literary' in the common imagination, and to uncover deeper features which explain why we group so many disparate and emerging genres under the heading of 'Literature'. The possibility then arises that writing not usually placed under that heading, including philosophy, turns out to share these deeper features and thereby deserve assimilation towards the literary paradigm.

Say, if you will, that 'literary' is being redefined, but it is not a *mere* or *arbitrary* redefinition, since it is motivated by a discovery of features underlying what is commonly recognised as literature. Say, too, that the distinction between the literary and the non-literary is being 'deconstructed': but deconstruction is not dissolution. Familar distinctions are not denied; people have not been *mistaken* in placing Kant and Wordsworth, Aristotle and Proust, on different shelves. Rather, these distinctions are revealed as *relatively* superficial, and as obtaining *within* a widened, but not arbitrary, category of the literary. The old polarity of the literary and non-literary is, as Jonathan Culler puts it, reinscribed 'within a general literarity or textuality', which then 'encourage[s] projects, such as the literary reading of philosophical texts'.[13]

If the assimilationist succeeds in discovering underlying dimensions of the literary which then turn out to characterise philosophical writing as well, it will be unimportant, in my view, whether we mark such a discovery by dramatic slogans like 'Philosophy is a literary genre' or 'Philosophy is reduced to poetry'. The important thing will be to appreciate the reasons which have inspired people, French people anyway, to make such proclamations. Derrida, it has been said, 'does not belong to those philosophers who like to argue':[14] and this could have been said of most assimilationists. What follows, therefore, is more a reconstruction than a report of their case. This case, put schematically, is that the features which identify works as literary are rhetorical ones, and that philosophical writing turns out to be imbued with those features too. The only difference is that, in philosophy, the features are less apparent and are standardly overlooked by its practitioners. The assimilationist, then, must do three things: articulate the rhetorical features in question; establish that these, or modulations of them, are distinctive of literature; and show that they also penetrate philosophy.

The assimilationist has, I think, four rhetorical features in mind: (i) the deployment of tropes, like metaphor and metonymy; (ii) the deployment of persuasive techniques other than 'straight' logical argument; (iii) unity of style and content, and what I shall call (iv) the deferral of reference. The first two require little comment. Aristotle defined rhetoric as 'the faculty of observing...the available means of persuasion' in areas where beliefs and decisions are not to be 'dictated by necessity'.[15] The importance he attached to metaphor etc. as a persuasive technique made it unsurprising that later rhetoricians built the study of tropes into the definition of their subject.[16] The importance of unity of style and content for rhetoricians is not merely or mainly the matter of speakers tailoring their style to the content of their speech – sombre for funeral orations, flirtatious for romantic advances. The point, rather, is that style may be less a *means* for expressing an already formulated content than a partial *determinant* of that content. As one writer puts it:

> ...our ends are themselves inextricably situated in a rhetorical medium, and are constituively shaped by that medium...discernment of what I want is inseparable from the words and manner of expression in which I express what I want.[17]

Thus the perfervid tones and gestures indulged in by members of a religious sect may serve to shape, as well as to reflect, their intolerant beliefs and aims.

By 'deferral of reference' I mean the strategy whereby an author's or speaker's reference to the real world is indirect, because refracted through an imaginary, or imaginatively presented one, which he sets up: as when Orwell writes of the Soviet Union through recounting the story of a farm. This way of talking of the actual world, not by directly describing it, but through the construction or creation of a domain from which inferences to the former might be made, is given much attention by recent rhetoricians. One of the most influential writes: 'Rhetorical discourse...is constrained by and refers to the order and relation of events in the world, but it also constructs a certain order and relation of elements within its own pattern of utterance.'[18] Poetry might perhaps be defined as that limiting case of rhetorical discourse where the author creates a domain for its own sake, or where the connection to reality is so radically refracted for talk of even *indirect* reference to be misleading. A.E. Housman's *Wenlock Edge*, 'yonder heaving hill' at which the Roman stared, is hardly the one which we might climb or picnic upon.

The more a text exhibits the four rhetorical features, so the assimilationist continues, the more it deserves to be called literary. The idea that figurative language is a mark of the literary is hardly novel; nor is the idea that a literary text, as against say a chemistry textbook, typically influences its readers' attitudes, not by straight assertion and transparent argument, but through such 'persuasive' devices as pathos, allegory, and emotive vocabulary. Nor is the idea that literature is marked by a peculiar unity of style and content startling. The Monty Python 'Proust Sketch', in which competitors have to summarise *À la Recherche du Temps Perdu* in ten seconds, would have been less effective if the competitors were summarising Newton's *Principia*. For while that, too, would have been impossible, there would not have been the same absurdity of trying to abstract a content from a book whose prose and very length are vehicles of the langour and decay it describes. The idea that deferral of reference should be a mark of the literary is, perhaps, a new one: especially when, as in the work of Richard Ohmann, it appeals to modern speech-act theory. His claim is that 'the quasi-speech acts of literature are not carrying on the world's business – describing, urging, contracting etc.', since the normal forces of words are 'bracketed' in the literary work. Instead, literature exercises a 'world-generating' capacity. 'A literary work creates a world', and can therefore describe or refer to the actual world only indirectly.[19] Such an approach goes smoothly, no doubt, with that cliché of modern literary criticism: meaning in a literary work is intratextual. The words in a poem, say, are to be understood not in terms of their reference to objects in the world, but through their interaction with other words in the text.

These claims about the distinctive marks of literature raise many questions. What, one wonders, has happened to the consideration of a text's *quality*? A football report in a tabloid newspaper will be as full of metaphor, 'persuasive' devices, and sheer fiction as anything by Shakespeare or Baudelaire – but is it literary? One wonders, too, if crucial terms are not badly stretched in the attempt to make them applicable to all literature. It is not very exciting to be told, as by Roland Barthes, that irony is the 'essence of literature', when irony is then defined as that feature of any text which makes its interpretation liable to some uncertainty. But I will waive such worries so as to get on to the third and most controversial stage of the assimila-tionist's argument: the purported discovery that philosophy is pervaded by the same four rhetorical features which distinguish texts as literary. Let me, somewhat im-pressionistically, illustrate the ensuing four components of this final stage. First, Derrida borrows the title of his essay on metaphor, 'La mythologie blanche', from Anatole France, who wrote that metaphysicians are 'sad poets, they take the colour out of ancient fables, and are mere assemblers of those fables. They create a white [colourless] mythology'. All the abstract ideas of 'schemas' of philosophers remain fraught with the 'images' from which they derive, and are therefore metaphorical. The idea of the soul or spirit, for example, is still governed by the image of the breath which animates the body.[20]

Second, Richard Rorty has the following to say on logic and persuasion in philosophy: 'The metaphysician thinks that there is an overriding intellectual duty to present arguments'. But the 'ironist' (like Rorty himself) recognises that 'logical arguments...are...in the end not much more than ways of getting people to change their practices'. The ironist will prefer honest 'redescription...in partially neologis-tic jargon, in the hope of inciting people to adopt and extend that jargon'.[21]

Third, Martha Nussbaum challenges Iris Murdoch's demand for a neutral, 'can-did' style of philosophical writing as follows: 'We can inquire either in the hard "philosophical" style or in a mode that lies closer to poetry and makes it appeal to more than one "part" of the person.... But no way is neutral, and it looks as if any choice will prejudice the inquiry in its own favour'. Plato was right, she suggests, to hold that a 'plain, hard' style of discussing ethics is prejudiced in favour of 'a conception of rational inquiry in which emotions and imagination play, at best, a decorative and subsidiary role'.[22]

Fourth, here is a much-quoted passage of Derrida's:

> ...reading...cannot legitimately transgress the text towards something other than it, towards the referent (a reality that is metaphysical...etc.) or towards a signifier outside...of language...of writing in general.... There is nothing outside of the text.[23]

Reference, in philosophy is permanently 'deferred', for the only 'world' it can be about is the one created or generated by a text. Philosophy, in the sense of 'poetry' stipulated earlier, is poetic. Rorty, I think, is right to hold that Derrida is not assert-ing a form of Idealism, but 'debunking' all metaphysical attempts to depict Reality and The World.

Piecing together the claims just cited, the following position emerges. Philosophy differs from literature only in the self-deception of its practitioners. The philosopher takes himself or herself to be offering, on the basis of logical argument, a literal and objective description of reality, and in a neutral style suited to that objective endeav-our. In fact, however, he is doing just what the author of a paradigmatically rhetorical, literary text is doing: persuading us, through the deployment of metaphor and a loaded style, to enter with him into a 'creation', a 'world' generated by his text. There have been many premature obituaries of philosophy: but with the recog-nition by Rorty's 'ironist', Heidegger's 'thinker/poet', and Derrida's 'deconstructor' that philosophical discourse is only self-deceived literature, that obituary is now overdue.

I came neither to praise nor to bury the assimilationist but, primarily, to diagnose and reconstruct his or her position. I do, however, want to indicate some considerations crucial to any appraisal of this thesis.

The first, obvious as it is important, is that the thesis rests on *philosophically* contentious views about the enterprise of philosophy. One cannot establish that philosophy is a literary genre merely by perusing its texts with the literary critic's eye, for one requires as well the judgements that philosophers *cannot* be describing Reality, *cannot* be presenting logically compelling arguments etc. And these judgements about what *cannot* be done are themselves philosophical ones. Now this may – I am not sure – place the assimilationist in a paradoxical position: for it is through philosophical argument that he attempts to subordinate philosophy to literary criticism, logic to rhetoric. Philosophy, it seems, must have the last laugh. Rorty, at any rate, appreciates the difficulty: and he admires Derrida for the latter's ability, shared perhaps with Zen masters, to resist any temptation to argue at all, relying instead on word-play, mockery and the poet's bag of tricks.

The second consideration is that the assimilationist's pivotal claim about philosophy's rhetorical character is the one about its non-referential nature. For unless he denies that philosophers can be referring to and portraying Reality, it is unclear how he can accuse their language of being irredeemably figurative, their style of being necessarily prejudiced, and their techniques of being only persuasive rather than logically compelling. Granted, for example, that the metaphysician's terms of art – 'substance', 'spirit', 'essence' etc. – originated through metaphorical derivation from familiar expressions, why deny that they have come to possess literal senses in their own right unless one thinks they cannot have the referential roles metaphysicians imagine? The debate must then, as Habermas sees, centre on the large issue of whether metaphysics is only a poetic exercise in 'world-creation', or whether it can after all provide an account of *the* world. I close with two remarks on the debate: one defending the assimilationist against a predictable objection; the other critical of the assimilationist's position.

Habermas objects to the assimilationist that philosophy surely belongs, alongside science, law economics etc., among what he calls the 'problem-solving' activities of men, and not among the 'world-disclosive' activities like poetry. 'Problem-solving' activities are not without their rhetorical elements, but these, he says, are 'tamed, as it were, and enlisted for the special purposes of problem-solving'.[24] Now it is certainly the case that most philosophers – we minnows – are busy for the most part tackling this problem, ironing out the difficulties, cast up by the great schemes propounded by men of genius – Descartes' dualistic metaphysics, Hegel's Idealism, Wittgenstein's Logical Atomism, and so on. What the assimilationist will insist, appealing to something akin to Kuhn's distinction between 'normal' and 'revolutionary' science, is that these great schemes cannot themselves be regarded as solutions to problems. They are inventions, creations, gigantic figures: so that we minnows are not, after all, solving problems about the nature of Reality, but problems of consistency and detail *within* world-creations. The assimilationist is therefore able to accommodate Habermas' distinction, but within a picture of philosophy as *essentially* disclosive and inventive, not descriptive and problem-solving. After all, she will say, many lesser composers are busy solving the problems raised by the great innovators: that hardly demonstrates that music is essentially a problem-solving enterprise. Indeed, an obsession with problem-solving is a sign of musical stagnation.

However – and this my second and critical point – there is something terribly crude in the dichotomy of 'world-creation' vs. 'world description', to which the assimilationist, as much as Habermas, is appealing. Are we obliged to assign philosophy, and much else besides, to just one or other of these categories? It is easy enough, perhaps, to decide into which pigeon-hole to put a Tolkien fantasy, a poem by Rimbaud, a chemistry textbook, or a report on yesterday in parliament. But what about Freud's account of the unconscious or a Chomskyan generative grammar? Are these just imaginative creations, figures for the depiction of mental processes, or just 'plain, hard' descriptions of those processes? Neither, surely. To the extent that such accounts regiment phenomena and provide models that are not forced on us by bare observation of behaviour or by introspection, they have affinities with the imaginative inventions of the poets. To the extent that they are responsive to bare observation and are tailored to solve puzzles and anomalies in earlier accounts, they have affinities with empirical, 'normal' science. If we are unhappy about slotting these theories into the pigeon-holes provided, should we be any happier about slotting the great philosophical systems into them?

There is irony in this criticism, since it in effect accuses those who parade their deconstructionist credentials of reliance on a rigid dichotomy. But if, stung by the criticism, they were to proceed too far in the direction of mellowing the distinction, their assimilation of philosophy to literature would look much less dramatic and interesting. The drama of their thesis requires, I think, a somewhat Manichean division into two kinds of intellectual enterprise: for what the thesis claims is that philosophy, having been for too long assigned to one kind, should be assigned to the other. Perhaps we no longer believe that philosophy is *sui generis*, that its propositions and arguments are unlike any others. But the sensible response need not be that philosophy is therefore 'really' literature – or 'really' science, linguistics, or whatever. Perhaps it is simply, and boringly, that philosophy has its affinities, its points of contact, with all of these.

Notes

1. Derrida, Jacques, 'Qual quelle: Valery's Sources', in *Margins of Philosophy*, trans. A. Bass (Chicago: University of Chicago Press, 1982) p. 293.

2. de Man, Paul, *Allegories of Reading: Figural Language in Rousseau, Nietzsche, Rilke and Proust* (New Haven: Yale University Press, 1979) p. 115.

3. Habermas, Jürgen, *The Philosophical Discourse of Modernity*, trans. F. Lawrence (Cambridge: Polity Press, 1987) pp. 190-1.

4. Op. cit., p. 115.

5. Ibid., p. 10.

6. Quoted in Jacques Derrida, 'Qual quelle', op. cit., pp. 293-4.

7. Op. cit., pp. 188-9.

8. Rorty, Richard, 'Philosophy as a kind of writing: An essay on Derrida', in *Consequences of Pragmatism, Essays 1972-80* (Brighton: Harvester Press, 1982) p. 94. Derrida's account of 'phonocentrism' and 'presence' is spelled out in his *Of Grammatology* (New York: Johns Hopkins University Press, 1976).

9. Murdoch, Iris, 'Philosophy and literature', in B. Magee (ed.), *Men of Ideas: Some Creators of Contemporary Philosophy* (Oxford: Oxford University Press, 1982) p. 265.

10. Kant, I., *Critique of Judgement*, trans. N.K. Smith (New York: St Martin's Press, 1963) p. 53.

11. Collingwood, *Philosophical Method* (Oxford: Oxford University Press, 1933) pp. 210-11.

12. de Man, Paul, *Allegories of Reading*, op. cit., p. 131. For an effective critique of de Man's fast and loose way with terms like 'rhetoric', 'trope', and 'metaphor', see Brian Vickers, *In Defence of Rhetoric* (Oxford: Oxford University Press, 1988). The relevant concluding chapter is reprinted in *Rhetorica* IV, 1 (1988).

13. Culler, Jonathan, *On Deconstruction: Theory and Criticism after Structuralism* (London: Routledge and Kegan Paul, 1983) pp. 184-5.

14. Habermas, Jürgen, op. cit., p. 193.

15. Aristotle, *Rhetoric*, trans. W.R. Roberts (Oxford: Oxford University Press, 1924) pp. 1355b 25-7 and 1357a 23-7.

16. What *is* surprising, and regrettable, is the way in which for eighteenth- and nineteenth-century rhetoricians like Dumarsais and Fontanier, rhetoric becomes virtually confined to the study of tropes. See Brian Vickers, *In Defence of Rhetoric* (Oxford: Oxford University Press, 1988).

17. Beiner, R., *Political Judgment* (London: Methuen, 1983) p. 95.

18. Michael Leff, quoted in Joseph W. Wenzel, 'The rhetorical view of argumentation: Exploring a paradigm' *Argumentation* I (1987) p. 76.

19. Ohmann, Richard, 'Speech-acts and the definition of Literature' *Philosophy and Rhetoric* 4 (1971) pp. 14ff.

20. France, Anatole, 'La Mythologie blanche', in *Marges de la Philosophie* (Paris: Minuit, 1972) p. 254.

21. Rorty, Richard, *Contingency, Irony, and Solidarity* (Cambridge: Cambridge University Press, 1989) p. 78.

22. Plato, *The Fragility of Goodness: Luck and Ethics in Greek Tragedy and Philosophy* (Cambridge: Cambridge University Press, 1986) pp. 16-7.

23. Derrida, Jacques, *Of Grammatology*, op cit., p. 158.

24. Habermas, Jürgen, *The Philosophical Discourse of Modernity*, op cit., p. 209. For a criticism of Habermas, see Jonathan Culler, *Framing the Sign: Criticism and its Institutions* (Oxford: Basil Blackwell, 1988) pp. 185-200.

11

Rhetoric, Feminism and Scientific Knowledge
Or From Either/Or To Both/And

Hilary Rose (University of Bradford)

Like others venturing into new intellectual territory I turned to the Oxford English Dictionary to find the official definition of rhetoric. Here was both guidance and exclusion:

> The art of using language to persuade or influence others.... The body of rules to be observed by a speaker or writer that he may express himself with eloquence.

How am I supposed to interpret this matter of the male pronoun – as a quaint historical residue, as absurd as using thee and thou in modern speech, or, as in the formulation much used in academic regulations: 'the use of the male pronoun embraces the female'? That this latter formulation is typically followed by smiles and sniggering on the part of at least some of the men present indicates that it should be unacceptable in an academic or any other context. Is it true that until the early nineteenth century the word 'they' was singular and that only later did 'he' become the universal pronoun. Do we need a ten minute pronoun repeal bill or cultural and social transformation? Suspecting that these are not tidy alternatives, and that this gendered pronoun continues to point unambiguously to those who are historical subjects worth persuading, relegating the others, who are merely objects of history to silence – and thence to nature. A mere pronoun should alert us to the possibility that rhetoric, like other analytical tools, is at best only partially friendly to feminist analysis, and that it always has to be made over to serve 'our' interests.

Gendering in the formation of rhetoric is not a new story. 'Rhetoric', suggested Walter Ong in 1972, '...developed in the past as a major form of ceremonial combat which is found among males.... Rhetoric became particularly attached to Latin which the male psyche appropriated to itself as an extrafamilial language when Latin ceased to be a "mother tongue" (that is was no longer spoken in the home by one's mother)'.[1] Yet if rhetoric is the *'science of persuasion'*[2] then many feminists –

however much women were excluded from rhetoric's origin stories – may well find that we have had a Molièrean relationship to the analysis of persuasion – for we have been doing it all our political lives.

For feminism, it has been precisely because of the domination of science and technology over womens' lives and bodies, accompanied by our exclusion from the production of science, that it has been politically necessary to be interested in the language and practices of science and technology. The renewal of scientific patriarchal rhetoric which seeks to persuade that biology is destiny, has mobilised feminists and their allies to criticise scientific texts in order to expose the poverty of science's ideological claim of gender-neutrality, while advancing androcentric and/or sexist science.[3] At the same time, feminism as a social movement has an understanding that the world is not entirely reducible to texts, even, or maybe especially, to scientific texts.

Thus although academic feminism remains a subordinated (though insubordinate) discourse within the academy, feminists because of their involvement in a powerful social movement and as holders of competing theoretical paradigms, are primarily addressing one another. In this situation, feminism cannot accept Wittgenstein's injunction that 'whereof we cannot speak, thereof we should remain silent', not least because the continuation of silence becomes a means of erasure of half of that claimed 'we'. The task has long been understood within the feminist movement as naming problems which have no name, a process of epistemological and political significance. In consequence, feminism – at least in its non-liberal variants – is not primarily concerned to engage in dialogue with the master world and its problematics. Nor has the movement remained monolithic in its theoretical and political preoccupations: during the 1980s black feminism successfully challenged white feminism. In consequence, that master world has been increasingly understood as white as well as bourgeois and patriarchal. Dialogue between the white master world and its discourses and the subordinated discourses of feminism is not possible, as they are divided, not by misunderstanding but by deep antagonism. This is not to say that this new social movement has only reached into womens' lives and changed our consciousness of who we are and what we might become; it has also unevenly, and with difficulty, reached into the lives and political consciousness of men, both black and white.

Let me make a partial analogy with the sixties, when the voices from the third world spoke with renewed force as historical subjects. Jean Paul Sartre was one of those who recognised the epistemological and political significance of these voices. In responding to *The Wretched of the Earth*, Sartre observed that Frantz Fanon was not speaking 'to us'. The third world, he went on, was speaking 'to itself'. Sartre then went on to advise the white first world to listen if they valued their own survival. The analogy can only be partial, as while Sartre was willing to listen to the black man, there is little evidence that he advised himself to listen to feminism in the same way – despite his longstanding relationship with Simone De Beauvoir. Yet *The Second Sex*, as with the rest of feminist knowledges, speaks first and foremost 'to itself' and not to the 'us' of the dominant gender.

As a feminist more familiar with the social studies of science than rhetoric, I found myself asking questions such as: how do mainstream rhetoricians speak/write without ironising even their own words out of the possibility of making provisional truth claims, instead of engaging methodologically in an endless series of mirrored refractions and reflections? Were they, like the hyper-reflectivists of the social studies of science, engaged – often very entertainingly – in sawing off the branch on which they sat?[4] My impression as I scan the rhetoric literature, is that it has not imploded in the way that the social studies of science has. In the latter's pursuit of new literary forms which can better meet the demands of social constructionism, some analysts have ended up, not merely talking, but co-publishing with themselves.[5] In this situation of imploding papers it is unsurprising that the discourse analysts of the social studies of science are beginning to hope for a beneficial convergence between their field and that of rhetoric.

The rhetoric of science

The rhetorical devices of the natural sciences have been a source of attention by philosophers and sociologists for some time now – and even by some natural scientists themselves. One of the most memorable is surely Peter Medawar's article asking: 'Is the scientific paper a fraud'?[6] In science, the adoption of the passive voice of authority and the exclusion of the 'I' both of subjectivity and of agency is central. Not only does the passive voice make the claim more true, but if the outcome is socially disastrous then the 'I' as the mere producer of scientific knowledge has no personal responsibility. The alchemy of words has made the living, breathing, experimenting, 'I' vanish. Ethics have left: only an aesthetic of science remains. Nor alas is this transmutation limited to natural science: the responsible 'I' disappears within the positive programme whether it is part of the natural or the social. Scientific sexism and racism always claim merely, and often reluctantly, to be speaking the facts. The sociobiologist David Barash washes his hands with: *'Nature is sexist, don't blame her sons'*.[7]

As the poet June Jordan[8] has observed, this depersonalisation of language in its removal of agency damages the possibility of democracy. Currently it extends from beyond the sciences into media punditry, until a discussion of a rising level of unemployment is transmuted into a natural event against which resistance becomes futile. Such a widespread natural determinism, even fatalism, weakens democracy. Not by chance is more money spent on reading the stars than studying them. By contrast with feminism's celebrated power to name, which has empowered women to act collectively, the lack of responsible language fails people in their need to have some control over their own lives. What in conventional analysis is seen as either the particular inability of young black working-class Americans to become literate, or more liberally is understood as the result of a failing school system, Jordan understands as a refusal to learn a language which offers no means of self or collective empowerment.

In similar vein E.O. Wilson opens the last chapter of *Sociobiology: the New Synthesis* with 'Let us now consider man in the free spirit of natural history, as though we were zoologists from another planet completing a catalogue of social species on the earth.' But the price of accepting that invitation to float above all social context, is to share uncritically Wilson's assumption that those zoologists from another planet will view this with exactly the same perspectives as those who presently propose the new synthesis. Fictional universalism guarantees itself, and this is the heart of the objectivity trick.

Nonetheless, whatever the impersonal public voice of science with its refusal of personal and collective responsibility for the products, back at the laboratory the names, and their ordering on the paper, together with matters of priority of publication are frequently matters of fierce property fights.[9] Long before the current talk of intellectual property rights, scientists were accomplished makers and breakers of property rights and rules. Scientific knowledge, despite the privileging words such as 'pure', 'disinterested', 'basic', 'neutral', has long been commodified; it is just that the official language system is catching up.

Origin stories

The power of modern science has lain in the success of its epistemological claim to generate objective – even if provisional – truth, hard facts which will come out the same way regardless of who tells the story. This abstract disembodied knowledge claims the mythic powers of a gaze which 'can represent without being represented'. The only issue for this objectivist science is whether science is 'good' or 'bad'. It is 'bad' science which lets bias in; science carried out properly removes the influence of interest.[10] Yet feminists have increasingly argued that this division serves to mask the mythic objectivity which presides over it, concealing the profoundly sexualised, racialised and class-biased practice of science from its origins in the seventeenth century to today. Indeed the problem is not so much with 'bad' science, where the bias is exposable within the canon of the scientific method, but with 'good' science. Marx's prescient aside, in which he observed that it would be perfectly possible to produce a history of technology which was a history of the means of repressing working-class struggle, would find among feminists a considerable number of takers, although they would radically extend the definition of those who had been repressed.

Here we find ourselves in Alice country where we are invited to believe at least two impossible things before breakfast. Simultaneously there is a widespread scepticism concerning the neutrality of science and technology, and also – above all in introductory textbooks on scientific method – a mythic account of universal and objective knowledge. The myth is powerfully supported by the ideologues of natural science, notably elite scientists and their organisations, and to a lesser extent a number of historians and philosophers of science. For others, science's incorporation into a militaristic and capitalist economy comes as no great surprise, but this chapter focusses on the profoundly gendered and gendering character of scientific knowledge – which has made possible the hurt done by objectivity to 'us'. From the origin stories of Francis Bacon in which he proudly proclaimed the power of the new 'masculine' knowledge, to the current feminist critique of the 'abstract masculinity of contemporary science'[11] developed over the last decade, there are profound and negative continuities. Yet, that it is possible to speak of a shift from proclamation to critique, points to an old *episteme* and even more to an old ideology now under seige. To follow the military metaphor, in some of the more enraged analyses currently made by the besieged, the traitor who let the seige armies into the castle was Thomas Kuhn.[12] Others think that the seige began more than 30 years before, with Hessen and Bukharin, but that their commanding officers shot them in the back,[13] which more than a little delayed the siege process. The abandonment of internalist history in the social study of science would suggest that 1968 was the *annus mirabilis* for a new or renewed critical attack.

In the origin stories of the birth of modern science, the seventeenth century is understood as moving away from a concept of nature which had purposes like human beings, to an insistence on nature as mere passive matter. Science – *scientia* – was the means by which mankind was to know and to master nature. Reconceptualising the world as Gaia, as attributing to her not merely intentionality but a sense of humour, attempts both to subvert such passivity and also to do quite alarming things to those of us who take this all very seriously. In this seventeenth-century story of the transformation from an active to a passive nature, nature itself was metaphorically sexualised, to be made as a female to submit and to yield her innermost secrets to man the knower. Carnal and scientific knowledge were as one. Bacon saw the task of the new masculine philosophy as 'leading you to nature with all her children to bind her to your service and make her your slave'.[14] Yet even while nature and women are thus to be subjugated by men, both were still cast as mysterious, unpredictable and thence dangerous. Nature and women were constituted as the Other. Children, it should not be forgotten, were cast as the even more subordinated Others, veritably the slave's slaves. To investigate this dangerous Other it was important to make a clear separation between the knower and the known, and to prescribe the relation between the two which can lead to knowledge. 'Not only', writes Keller, 'are mind and nature assigned gender but in characterising science and objective thought as masculine, the very activity by which the knower can acquire knowledge is also genderised'.[15]

While Keller emphasises this dichotomous relation through a metaphor of marriage, the nature of this metaphorical marriage is not only one of difference and separation, but violence. Here Bacon speaks of: 'The chaste and lawful marriage between Mind and Nature (that) is consummated through reason rather than feeling, and observation rather than sensory experience'. Brian Easley's[16] reading is less forgiving; he stresses the violent sexuality of masculine philosophy. Carolyne Merchant[17] points in a way that anticipates current research on sex and gender in the organisation, to the patriarchal and hierarchical structure of the Baconian utopia. The refrain that men's utopia is womens' distopia returns. Feminism's insistence on stating and restating the ugly fact that lawful and chaste marriage within the Baconian metaphor included rape (for it was through men's force that nature had to be made to yield her secrets, nature's willingness being a matter of indifference) has been seized upon by some and criticised as overdone. It would be easier to share the criticism that feminism had spoken too long and too loud at this unthinkable elision were it not for the historical fact, that it is only this year (more than three centuries after Bacon's apologia for science) that the willingness or unwillingness of a wife to be 'known' has become as matter of legal concern. The taken for granted right of a husband to rape, that is to have forcible sex with his wife, has been so profoundly naturalised that it is only with immense political effort that this violence has been pulled out of silence and masculinist nonexistence into the public arena. At the very least, this example should indicate caution before it is assumed that the overt violence of the programme of seventeenth century science has been transformed by the mere passage of time into sensitivity to either women or nature. Indeed there is a remarkable fit between the programme of that most abstract (most masculine?) of sciences – physics – and militarism, whether the planned violence of Mutually Assured Destruction or the 'accidental' violence of the power and bomb-material production systems of Sellafield, Three Mile Island and Chernobyl.

Increasingly the scientific revolution has been read as imbued with the metaphors of violent and masculinist sexuality and domination. The key dualism of Man as Mind, Woman as Nature, came into existence, was elaborated within nineteenth-century evolutionary biology and anthropology[18] and was later augmented by the sexist metaphorical transfusion given by sociobiology, a transfusion all too evident in contemporary science. While some feminists have resisted the dualism, insisting on the right of women to study 'masculine' subjects, others have used dualism, and women's closeness to nature, as a political resource. In this way the nineteenth-century feminist, Frances Power Cobbe was a leading protester against the new experimental physiology – the method of cruelty – and against wife battering. Her argument was that, if men generally and scientists in particular were inherently brutal then it was women, closer to nature and inherently kinder, who must modify them. Dualism is by no means played out in contemporary scientific sexism nor within its feminist opposition for dualism is inscribed within sociobiology and serves as an oppositional resource within much of radical feminism. De Beauvoir's pioneering text adheres to such a biological dualism, for she sees women as enslaved by their bodies, held back from creativity by motherhood. Woman's reproductive capacity leaves her closer to nature whereas men are the makers of culture. If objectivity is an achievement of men then subjectivity is constructed as a resource of women. This essentialist strand is a continuing but ambiguous presence in feminist politics; as a defence, a woman's body is a necessary element in feminist opposition to male domination. 'Mutterlichkeit' or 'Motherliness', last spoken of within Nazi discourse and a New Right project within West Germany (CDU) during the 1980s, is contested by the Greens' support for the still ambiguous project of the Mother's Manifesto.[19] These theoretical and political tensions between radical and socialist feminisms are fruitful; for while socialist feminism is rightly opposed to biology as destiny, nonetheless it owes a certain debt to radical feminism's outright refusal to let women's bodies disappear. Of course both, and maybe the entire feminist project, are put into difficulties by a radical deconstructionism which renders the concept of 'woman' problematic, but that is another, although connected, problem.

Except for liberal feminism which wants an equal slice of today's pie, and equal access to the bakery, both radical and socialist feminists together with feminist deconstructionism, view science not only as having a highly sexualised origin story but also a sexualised present. They neither like the pie nor the social organisation of the bakery. Sharon Traweek's anthropological account of a high energy physics laboratory reports on both the persistently sexualised language of scientists when they talk about nature and their peculiarly impersonal language when they talk about one another. She quotes Richard Feynman's 1966 Nobel acceptance lecture in which he talks about an idea,

> as so elegant that I fell deeply in love with it. And like falling in love with a woman it is only possible if you don't know much about her, so that you do not see her faults. The faults will become apparent later, but after the love is strong enough to hold you to her...so what happened to the old theory? Well I would say it's an old lady.... But we can say the best we can for any old women, she has become a very good mother and has given birth to some very good children.[20]

Gendered representations similarly suffuse biology. These have been the subject of scholarly analysis in, for example, Donna Haraway's powerful *Primate Visions*, and the subject of professional fights. During the 1980s, the rise of the feminist movement ensured that biological language in professional journals became a contested zone. After fierce protests, leading ethology journals prohibited the term 'rape' to describe the intercourse of mallard ducks. A critical analysis of the discourse of cell biology illustrates the near Aristotelian language of the 'active sperm wakening the slumbering egg' which has run for almost two centuries, and which begins to be contested by the representation of 'the active egg', to replace the fusion of female-ness and passivity.[21] However even if the fertilisation story can be rewritten, the new genetics and their loose kin, biotechnology are suffused with the language of masculinist power, and, it goes without saying, command immense material resources. The Gender and Biology Group write:

> The master-molecule of DNA has become the unmoved mover of the changing cytoplasm. In this cellular version of the Aristotelian cosmos, the nucleus is sufficient cause (like Aristotle's conception of the unmoved mover), the female substrate is merely the material cause. The nuclear DNA is the essence of domination and control. Macromolecule as machomolecule[22]

Language and above all metaphor frame scientific fact; the struggle is to change the frame. Within the new genetics, the language of the market sets the frame for the mega-dollar Human Genome (HUGO) Programme, with its potential for massively appropriating both procreation and the labour market to technology and its owners. That the programme is headed by Jim Watson whose *obiter dicta*, 'the best home for a feminist is another person's lab' suggests that the burgeoning alliance of a gendered biology with domination and profit could scarcely be more complete.

Silences and the social studies of sciences

If this is the rhetoric of the founding and indeed continuing practice of science, not least of the Royal Society with its motto *Nullius in Verba* (sic), then what of the new and widely regarded as exciting field of the social studies of science (SSS)? Here, there remains a stubborn silence. With certain notable exceptions, mainstream (male stream, to borrow Mary O'Brien's pun)[23] SSS locates science and politics as public knowledge and public politics and continues to relegate gender to the naturalised realm of the private, and thence to silence. Instead, the mainstream social studies of science are locked into a dichotomising debate between realism on the one hand (the claim to rephrase Gertrude Stein 'a gene is a gene is a gene') and on the other an examination of the technical and social processes (above all the process of inscription) through which the 'gene' became an established 'fact'. Indeed, given the history of Lysenkoism, the gene is a singularly good example of the social construction of a scientific 'fact'; for it was attacked as bourgeois idealism with no correspondence in nature, and Soviet geneticists, unless they wished to share Vavilov's fate, had to call themselves radiation biologists.

The stubborn refusal by most SSS to treat seriously the literature produced by the feminist studies of science over the last two decades requires explanation. It is almost embarrassing that it is easier for a feminist contribution to the social studies of science to be reviewed in say *Science*, or even *Nature*, as journals of science, than it is to be reviewed in the journal *The Social Studies of Science* itself. *Science* in particular, with its special place as the journal of the American Association for the Advancement of Science (AAAS), has a 24-year track record of discussing the under-representation of women in science as a social problem. It was as long ago as 1965 that Alice Rossi published her germinal article in *Science*, entitled 'Why So Few?', in which she explored the reasons for the under-representation of women in the sciences. Both the timing of the article and its strategic location are important for an understanding of the debates about gender within science in the subsequent period. It was published in the socially optimistic context of the 1960s, when the domain assumption of the plasticity of individual human beings fused with the corresponding assumption concerning the collective capacity for societal self-reorganisation along more socially just lines. Further, while it would be an error to assume that a feminist utopia has broken out in American scientific institutions, it is true that *Science* has maintained this public voice on the need to make science accessible to women. Thus an editorial by Daniel Koshland discussed 'women's needs for child care, flexible work hours and a change in the attitudes and practices of men both as colleagues and as partners'.[24] In the same year the AAAS was, for the first time, headed by a woman committed to increasing women's representation in science. An editorial such as Koshland's would be quite unthinkable in *Nature*, and it would be hard to envisage a comparably senior elective position occupied in Britain by a woman scientist publicly committed to advancing women scientists.

However, both *Nature* and even more *New Scientist* regularly review feminist

210

work. Of course it is true that a certain ambivalence, not to say double standard, can be discerned in *Nature*, in that an apparent commitment to liberal equal-opportunities reform means that theoretical texts such as Sandra Harding and Jean O'Barr's[25] collection can be trashed by in-house journalists for not being directly oriented towards practical help for women; while the editorials which might (like those of *Science*) address those self-same practical matters, remain unwritten. However the adage that all publicity is good publicity holds, and hostile reviews *can* flag attention to a book that needs to be read. Feminist writing at least gets the oxygen of publicity in the natural science journals – from SSS it receives silences.

Two searches through the SSS literature, carried out by Sara Delamont[26] and Evelyn Fox Keller[27] document the absence of gender. Delamont's self-styled outsider account was published in the journal *Social Studies of Science* and surveyed the reviews and articles published since 1980 in four journals *(British Journal for the History of Science; History of Science; Studies in the History and Philosophy of Science* and *Social Studies of Science)* and came to three conclusions. These were that there was: (i) a failure to draw on the wealth of research on the sociology of occupations; (ii) a lack of attention to the learning of science by novices; and (iii) a failure to examine gender divisions in scientific practice and knowledge, especially the division of labour in science. While Delamont's feminist analysis of the orthodox British publications is on target, she, and also the SSS editors and referees, are unaware that outside the carefully defended journals of orthodoxy there is a very different and richer story told by the heterodoxies of feminism.

In parallel pursuit, Evelyn Fox Keller searched through the journal SSS over a 12-year period – an exercise which yielded a score of two entries, by contrast the US journal ISIS contained some thirty over the same period.

Sexual divisions in democratic sensibilities?

While SSS has a distinctly undemocratic relationship with the heterodoxies of feminism, it has taken a particular interest in what it speaks of as 'heterodox' scientific claims, and is concerned to ensure that orthodox science behaves tolerantly and democratically towards them. Thus there has been a long standing and tolerant interest in the claims of fringe science – from say Velikovsky and Uri Geller to the worm-runners. The argument is that the way science manages these 'outsider' truth claims is, as Harry Collins puts it in his discussion of *L'Affaire Benveniste*, nothing less than 'epistemology in action'.[28] This controversy arose in the wake of the publications in *Nature* by the biologist Jacques Benveniste of results that seemed to support the possibility of homeopathy. The editor, John Maddox, had apparently only agreed to publication on condition that the French laboratory submitted itself to a visit from a 'fraud squad' appointed by Maddox himself. Collins argued that only 'outsiders' to the production of science – such as the *Nature* group – could conceive of scientific experiments as yielding unequivocal results. Neither heterodox nor orthodox science, he argued, can stand up to such an approach. In consequence, Collins reads the story as bad news for the democratic organisation of science.

Instead of the heterodox claim – represented here by the publication of just one article – falling into the vast category of the more or less unread where some 90% of all scientific papers lie, *Nature*'s 'Editorial Leviathan,' feeling threatened by any credence being given to the outsider knowledge of homeopathy, abruptly imposed its orthodoxy. The not dissimilar approach to the administrative suppression of heterodox claims on an earlier occasion (but on the side of scientific fraud and with lethal rather than embarrassing outcomes for the losers) had of course been played been out by the 'Stalinist Leviathan' in the Lysenko affair. However, in that a very considerable section of the reaction to the Benveniste affair (expressed in letters to *Nature* and in editorials within other prestigious scientific journals) criticised *Nature*'s editor as robustly as Collins had, it seems that epistemology in action in the natural sciences is more tolerant of heterodoxy than SSS.

The interest, even sympathy, of SSS seem to be warmest for those who are often very marginal, not least in terms of the social significance of their heterodox claims. It seems that by celebrating the male fringe within natural science, feminism, with its serious political and theoretical concerns, can be marginalised within the mainstream social studies of science to the point of invisibility. SSS's erasure seeks to outdo *Nature*'s fraud squad.

The epistemology of SSS

The androcentricity of orthodox SSS is particularly acute within the sociology and the philosophy of science – in books as well as journals – while history has made a rather better accommodation with the new analytical categories. Nowhere is this more marked than within the masculinist philosophers' debates. Thus in a recent and very elegant collection *Dismantling Truth*[29] which sets out the dichotomy between the realists and the social constructionists, no feminists have been included. The 'Either/Or' choice of masculinist dichotomies is left unquestioned; feminism's ability to work with 'Both/And' positions is safely neglected. Thus in their masculinist epistemology, action and theory mutually reinforce one another. These strongly relativist views were anticipated within the radical science movement[30] (which has to be understood as a radical mens' science movement) a decade before. These views were criticised as exposing the new social movements to the political danger and theoretical absurdity of a hyper-reflexivity that denied the possibility of objective truth while engaging in literary activity which sought to persuade its reader that this account was to be preferred.[31]

Unlike those who see the new grouping of SSS as the inheritors of the radical science movement,[32] I read SSS as a rather professionalised, politically unengaged group. Indeed the politically engaged who work on science and are part of the new social movements are much less close to the profound relativism of the highly professionalised.[33] They offer instead a conception of scientific knowledge in context. But it has been thorough-going relativism which seeks to manufacture scientific facts which is at once revealing and disturbing. It leaves no grounds to distinguish between different stories about nature; thus the transmission mechanisms of AIDS becomes a story among stories – rather than an effective guide to protect health. Yet even this apparently radical historicising of all truth means that the new relativists are sensitive to every nuance of the social production of knowledge – except the profound social cleavages of race and gender. For all its claims to reflexivity, an androcentric and ethnocentric science is considered through a discourse unconscious of its own androcentricity and ethnocentricity.

Both the old sociology of science and the new have for all the latter's radical epistemology shared the scientists' privilege-maintaining definition of themselves as the sole producers of scientific knowledge. When the new SSS invokes the apparently secular metaphor of the 'factory' to frame the analysis of the production of knowledge, the factory is rendered both privileged and sacred, for the metaphor is restricted to the specific sector of the scientific workforce with the right to inscribe their names on the artifacts. All others are erased. The SSS factory has parallels with the Greek polis in which the theory of democracy fails to include either the women or the helots as citizens. By contrast, when feminists use a 'factory' metaphor they include the entire scientific labour force from the cleaners and technicians (typically women and not infrequently black) to the Nobel Laureates (almost entirely white men). While Left theorists have noted that industrialised and indeed globalised science has become less critical, feminists theorists[34] note that as science has become more industrialised it has excluded women from its leadership with greater efficiency.

Those old entrées into science through a sympathetic and scientific father or husband are being closed off as the industrialisation of science has spread. Big science is pretty much men's science. Even where feminist scientists do work within science, as Ruth Hubbard points out,[35] they exist by paying lipservice to the dominant ideology and keep their politics for after-hours. But for the most part, where science equals a high technological and capital-intensive knowledge production system, there are likely to be relatively few women present except as the soft-money underlabourers. Feminist knowledge by contrast has been most effectively produced on a craft model of single or small groups of research workers, with a modest capital-labour ratio.

Initially, the new SSS researchers read the scientific papers and interviewed scientists. In consequence, the continuing silence about the other workers in the factory has been rather more surprising as the research methods have shifted to include detailed ethnographies where it would seem more difficult to exclude sections of laboratory life. But perhaps, conscious of the history of anthropology, it is not really so hard to believe; as some anthropologists have talked only to rulers, men only to men and so on). Nonetheless the case of Bruno Latour and Steven Woolgar's[36] ethnography of a laboratory, written from the location of field workers employed as laboratory technicians, makes it clear that technicians are still not 'seen'. The ethnographer/technician provides a clue, for he takes an inverse pride in his lack of dexterity as a technician. There is a strong sense that feminism has been here before. Pat Mainardi's aphorism summing up the capacity of men to buckpass domestic labour comes vividly to mind: 'his resistance is the measure of your oppression'.

The ethnographers consider whether certain forms of help are indispensable to the production of the science. They report, but leave unexamined, the conflicting claims of the scientist (a man) and the technician (a woman) concerning the indispensability of the technician's contribution, itself a critical debate for solving the issue of which names go on the paper. This neglect is all the more marked if we look outside the occupation of science where we clearly see that skill is not a given but is socially constructed, and where sexism and racism, to say nothing of class are routinely institutionalised. Both American legislation of 'comparable worth' and British 'work of equal value' contest this. It is surely unusual to find legislation more conscious of social constructionism than the social constructionists themselves?

Masculinist metaphors

The metaphors of mainstream SSS are not exactly woman friendly. One extensively used is of capitalist economic processes in which ideas of investment and profitability are used to illuminate the scientific production process. SSS shares this fascination with the market with sociobiology which takes the language of investment and spreads it over our sexual and procreative lives. But even this is small-talk compared with the metaphor of war which even more effectively directs our minds towards thinking naturalistically about men as warriors. Such a metaphor has been deployed by Bruno Latour,[37] arguably the most influential of the social constructionists, to extend his ethnographically-based account of the science production process. Latour entirely rejects epistemological realism and collapses the distinction between the social and the technical in his analysis of scientific practice. Here I use Steven Shapin's[38] review of *Science in Action* because he picks up and amplifies the masculinism of the metaphor. Shapin says of Latour:

> The recalcitrant reader has now been shown the forces arrayed against *his* resistance, and therefore the price to be paid should *he* continue to deny the truth of what is asserted. As *he* persists in *his* resistance the debate becomes at once more technical and more social. It becomes more technical because the doubter has to be shown in the text what claims (and who) *he* must also doubt if *he* wants to doubt this one. It becomes more social because allies are being mobilised and enemies are being isolated. [my emphases]

Latour writes:

> In general the technical appearance of the scientific literature...is nothing but its social character, its display of phalanxes of armed allies making it pointless to resist. If being isolated, besieged, and left without allies and supporters is not a social act, then nothing is. This literature is so hard to read and analyse not because it escapes from all normal social links but because it is more social than so-called normal social ties.

Shapin again:

...the show of the instruments of torture may not be enough for the committed heretic: they may have to be applied to *his* flesh. The doubter may resist all rhetorical tricks; *he* may want to follow the scientists into the actual place where the work is done: the laboratory. *He* may want to see the reality that is said to 'lie behind' the text. What *he* sees there raises the cost of resistance further. If you don't believe the representations produced by your antagonist, you will ultimately have to learn to make them yourself, more than that you will be obliged to build your own instruments and to gather them in one place. You will have to secure the resources to construct a 'counter laboratory'. [my emphases]

I want to do more than make the obvious point that the pronoun 'lapse' on the part of a sociologist of some sophistication should not be ignored; I want to stress the power of the metaphor. Women are simultaneously erased by the war metaphor even while it also ties in with feminist experience at the hands of orthodox SSS. The vision of the armed phalanxes moving forward to annihilate the individual expression of dissent sounds like an action replay of many of our lives. War – or politics by other means – all too vividly recalls the powers of the academy – which gender-controls the jobs, grants, the journals and the language. Feminism by contrast has to start not so much by asking for a laboratory but by looking for its mud and straw.

Feminist laboratories

Thus Latour's metaphor and his appeal '*Give me a laboratory and I will raise the world*'[39] is full of resonance for feminists: for in order to challenge the claims of those who control the scientific knowledge production system it is necessary to have the full panoply of the laboratory and the scientific workers. Yet while no-one gave feminism a laboratory, although Virginia Woolfe did put in a request for a room to make literary production possible, feminist knowledges have proposed different world-views. Unquestionably, it is the immense, fragile and collective resources of the feminist movement which constitute our 'laboratory'. The history of the preparation of the instruments of analysis of feminist research is rather different from that of the high-tech contemporary laboratory. Its prescriptions for successful work speak of disclosure and self-disclosure; the boundary between the knower and the known is permeable. Evelyn Fox Keller's biography of the plant geneticist Barbara McClintock (although she is careful to insist that McClintock in no way regards herself as a feminist) reports the geneticist as describing her research approach as 'hearing what the material has to say to you'.[40] McClintock's nature is active, the material/nature will chat to a good listener. Such alternative approaches, or subordinated discourses, can be traced within many areas of biology, they can be the product of men and women and, like McClintock's jumping genes, they can command widespread respect; they live in opposition and are subordinate to the mainstream – or aggressive science as usual.

For feminist knowledge production, the first phase of consciousness-raising groups was seen as a collective method for generating alternative conceptualisations.

With so many of the concerns of women relegated by men to the trivial or the hateful, both the trivial and the hateful have entered the problematic and have been celebrated (some feminist journals delight in such anti-titles from *Trivia* to *Trouble and Strife*). Not surprisingly, such an alternative laboratory is unlike both normal science or even normal SSS, as its interpretations, knowledges and truth claims concerning the social and natural worlds are written from below. Subjugated knowledges are seen as potentially having something more truthful to say. SSS holds open the possibility that, given the same resources or rather the same skill at mobilising resources, scientist A might have produced science which claimed equally strong factual status as the actually triumphant B's claims. As well as being self-protectively funny, SSS is almost voluptuous in its appreciation of power. It is overwhelmed by the capacity of the scientists to secure all these immense resources which sustain their construction of scientific facts, and their powers to persuade that these and only these are facts. Nothing could be more different from the voices of academic feminism which, while speaking to academic feminism, are also continuously related to the social movement. Such accountability is anathema to the gatekeepers of the dominant masculinist knowledge system. In consequence, these alternative accounts are constantly under siege. As the historian Linda Gordon observed: 'Existing in between a social movement and the academy, women's scholarship has a mistress and a master and guess which one pays the wages?'[41]

The conclusion to which many radical feminists have come, that it is a mistake to waste further precious time trying to promote change in men is articulated most strikingly in the separatist feminist utopias of feminist science fiction, such as those of Joanna Russ' *Whileaway* or Sally Gearhart's *Hillwomen* which refuse both men and their science.[42] It is also present in the enrage politics of FINNRAGE – the Feminist International Network against the New Reproductive Technology and Genetic Engineering – which seeks to opposes all genetic screening, *in vitro* fertilisation and embryo research. This fundamentalist feminist antiscience stance, while profoundly flawed, cannot be dismissed as it has powerfully helped to bring the issues of reproductive technology to the fore-front of political debate. It has made alliances, both positively with expanding Green politics which seek to protect 'nature', and more negatively (not least through the concepts of femicide and gynaecide used to denounce selective female foetus abortion), to support right-wing 'pro-life' groups with their defence of the foetus as a person. Foetal personhood is a crucial element in restoring patriarchal control over women's bodies. Fortunately the cultural and political battle played out over women's bodies can at least declare a partial victory in Britain with the recent confirmation of legal abortion.

Yet this feminist fundamentalism, which campaigns globally with universal slogans, is a politics fashioned in the runaway technological environment of America, transferred and imposed on all women who are not only located in very different economic and political contexts but who have different personal biographies and needs. Within a world science-production system where the market, rather than democracy is sovereign, the politics of refusing the work to be carried out within the national frontiers of one advanced industrial society under some measure of control, rather than accelerating its exportation to a poorer country with few or none, has not been adequately addressed by radical feminism. Such universalistic politics of re-production obliterates and negates difference between women. Women who are always being asked to sacrifice their needs – or at least those who are infertile and who wish for a child – are once more being asked to sacrifice their needs to serve some other project, this time universal woman. Yet even while criticising these politics which defend a universal woman, it must be recognised that they emerge as an enraged response to a masculinist science and technology which seeks to domi-nate and make profits from the bodies and minds of women.

In the 1980s, science and technology have been central arenas of struggle for feminism, both in reproduction but also in production. There is both a struggle about political issues and a struggle about meaning as our conceptions of who we are continuously change. With *in vitro* fertilisation, the concept of motherhood moves from two meanings to three (from the biological and care mothers to the biological, carry and care mothers); images of the unborn become part of the proud set of baby pictures of the comfortably-off parents in the West; the electronic factory in the newly industrialising countries presiding over the new international and sexual divi-sion of labour. Women's lives and the social meanings of gender are being transformed by rapidly changing technologies in alliance with a footloose and inter-national capital. Women's bodies, whether through the increasingly industrialised birthing for American women, or the eyesight of the very young women working in the electronic factories in Taiwan, are the terrain of struggle.

Yet science and technology were relatively slow to appear as a significant con-cern of the feminist movement. For a long time the radical feminist Shulamith Firestone's[43] text which saw women's liberation advancing through reproductive technology stood alone. Although the science fiction novel *Woman at the Edge of Time* by Marge Piercy played with a similar theme, as a socialist feminist, Piercy was very clear that the social and economic context also required transformation before it was safe to modify birth and enable men to lactate as technological aids to a post-gendered utopia. Feminist science-fiction and fantasy have continued to make a dramatic contrast with their masculinist counterpart. It is not only that their utopias and dystopias offer a safe space to project different relationships with nature, and different solutions to relationships between people; they also are located within different epistemologies, from the realism of Marge Piercy to the postmodernism of Joanna Russ and the cyborg fantasies of the black feminist Octavia Butler.[44] Such books have had massive sales throughout the 1970s and 1980s, and have introduced hundreds of thousands of readers to the feminist debates about epistemology and science.

Where between men the realist/social constructionist debate has led to a harden-ing of positions with battle lines drawn, feminism has been slow to foreclose options. New theoretical projects, such as the rise of postmodernism, which have operated not unlike Paulinian conversion in the mainstream social sciences, are rarely accepted within feminism without first, and very openly, being very carefully considered as to what they potentially offer theoretically and politically to feminism.

Thus while few feminists are willing to ignore the powerful tools of deconstruc-tionism, it has not passed unnoticed by feminists that postmodernism's claim that realism is dead, has only arisen when women and non-western people have begun to speak for themselves. Is postmodernism singularly the theory of white men whose universalistic project is (rightly) seriously under question? Feminism increasingly questions this timely appearance of relativism as a political response which acts to preserve the hegemonic voice of white men. Relativism, unhinged to any declared political project, serves an old master.

It is within the oppositions to this masculinist epistemology, its theories, methods and 'facts', that the practice and theorising of a distinctively feminist epistemology have been created. As against the tradition of argument and rebuttal which serves to make each position both plain and maximally far apart, conveniently generating an intellectual product-differentiation which can then be niche-marketed, feminist theorising is ambiguous to read. While it would be disingenuous to claim that feminists listen to one another with quite McClintock's respect for nature, there is less concern with product-differentiation and a greater concern with theorising both difference and commonality. Keller's biography, for example, seems to skirt close to essentialism in that she suggests a distinctively feminine perspective while scrupulously reporting the scientist's explicit refusal of feminism. She speaks against a single hegemonic voice and yet throughout her writing privileges the truth claims of science. Elsewhere from within a feminist-marxist tradition, something like the 'two science thesis' – of proletarian vs. bourgeois science – has been restated for feminism but with a recognition that there are potential connections with other radical epistemologies which need to be taken into account. Thus there is both a return to marxist preoccupations with the class basis of science and imperialism (and, what is often forgotten in the discussion of the two science thesis, a potentially co-operative relationship between proletarian culture and nature) and also a recovery and new respect for the non-violent relationship, indeed mutual interdependence between nature and culture, characteristic of Aboriginal, traditional Chinese, African and native American thought. These are set positively as resources for green theorising against the 'domination of nature' which threatens the planet itself.

A major feminist project of the 1980s was to locate a distinctively feminist epistemology from within women's experiences rather than from exclusively within women's biologies, yet to do so in a way which refuses the Cartesian dichotomy and so admits bodily along with other differences. 'Standpoint' theory suggests that it is within the commonality of women's experience in reproductive labour that the possibility of a feminist epistemology is offered, a commonality which is also capable of paying systematic attention to difference. To the old claim and aspiration of the workers' movement to bring together the knowledges derived from mental and manual labour as sensuous practices in the world is added the feminist claim of the knowledge derived from emotional labour, a knowledge of relationality and of interconnectedness between the knower and the known. To restate a metaphor I have used before, the goal is to bring together the knowledges of hand, brain and heart.

What Nancy Hartsock claims as 'standpoint' theory has, not least in contesting the power of masculinist science, the strength of the claims of a successor science and is very much part of an Enlightenment tradition. Yet this formulation has given rise to an unease, lest standpoint feminism seeks to replace the one true story of white men with the one true story of white women. Such unease has been considerably assuaged by Patricia Collis Hills *Signs* article which indicates that standpoint theory can be used to sustain the theoretical and political project of black feminism.[45] At the same time where do the highly theoretical approaches to science locate the black feminists, particularly biologists who have been active in exposing and denouncing biased sexist science? Are they denounced as mere empiricists who preserve masculinist hegemony by using its canon against itself, or are they seen as part of the complex struggle against masculinist science?[46] Certainly, the feminist biologists are not easily written off as mere positivists, for positivism is frontally challenged by their explicit insistence on the importance of the knower's stance. Sandra Harding is among those who see a linkage between the standpoint theorists and those feminist biologists whom she speaks of as feminist empiricists. However, I think I would want to replace both categories of standpoint theorist and empiricist with the concept of critical realism. Critical realism more fully grasps the connection between political stance and truth claim than does the notion of flawed (if feminism can be said to be a flaw?) empiricism. At the same time, postmodernist strands of feminism enter the critique of science, decentering both the unitary voice of dominant white male science and the universalistic claims of both standpoint theory and critical realism. There are dangers, as postmodernism can invoke an equality between the discourses and so dissolve, within the text if alas not within the world, the issue of power.

Words and bodies

Yet in practice the realists and the postmodernists handle the arguments about truth claims with exceeding care, not dismissing the other, but insisting on the common feminist project. The value of these apparently contradictory claims/stories to the defence of women and the creation of space for women is evident to all. Indeed classifying feminist theorists of science is probably a mistaken enterprise, because of the interesting inconsistencies and complexities within the accounts. Keller, for example, has strong postmodernist strands but is unwilling to abandon the privileged truth claims of science, and so are Harding and Rose, but nor do they wish to jettison the analytic power of social constructionism and they evidently anguish over postmodernism lest its deconstructionist tendencies remove the ground on which feminism itself stands. Haraway, the most radical of the feminist deconstructionists, tells science as stories but mounts a robust defence of a distinctively feminist objectivity as situated knowledge. There is a strong theory of political economy suffusing her work which gives force to her support for subjugated knowledge; arguably political economy has a privileged truth status within her work. But whatever the theoretical emphasis, because body politics remains at the centre of feminist political struggle, the body serves to limit the capacity of words/texts to run off with everything.

For it has been particularly through body politics that fluid accommodations are made between those committed to postmodernism and to realism. Feminists, in a way that most men writers find very hard to do, not only reflect on bodies out there, but are much more conscious of those that we ourselves live within. The title and the text of Emily Martin's *The Woman in the Body* speak to this process. Thus while the science of masculinism is a singularly disembodied knowledge, feminist knowledge is disembodied, situated knowledge. It is not easy even now at the beginning of the 1990s to discuss science within feminism; for the political poles have at one end a widespread hostility to science, and at the other, a demand for 'hard' and often missing scientific facts which relate to women's daily lives, particularly to issues of health and illness. In consequence, feminism's theoretical debate is not only concerned with analysing the scientific and literary practices but with supporting their transformation.

There are a number of encouraging signs, from the world-wide success of the women's health book *Our Bodies Ourselves* as a practical demonstration of a new epistemology in action, to the widespread interest in the attempts currently being made to design reliable experiments other than the classical double-blind trial. The latter turns both the patient and the doctor into impersonal objects and has produced recent outcries, particularly in the case of the Vitamin B Cystic Fibrosis and the AZT trials. In the AZT case, patients shared their medication, mixing placebo and active pharmacological agents, on the moral grounds that no-one should be left out. Such an act of resistance produced no hard facts but it did maintain patients' dignity and autonomy, but it also dramatically pointed to the need for some other experimental method. It is not by chance that both protests are linked to new social movements strongly concerned with body politics. The presence of the gay movement is particularly important in closing the gap between the knower and the known, as men, albeit with a 'flawed' sexual identity, are present on both sides of the divide. Gay men as scientists are among the active/knowers, and gay men with AIDS are, or are supposed to be, the passive/known. The attempt to develop a reliable alternative to the double-blind trial, to give all the actors a part in a different science story, so that no-one is relegated to a passive nature, are crucial elements in an overall project of changing scientific practice. Whether these are odd swallows or the harbingers of something rather larger depends on political choices and how we mobilise and draw on the theoretical resources available to us.

It is time for the mainstream social studies of science to move away from masculinism's dichotomising choice between *either* abstract objectivity *or* a relativism which often retreats to becoming a cynical joker at the court of power, and join feminism's search *both* for a situated objectivity *and* a politically located relativism. Meanwhile, back in the alternative laboratory there is a sign up for old and new masculinisms: Beware! Feminists at Work.

Notes

1. Cited in Adrienne Rich, *On Lies, Secrets and Silence: Selected Prose 1866-78* (New York: Norton, 1980) p. 218.

2. A definition borrowed from Michael Billig, *Arguing and Thinking: A Rhetorical Approach to Social Psychology* (Cambridge: Cambridge University Press, 1987) p. 51.

3. There is an immense literature contesting a renewed biological determinism. For example, see: Ann Arbor Science for the People Collective, *Sociobiology as a Social Weapon* (Minneapolis: Burgess Publishing, 1977); the influential series *Genes and Gender*, Ethel Torbach and Betty Rossoff (eds) (New York: Gordian Press) vol. I, 1978; vol. II, 1979; vol. III, 1981; vol. IV, 1981; (vol. II, guest eds Ruth Hubbard and Marion Lowe); Brighton Women and Science Group, *Alice Under the Microscope* (London: Virago, 1980); Ruth Hubbard, Mary Sue Henifin, Barbara Fried (eds), *Women Look at Biology Looking at Women* (Cambridge, MA: Schenkman, 1979); Ruth Bleier, *Science and Gender: a Critique of Biology* (Oxford: Pergamon, 1984); Sarah Hardy, *The Woman that Never Evolved* (Cambridge, MA: Harvard University Press, 1981); *Science for the People, Biology as Destiny?* (Cambridge, MA, 1984). Helen Longino and Ruth Doell, 'Body Bias and Behaviour' *Signs* 9, 2 (1983) pp. 206-27; Steven Rose, Richard Lewontin and Leo Kamin, *Not in our Genes* (New York: Pantheon, 1984); Donna Haraway *Primate Visions* (London: Routledge, 1989).

4. Joking is big in mainstream SSS, and merits sociological investigation in its own right. Michael Ashmore gets A grades for jokes, see 'The Life and Opinions of a Replication Claim: Reflexivity and Symmetry in the sociology of Scientific Knowledge' in Steven Woolgar (ed.), *Knowledge and Reflexivity* (London: Sage, 1988) pp. 125-53. But it is Woolgar who is particularly aware of the potentiality of rhetoric – maybe as a way out of the punning – see Steve Woolgar, 'What is the analysis of scientific rhetoric for? A comment on the possible convergence between rhetorical analysis and social studies of science' *Science Technology and Human Values* 14 (1989) pp. 47-9 (special issue on rhetoric of science).

5. Pinch, Trevor, 'Reservations about Reflexivity and New Literary Forms or Why Let the Devil have all the Good Tunes?', in Steven Woolgar, op. cit., pp. 178-97.

6. Medawar, Peter, 'Is the scientific paper a fraud?' *The Listener* (12 September, 1963) pp. 377-8.

7. Barash, D.P., *Sociobiology and Behaviour* (Amsterdam: Elsevier, 1977).

8. Jordan, June, *Moving Towards Home: Political Essays* (London: Virago, 1981) pp. 126-36.

9. Hartsock, Nancy, *Money, Sex and Power* (London and New York: Longman, 1983).

10. Steven Jay Gould, Marxist and brilliant evolutionary theorist, in an otherwise supportive review of Ruth Bleier's book reduces much of the feminist critique of science to the presence of 'bad science'. Feminists and others may well enjoy the irony in that Gould's evolutionary theories were central in a recent furious debate concerning a 'marxist take-over' at the London Natural History Museum.

11. Hartsock, Nancy (1983); as in note 9.

12. Kuhn, Thomas, *The Structure of Scientific Revolutions* (Chicago: University of Chicago Press, 1970).

13. Bukharin, N., *et al.*, *Science at the Cross Roads* (1931; reprinted London: Cass, 1972). Bukharin was disgraced and eventually posthumously rehabilitated in 1989.

14. Bacon, Francis, *The New Atlantis*, quoted in Evelyn Fox Keller 'Feminism and Science' *Signs* 7 (1982) pp. 589-602.

15. Op. cit., Evelyn Fox Keller (1982).

16. See Brian Easley, *Science and Sexual Oppression* (London: Weidenfeld and Nicholson, 1981).

17. Merchant, Carolyn, *The Death of Nature* (London: Wildwood House, 1982).

18. For an overview see Londa Scheibinger, 'History and Philosophy of Women in Science a Review Essay' *Signs* 12 (1987) pp. 305-32.

19. Green, Prudence, *Critical Social Policy* (Summer, 1990).

20. Traweek, Sharon, *Particle Physics Culture* (Cambridge, MA: Harvard University Press, 1989).

21. Biology and Gender Study Group, 'The Important of Feminist Critique for Contemporary Cell Biology' in Nancy Tuana (ed.), *Feminism and Science* (Bloomington: Indiana University Press, 1989).

22. Biology and Gender Study Group (1989), op. cit., p. 181.

23. O'Brien, Mary, *The Politics of Reproduction* (London: Routledge and Kegan Paul, 1981) p. 5.

24. Koshland, D., editorial, *Science* (1989).

25. Harding, Sandra, and O'Barr, Jean (eds), *Sex and Scientific Inquiry* (Chicago: Chicago University Press, 1987).

26. Delamont, Sara, 'Three Blind Spots? A Comment on the Sociology by a Puzzled Outsider' *Social Studies of Science* 17 (1987) pp. 163-70.

27. Keller, Evelyn Fox, *Reflections on Gender and Science* (New Haven: Yale University Press, 1985).

28. Collins, Harry, 'Perspective' *Times Higher Educational Supplement* (21 October 1988) p. 14.

29. Lawson, Hilary, and Appignagnesi, Lisa (eds), *Dismantling Truth: Reality in the Post-Modern World* (London: Weidenfeld and Nicholson, 1989).

30. The central and much debated article was that by R.M. Young, 'Science *is* Social Relations' *Radical Science Journal* 5 (1977) pp. 65-129.

31. Rose, Hilary, 'Hyper-reflexivity: a New Danger for the Counter Movements', in Helga Novotny and Hilary Rose (eds), *The Countermovements in the Sciences* (Dordrecht: Reidel, 1978).

32. Ross-Hansen, Nils, 'The Practice Criterion and the Rise of Lysenkoism' *Science Studies* 2 (1989) pp. 3-16.

33. The environmentalist movement takes very seriously the 'facts' of pollution and continues to privilege objective knowledge. The women's health movement, as well as deconstructing the discourse of masculinist medicine, is also preoccupied with finding out 'hard facts' such as the hazards of foetal screening.

34. See Hilary Rose 'Women's Work and Women's Knowledge', in Juliet Mitchell and Ann Oakley (eds), *What is Feminism?* (Oxford: Blackwell, 1986); Sandra Harding, *The Science Question in Feminism* (Milton Keynes: Open University Press, 1986).

35. Hubbard, Ruth, 'Science, Facts and Feminism' in Nancy (ed.) (1989) op. cit., *Tuana* pp. 119-31.

36. Latour, Bruno, and Woolgar, Steve, *Laboratory Life: the Construction of Scientific Facts* (London: Sage, 1979).

37. Latour, Bruno, *Science in Action* (Milton Keynes: Open University Press, 1987).

38. Shapin, Steven, 'Following Scientists Around' *Social Studies of Science* 18 (1988) pp. 533-50.

39. Latour, Bruno, 'Give me a Laboratory and I will Raise the World', in Karin Knorr and Michael Mulkay (eds), *Science Observed: Perspectives on the Social Study of Science* (London: Sage, 1983).

40. Keller, Evelyn Fox, 'Feminism and Science' *Signs* 7 (1982) pp. 589-602.

41. Gordon, Linda, 'What's New in Feminist History?', in Teresa De Laurentis (ed.), *Feminist Studies/Critical Studies* (Bloomington: Indiana University Press, 1986) p. 21.

42. These separatist utopias are to be found in Joanna Russ, *The Female Man* (London: Virago, 1985) and Sally Gearhart, *The Wanderground: Stories of the Hill Women* (London: The Women's Press, 1985), but this entire genre of feminist SF and fantasy distinguishes itself from the mainstream by offering genuinely alternative social utopias and dystopias and new technologies as against merely the latter, with the existing but even worse social relations.

43. Firestone, Shulamith, *The Dialectic of Sex* (London: Cape, 1971).

44. Butler, Octavia, *Imago: Ectogenesis 3* (London: Gollancz, 1989).

45. Collis Hill, Patricia, 'The Social Construction of Black Feminism' *Signs* 14 (1989) pp. 875-84.

46. A number of commentators have discussed this co-operative relationship between 'empiricists', 'standpoint theorists' and 'deconstructionists'. Harding (1986) provides a very good account. This contrasts with the more negative debate within the left in the late 1970s. See Hilary Rose and Steven Rose 'Radical Science and its Enemies', in R. Miliband and J. Saville (eds), *The Socialist Register* (London: Merlin, 1979).

12

Rhetoric and the Resurgence of Capitalism

Richard H. Roberts (University of St Andrews)

Introduction

The study of 'capitalism' is not a discipline as such; yet the effective appraisal of the modern system of the market economy and its social and cultural correlates demands levels of interdisciplinary commitment that relatively few are willing or capable of sustaining. Seen historically, many of the theories of capitalism that have arisen from the time of Adam Smith's *Wealth of Nations* onwards have contained powerful rhetorical features through which their formulators have sought to impose persuasive order upon a mass of complex evidence. Rhetorical analysis of the texts of the great exponents of capitalism lies, however, beyond the scope of this paper. Our aim here is more limited, in that attention is directed towards a subgenre of representations of capitalism produced by a succession of English critics who sought to confront the ethical vacuum brought about by a continuing historical transformation, in the face of which traditional society had proved impotent.

In recent years a remarkable revival of interest in rhetoric has become apparent, characterised in this collection as the 'recovery of rhetoric'. This 'recovery' of rhetoric has taken on contrasting forms and this raises a general question as to the limits and utility of rhetorical analysis when it is directed at a topic rather than when seen in the discourse of individual disciplines as such. To what extent is the 'rhetoric of inquiry' more than a *Hilfswissenschaft*, a latter-day equivalent to Locke's intellectual underlabourer who clears away the growth of misconception and disturbs the unacknowledged residues of disciplinary power-play? In this paper we see how the extreme complexity of the 'rise', 'decline', 'persistence', and 'resurgence' of capitalism gave rise to critical strategies, the rhetorical characteristics of which can be seen to reflect the methodological limitations of their proponents. The use of rhetorical devices as a means of managing the unmanageable thus provokes questions as to how the human sciences might better perform their communicative task. In a more complex sense we need to test some of the claims made for the rhetoric of inquiry in order to try and see if this form of analysis contains theoretical potential beyond the cautionary or deconstructive exposure of the linguistic mechanisms that encode strategies of power.

The contemporary 'rhetoric of enquiry' that has influenced the approach adopted in this paper is bold in its pretentions. On the level of ambition some proponents of the rhetoric of inquiry lack nothing. For example, the amplitude of working definitions of 'rhetoric' in the 'rhetoric of inquiry' is generous to a fault. Thus Herbert W. Simons introduces rhetoric as 'about persuasion', the examination of discourse 'as persuasion'; more broadly 'we may wish to characterise a given economic theory, or philosophy, or historical account as a rhetoric'; rhetoric is 'the form that a discourse takes when it goes public' and 'it relies on something more than fact or logic or feeling to accomplish its ends'. Rhetoric as a pragmatic art functions in the realm of judgement and what Herbert W. Simons terms 'symbolic inducement'.[1] This conceptual expansion recognises few boundaries, Simons adds that:

> ...rhetoric is not just an individual practice: that there are rhetorics of organisations, of social movements, of professions, and of scientific schools and disciplines. With but a bit of casuistic stretching, we might conceive of the products of the mass media, and of entire cultures or cultural epochs, as collective rhetorics.[2]

The implications of such an extension are considerable inasmuch as 'rhetoric' would appear to encroach upon 'ideology' as an interpretative tool in the social sciences. Simons' representation of the potential of the rhetoric of inquiry is, if it can be sustained, a pragmatics grounded in a textuality that is bounded in its power only by the limits of the 'text' itself. For the purposes of this analysis we may, however, isolate three levels of 'rhetoric' in the rhetoric of inquiry which reflect both its critical and prescriptive functions. These are: first, technical rhetorical analysis of the available means of persuasion; second, rhetoric as the 'rhetoric' or systematically exploited commonplaces (in effect, its organisational paradigm and implicit presuppositions) of a given discipline or sphere of discourse; and, third, 'rhetoric' conceived as the totality of a culture in Simons' last expanded sense.

The rhetoric of inquiry is putatively endowed with great power: deconstructive, explanatory and negative on the one hand; but also, on the other, constructive, positive and prescriptive. Can we not recognise here, if we are honest with ourselves, an opportunity for that creative misprision,[3] the agonistic struggle to reread and overwhelm precedent within the human sciences, which does not merely deconstruct the rhetoric of others but also strives to create new and effective rhetorics that may transmute mere analysis into the agent of social change?

In the British context it was the recent assertion of outright rhetorical power by the 'enterprise culture' which posed important questions about the ethos and fundamental ethics of socio-economic and political power. It is plausible to suggest that the political disempowerment of Marxism and the declension of the concept of ideology are parallel, if not necessary causally linked phenomena. In consequence, the era of postmodernity has become a *rhetorical*, rather than an ideological battleground in the classic post-war sense. If the rhetoric of inquiry is to transcend its merely subsidiary employment as intellectual underlabourer then it must needs confront and conquer the crude anti-rhetoric that denigrates all rhetoric (other than the speaker's own purportedly non-rhetorical rhetoric) as 'mere rhetoric', and assume at least some of the powers of analysis possessed by the theory of ideology.[4] The task is formidable.

There are definite cultural ambitions expressed in the revival and recovery of rhetoric. Both the North American and West German projects (which were conceived independently)[5] are committed to the belief that rhetoric and rhetorical analysis are not merely pragmatic tools but may be capable of providing the intellectual means of managing at least in part the socio-cultural fragmentation characteristic of the postindustrial era and the postmodern condition. The testing of such a contention in the contemporary context would raise global theoretical questions as to limits of textuality and the corresponding status of sociological explanation.

My goal in this chapter is to approach the 'resurgence of capitalism', a conception which is itself the most recent extension of the metaphorical representation of an economic and socio-cultural phenomenon, the scale and complexity of which almost defeats representation. Eschewing the temptations offered by the mighty metaphor of reality, the world as total text, we engage in rhetorical analysis of a limited sub-genre of texts that offer circumscribed accounts of capitalism and its role in the transformation of culture and social norms. We shall subject to rhetorical analysis, and comment in passing upon three texts: R.H. Tawney's *Religion and the Rise of Capitalism*[6] and the lesser known Anglican theologian V.A. Demant's, *Religion and the Decline of Capitalism*[7] and R.H. Preston's *Religion and the Persistence of Capitalism*.[8] These writers locate the term 'resurgence of capitalism' in the self-conscious continuation of a tradition which has for 60 years operated with the processual metaphor of the 'rise', 'decline', 'persistence', and now the 'resurgence' of the dominant reality of our time.

With the passage of time these texts by Tawney, Demant and Preston have doubtless come to occupy an increasingly marginal status in relation to the mainstream of sociological reflection. Yet we ought also to interrogate the latter in order to determine whether it has ventured to undertake the normative and evaluative tasks proper to a human science. These three books are not as such great works (in the sense of establishing dominant, internationally-recognised paradigms) but texts which have nevertheless sought to establish and sustain a distinctive but 'mixed' set of objectives. Each writer has in his own way tried to defend the integrity of human nature through an account of the religious dimension as this responds reciprocally with the changing condition of capitalism itself. Our target texts are not so much formal analyses of contemporary capitalism in various stages of its recent evolution as partial insights and attempted corrections, in so far as each seeks to persuade, to posit and to sustain 'rhetorics' of the ethical and the human in the face of the dehumanising power of the capitalist project and its consequences.

In the light of these introductory remarks we shall proceed as follows. We shall first of all subject the texts that represent the 'rise', 'decline' and 'persistence' of capitalism to rhetorical analysis in order to isolate the main features of their respective strategies of persuasion. This will allow us to draw out the implications of the rhetorical turn for the later study to be undertaken elsewhere of the major, paradigm-setting representations of capitalism (for example, those of Karl Marx, Max Weber, Werner Sombart, Böhm-Bawerk, Hilferding, Ferdinand Braudel, David Bell, Friedman, Jürgen Habermas, Niklas Luhmann, Nicholas Abercrombie, Scott Lash and John Urry and so on).[9] In the present paper, however, we shall re-apply our insights to a patently rhetorical exercise in public persuasion, that is to the distinguished British industrialist Mr Peter Morgan's address to the Institute of Directors,[10] in which he spelt out the socio-cultural implications of the triumph of resurgent capitalism at the height of the Thatcher era. On this basis we shall have set in a reasonably generous setting the questions that arise when a new rhetoric displaces the scarcely inhabited ruins of its predecessor. My own goal lies visible on the horizon at this last juncture: how may a new rhetoric arise despite the triumphant and totalitarian commonplaces of the 'resurgence of capitalism'?

'Rise', 'decline' and 'persistence' – the career of a processual metaphor

The rise of capitalism

R.H. Tawney's *Religion and the Rise of Capitalism* was a remarkably successful exercise in indirect rhetorical communication, a strategy revealed in the humble disclaimers to be found in the Preface to the 1936 edition in which Tawney replied to a decade of criticism of the 'Weber–Tawney thesis'. In this 'apology' we are informed that:

> The most suitable beginning for a foundation established to commemorate him [Henry Scott Holland] would have been either an examination of the spiritual problems concealed behind the economic mechanism of our society, or a philosophical discussion which religion can make to their solution. Discretion compels one who is competent neither to inspire to action nor to expound a system, to refrain from meddling with these high matters. I have therefore chosen the humbler task of trying to give an account of the history of opinion during one critical period.[11]

On the level of first-order rhetorical analysis, that is in terms of the trope employed, the 'rise' of capitalism in the seventeenth century functions through synecdochal displacement[12] as a representation of the capitalism of Tawney's own time and its immediate precedent in the late nineteenth and early twentieth century. Tawney's second-order level of overall persuasive strategy can be characterised as a rhetoric of humility; in a characteristically English way the historical underlabourer is seen as refraining from both action and 'system' (i.e., theory) and simply resorting to the plain facts. Such a seemingly disingenuous approach most notably did not prevent an at times fairly ferocious controversy from breaking out, in which Tawney and the 'Weber–Tawney thesis' were castigated as hostile to capitalism. The very use of the term 'capitalism' had been depicted as a 'political catch-word, betraying a sinister intention on the part of the misguided author'.[13]

The synecdochal diversion exploited by Tawney when he let the sixteenth and seventeenth centuries stand for the twentieth, a step undertaken on the assumption that 'men were asking the same questions, though in different language',[14] allowed his peculiar expertise as a historian full play and informed his indirect polemical strategy. Tawney's resistance to theory was, however, a more serious matter. To grant that capitalism is a 'fact' and not to shrink from the term helped give him the ethical grasp upon the real which Tawney, as a socialist, intended to invest in his argument. His refusal to theorise the term, so as, for example, to tackle the histori-cally understood growing disjunction between economic and ethical discourse weakened his position, even as now similar refusals continue to sap the efforts of those who would engage both negatively and positively with resurgent capitalism. Do subsequent developments in ethics, economics and sociological reflection on capitalism in the British context indicate that the disjunction (the genesis of which Tawney explained historically) has been overcome? The current triumph of free market rhetoric would indicate that it has, albeit by fiat, but not perhaps so as to command universal agreement. Tawney's concluding passage in *Religion and the Rise of Capitalism* has about it an acutely contemporary ring, which, as we shall shortly see, makes his successors V.A. Demant (1949) and R.H. Preston (1977) dated by comparison. For:

> Few who consider compassionately the facts of social history will be disposed to deny that the exploitation of the weak by the powerful, organised for the purposes of economic gain, buttressed by imposing systems of law, and screened by decorous draperies of virtuous sentiment and resounding rhetoric, has been a permanent feature of the life of most communities that the world has yet seen. But the quality in modern societies, which is most sharply opposed to the teachings ascribed to the Founder of the Christian Faith, lies deeper than the exceptional failures and abnormal follies against which criticism is most commonly directed. It consists in the assumption, accepted by reformers with hardly less naiveté than by defenders of the established order, that the attainment of material riches is the supreme object of human endeavour and the final criterion of human success.[15]

The return to political economy in our own, post-welfare era resonates with this passage, and Tawney in his time did not hesitate to draw out its moral and religious implications in terms which provide one plausible point of departure for a critical response to the resurgence of capitalism. Tawney caps his argument with the moral conclusion that:

> Such a philosophy, plausible, militant, and not indisposed, when hard pressed, to silence criticism by persecution, may triumph or may decline. What is certain is that it is the negation of any system of thought or morals which can, except by a metaphor, be described as Christian. Compromise is as impossible between the Church of Christ and the idolatry of wealth, which is the practical religion of capitalist societies, as it was between the Church and the State idolatry of the Roman Empire.[16]

Tawney thus provides a no-nonsense base-line for the critique of those who within the contemporary resurgence of capitalism would seek to revive 'religion' in order to create a normative basis of a society now largely cut off from the remnants of its organic structures and supposed original moral consensus.

Tawney never showed much interest in the metaphysical aspects of his un-doubtedly Christian outlook, nor, moreover, did he enter into the theological controversies of his time, and such hesitance corresponds with his distinctively English and historicist resistance to theory. Tawney's continuing topicality contrasts with the context-bound attitudes of Demant and Preston who depict the 'decline' and 'persistence' of capitalism through rhetorics that now seem to have lost the power to articulate, and thus to command the commonplaces of the life-worlds of contemporary humanity.

The decline of capitalism
In 1949 in the aftermath of World War II, V.A. Demant, Regius Professor of Moral Theology at Oxford, consciously took up where Tawney had left off, but from a markedly different standpoint. Both lectured and wrote under the aegis of the Scott Holland Memorial Lectures. Whereas Tawney's ethos was that of the Balliol of T.H. Green, purged of residual Oxford idealism, Demant entered the field by admitting a far more serious engagement with the statutes governing the content of the lectures, that is with 'the religion of the Incarnation in its bearing on the social and economic life of man'.[17] This sentence can without undue exaggeration be taken in a metony-mous sense as the coded bearer of both the supposed promise and the ultimate failure of the interwar discussion of society within English, and in particular Angli-can Christianity. The latter struggled with the then so-called Social Question with good intent but it was hampered by inadequate theoretical tools and an ineffective research base. Demant's main resource was the Christological postulate which en-couraged belief in the intrinsic and humanly-unaided social efficacy of a metaphysical Incarnation.

As a historian, Tawney propounded an ethical socialism of Christian inspiration through synecdochal displacement and a critical (if largely implicit) juxtaposition of epochs; his rhetoric thus subsumed plain historical argument of a high quality into an indirect critique. Demant was, however, caught in the theologian's perennial dilemma expressed in the initial juxtaposition of Incarnation and the contemporary 'social and economic life of man'. Whilst Demant accepted Tawney's problem from the outset, that is the disjunction of ethics from economics and the attendant phen-omena of secularisation, his 'rhetoric' involved a recovery of the conceptuality of natural law in a compounded quasi-metaphysical form and the continued, but subor-dinate use of incarnational analogies as the basis of ethics and defence of a conception of persisting 'human nature'.

The exploitation of recovered natural law (under the influence of Maratain and Catholic Neo-Thomism) and the incarnational motif beloved of Anglicans implied a problematic juxtaposition of the distant past (the Incarnation), and the not so distant past of medieval Christendom, with a 'declining' capitalist present. The latter was a complex set of phenomena rendered conceptually visible by a positivistic and evol-utionary English sociological tradition that had by implication consigned Demant's conceptual vocabulary and its 'rhetoric' to the pre-scientific era. How could an

229

Anglican clergyman, burdened with the sympathy born of his upbringing in and experience of industrial conditions in the North of England and shackled with an archaic conceptual apparatus, hope to communicate and persuade his audience. What then was his rhetorical strategy under these circumstances?

Demant's 1949 Holland Lectures are difficult to summarise, but his basic argument is a variation on the 'contradictions of capitalism' theme. The turgid and unresolved character of these lectures stems not merely from the lesser stature of Demant as against Tawney but also from the far more difficult task that he set himself. Demant's interpretation of the present involves disentangling self-involvement rather than an oblique approach through the indirectness of historical diversion and synecdoche. Tawney, moreover, was the freer man for he was not burdened in the sphere of public persuasion, as was Demant, with the residual transhistorical rhetoric of an incarnational principle, a commonplace assented to, but increasingly under challenge within the community of the Church. Tawney confronted the reality of secularisation and the disjunction of religion and ethics from the social and above all the economic spheres, and he succeeded in reconstructing certain values in social ethics without recourse to the quasi-metaphysical realities to which Demant was bound. The latter could on occasion assume all too easily the transcendental standpoint of the theologian and pronounce *sub specie aeternitatis* that the decline of capitalism should be regarded 'not so much as the beginning of a new order of history but as the end of a short-lived experiment'.[18]

Read from our distinctive standpoint, Demant can be said to develop a rhetoric of natural law on all of the three levels we outlined earlier. First, he attempts to re-install a normative commonplace; second, this commonplace, natural law, provides the continuity within the whole structure of this exercise in public persuasion; and, third, Demant moves onto the comprehensive cultural level, the analysis of which constitutes the 'base' and the dialectical ground of the whole argument. Implicit in this position is a pointed inversion of the Marxist conception of bases (*Base*) and superstructure (*Überbau*).[19] The rise and decline of capitalism are not conceived directly on the economic level (although this dimension is not wholly circumvented) but as 'culture' subsumed under the category of 'natural law'. Natural law was initially displaced by the economic rationality of capitalism, yet it reappeared within the latter when capitalism itself presented its workings as an 'operation of natural law rather than a system developed by men',[20] central to which was, of course, the doctrine of the 'hidden hand'. Thus the internal contradictions of capitalism rest not upon the formulation of laws of economic inevitability (as in Marxism) but upon the alleged fact that its initial success depended upon certain social relations. These latter relations would, given consistent capitalism, be destroyed by the economic rationality that tends to reduce all human life to the cash nexus in the market-place:

> It was only because society by its toughness was not completely amenable to market economy that capitalism was possible even for a short time and has some great achievements in the productive field to its credit. A self-regulating market society never existed in its entirety; it could be approached and could achieve solid results only

so far as there were underneath it non-contractual bonds (legal, moral and religious).[21]

For Demant, the history of capitalism is not primarily the record of changing competitive economic relations, that is transformations in the division of labour and the accumulation of capital, so much as the record of society's attempt to protect itself from the ravages of such developments; thus 'this twentieth century history of ours is witnessing on a widespread scale the disappearance of the economic victory of the capitalist era'.[22] Conceiving capitalism as a basically disorganised phenomenon on the level of civil society, Demant constructs his public persuasion around the possibility of recreating the community in which the commonplace consensus of natural law (a kind of common culture) would flourish. This culture would, rightly enacted, overcome the self-stultifying dialectic of the capitalist project through an organic coalescence of a social *caput et corpus*, an Augustinian ecclesial head and body, and a renewed role for the integrative intellectual leader:

> Where planning now mostly takes the form of collectivising an atomistic society already *disorganized* in the literal meaning of the word, a real leadership commensurate with the scale and depth of the problem would envisage the formidable task of re-creating a more natural community so well grounded in its biological, community and spiritual foundations, that it can use technique and exchange as enrichments without drying up the sources of social living.[23]

We need scarcely mention the interesting correspondences of this view with the Beveridge proposals for the welfare state, the anti-establishmentarian arguments surrounding Raymond Williams' conception of the lack of a 'common culture',[24] and Richard Hoggart's classic portrayal of English working class culture. Demant's four main reasons for the decline of capitalism are all components of the assumed inability of capitalism to generate its own culture.[25] Thus: 'the hostility it has brought on against itself; the break-up of its own institutional framework; its parasitism on the non-economic foundation of society; and the dissipation of the disposition which reared and sustained it'[26] all emphasise the apparently indisputable role of culture in the continuation of capitalism and the civil life-world. Out of this crisis a dilemma presents itself: 'We may then ask: in what sense is humanity's struggle to recover from the dissociation represented by the rise of capitalism, a reversion to a state of life which classical and Christian life transcended?'[27]

It is no accident that this passage reminds us of T.S. Eliot's *The Idea of a Christian Society*; this is the cry of ancestral Christian England at bay. Given the then apparent crisis of capitalism and its disentigration along the fissures of its own contradictions, would the remaining natural community revert to classical and Christian values or regress into the contemporary analogate of a pre-Christian paganism? Whilst the reader might not share Demant's vision of England, it would appear that he had laid hold of at least some of the elements of the crisis of modernity. Demant wanted to be midwife assisting at the rebirth of a renewed comprehensive 'rhetoric' of English Christian culture and to empower through traditional leadership roles those rhetoricians capable of re-articulating the verbal and social web damaged, but not destroyed by usurping capitalism. This was to be the role of Demant's reconstituted clerisy, one which has now broadened and been embodied in what the economic *samurai* of the new enterprise culture of the 1980s came to see as a reluctant, self-serving salariat.

The strength and courage in Demant's work lay in his willingness to investigate and criticise, rather than merely assume the benefits of capitalism. He wanted to reinvigorate a benevolent ideological hegemony, rebuild the core of social values and beliefs and recommit the Church of England to its task of spiritual and ethical leadership. Demant cites Tawney, and from him draws the subliminal impulse for his own motivation: 'The social teaching of the Church had ceased to count, because the Church itself had ceased to think'.[28] Would that thought alone might conquer!

In 1949, during the mid-term of the post-war Labour Government, Demant was naturally aware of the political will to dismantle capitalism and of the then available means for creating the collectivist social structures of the Welfare State. The transition to a controlled economy was a change in overall economic organisation which would be manageable provided the cultural 'base' remained sufficiently intact, for:

> However great that change in organisation, it takes place within a common factor of social culture which had already given the new society a structure quite unlike that of the past. We may call this new structure and its culture, which is common to both capitalist and socialist phases, by the name of Bourgeois Society, in spite of the determination of socialist analysis to confine it to the former.[29]

Demant relied upon the relative and persisting power and integrity of a non-pluralistic cultural ground-rhetoric, a 'base' inherited, albeit in modified form, from the lost pre-industrial world. Demant wondered if this 'culture' could survive, but 'Such an estimate can only be reached by assessing how far bourgeois society can stand on its own feet, even with the crutch of state socialism, after it has all but destroyed the pre-economic social bonds'.[30] The socio-cultural 'axioms' which Demant then adumbrated had been mistakenly attributed by Enlightenment modernity to Nature, but in reality they have a culture-specific normative status. In a manner directly reminiscent of Aristotle, they are seen to function as the commonplaces of culture, the categorical framework of integral thought:[31]

> The axioms...are the presuppositions that men have about the nature of things, their unquestioned outlook concerning existence, the unformulated certainties they take for granted as to what the world and man and history are. Axioms may be formulated in doctrines which are the subject of teaching, discussion and proclamation. At their most influential they are, however, not formulated at all but assumed as the datum from which all formulation and discussion proceed.[32]

Demant was the last of a line, his approach was an attempt to turn socio-cultural concern into an informed policy. This was doubtless archaic in certain respects but in other ways it is an outlook valuable for the light it casts upon what happens when an established tradition under attrition attempts to cope with modernity. Demant does not provide a *theory* about the clash of tradition and modernity, but his work is

232

an *instance* of such an encounter. As such, his strategy can be readily subsumed under the rubric of rhetoric, although it is concerned with the defence of the commonplaces of a culture rather than the manipulation of synecdochal displacement. It is necessary to ask if such a strategy can survive in an era fully informed by socio-scientific methods that trade in the currency of theory and empirical data. Our last example brings us closer to this form of test.

The persistence of capitalism

In 1977, R.H. Preston, a professor of social ethics who studied under Tawney at the London School of Economics, began his analysis of the state of capitalism by returning once more to Tawney and Demant. Preston also recognised the difficulties in generating an analysis of a contemporary context in which the investigator is self-involved, and he made no attempt at the scale of inquiry which would be necessary to sustain a direct socio-scientific analysis of capitalism. As with Demant, so with Preston the reader learns little about the contemporary circumstances of the writer. Preston gives away little that might suggest that as he wrote the British economy and its industrial base were entering one of the greatest crises in its history. Preston, like Tawney, argues through a diversion rather than directly. Rather than looking at the contemporary nature of capitalism by recourse to an earlier century or the repristination of an archaic commonplace, Preston abandons the empirical problems inherent in his home context and appropriates the ethos of the World Council of Churches and its absorption of the principles put forward in the Club of Rome report of 1972, *The Limits to Growth*[33] and *A Blueprint for Survival*,[34] likewise published in 1972. By making the notion of a 'just and sustainable society' the normative commonplace of an attempted new rhetoric operating at the second and third levels (that is in disciplinary pragmatics and global culture), Preston avoids the first level of rhetoric where the clash of rival persuasive strategies might take place. Preston's gestures of support for the culture-focused approaches of Demant and Hirsch[35] are insubstantial and not matched with adequate effort directed at the interpretation of the cultural matrix. Where, however, Preston gets into evident difficulties is when the positivistic orientation of his own training in economics appears to lead him into the death by a thousand qualifications, once he is obliged to try to give content to ethical commonplaces like the 'common good' and 'just and sustainable'. As with the accountant's 'true and fair' appraisal of the financial state of a company, so the rhetorics of these forms of human science demand, if they are to secure the basis of consensus, a cultural aggregation. This must itself be the object of inquiry if rhetoric is to be used responsibly. We may add that as regards the wider issues a theoretical dialogue is required, for as Margaret Archer shows in her recent book,[36] the analysis of theories of social action and cultural formation have to be brought into mutual conjunction.

Preston follows an agenda suggested by Dietrich Bonhoeffer's understanding of the Church exercising its secular faith-witness in a 'post-religious' and culturally diverse world. The problems this implies are barely hinted at in the awkward juxtaposition of a set of theologically-inspired injunctions to which is ascribed absolute validity (these are: justice and sustainability; a concern or bias for the poor; equality in the sight of God; a conception of humankind articulated in terms of integral dignity; and a positive role for the state) with the ethical *Sitz im Leben* informed by the relatively secularised contractual basis of justice formulated by John Rawls.[37]

Preston scarcely touches upon the problem of the disjunction of ethical and economic argument inherited from Tawney, but when he does so it is from a time and place in which the cultural 'basis' has become even more attenuated than it was 30 years earlier with Demant. Preston has in principle to draw down his third order rhetoric, a set of global commonplaces now *divorced* from any cultural matrix (other than the subculture of multi-national ethical agencies like the World Council of Churches) so as to apply it in an increasingly secular and plural society, the exact, socio-scientific analysis of which was *not* in fact part of his original agenda. Preston's expertise in economics did not ensure his capacities as a prophet in 1977: he failed to intimate the possibility of a revolution from the Right in political economy and the triumph of resurgent capitalism. Nor did Preston grasp the cultural questions inherited from Demant's earlier qualification of Tawney's position: can capitalism generate its own culture? This leads us to the contemporary question: can the capitalist world system now come to terms with its own cultural dialectics, given its apparent global triumph on the political and economic fronts?

These questions lead us to the threshold of our present situation. Given the scale and complexity of the undertaking, we cannot but resort in turn to a form of metonymy, a small part has provisionally to represent the whole. In the conclusion of this paper we shall therefore explore and articulate the rhetoric of triumphant capitalism through a modest exercise in the textual analysis of elements in the rhetoric of the 'enterprise culture' that possessed unusual power in the Thatcher era in Britain (1979-90).

The triumph of capitalism

On the 27th February 1990, Mr Peter Morgan, Director General of the Institute of Directors, addressed the annual convention of the Institute and provided in microcosm a vision of the 'enterprise culture' in a speech which is as interesting for its elisions and hidden assumptions as for its normative prescriptions and combative metaphors. Morgan's style is not that of the chattering classes: he favours the short explosive sentences of the *Sun* and the *Mirror*. These are the verbal expressions of an assumed consensus, a commonplace normativity, exclusion from which might well prove uncomfortable or even dangerous. Unlike Tawney, Demant or Preston, Morgan begins with an assertion of the total claims of the market:

> Since this convention was planned, Eastern Europe has had its revolution. The market economy has triumphed.[38]

Here is no hesitance for in the end is the beginning: the stunning reversal of socialism might suggest a well-earned rest, but far from it: 'the enterprise culture has not yet won the battle for Britain'.[39] With the military metaphor once launched, a few choice statistics are called up to show that an undue proportion of the British people (one in five) still evinced some sympathy for communism and thereby fail fully to embrace capitalism. On a general level does this country really believe in capitalism? Turning to his colleagues in the manner of a revivalist preacher addressing likely backsliders in a lukewarm church, Morgan finds that 'not all our members have a coherent vision of the enterprise culture'.[40] The presentation and effective internalisation of this vision must be the prelude to the removal by government and business of the obstacles in its way.

Morgan's vision of the enterprise culture consists in the forceful assertion of an invasive, all-conquering metaphor that is the comprehensive paradigm in accordance with which society in its totality is to be re-organised:

> An enterprise culture is one in which every individual understands that the world does not owe him or her a living, and so we act together accordingly, all working for the success of UK PLC.[41]

The enterprise culture has its 'flagships' (successful companies), 'heroes' (the directors who lead), its 'pride' (the products); the whole nation must understand that it is locked in global economic war in which there are in principle no non-combatants. The education of the 'economic warriors' is imperative but obstructed by three obstacles: establishment attitudes, the middle class salariat and the 'lumpenproletariat'. The first is epitomised by the bishop who denigrates wealth creation and praises wealth distribution; the second is that sector of the population which parrots the liberal establishment and commands such propaganda methods as lie at its disposal in classroom, pulpit, the press and the state; the third is the last 40% which has nothing and has no stake in society other than a parasitic dependency.

The capitalist commonplace is all-embracing: interlocking but unargued propositions combine to reinforce the subliminal conviction frequently uttered by Mrs Margaret Thatcher that 'there is no alternative'. There is no basis in the rhetoric for any resistance to consistent *Gleichschaltung*.[42] In the global economic war the whole population, the 'warriors' and the 'players' and the 'educated citizens' required for production and consumption must work together to further the enterprise culture. The old establishment responsible for the 'decline of UK PLC' and its salariat allies have to be brought into conformity with the enterprise culture. In principle there can be no exceptions: the rhetoric of triumphant capitalism must become reality, the revolution must be consistent and complete.

Conclusion

The rhetorical commonplaces of triumphant resurgent capitalism at the height of the Thatcher era knew no bounds; they were in my view intrinsically totalitarian. Yet the inconsistencies of contemporary capitalism and its ethical failures are still as real as they were in Tawney's day. Now, however, the global totalising power of capitalism is greater, its invasive capacities enhanced through lessons learned, and money and effort well invested in the practical furtherance of the invasive metaphors that preclude alternatives. The astonishing clarity of the rhetoric of resurgent British capitalism suddenly dimmed with the resignation of the Prime Minister, Mrs Margaret Thatcher, on the 22nd of November 1990. The return of the grey men of British politics, and the renewal, however vacuous or problematic, of a form of the rhetoric of consensus have apparently brought to an end an unprecedented public experiment with discourse. The rhetoric of resurgent capitalism is now but one discursive strategy amongst others. In the era of John Major, socio-economic transformation is achieved through the less strident but more effective means of government by management.

Rhetorical analysis clearly provides a singularly appropriate way of entering the interpreting styles of representation of capitalism. As such, it assists the de-mystification of the political process. The sheer scale of capitalism is such that the use of metaphors, synecdoche and metonymy are essential if the human experience constructed within its bounds is to be understood. Such strategies have, however, their limitations and need to be relativised by properly informed socio-scientific accounts of the phenomena. Effective representations of capitalism will have to embrace the intrinsic rhetorical dimensions of the human sciences. More than this is required, however. The representation of capitalism must draw upon the full range of the theoretical and methodological resources of the human sciences. Only then, in our post-Marxian era, are we likely to comprehend, and respond effectively to, the ethical void that Michael Novak exposes in the 'empty shrine' of resurgent 'democratic capitalism'.[43]

Notes

1. Simons, H.W., 'Introduction', in H.W. Simons (ed.), *Rhetoric in the Human Sciences* (London: Sage, 1989) pp. 2-3.

2. Simons, H.W., op. cit., p. 3.

3. Harold Bloom's useful neologism drawn from *The Anxiety of Influence. A Theory of Poetry* (London: Oxford University Press, 1973) carries with it many helpful insights into the processes that take place when one poet re-reads his/her predecessor and thus, by analogy, what happens when a paradigm in the human sciences is overwhelmed and supplanted.

4. See J. Thompson, *Studies in the Theory of Ideology* (Cambridge: Polity, 1984).

5. The two most influential North American projects are the major ongoing programme at Iowa originally associated with J.S. Nelson, Allan Megill, and D.N. McCloskey (eds), *The Rhetoric of the Human Sciences* (Madison: University of Wisconsin Press, 1987) and the Temple project which is strongly linked with communication studies, see Herbert W. Simons (ed.), op. cit. A monumental *Historisches Handbuch der Rhetorik* is in preparation, Walter Jens and Gert Ueding (eds), Seminar für allgemeine Rhetorik, University of Tübingen.

6. Tawney, R.H., *Religion and the Rise of Capitalism. A Historical Study* (London: John Murray, 1926). This book contains the Holland Memorial Lectures of 1922. The 1936 edition contains an important New Preface.

7. Demant, V.A., *Religion and the Decline of Capitalism. The Holland Lectures for 1949* (London: Faber and Faber, 1952)

8. Preston, R.H., *Religion and the Persistence of Capitalism. The Maurice Lecture for 1977 and other studies in Christianity and Social Change* (London: SCM, 1979).

9. I undertake a systematic review of the relevant texts in my forthcoming book, *Religion and the Resurgence of Capitalism* (London: Routledge, 1994).

10. See undated Institute of Directors Press Release.

11. Tawney, R.H., op. cit., p. 3.

12. 'Synecdoche': 'A figure by which a more comprehensive term is used for a less comprehensive or vice versa; as a whole for a part or part for a whole, genus for species, or species for genus, etc.' Oxford English Dictionary. Brian Vickers succinctly puts it thus: 'where one thing is substituted for another', *In Defence of Rhetoric* (Oxford: Clarendon Press, 1988) p. 498.

13. Tawney, R.H., op. cit., p. xi.

14. Tawney, R.H., op. cit., p. 14, where he reviews the responses in the New Preface of 1936 edition of *Religion and the Rise of Capitalism*.

15. Tawney, R.H., op. cit., p. 286.

16. Ibid.

17. Demant, V.A., op. cit., p. 13.

18. Demant, V.A., op. cit., p. 20.

19. The discussion of this distinction stems from Marx and Engels' *The German Ideology*. See S. Hall, 'Rethinking the "Base and Superstructure" Metaphor', in J. Bloomfield (ed.), *Class, Hegemony and Party* (London, 1977).

20. Demant, V.A., op. cit., p. 22.

21. Demant, V.A., op. cit., p. 24.

22. Ibid.

23. Demant, V.A., op. cit., p. 28.

24. Williams, R., *Culture and Society 1780-1950* (London: Chatto and Windus, 1958).

25. Hoggart, R., *The Uses of Literacy* (London: Chatto and Windus, 1957).

26. Demant, V.A., op. cit., p. 31.

27. Demant, V.A., op. cit., p. 32.

28. Demant, V.A., op. cit., p. 50.

29. Ibid.

30. Demant, V.A., op. cit., p. 51.

31. See Aristotle, *Rhetoric* 1358a ff.

32. Demant, V.A., op. cit., p. 62.

33. Meadows, D.H., *et al. The Limits of Growth* (London: Pan, 1974).

34. Commissioned by *The Ecologist* (Harmondsworth: Penguin, 1972).

35. Hirsch, F., *The Social Limits to Growth* (London: Routledge and Kegan Paul, 1977).

36. Archer, Margaret, *Culture and Agency. The Place of Culture in Social Theory* (Cambridge: Cambridge University Press, 1988).

37. Rawls, J., *A Theory of Justice* (Cambridge, MA: Belknapp Press of Harvard University Press, 1971).

38. Morgan, P., op. cit., p. 1.

39. Ibid.

40. Ibid. Peter Morgan confirms Hilary Rose's exposure of the all-inclusive gender-blindness of militaristic metaphors and commonplaces (see ch. 11 above).

41. Morgan, P., op. cit., p. 2.

42. Political co-ordination, a bringing into line. This is a word strongly affected by its use within National Socialism.

43. Novak, M., *The Spirit of Democratic Capitalism* (London: Institute of Economic Affairs, 1982/8).

13

Quests for Interdisciplinarity: The Rhetorical Constitution of Social Psychology[1]

James M.M. Good (University of Durham)

Introduction

The idea of an interdisciplinary social psychology (hereafter IDSP) is, we are often told, as old as social psychology itself.[2] But to what terrain of the human sciences, indeed, do we refer by the term social psychology? And which disciplines does this Janus-faced interstitial activity bring together? How has this idea of an IDSP been expressed and with what consequences? Has such an IDSP been developed? Or are there still two (or more) social psychologies with quite separate roots in sociology and psychology?

Nowadays we are ready to acknowledge the arbitrariness of answers to questions about 'origins' and we are ever alert to the dangers of the 'retrospective' imposition of disciplinary boundaries.[3] Yet it is difficult to discard the belief that both sociology and psychology are indeed the parents of the child and that the discipline of social psychology, having come of age, now bears some responsibilty for effecting a reconciliation between the estranged parents. Indeed it is now some 40 years since Hans Gerth and C. Wright Mills remarked that it was:

> ...one of the special obligations of the social psychologist to bridge the departmentalized gap which unfortunately separates sociological and psychological approaches.[4]

In my view, there are many similar gaps to be bridged in the human sciences, other pressing obligations to take note of. In the introductory chapter to this volume it was noted that the emergence and institutionalisation of psychology did not end its intellectual and social embeddedness but only changed the structure of that embeddedness.[5] The problems of social psychology represent a special case of a more general problem of the division of labour in the human sciences, of the 'disciplinary specialism' which has ensued with its resulting fragmentation of knowledge.[6] It was just such a fragmentation of knowledge that Marcel Mauss had in mind when, addressing members of the French Psychological Society nearly 70 years ago, he remarked that:

> The study of the complete man is among the most urgent of these studies we would ask you to make...may we sociologists be allowed to beg you for our own good, and the mutual advantage of all of us, to be prepared to work even more now, and in your normal field, in the domain opened up by the psychopathologists of the study of the complete, non-compartmentalized man.[7]

This chapter begins with a brief discussion of the relationship between knowledge and academic disciplines. I next clarify why social psychology is often taken as an example of an inter-discipline in the human sciences. This is followed by an analysis of some of the ways in which social psychology is constituted rhetorically. This analysis draws examples from a variety of sources – introductory textbooks, disciplinary histories, handbooks, disciplinary debates and discussions of teaching and postgraduate training. I shall also try to bring out some of the tensions between disciplinary and interdisciplinary discourses. In a final section I consider some of the implications of the analysis for the disciplinary futures of social psychology in their attempts to comprehend the 'complete' person.

Knowledge, disciplinarity and interdisciplinarity

The book series of which this volume is a part reflects the recent and rapidly developing interest in the systematic study of disciplines as agencies for the production and dissemination of knowledge. From earlier chapters in this volume it should already be clear that disciplines influence how their practitioners both view and engage with the world. And that disciplines bestow legitimate authority upon their practitioners.[8] Disciplines also have to be seen as rhetorically constituted, historical products. But where do we locate the essential features of disciplinarity? In shared beliefs and representations of the world or in disciplinary practices? How do disciplines mediate and embody the relationships between knowers and what is known? What prompts scholars to cross disciplinary boundaries and what are the distinctive features of interdisciplinarity? In this section I consider some of the essential features of disciplinarity, focus on the embodiment of knowledge not just in texts or discourse but also in disciplinary practices, and identify some of the reasons why scholars are motivated to cross disciplinary boundaries. With this framework in place, the rhetorical constitution of social psychology will then be examined in the following section.

Describing disciplines: Some essential features
William Bechtel has recently suggested that the criteria used to define the basic units of science fall on three major dimensions: the objects studied, the cognitive activities involved, and social and institutional organisation.[9] The first of Bechtel's

criteria concerns the most common way in which people describe disciplines – in terms of the things they study. However such objects do not simply reveal themselves to scientists. Scientists must decide which 'items' to group together into different 'domains' of study. However, even when the same entities or phenomena are involved, different disciplines may tackle the common domain differently. Thus while 'objects of study' constitute an important part of what characterises disciplines, it is also necessary to consider the factors which lead scholars to group different phenomena together. As Bechtel puts it 'some of these factors have a basis in nature, but they are also influenced by both the cognitive and social features of disciplines'.[10]

The second dimension focuses on the cognitive tools developed by a discipline to describe and investigate the phenomena in its domain. Here Bechtel identifies a variety of factors – theories and laws; problems addressed; methods, techniques and tools for investigating these problems; and the procedures for presenting solutions.

While the intellectual dimension of research is clearly central, over the past decade especially, social historians and sociologists of science have persuasively demonstrated the ways in which scientific activity is embedded in social and institutional contexts.[11] Bechtel draws attention to the following features of such contexts: the role of the social structure of disciplines in regulating the activities of individual scientists to insure compliance with accepted disciplinary principles; the role of academic departments in the formation of disciplinary identity, for example, in securing the cognitive and social allegiances of members of a discipline and in providing the framework in which one acquires the cognitive tools of the discipline – i.e., theories and accumulated knowledge; professional organisations and journals as outlets for the dissemination of information; disciplinary 'specialities' as the important units of communication and interaction in research.

Bechtel also proposes that it is useful to follow the suggestion of David Hull and view disciplines 'as historical individuals or lineages, characterised not by a defining property but by their historical continuity'.[12] Hull rejects the view that agreement on basic principles is a major factor in determining (research) group membership. Rather he suggests that scientific communities should be treated ontologically as *individuals* (entities with parts), not as *sets* (entities with members). As an individual researcher, then, what determines membership in a scientific community is not the characteristics which one shares with other members of one's research group or discipline, but being spatially–temporally integrated into the group. Hull does not offer an analysis of how one becomes a member of such communities but it is clear that disciplinary socialisation practices and such chance factors as which graduate school one choses or where one finds a job are likely to be involved.

Embodied disciplinary practices
In the introductory chapter, attention was drawn to the growing awareness of the ways in which disciplinary knowledge is embodied not only in linguistic and social practices but also in standardised technical practices and skills. In a recent monograph and a series of papers, the American philosopher of science Joseph Rouse has

attempted to develop a political philosophy of science.[13] In an impressive and powerful synthesis of both pragmatist and Heideggerian thought, contemporary philosophy of science, and of recent empirical studies in the sociology of science, Rouse develops a view of science in which '...power and knowledge or truth are [seen as] internally related....where the power relations that open up a field of scientific practice are also relations of disclosure, of truth'. On Rouse's account:

> ...in working on the world, we find out what it is like...it is what shows up in our practices, what resists or accommodates us as we try to act upon it. Scientific research, along with the other things we do transforms the world and the ways it can make itself known. We know it not as subjects representing to ourselves the objects before us, but as agents grasping and seizing upon the possibilities among which we find ourselves.[14]

Unlike the early Heidegger, Rouse does not exempt the sciences from his practical hermeneutics. To do this, he maintains, would be 'to overlook both the engaged opportunistic character of scientific research and also the concrete, contextual nature of scientific theorizing'.[15]

Rouse also attempts to bring out the cognitive significance of *narrative* for knowledge not only in the human sciences but also, more unusually, in the natural sciences. He does this not by focussing on narrative as a literary form but as the temporal organisation of the understanding of practical activity. Science is portrayed by Rouse as a social practice through which practitioners structure the 'narrative context' in which past work is interpreted and possibilities for future work are projected. He is not saying that scientific papers are really narratives in disguise: 'papers do not *tell* stories about how the current research situation came about and where it seems to be heading. They are instead more complicated speech acts, which can only be understood in the *context* of a story.'[16] Rouse emphasises the fact that such papers are written for an audience – but an audience with closely related concerns – and the papers are written to address issues in terms that are of interest to and understandable by other workers in the field. Such papers are very context-bound because the context is assumed to be supplied by the reader.[17] Moreover if a scientific paper is to make its mark, it must also have implications for the work of others: 'Scientific papers are attempts to reshape...the situation in which scientists in [a] field see themselves working, and the possibilities for further investigation which arise out of that situation'.[18] Rouse also draws attention to more explicit reconstruction of the scientific literature in review articles and textbooks.

Rouse is anxious to distance himself from both realist and anti-realist interpretations of scientific knowledge, while also challenging the ironic stance adopted by many sociologists of science to the task of the global legitimation of science. Insofar as both the social constructivist and the realists emphasise 'world-views', they both utilise a Cartesian notion of an subject viewing the world and a world as object viewed. Rouse thus provides a basis for the development of a more 'mutualist' approach to an understanding of the role of disciplines in the *joint constitution* of the knower and the known.

Richard Harvey Brown has also recently drawn attention to the way in which a 'critical rhetoric' of science which reveals homologies between stylistic and social practices can illuminate relationships between knowledge, power and legitimation in disciplines, and thus illustrate how 'the creation and transmission of knowledge recreates and transmits forms of power, and how power shapes and deploys knowledge'.[19] The focus of this fusion of 'poetics and politics' is on how reality and truth are constructed both textually and socially. Brown is concerned with the 'politics' of representation, with the 'transparent' practices by which things take on meaning and value. For a discourse to become hegemonic, Brown suggests that there appear to be two conditions to be met (the first he terms political, the second poetic): 'it must be capable of articulating a reality consonant with the habitus and interests of dominant groups; and it must possess sufficiently occult or formal properties to bar unwanted persons from its legitimate deployment'.[20] In a later section I shall illustrate these different aspects of disciplinarity in relation to the constitution of the discipline(s) of social psychology.

Reasons for crossing disciplinary boundaries and how such activity should be described
Scholars are prompted to cross disciplinary boundaries for a variety of reasons:[21] to share common interests with members of other disciplines; to overcome the 'ethnocentrism' or ingroup partisanship of disciplines or university departments;[22] to seek help, theoretical or procedural, where the problem one is encountering cannot be adequately dealt with within one's own discipline; to engage in collaborative problem solving; to develop synthetic theories that straddle disciplines; and in circumstances where one is trying to explain the origin of a phenomenon that has traditionally fallen within the domain of one discipline, but where explaining the origin requires entering the domain of another discipline.

At the same time, it is clear that much cross-disciplinary work is dependent on disciplinary skills and that it is also constrained by disciplinary loyalties. There is thus a tension between disciplinarity and interdisciplinarity which Julie Klein refers to as the 'disciplinary paradox'. While the effect of interdisciplinary fields 'is to make boundaries seem looser, inquiry tends to be rooted in a given discipline and institutional setting'.[23] Fundamental disciplinary divisions retain their force, a force which Klein suggests has both positive and negative consequences. 'It ensures the kind of concentrated effort necessary to conduct research in depth, yet it holds cross-disciplinary inquiry hostage to the disciplines.'[24]

In the introduction to this volume it was noted that there was as yet little consensus as to how intellectual activity which crosses disciplinary boundaries should be described. For the purposes of this chapter we shall use the classification outlined in the introduction to this volume: *Cross-disciplinarity* – where individuals from different disciplines tend to get together because they have common interests; *Interdisciplinarity* – where expertise from more than one discipline is required in order to achieve a common aim; and *Trans-disciplinarity* – conceptual frameworks that transcend the narrow scope of disciplinary world views. As will become clear, most proponents of an IDSP have the latter two forms of boundary crossing in mind.

Social psychology – an exemplary inter-discipline?

According to a definition currently influential in Europe, 'social psychology is...a discipline which aims at an integration of the psychological functioning of individuals with the social settings, small and large, in which this functioning takes place'.[25] The achievement of such an integration would seem to require at least interdisciplinary, if not trans-disciplinary, styles of work. Social psychology does seem to enjoy an unique status as an academic discipline in having emerged in the course of the twentieth century as a branch of two human sciences – sociology and psychology.[26] Its 'origins' are often traced to the year 1908 in which two books were published whose titles included the name social psychology.[27] While this particular 'origin myth' serves a useful purpose in allowing the reconstruction of a dual-heritage history, it fails to take account of earlier 'social psychological' developments such as the *Völkerpsychologie* of Moritz Lazarus, Hermann Steinthal and Wilhelm Wundt and the crowd psychology of late nineteenth-century Italian and French writers such as Gabriel Tarde and Gustave LeBon.[28]

What is clear, is that by the second decade of the century when both psychology and sociology were well-established as academic disciplines in the United States, sociological and psychological traditions of social psychology were already developing independently from one another. Indeed, by the middle of the third decade, concern was being expressed about the relative isolation of the two traditions from one another and proposals were being made to facilitate more communication and closer cooperation between the 'two social psychologies'.[29] The Second World War brought a rapid expansion of social psychology and fostered a period of cross-disciplinary activity which led to a variety of post-war institutional developments promoting an interdisciplinary social psychology.

Arising out of the experiences of social psychologists engaged in interdisciplinary research on the adjustments of the American soldier and on the American strategic bombing surveys in Germany and Japan,[30] there began what recently has been called by William Sewell 'a golden age of interdisciplinary social psychology'.[31] This led to the setting up of interdisciplinary graduate training programmes in social psychology at Michigan, Harvard, Yale, Cornell, Berkeley, Columbia, Minnesota, Wisconsin and other universities.[32] In addition, a variety of interdisciplinary research centres were also set up.[33] As Sewell notes however, by the late 1960s, these interdisciplinary programs in social psychology had all but vanished leaving 'a fractionated set of social psychological traditions returning to their original disciplinary moorings once the interdisciplinary arrangements had faltered'.[34] By the late 1960s most of these arrangements had collapsed and, despite the continued expansion of social psychology, a period of disciplinary soul-searching began – the so-called 'crisis of social psychology'.

The roots and symptoms of this crisis were diverse and reflected a variety of concerns about the task of social psychology – about the topics studied, the nature and status of those who took part in social psychological studies (the 'subjects' who took part in the ubiquitous laboratory experiments were predominantly college students), the lack of integrative theory, the dominance of experimentation, the nature and consequences of experimental 'artifacts', the neglect of ethical issues, and the apparent lack of relevance, etc.[35]

A central theme was captured in a celebrated question: 'How social is social psychology?' posed in 1972 by Serge Moscovici.[36] Some 20 years later, the 'social dimension' in social psychology (to use Henri Tajfel's apt phrase)[37] is, I believe, now richer and better cultivated and this, in some measure at least, reflects some impact on psychological social psychology (hereafter PSP) of more sociological, and to a lesser extent, anthropological traditions. Indeed many of the so-called 'new social psychologies' can be seen as reflecting a discovery by psychological social psychologists of the 'social behaviorism' of G.H. Mead and of such sociological perspectives as symbolic interactionism, ethnomethodology, critical theory, etc.

A recurring theme of the post-crisis debates has been the relationship between psychological traditions of social psychology – focusing on the psychological properties and processes of indidividuals and studied predominantly in the laboratory and sociological traditions of sociological psychology – focusing on the reciprocal relations of the individual and society, the mutuality of social interaction and on the 'emergent' products of such interaction. Considerable attention has been directed to the notion that there are 'two social psychologies', differentiated by origins, institutional base, topics, theories and concepts, and disciplinary practices.[38]

There is as yet little agreement as to how these traditions should be described.[39] Some sensitivity to differentiation within the psychological and sociological traditions is to be found, with PSP tending to be presented in a more monolithic way.[40] However, it is important to exercise caution with regard to the classification of such disciplinary collectivities. As S. Woolgar has noted, the division of scientists into categories of various kinds is a prerequisite for social and historical studies of science. Such categorisations are usually not regarded as being problematic;[41] category discourse should be seen, however, as serving a variety of pragmatic and evaluative functions.[42]

Over the past two decades, in the wake of the decline of the hegemony of logical empiricism and Kuhnian postempiricism, social psychologists have been exploring realist and social constructionist philosophies of science.[43] They have also begun assessing the significance of the revival of rhetoric which is the focus of this volume. A fascination with narrative forms of explanation and with discourse is much in evidence and there is a growing awareness of the impact of 'culture' on the development of social psychological processes and outcomes.[44] Social psychologists from both major traditions have also begun to come to terms with the implications of postmodernism.[45]

The rhetorical constitution of social psychology

In earlier chapters of this book we have already taken note of the role of rhetorical factors in the constitution and legitimation of disciplines. Such factors were seen to be especially prominent in disciplinary socialisation practices, in disciplinary histories and in times of disciplinary crisis. In this section I shall examine some features of the rhetorical constitution of social psychology, drawing examples from disciplinary debates about the task of social psychology, from accounts of disciplinary histories, and from discourses about the need to develop an interdisciplinary social psychology.[46] In doing so it will be necessary at times to keep in mind Potter's warnings about category discourse (noted above) and also to consider the communication process as a whole: what is said, to whom, in what way and with what consequences.

Disciplinary debates

Many of the disciplinary debates over the past two decades have concerned social psychology's 'objects of study' which are revealed, for example, in conceptions of the 'social', of the 'psychological' and of the 'interfacing' of the 'social' and the 'psychological'. Thus, social psychology has been seen as insufficiently 'social': in Graumann's memorable phrase, there has been an 'individualisation' of the social and a 'desocialisation' of the individual.[47] Too little attention has been paid to the 'emergent' (social) products of interaction – relationships, groups and crowds; too much attention has been paid to the (individual) attributes of attitudes, attributions, schemas and stereotypes. Concerns about other dualisms are not too hard to discern. Thus when Markus and Zajonc equate social psychology with cognitive social psychology they dismiss (or are unaware of) attempts to develop 'noncognitivist' approaches to social cognition.[48]

In these debates we can also see the operation of the 'cognitive' and 'social' features of science noted in an earlier section of this chapter. There are debates about whether social psychology is a 'natural' science, or an 'historical' discipline.[49] There are concerns expressed about the ethics of research (mainly laboratory research but also about the use of role-playing), about 'relevance' and the need for a more applied and a more 'critical' social psychology.[50] These debates about the 'social' and the 'psychological' may be seen as involving what Billig has termed disciplinary 'argumentative common-places'. By means of an appeal to such *topoi*, social psychologists attempt to justify their preferred style of work and its justificatory principles, and to argue against the counter principles.[51]

The emphasis in such debates varies with the disciplinary affiliation of the writer: we can see the influence of the different disciplinary origins of social psychologists, psychological and sociological. Disciplinary identity is also revealed in membership of different professional organisations, publication in different journals and attendance at different conferences and meetings.[52] Yet as social psychologists look beyond their own disciplines for theoretical guidance, they often discover new allegiances: a 'critical' or discourse-oriented social psychologist may have more in common with a sociological colleague than with a psychological colleague, for example.

In these disciplinary debates we also find rhetorics of 'exclusion' and of 'incorporation'. Thus E.E. Jones in his article on major developments in social psychology since the 1930s (in the third edition of *The Handbook of Social Psychology*) characterises social psychology as primarily a subdiscipline of psychology. He excludes sociological social psychologists from serious consideration on a variety of grounds, including the proportionate volume of social psychological literature in psychological journals, a history of failed interdisciplinary arrrangements, and because 'the ultimate interests of the two approaches are distinctive' (i.e., sociological social psychologists are not really social *psychologists*).[53] Rob Farr argues for the incorporation of the sociological in the psychological in terms of the development of an essentially 'social' theory of mind (the symbolic interactionist model of the individual) rather than dealing with the 'social' and the 'psychological' in terms of different levels of analysis.[54]

Sociological social psychologists are concerned to secure their disciplines 'core message' about the impact of 'social structure',[55] or they wish to 'rekindle the sociological imagination' linking biography and history.[56] Others wish to purvey the message that 'social structure and cognitive structure go hand in hand' thus offering sociological social psychologists 'a chance to make a distinctively sociological contribution to the cognitive revolution'.[57] Finally, in these debates we can see examples of the reconstruction of historically continuous traditions of both psychological and sociological social psychology, although the central problems under study may have changed over the decades.[58]

Accounts of the emergence of social psychology during the inter-war years

In terms of a mutualist approach to history, historical reality is not the true narrative waiting to be uncovered nor is it a web spun within the minds of historians. Rather, it has to be seen as mutually constituted by the undifferentiated relationship between the historians and historical objects. Arthur Still and James Good have suggested that the history of an academic discipline lies somewhere between the history of a building and the history of a legal system. Thus the historian starts with different plans or agendas or programmes, then goes on to the construction itself, bringing in questions about interest groups, competition for limited resources, gender bias, traditional practices etc. With the help of these similes, a return to traditional teleological histories is avoided, where what has evolved is the one true, correct building (or discipline) for the fundamental needs (or facts) that are served (or represented).

In such an account metaphors are useful not just to uncover similarities but also differences.[60] Buildings and legal systems are fairly universal aspects of human societies, but academic disciplines are more local. There may be other ways of channelling curiosity about the world, and much may be lost when methods become established and an academic discipline is constituted. What might have been lost is shown to some extent in the debates that went on at the beginning. Often these are debates we can still resonate to, and we may begin to recognise ourselves as critics of a disciplinary system that has moulded our thinking.

The inter-war years (1919-38), and the 1930s in particular, were a period during which agendas for subsequent developments in social psychology were laid down.[61] This is a period in which the transition to modern social psychology is often located,[62] a point of demarcation of the 'long past' of social psychology from its 'short history'. Still and Good draw attention to Farr's identification of the positivistic bias in the use of Ebbinghaus' famous dictum to distinguish between the long past of social psychology as part of the Western (mainly European) tradition of thought and its short history (since 1935) as an experimental science that is characteristically American.[63]

While Still and Good accept Farr's argument, they do not agree that the 'long past' and the 'short history' can or should be eliminated from the historiography of psychology. They suggest that when we are dealing with periods and movements, rather than identifiable products, and take a diachronic rather than a synchronic approach, it almost becomes a necessity of thought to use the mathematical metaphor that Farr sees as implicit in the distinction, that of *points of inflection*. In historical studies we inevitably pick out significant events, and these are naturally troped as points of inflection, points at which the rate of change rapidly shifts. Thus points of inflection are a basic and natural way of constructing narratives, though we must of course beware of taking one's chosen point to convey a unique and exclusive truth – that and not the inflection per se (as Farr argues), is the mistake of positivism.

Sometimes the point of inflection is a single event, for example, Vygotsky's famous speech against physiological reductionism at the 1924 Psychoneurological Congress marking his entrance, centre stage, into Russian psychology, and the beginnings of a movement that launched Luria and Leont'ev as well as Vygotsky. Sometimes the point of inflection is the publication of a single book as in the case of Farr's analysis of his positivist historians – Murchison's (1935) *Handbook of Social Psychology*. Again this is a useful beginning for constructing a narrative, but a further decision is necessary before it can be unfolded. The significant event may either be seen as a choice point which determines the future course of events, or as a trigger for the crystallisation (Apfelbaum) of previously latent (but inexorable) tendencies. In the first case the event changes the direction of history, and the perpetrator is the great man or woman whom William James championed against the sociological reductionism of Herbert Spencer. In the second case the event may fortuitously precipitate the coming change, but only as part of the inevitable crystallisation process, which can be set off and sustained by a wide variety of small changes.

Still and Good show how these two versions of narrative can be exemplified in the recent historiography of social psychology during the inter-war years: the former in Graumann's discussion of the significance of Floyd H. Allport's 1924 book *Social Psychology* and its role in the 'desocialization of the individual';[64] the later in Erika Apfelbaum's 'Prolegomena for a history of social psychology' where she writes:

> The 1930s, I feel, may be characterized with respect to the development of social psychology as a major – and perhaps even the first true – crystallization period for the discipline. This period combined an effervescent shot of leftist, socialist, and Marxist ideas with the formation of SPSSI (*Society for the Psychological Study of Social Issues*). The latter event proved an important step towards giving structure to the discipline, so as to permit the congregation of otherwise isolated and marginalized social psychologists. The 1930s combined intellectual ferment, economic uncertainty, and, as well, a developing sense of 'we-ness' and the beginnings of a social identity as a social psychologist.[65]

Thus different narratives about the development of social psychology are constructed around different points of inflection, which may be the result of a speech, or a book, or the formation by social psychologists of a society. Assuming a narrative is not marred by faulty scholarship, the question to ask is not 'is this the true account?' but 'is it readable or thought-provoking?' or 'does it throw light on the period and on the social psychology that has resulted?'. For the result itself varies with the narrative – Graumann's 'individualization of the social' refers to a social psychology that is a far cry from the politically-oriented discipline of Apfelbaum's account.

The idea of an interdisciplinary social psychology
There is only space to present a sample of the persuasive discourse in terms of which notions of IDSP have appeared. In the introduction to this volume it was noted that while the beginning of the formation of autonomous human sciences undoubtedly began in the nineteenth century, these processes were by no means completed until well into the twentieth century. It is my belief that it does not make sense to talk about the idea of an IDSP which integrates psychological and sociological approaches, until there are clearly identifiable separate traditions of social psychology within each parent discipline, together with an expressed concern about the absence of contact and integration. That condition begins to be met in the 1930s.

One of the earliest examples of this debate, a paper by Steuart Britt which appeared in 1937, unusually, in both the *Journal of Abnormal and Social Psychology* and the *American Sociological Review*.[66] This paper represents one of the earliest expressions of concern about the negative consequences of the existence of 'two social psychologies'. Britt presents three lines of evidence for social psychologists being divided into two separate camps: the division of social psychologists as to membership in the American Sociological Society and the American Psychological Association; the separate meetings of the two groups and lack of formal contact; and their divergent reading and research habits. Britt draws attention to 'the lack of understanding, and sometimes even jealousy, between the two groups.' 'Surely', he writes, 'the time has come for the two groups of social psychologists to form a united front to attack their mutual problems. Differences in points of view should not prevent coordination of interests and activities'.[67] Britt innocently surmises whether the field has been dubbed 'social psychology' perhaps because 'social' was a more convenient adjective than 'psychological' and wonders whether it really would make any difference if the word order were reversed and the field were called 'psychological sociology'. It is interesting to contrast Britt's remarks with those of Holland who, writing some 40 years later, notes:

>...the extent to which the disciplines [of social psychology] are professionalised, making it necessary to draw boundaries which locate a monopoly of certain kinds of research and practice, and the extent to which these professional property rights are deeply and historically institutionalised.[68]

Britt concludes by proposing an 'united group' – a 'Society of Social Psychologists', a proposal which was to be made more than once in the following decades.

A recent example of the debate which suggests that not all that much has changed in 54 years comes from *The Future of Social Psychology*.[69] In this even-handed volume, the seven contributors are prominent Amerian social psychologists – four sociological social psychologists (Backman, House, C.W. Stephan, and Stryker) and three psychological social psychologists (Pettigrew, Schooler and W.G. Stephan) and they are largely in agreement that a major schism still exists between the sociological and psychological traditions of social psychology and that its continuation has 'negative consequences' for both traditions.[70]

In an authoritative, but appropriately ecumenical final chapter titled 'Is unity possible?', Pettigrew identifies various problems and barriers to greater communication.[71] These include the now familiar factors of disparate histories, intellectual traditions and epistemologies, one-way communication (especially evident in journal citations – articles in sociological social psychology journals such as *Social Psychology Quarterly* being much more likely to cite psychological sources than are PSP articles likely to cite sociological sources) and above all, the way these differences are embedded in institutional arrangements (discussed earlier in this chapter) – separate departments, journals, professional organisations and meetings, research funding councils, etc.

Pettigrew rejects the idea of separate 'interdisciplinary' departments of social psychology and, bringing together a number of proposals that have been made over the years, suggests instead that attention be focussed on the 'gate-keeping nodes of the discipline' – graduate training, research institutes, the journals, the research funding agencies, and professional organisations and meetings. Each of these has, at one time or another, already been singled out as having a contribution to make to the solution of social psychology's problems.[72]

There is only space to comment on only a few general historical and rhetorical aspects of this literature. First of all, the regularity of the debates suggests that the matter has been, and continues to be of concern to social psychologists from both traditions of social psychology. It can be no coincidence, surely, that the flow of papers increases during the 1970s and 1980s, following the collapse of most of the interdisciplinary arrangements.[73] There is little agreement, however, about possible remedies.[74] It seems that we have as yet been unable to develop a social psychology which effectively brings sociological and psychological expertise together in a 'trans-disciplinary' framework. Though more limited examples of 'cross-' and 'interdisciplinarity' can be found.[75] It may indeed be the case that the social psychologist's 'special obligation' to bridge the gap between sociology and psychology is, as Jos Jaspers once suggested,[76] a goal beyond our reach, a task that can never reasonably be achieved, given the diversity and complexity of the parent disciplines. It may thus be a goal, like that of a general integrative theory, to which we should not aspire.[77]

Secondly, if some of the characteristics of what communication there exists between the separate traditions of social psychology are examined, it is found that much of the traffic is one-way. Sociological social psychologists tend to cite studies in PSP, but not the reverse.[78] The *American Sociological Association* sponsored social psychology journal *Social Psychology Quarterly* has at least a sprinkling of psychological social psychologists on its editorial board, whereas the *Journal of Personality and Social Psychology* and *Personality and Social Psychology Bulletin* do not. More surprisingly, or alarmingly (depending on where one stands), is the fact that many of those who have contributed to the debate (or at least the 'two social psychologies' strand) come from sociological traditions and the audience they have been addressing has tended to be one of sociologists.[79] Despite their genuine concerns about the 'psychologizing' and 'dissipation' of sociological social psychology[80] and their 'minority' status,[81] it is sociological social psychologists who seem most keen to pursue closer co-operation.[82]

At this point it is appropriate to apply, reflexively, some social psychological principles from intergroup conflict theory to the discipline(s) of social psychology. What we are considering here is a form of intergroup behaviour – between two groups with similar interests but differing in size and perceived status. The restricted contact and largely one-way communication noted above provide appropriate conditions for the development of gross misconceptions, negative outgroup stereoytpes and resistance by both groups to ideas of unity and integration.[83] But it is also clear from the intergroup literature that mere intergroup 'contact' is not sufficient in this, as in other domains, to improve poor intergroup relations, especially in circumstances where there is a long history of institutionally reinforced suspicion, prejudice and rivalry for scarce resources.[84]

Thirdly, although keen to pursue greater communication, some social psychologists (e.g., Stryker) are opposed to integration – especially in the form of single departments of social psychology – fearing the loss of both their own distinctive disciplinary perspective and of contacts with the parent discipline.[85] Stryker suggests that 'thorough institutional integration would be disastrous' because sociological social psychology's 'core message' (that social psychological processes are crucially affected by social structural settings) would be lost in the process of integration. In a passage which is worth quoting at length, he beautifully captures the tension between disciplinary and interdisciplinary forms of knowing:

> ...the two social psychologies need one another, and they need one another in something approximating their current form rather than in a blend of the two. I am not arguing that efforts to bridge the gap between the two social psychologies should be aborted: the dialectic that I claim is healthy requires that communication between the two takes place, almost certainly on a level more extensive than is currently accomplished, and that means more forums bringing together representatives of the two social psychologies. Their coming together, however, must be against a context of support from their parent disciplines, and the continued separate disciplinary identification that implies. What we should not be looking towards is a disappearance of the two social psychologies.[86]

In other words, dialogue between the two 'social psychologies' (indeed between various social psychological 'traditions') should be seen as an essential part of the discipline(s) of social psychology.[87]

Lastly, in much of this literature, a 'rhetoric of interdisciplinarity' can be seen to be employed in relation to the crossing of the disciplinary boundaries of the social psychologies – there is talk of 'sharing' and 'borrowing', of 'bridge-building' and 'integration'. 'Geopolitical' metaphors are evident – there is reference to 'trespassing', 'property rights', and 'territorial struggles'.[88] These attempts to promote an IDSP also reveal, I believe, the danger of the progressivist trap of critical history: an IDSP on which we pin our hopes for the future but which itself acquires many of the characteristics of the separate disciplines from which it has been spawned. It retains, above all, a 'disciplinary' character.

Some implications for the disciplinary futures of social psychology

This chapter ends on a shamelessly presentist note, with a consideration of some of the implications of the analysis for current practice. Earlier in this chapter the reader was alerted to the dangers of disciplinary categories and cautioned to examine carefully the uses to which such categorisations were being put. The reader is thus encouraged to do so with respect to this chapter as a whole but especially to this final section.

First of all, I question the feasibility and desirability of the various calls for unity, synthesis or integration. This 'integration fantasy', as Holland has called it,[89] fails to recognise the powerful (disciplinary) institutional constraints that stand in the way of such unification. At times of financial or intellectual uncertainty 'disciplinary' loyalties tend to prevail, with unfavourable implications for staff appointments, research funding, publications etc.[90] Time and time again, such constraints have undermined even the most successful of interdisciplinary initatives (e.g., the programmes at Harvard and Michigan).[91']

Secondly, even if these constraints could be overcome another problem, noted in the introduction to this book, has to be faced. Social psychology still embodies many of the features of the legacy of Cartesian philosophy – an individualistic, representational theory of mind.[92] It thus wrestles with a variety of dualisms that have dominated the intellectual life of many of the human sciences during the past three centuries – body/mind, subject/object, individual/collective, biological/social, organism/environment, fact/value, knowledge/action, etc. Given that the terms of these dualisms are often differently patterned within the various human sciences, a greater emphasis on border crossing would undoubtedly be beneficial but would tend to redistribute the dualisms rather than transcend them.

In order to transcend these dualisms I believe it to be necessary to embrace a *mutualist* perspective in which mind, body and environment cannot be understoood as separate entitities. The foundations for such a perspective are to be found in the writings of William James, John Dewey, G.H. Mead and Lev Vygotsky. More recent inspiration can be drawn from James Gibson.[93] To achieve the implementation of such a perspective, I also believe it to be necessary to foster a strategic 'undisciplining'[94] of the human sciences. Such a view is, I believe, consonant with Serge Moscovici's recent proposals for dealing with the 'crisis of the representation of the social' in the human sciences by means of 'a flexible union of sociology, economics, psychology, history'.[95] Given the 'constructed' character of the objects of social psychological enquiry, I agree with Danziger's recent conclusions that for greater access to the social and psychological realities we study, we need to ensure a:

> ...mutual confrontation of divergent empirical domains and the different investigative practices that constitute them. This would have to include domains that, for entirely extraneous reasons, have become identified with other disciplines, like linguistics, sociology, or anthropology.[96]

While I reject the notion of an IDSP, I nonetheless believe that both the intermittent quest for an IDSP and the 'two social psychologies' debate have served a useful purpose in the history of social psychology in drawing attention to the false sense of self-sufficiency of 'disciplined' social psychology, sociological or psychological.

Conclusion

In this chapter I have analysed rhetorical aspects of social psychology, viewed as an exemplar of an 'inter-discipline' in the human sciences. Beginning from a consideration of some features of 'disciplinarity' and also the tension between disciplinarity and interdisciplinarity, I have looked at the politics of the disciplinary representation of various traditions of social psychology, discussed the role of metaphor in the historical reconstruction of social psychology, and have examined aspects of the attempts to foster an interdisciplinary social psychology, noting the persisting attraction of the goal of interdisciplinarity. I also have identified some of the functions of such disciplinary and interdisciplinary rhetorics. While I do not share the belief that 'interdisciplinarity' will provide a solution to social psychology's long-standing disciplinary problems, I have concluded by advocating recourse to Moscovici's notion of 'flexible unions' in and between the human sciences. In such a way we can, I believe, respond to Marcel Mauss' challenge to study the complete 'non-compartmentalised man' and avoid some of the negative consequences of disciplinary specialism and isolation. Over 10 years ago I wrote a paper on the relationship between sociology and psychology. Its conclusion still seems timely:

> ...if in the past psychologists have erred in their studies of social life by overemphasizing constraint and neglecting social context, then sociologists in their turn have erred by overemphasizing autonomy and neglecting the characteristics of the actors who generate patterned social life. Does this amount, then, to promise unfulfilled? I fear that the answer must be yes. And is it not possible that, in failing to explore fully the potential mutual relevence of psychology and sociology, each discipline has itself achieved less than it might have otherwise? Indeed, promises unfulfilled.[97]

Notes

1. Some of the material in this paper has appeared in *Canadian Psychology* and in the British Psychological Society *History and Philosophy of Psychology Newsletter*. I am grateful to Arthur Still, Irving Velody and Richard Roberts for numerous helpful conversations about many of the themes in this paper.

2. Jaspars, J.M.F., 'The task of social psychology: Some historical reflections' *British Journal of Social Psychology* 22 (1983) pp. 277-88. Jaspars writes: 'From the very beginning social psychology has regarded it as its task to integrate the knowledge of the individual and of society' (p. 278).

3. See R. Smith, 'Does the history of psychology have a subject?' *History of the Human Sciences* 1 (1988) pp. 147-77.

4. Gerth, H., and Wright Mills, C., *Character and Social Structure: The Psychology of Social Institutions* (London: Routledge and Kegan Paul, 1954) p. xviii.

5. I believe that this point is just as appropriate to the position of social psychology.

6. The term 'disciplinary specialism' derives from Nicholas Maxwell. See N. Maxwell, 'Science, reason, knowledge, and wisdom: A critique of specialism' *Inquiry* 23 (1980) pp. 19-81.

7. In a communication to the Société de Psychologie on 10 January 1924. Mauss, M., 'Address to the Société de Psychologie' (10 January 1924). Reprinted in M. Mauss, *Sociology and Psychology: Essays* (London: Routledge and Kegan Paul, 1979).

8. See D.R. Shumway and E. Messer-Davidow, 'Disciplinarity: An introduction' *Poetics Today* 12 (1991) pp. 201-25. The contribution of Foucault to our understanding of disciplinary authority has already been noted in the introduction and elsewhere in this volume.

9. Bechtel, W., 'The nature of scientific integration', in W. Bechtel (ed.), *Integrating Scientific Disciplines* (Dordrecht: Martinus Nijhoff, 1986).

10. Bechtel, W., op. cit., p. 10.

11. For example, S. Shapin, 'History of science and its sociological reconstructions', *History of Science* 20 (1982) pp. 157-211; K.D. Knorr-Cetina and M. Mulkay, *Science Observed: Perspectives on the Social Study of Science* (London: Sage, 1983); R. Whitley, *The Intellectual and Social Organization of the Sciences* (Oxford: Clarendon Press, 1984).

12. Hull, D.L., 'Exemplars and essences', unpublished manuscript (1982), cited in W. Bechtel, op. cit., p. 19; Hull, D.L., *Science as a Process: An Evolutionary Account of the Social and Conceptual Development of Science* (Chicago: University of Chicago Press, 1988).

13. Rouse, J., *Knowledge and Power: Toward a Political Philosophy of Science* (Ithaca: Cornell University Press, 1987); Rouse, J., 'The narrative reconstruction of science' *Inquiry* 33 (1990) pp. 179-96; Rouse, J., 'The politics of postmodern philosophy of science' *Philosophy of Science* 58 (1991), 607-27; Rouse, J., 'Philosophy of Science and the persistent narratives of modernity' *Studies in History and Philosophy of Science* 22 (1991) pp. 141-62.

14. Rouse, J., (1987) p. 25.

15. Rouse, J., op. cit., pp. xii-xiii.

16. Rouse, J., (1990) p. 188.

17. Scientific papers thus rely on *tacit knowledge*. See T. Becher, *Academic Tribes and Territories: Intellectual Enquiry and the Culture of Disciplines* (Milton Keynes: SRHE and Open University Press, 1989) ch. 2, pp. 25-6.

18. Ibid., p. 189.

19. Brown, R.H., 'Poetics, politics and professionalism in the rise of American psychology' *History of the Human Sciences* 5 (1992) pp. 47-61. [p. 47]

20. Steve Fuller also draws attention to the way in which 'science exercises wordly power by rhetorically drawing our attention to the fact that scientific knowledge represents the world and away from the fact that it also intervenes in the world' (Fuller, S., 'Disciplinary boundaries and the rhetoric of science' *Poetics Today* 12 [1991] pp. 301-25).

21. For some recent discussions see J.T. Klein, *Interdisciplinarity: History, Theory and Practice* (Detroit: Wayne State University Press, 1990); T. Becher, *Academic Tribes and Territories: Intellectual Enquiry and the Culture of Disciplines* (Milton Keynes: SRHE and Open University Press, 1989); W. Bechtel, *Integrating Scientific Disciplines* (Dordrecht: Martinus Nijhoff, 1986).

22. The term comes from Donald Campbell who defines disciplinary ethnocentrism as 'symptoms of tribalism or nationalism or ingroup partisanship in the internal or external relationships of university departments, national scientific organisations, and academic disciplines.'. (Campbell, D.T., 'Ethnocentrism of disciplines and the fish-scale model of omniscience', in M. Sherif and C.W. Sherif [eds], *Interdisciplinary Relationships in the Social Sciences* [Chicago: Aldine, 1969]).

23. Klein, J., 'Across the boundaries' *Social Epistemology* 4 (1990) pp. 267-80. [p. 277]

24. Klein, J., ibid., p. 277.

25. Tajfel, H., and Fraser, C., *Introducing Social Psychology* (Harmondsworth: Penguin, 1978) p. 17.

26. There is no adequate critical history of the disciplines of social psychology. I share Farr's view that it is impossible to write a history of social psychology without at the same time writing a history of psychology and sociology (see R.M. Farr, 'Editorial' *British Journal of Social Psychology* 22 [1983] pp. 273-5). An impressive start has been made by C.F. Graumann, 'Introduction to a history of social psychology', in M. Hewstone, *et al.* (eds), *Introduction to Social Psychology* (Oxford: Blackwell, 1988), but other 'disciplinary interests' also need to be represented, especially anthropology.

27. McDougall, W., *Introduction to Social Psychology* (London: Methuen, 1908); Ross, E.A., *Social Psychology* (New York: Macmillan, 1908).

28. See C.F. Graumann, op. cit.; I. Lubek, 'Psychology and its history in various countries', paper presented at the XXnd International Congress of Psychology (Leipzig, 1980).

29. Britt, S.H., 'Social psychologists or psychological sociologists – which?' *Journal of Abnormal and Social Psychology* 32 (1937) pp. 314-18.

30. Stouffer, S.A., Suchman, E.A., De Vinney, L.C., Star, S.A., and William Jr, R.M., *The American Soldier: Studies in Social Psychology in World War II* vol. I

(Princeton: Princeton University Press, 1949); and US. Strategic Bombing Survey, *The Effects of Strategic Bombing on German Morale* (Washington, DC: USGPO, 1946); US Strategic Bombing Survey, *The Effects of Strategic Bombing on Japanese Morale* (Washington, DC: USGPO, 1947).

31. See W.H. Sewell, 'Some reflections on the golden age Interdisciplinary social psychology' *Annual Review of Sociology* 15 (1989) pp. 1-16. One early discussion of 'who teaches social psychology?' advises social psychologists to 'attempt to apprise their faculty committees, administrative officials, and governing bodies of the desirability of financial and moral assistance in developing a more unified field of study and instruction' (Cameron, W.B., Lasley, P., and Dewey, R. 'Who teaches social psychology?' *American Sociological Review* 45 [1950] pp. 553-5).

32. A convenient source for details of some of these graduate training programmes can be found in S. Lundstedt (ed.), *Higher Education in Social Psychology* (Cleveland: Case-Western Reserve Press, 1968).

33. For example, the *Institute for Social Research* at the University of Michigan and the *Bureau of Applied Social Research* at Columbia University.

34. Sewell, W.H., op. cit., p. 3.

35. For some contrasted commentaries see R.L. Rosnow, *Paradigms in Transition: The Methodology of Social Inquiry* (New York: Oxford University Press, 1981); *Social Psychology, Past and Present: An Integrative Orientation* (Hillsdale: Erlbaum, 1988, ch. 5) and I. Parker, *The Crisis in Modern Social Psychology – and how to End it* (London: Routledge, 1989).

36. Moscovici, S., 'Society and theory in social psychology', in J. Israel and H. Tajfel (eds), *The Context of Social Psychology* (London: Academic Press, 1972).

37. Tajfel, H. (ed.), *The Social Dimension: European Developments in Social Psychology* (Cambridge/Paris: Cambridge University Press/Maison des Sciences de l'Homme, 1984).

38. In the period between the Britt paper with its call for the formation of an ecumenical 'Society of Social Psychologists' and the Stephan volume, there have appeared with some regularity, discussions of these two separate traditions of social psychology, of their relative isolation, and of the need to bring them together. There have also been intermittent calls for the development of a properly interdisciplinary social psychology. Elsewhere I have argued that this 'two social psychologies' thesis and the quest for an interdisciplinary social psychology are not post-Second World war phenomena (and consequences of the 'crisis') but can be traced back to earlier expressions of concern about the existence of two ostensibly autonomous social psychologies – at least to the 1930s (see J.M.M. Good and A.W. Still, 'The idea of an interdisciplinary social psychology: An historical and rhetorical analysis' *Canadian Psychology* 33 [1992] pp. 43-8.

39. See J. House, 'The three faces of social psychology' *Sociometry* 40 (1977) pp. 161-77; R.M. Farr, 'On the varieties of social psychology: An essay on the relationships between social psychology and other social sciences' *Social Science Information* 17 (1978) pp. 503-25.

40. There always has been much greater diversity within each of these allegedly monolithic social psychologies than such a view would suppose. See J.M.M. Good, 'Sociology and psychology – promise unfulfilled?', in P. Abrams and P. Lethwaite (eds), *Development and Diversity: British Sociology 1950-1980* (London: British Sociological Association, 1981); T.F. Pettigrew, 'Is unity possible? A summary', in C.W. Stephan, W.G. Stephan, and T.F. Pettigrew (eds), *The Future of Social Psychology: Defining the Relationship between Sociology and Psychology* (New York: Springer-Verlag, 1991).

41. Woolgar, S., 'The identification and definition of scientific specialities' in G. Lemaine, R. MacLeod, M. Mulkay/and P. Weigart (eds), *Perspectives on the Emergence of Scientific Disciplines* (The Hague: Mouton, 1975).

42. Jonathon Potter provides a interesting example of psychologists' category discourse in a study of the use of the categories 'mechanist' and 'humanist' in the transcript of an international psychology conference. Potter is able to demonstrate a flexibility of category definition with respect to the subject matter, the research methods and the metaphysical assumptions of the putative membership as well as the involvement of categories in practical tasks of criticism and evaluation (Potter, J., 'Cutting cakes: A study of psychologists' social categorisations' *Philosophical Psychology* 1 [1988] pp. 17-33).

43. Harré and Secord's (1972) monograph, with its (for some) intoxicating blend of realist philosophy of science, social theory, and analytical philosophy provided the initial impetus (Harré, R., and Secord, P.F., *The Explanation of Social Behaviour* [Oxford: Blackwell, 1972]. For a recent example see J.D. Greenwood, 'Realism, empiricism and social constructionism: Psychological theory and the social dimensions of mind and action' *Theory & Psychology* 2 (1992) pp. 131-51.

44. On rhetoric, see M. Billig, *Arguing and Thinking: A Rhetorical Approach to Social Psychology* (Cambridge/Paris: Cambridge University Press/Editions de la Maison des Sciences de l'Homme, 1987); on narrative, see T.R. Sarbin, *Narrative Psychology: The Storied Nature of Human Conduct* (New York: Praeger, 1986); on discourse, see D. Edwards and J. Potter, *Discursive Psychology* (London: Sage, 1992); on culture, see A. Pepitone, 'The role of culture in theories of social psychology', in C. Kagitcibasi (ed.), *Growth and Progress in Cross-Cultural Psychology* (Lisse: Swets and Zeitlinger B.V., 1987) and G. Jahoda, 'Nature, culture and social psychology' *European Journal of Social Psychology* 16 (1986) pp. 17-30.

45. For a sample see N.K. Denzin, 'The spaces of postmodernism: Reading Plummer on Blumer' *Symbolic Interaction* 13 (1990) pp. 145-54; M. Michael, 'Some postmodern reflections on social psychology' *Theory & Psychology* 1 (1991) pp. 203-21; I. Parker and J. Shotter, *Deconstructing Social Psychology* (London: Routledge, 1990).

46. For a more extended analysis which examines the rhetorical constitution of social psychology in texts, handbooks and discussions of teaching see J.M.M. Good, *The Quest for an Interdisciplinary Social Psychology* (manuscript in preparation).

47. Graumann, C.F., 'The individualization of the social and the desocialization of the individual: Floyd H. Allport's contribution to social psychology', in C.F. Graumann and S. Moscovici (eds), *Changing Conceptions of Crowd Mind and Behavior* (New York: Springer-Verlag, 1986).

48. 'Social psychology and cognitive social psychology are today nearly synonymous. The cognitive approach is now clearly the dominant approach among social psychologists, having virtually no competitors.... The social psychology of the seventies and of the eighties takes it for granted that internal representations mediate between the stimulus and its behavioral consequences and that these representations dominate the entire process' (Markus, H., and Zajonc, R.B., 'The cognitive perspective in social psychology', in G. Lindzey and E. Aronson (eds), *Handbook of Social Psychology* 3rd edn, vol. 1 [Hillsdale: Erlbaum, 1985] pp. 137-8). For one positive view of the strength of the competition, see G.P. Ginsburg, 'The ecological perception debate: An affordance of the *Journal for the Theory of Social Behaviour*', *Journal for the Theory of Social Behaviour* 20 (1990) pp. 347-64.

49. Gergen, K.J., 'Social psychology as history' *Journal of Personality and Social Psychology* 26 (1973) pp. 309-20; Blank, T.O., 'Reflections on Gergen's "Social psychology as history" in perspective' *Personality and Social Psychology Bulletin* 14 (1988) pp. 651-63; R. Harré, 'Metaphysics and methodology: Some prescriptions for social psychological research' *European Journal of Social Psychology* 19 (1989) pp. 439-53.

50. Pettigrew, T.F., 'Influencing policy with social psychology' (The 1987 Kurt Lewin Memorial Address) *Journal of Social Issues* 44 (1988) pp. 205-19; Stephenson, G.M., 'Applied social psychology' in M. Hewstone, *et al.* (eds), *Introduction to Social Psychology* (Oxford: Blackwell, 1988); P. Wexler, *Critical Social Psychology* (Boston: Routledge and Kegan Paul, 1983).

51. Billig, M., 'Rhetoric of social psychology', in I. Parker and J. Shotter (eds), *Deconstructing Social Psychology* (London: Routledge, 1990).

52. Wilson, D.W., and Schafer, R.B., 'Is social psychology interdisciplinary?' *Personality and Social Psychology Bulletin* 4 (1978) pp. 548-52.

53. Jones, E.E., 'Major developments in social psychology during the past five decades', in G. Lindzey and E. Aronson (eds), *Handbook of Social Psychology* vol. 1, 3rd edn (New York: Random House, 1985).

54. Farr observes that 'the attempt initially to distinguish social psychology from psychology, and subsequently also sociology from psychology in terms of a difference in levels, is the cause rather than the antidote of the problems [in the relationships between psychology and other social sciences]' (R.M. Farr, 'On the varieties of social psychology: An essay on the relationships between social psychology and other social sciences' *Social Science Information* 17 [1978] pp. 503-25). [p. 513]

55. For example, J. House, op. cit.; M.L. Kohn, 'Social structure and personality: A quintessentially sociological approach to social psychology' *Social Forces* 68 (1989) pp. 26-33; S. Stryker, 'The two social psychologies: Additional thoughts' *Social Forces* 68 (1989) pp. 45-54.

56. Gecas, V., 'Rekindling the sociological imagination in social psychology' *Journal for the Theory of Social Behaviour* 19 (1989) pp. 97-115.

57. Morgan, D.L., and Schwalbe, M.L., 'Mind and self in society: Linking social structure and social cognition' *Social Psychology Quarterly* 5 (1990) pp. 148-64. [p. 162]

58. A recent volume devoted to a detailed examination of the 'two social psychologies' provides a convenient example, see C.W. Stephan, W.G. Stephan, and T.F. Pettigrew (eds), *The Future of Social Psychology: Defining the Relationship between Sociology and Psychology* (New York: Springer-Verlag, 1991).

59. In this section I draw upon a mutualist approach to historical work developed in conjunction with Arthur Still. In previous papers we have described mutualism as a perspective which has its source in Hegel and in the anti-mechanistic philosophy of Romanticism (see A.W. Still, 'Mechanism and Romanticism: A selective history', in A.W. Still and A. Costall [eds], *Against Cognitivism: Alternative Foundations for Cognitive Psychology* [Hemel Hempstead: Harvester Wheatsheaf, 1991]; and A.W. Still and J.M.M. Good, 'Mutualism in the Human Sciences: Towards the implementation of a theory' *Journal for the Theory of Social Behaviour* 22 [1992] pp. 105-28). In recovering and developing this perspective we have drawn upon the writings not only of the Pragmatists (especially James, Dewey and Mead) but also of Vygotsky and James Gibson. From this perspective mind, body and environment cannot be understood in isolation but are constructions from the flow of purposive activity in the world (See J.M.M. Good and A.W. Still, 'Accounting for histories of social psychology: A case study in post-critical history', paper presented at the Symposium on *History and Social Psychology*, British Psychological Society Social Psychology Section Annual Conference [University of Surrey, September 1991]).

60. For a discussion of the role of metaphor in the history of psychology see D.E. Leary (ed.), *Metaphors in the History of Psychology* (New York: Cambridge University Press, 1990).

61. Apfelbaum, E., 'Prolegomena for a history of social psychology: Some hypotheses concerning its emergence in the 20th century and its raison d'être', in K.S. Larsen (ed.), *Dialectics and Ideology in Psychology* (Norwood: Ablex, 1986).

62. Jones, E.E., 'Major developments in social psychology during the past five decades', in G. Lindzey and E. Aronson (eds), *Handbook of Social Psychology* vol. 1, 3rd edn (New York: Random House, 1985).

63. Farr, R.M., 'The international origins of a science: Social psychology' *British Psychological Society History and Philosophy of Psychology Newsletter* no. 8 (1989) pp. 13-21.

64. Graumann, C.F., op. cit. (1986).

65. Apfelbaum, E., op. cit., p. 11.

66. Britt, S.H., 'Social psychologists or psychological sociologists – which?' *Journal of Abnormal and Social Psychology* 32 (1937) pp. 314-18.

67. Britt, S.H., op. cit., p. 318.

68. Holland, R., *Self and Social Context* (London: Macmillan, 1977) p. 286.

69. Stephan, C.W., Stephan, W.G., and Pettigrew, T.F. (eds), op. cit.

70. These 'negative consequences' are seen to include duplication of effort, loss of valuable theoretical and methodological resources, intellectual isolation etc.

71. Pettigrew, T.F., op. cit. (1991).

72. For a sample see S.H. Britt, op. cit; T.M. Newcomb, 'The training of social psychologists', in J.E. Hulett Jr. and R. Stagner (eds), *Problems in Social Psychology: An Interdisciplinary Inquiry* (Urbana: Illinois, 1952); J.M.F. Jaspars and

E. Ackermans, 'The interdisciplinary character of social psychology: an illustration' *Sociologia Neerlandica* 4 (1966) pp. 62-79; S. Lundstedt, op. cit.; S. Stryker, 'Developments in "two social psychologies": Toward an appreciation of mutual relevance' *Sociometry* 40 (1977) pp. 145-60; C.W. Backman, 'Toward an interdisciplinary social psychology' *Advances in Experimental Social Psychology* 16 (1983) pp. 219-61.

73. See R.G. Boutilier, J.C. Roed, and A.C. Svendsen, 'Crises in the two social psychologies: A critical comparison' *Social Psychology Quarterly* 43 (1980) pp. 5-17; and A.M. McMahon, 'The two social psychologies: Postcrises directions' *Annual Review of Sociology* 10 (1984) pp. 121-40.

74. The main institutional choice is between independent interdisciplinary departments of social psychology, separate disciplinary-based social psychology courses or joint programmes run by social psychologists located in psychology and sociology departments.

75. In the fields of intergroup relations (H. Tajfel [ed.], *Social Identity and Intergroup Relations* [Cambridge/Paris: Cambridge University Press/Maison des Sciences de l'Homme, 1982]); collective behaviour (G. Gaskell and R. Benewick [eds], *The Crowd in Contemporary Britain* [London: Sage, 1987]), social representations (R.M. Farr and S. Moscovici [eds] *Social Representations* [Cambridge/Paris: Cambridge University Press/Maison des Sciences de l'Homme, 1984]) and discourse (J. Potter and M. Wetherell, *Discourse and Social Psychology: Beyond Attitudes and Behaviour* [London: Sage, 1987]), for example.

76. See J.M.F. Jaspars, op. cit.

77. See L.H. Strickland, F. Aboud, K.J. Gergen, G. Jahoda, and H. Tajfel, 'General theory in social psychology' *Personality and Social Psychology Bulletin* 2 (1976) pp. 148-53.

78. See T.F. Pettigrew, op. cit. (1991).

79. Among the most frequent 'sociological' contributors to these debates are Guy Swanson, James House, Sheldon Stryker and Carl Backman.

80. On the 'psychologizing' and 'dissipation' of sociological social psychology see A.E. Liska, 'The dissipation of sociological social psychology' *American Sociologist* 12 (1977) pp. 2-8.

81. In both the USA and Europe there are far more social psychologists whose professional disciplinary affiliation is psychology rather than sociology. See C.W. Backman, 'Interdisciplinary social psychology: Prospects and problems', in C.W. Stephan, W.G. Stephan, and T.F. Pettigrew (eds), op. cit.

82. There are some notable exceptions – both European (e.g., Henri Tajfel, Serge Moscovici, Willem Doise, Jos Jaspars) and North American (e.g., Thomas Pettigrew, Ian Lubek, Paul Secord, Henry Minton).

83. See T.F. Pettigrew, op. cit., pp. 104-5 and C.W. Stephan and W.G. Stephan, 'Social psychology at the crossroads', in (eds) C.W. Stephan, W.G. Stephan and T.F. Pettigrew (eds), *The Future of Social Psychology: Defining the Relationship between Sociology and Psychology* (New York: Springer-Verlag, 1991).

84. For an assessment and reworking of the 'contact hypothesis' see M. Hewstone and R. Brown, 'Contact is not enough: An intergroup perspective on the

"contact hypothesis" ' in M. Hewstone and R. Brown (eds), *Contact and Conflict in Intergroup Encounters* (Oxford: Blackwell, 1986).

85. See S. Stryker, 'The two social psychologies: Additional thoughts' *Social Forces* 68 (1989) pp. 45-54 and S. Stryker, 'Consequences of the gap between the "two social psychologies" ', in C.W. Stephan, W.G. Stephan, and T.F. Pettigrew (eds), op. cit.

86. Stryker, S. (1991), op. cit., pp. 96-7.

87. On traditions of inquiry and their comparison see A. MacIntyre, *Whose Justice? Which Rationality?* (London: Duckworth, 1988).

88. On sharing, see G.E. Swanson, 'On sharing social psychology: A problem in graduate education', in S. Lundstedt (ed.), *Higher Education in Social Psychology* (Cleveland: Case-Western Reserve Press, 1968); on bridge-building see Wilson and Schaffer, op. cit.; on integration and property rights, see W.P. Archibald, 'Psychology, sociology and social psychology: Bad fences make bad neighbours' *British Journal of Sociology* 27 (1976) pp. 115-29.

89. Holland, R., op. cit.

90. See W.H. Sewell, op. cit; T.F. Pettigrew, op. cit. These examples provide effective illustrations of Julie Klein's observations about the 'disciplinary paradox' (cited earlier in this chapter).

91. See E.E. Jones, op. cit. Theodore Newcomb, reflecting on the factors which led to the dissolving of the University of Michigan's highly successful interdepartmental doctoral program in social psychology (which he had directed for nearly 20 years) notes that though the 'structural' fact that far more psychologists than sociologists were available to run the program had, from the beginning been a source of potential threat to some members of the sociology department, 'the crucial, irreversible steps were not explainable primarily in such terms. Individuals of strong determination, on both sides, moved toward irreconcilable positions on issues that had previously been negotiable...a budgetless organization, serving to promote the overlapping interests of two strong parent organizations, cannot long survive beyond the time when those organization's representatives, who must work together, have ceased to trust one another' ('Theodore M. Newcomb', in G. Lindzey (ed.), *A History of Psychology in Autobiography* vol. VI [Englewood Cliff: Prentice-Hall, 1974] p. 384).

92. On the identity of social psychology and cognitive social psychology, see the passage cited from Markus and Zajonc, in note 48.

93. For an outline of such a mutualist psychology, and an attempt to implement it see A.W. Still and J.M.M. Good, 'Mutualism in the Human Sciences: Towards the implementation of a theory' *Journal for the Theory of Social Behaviour* 22 (1992) pp. 105-28.

94. By this I mean a strategic and selective focus on limited topic areas, often but by no means always of a 'social problems' nature.

95. Moscovici, S., op. cit. (1990) These proposals are also echoed by Tomas Ibanez in his uncompromising appeal for the espousal of a post-modernist perspective in developing a properly 'social' social psychology (Ibanez, T., 'Henri, Serge...and the next generation' *British Psychological Society Social Psychology*

Section Newsletter no. 24 [1990] pp. 5-14; Ibanez, T., 'Social psychology and the rhetoric of truth' *Theory and Psychology* 2 [1991] pp. 187-201).

96. Danziger, K., *Constructing the Subject: Historical Origins of Psychological Research* (Cambridge: Cambridge University Press, 1990).

97. Good, J.M.M., 'Sociology and psychology – promise unfulfilled?', in P. Abrams and P. Lethwaite (eds), *Development and Diversity: British Sociology 1950-1980* (London: British Sociological Association, 1981).

Bibliography

Ad Herennium, trans. H. Caplan (London: Loeb Classical Library, 1954).

Aho, J.A., 'Rhetoric and the Invention of Double Entry Bookkeeping' *Rhetorica* 3 (1985) pp. 21-44.

Aristotle, *Rhetoric and Poetics*, trans. W.I. Roberts and I. Bywater, and F. Solmsen (ed.) (New York: Random House, 1954).

———— *Rhetoric* (Oxford: Oxford University Press, 1924, etc.).

Atkinson, P., *The Ethnographic Imagination: Textual Constructions of Reality* (London: Routledge, 1990).

Augustine (St), 'Principia Rhetorices' *Patrologie latine de Migne* vol. XXXII, columns 1439-48 (Paris, 1865).

Ballweg, Ottmar, 'Rhetorik und Res humanae', in R. Hauser, J. Rehberg, and G. Stragenwerth (eds), *Gedächtnisschrift für Peter Noll* (Zürich, 1984) pp. 13-26.

Ballweg, O., and Seibert T.-M. (eds), *Rhetorische Rechtstheorie* (Freiburg: Alber Verlag, 1982).

Barnes, Jonathan, 'Is Rhetoric an Art?', in *darg Newsletter* (Discourse Analysis Research Group, University of Calgary; 2/2 Fall, 1986).

Barthes, R., 'L'Ancienne rhétorique: aide-mémoire' *Communications* 16 (1970) pp. 179ff.

———— 'To Write: An Intransitive Verb?', R. Macksey, E. Donato (ed.), *The Structuralist Controversy* (Baltimore: Johns Hopkins University Press, 1972).

Bateson, G., *Steps to an Ecology of Mind* (St Albans: Paladin, 1973).

Bauman, Zygmunt, 'Philosophical affinities of postmodern sociology' *Sociological Review* 38 (1990) pp. 411-44.

Becher, Ilse, 'Rhetorik', in Johannes Irmscher (ed.), *Lexikon der Antike* (Leipzig, 1972).

Becher, Tony, *Academic Tribes and Territories: Intellectual Enquiry and the Cultures of Disciplines* (Milton Keynes: SRHE and Open University Press, 1989).

Bechtel, E. 'The Nature of Scientific Investigation', in E. Bechtel (ed.), *Integrating Scientific Disciplines*, (Dordrecht: Martinus Nijhoff, 1986) pp. 3-52.

Beer, G., and Martins, H. (eds), 'Introduction' to special issue *Rhetoric and Science* of *History of the Human Sciences* 3 (1990) pp. 163-75.

Bergner, Jeffrey T., *The Origin of Formalism in Social Science* (Chicago: Chicago University Press, 1981).

Bhaskar, Roy, *Reclaiming Reality A Critical Introduction to Contemporary Philosophy* (London: Verso, 1989).

'Bibliographie zur deutchsprachigen Rhetorikforschung', in *Rhetorik* 3ff. (1983).

Billig, M., *Arguing and Thinking: A Rhetorical Approach to Social Psychology* (Cambridge: Cambridge University Press, 1987).

———— 'Conservatism and the rhetoric of rhetoric' *Economy and Society* 18/2 (1989) pp. 132-48.

Bitzer, L., 'The Rhetorical Situation' *Philosophy and Rhetoric* 1.1 (1968), reprinted in D. Ehninger (ed.), *Contemporary Rhetoric* (Glenview, Illinois: Scott Foreman, 1972) pp. 39-78.

Black, E., *Rhetorical Criticism: A Study in Method* (New York: Macmillan, 1965).

Blair, Carole, 'Nietzsche's Lecture Notes on Rhetoric: a Translation' *Philosophy and Rhetoric* (1983) vol. 16/2, pp. 94-129.

Blair, Hugh, *Lectures on Rhetoric and Belles Lettres* (London, 1783).

Bloch, Ernst, 'Sokrates und die Propaganda', in *Vom Hasard zur Katastrophe: Politische Aufsätze aus den Jahren 1934-1939* (Frankfurt a. M.: Suhrkamp, 1972).

Bonebakker, S. A., *Materials for the History of the Arabic Rhetoric* (Naples, 1975).

Booth, Wayne C. *Modern Dogma and the Rhetoric of Assent*, (Chicago: University of Chicago Press, 1974).

———— *The Rhetoric of Fiction* (Chicago: University of Chicago Press, 1961).

———— *The Rhetoric of Irony* (Chicago: University of Chicago Press, 1974).

Bosmajian, Haig A. (ed.), *The Rhetoric of Nonverbal Communication*, (Glenier, Illinois: Scott Foresman, 1970).

Boyne, Roy, and Rattansi, Ali (eds), *Postmodernism and Society* (Basingstoke: Macmillan, 1990).

Brandt, William J., *The Rhetoric of Argumentation*. (New York: Bobbs-Merrill, 1970).

Brockriede, Wayne E., 'Dimensions of the Concept of Rhetoric' *Quarterly Journal of Speech* 54 (1966) pp. 33-40.

Brooks, Cleanth, and Penn Warren, Robert, *Modern Rhetoric* (New York: Harcourt Brace Jovanovich, 4th edn, 1979).

Brown, R.H., *A Poetic for Sociology* (Cambridge: Cambridge University Press, 1977).

———— *Social Science as Civic Discourse: Essays on the Invention, Legitimation, and Uses of Social Theory* (Chicago: Chicago University Press, 1989).

———— *Society as Text: Essays on Rhetoric, Reason and Reality* (Chicago: University of Chicago Press, 1987).

Brummett, B., 'Postmodern Rhetoric' *Philosophy and Rhetoric* 9/1 (1976).

Bryant, Donald C., 'Rhetoric: its function and its scope', in D. Ehringer (ed.), *Contemporary Rhetoric* (Glenier, Illinois: Scott Foresman, 1972).

Burke, K. A., *A Grammar of Motives* (Berkeley: University of California Press, 1945).

———— *Counter-Statement* (Berkeley: University of California Press, 1968).

———— 'Rhetoric – Old and New', in Martin Steinmann (ed.), *New Rhetorics* (New York: 1967).

———— *The Philosophy of Literary Form: Studies in Symbolic Action* (Louisiana: Louisiana State University Press, 2nd edn, 1967).

———— *Language as Symbolic Action: Essays on Life, Literature and Method* (Berkeley: University of California Press, 1969).

———— *A Rhetoric of Motives* (New York: George Braziller, 1950).

———— 'Rhetoric Old and New' *Journal of General Education* 5 (1950-1) pp. 203-9.

Burks, D.M. (ed.), *Rhetoric, Philosophy and Literature* (Indiana: W. Lafayette and Purdue University Press, 1978).

Butler, H.E., *The Institutio Oratoria of Quintilian* (London: Loeb Classical Library, Heinemann, 1990-2).

Cahn, Michael, *Kunst der Überlistung: Studien zur Wissenschaftsgeschichte der Rhetorik* (München: Fink, 1986).

Campbell, George, *The Philosophy of Rhetoric*, (London, 1776).

Campbell, Kathryn K., 'The Ontological Foundations of Rhetorical Theory' *Philosophy and Rhetoric* 3 (1970) pp. 97-108.

———— *Critiques of Contemporary Rhetoric* (Belmont, California: Wordsworth, 1972).

Campbell, P.N., 'Poetic-Rhetorical, philosophical, and scientific disourse' *Philosophy and Rhetoric* 6 (1973) pp. 1-29.

Caplan, Harry, *Of Eloquence: Studies in Ancient and Mediaeval Rhetoric*, Anne King and Helen North (eds) (Ithaca: Cornell University Press, 1970).

Carnap, Rudolf, 'Logical Foundations of the Unity of Science', in O. Neurath, R. Carnap, and C. Morris (eds), *International Encyclopedia of Unified Science* (Chicago: Chicago University Press, 1938) vol. I.

Carroll C., Introduction to the *Realm of Rhetoric* (Notre Dame: University of Notre Dame Press, 1982).

Cherwitz, Richard A., and Hilkins, James W., *Communication and Knowledge: An Investigation in Rhetorical Epistemology* (Columbia: University of South Carolina Press, 1986).

Cicero, *De Inventione*, trans. H.M. Hubbell, (London: Loeb Classical Library, Heinemann, 1949).

Classen, Carl Joachim (ed.), *Sophistik* (Darmstadt: Wissenschaftliche Buchgesellschaft, 1976).

Cleary, James W., and Haberman, Frederick W. (eds), *Rhetoric and Public Address: a Bibliography 1947-1961* (Madison: University of Wisconsin Press, 1964).

Cope, E.M., *An Introduction to Aristotle's Rhetoric* (Cambridge: Cambridge University Press, 1867).

Corbett, Edward P.J., *Classical Rhetoric for the Modern Student* (New York: Oxford University Press, 2nd edn, 1965).

———— 'The Rhetoric of the Open Hand and the Rhetoric of the Closed Fist.', in

Douglas Ehninger (ed.), *Contemporary Rhetoric* (Glenier, Illinois: Scott Foresman, 1972) pp. 202-10.

——— (ed.), *Rhetorical Analysis of Literary Works* (New York: Oxford University Press, 1969).

Covino, William, *The Art of Wondering: A Revisionist Returns to the History of Rhetoric* (Portsmouth: Boynton, 1988).

de Man, Paul, *Blindness and Insight: Essays in the Rhetoric of Contemporary Criticism* (2nd edn rev., London: Methuen, 1983).

——— *The Resistance to Theory, Theory and History of Literature* (Manchester: Manchester University Press, 1986).

Dockhorn, Klaus, *Macht und Wirkung der Rhetorik: Vier Aufsätze zur Ideengeschichte der Vormoderne* (Berlin, 1968).

——— 'Rhetorik und germanistiche Literaturwissenschaft in Deutschland', in *Jahrbuch für Internationale Germanistik* 3 (1971) pp. 168-85.

——— 'Luthers Glaubensbegriff und die Rhetorik: Zu Gerhard Ebelings Buch. Einführung in theologische Sprachlehre', in *Linguistics Biblica* 21/22 (1973) pp. 19-39.

Dubois, J., *Rhetorique générale* (Paris: Libraire Larousse, 1970).

Dyke, Joachim, 'Bibliographie zur Argumentationsforschung 1966-1978' *Rhetorik* 1 (1980) pp. 153-60.

Edmondson, Ricca, *Rhetoric in Sociology* (London: Macmillan, 1984).

Ehninger, Douglas, *Contemporary Rhetoric: A Reader's Course Book* (Glenier, Illinois: Scott Foresman 1972).

——— 'On Systems of Rhetoric' *Philosophy and Rhetoric* 1 (1968) pp. 131-44.

Erikson, K. (ed.), *Aristotle: The Classical Heritage of Rhetoric* (Metuchen: Scarecrow Press, 1974).

Fish, Stanley, *Doing What Comes Naturally: Change, Rhetoric, and the Practice of Literary and Theory in Legal Studies* (Oxford: Clarendon Press, 1990).

——— *Is there a Text in this Class? The Authority of Interpretive Communities* (Cambridge, MA: Harvard University Press, 1980).

——— 'Rhetoric', in Frank Lentricchia and Thomas McLaughlin (eds), *Critical Terms for Literary Study* (Chicago: Chicago University Press, 1990).

Fisher, W.R., 'Rationality and the Logic of Good Reasons' *Philosophy and Rhetoric* 13/2 (1980).

Florescu, Vasile, 'Rhetoric and its Rehabilitation in Contemporary Philosophy' *Philosophy and Rhetoric* 3 (1970) pp. 193-224.

Fogarty, Daniel, *Roots for a New Rhetoric* (Bureau of Publications, Colombia Teachers College, 1959).

Foss, Sonja (ed.), *Contemporary Perspectives on Rhetoric* (Prospect Heights, Illinois, 1985).

France, P., *Rhetoric and Truth in France: Descartes to Diderot* (Oxford: Clarendon Press, 1972).

——— 'Roland Barthes, A Rhetoric of Modernity', in *Proceedings of the Cana-*

dian Society for the History of Rhetoric 2 (1989) pp. 67-84.

——— 'The Uses of Rhetoric' *History of European Ideas* I/2 (1981) pp. 133-41.

Friedman, Norman, 'The Rhetoric of Logic' *Journal of General Education* 17 (1965-6) pp. 287-94.

Fumaroli, Marc, *L'âge de l'élequence: Rhétorique et 'res literaria' de la Renaissance au seuil de l'époque classique* (Paris/Geneva: Champion/Droz, 1980).

Gadamer, Hans-Georg, 'Rhetorik, Hermeneutik und Ideologiekritik: Metakritische Erörterungen zu Warheit und Methode', in Karl-Otto Apel, Claus von Bormann (eds), *Hermeneutik und Ideologiekritik* (Frankfurt a. M.: Suhrkamp, 1971).

——— 'Replik' ('Rhetorik, Hermeneutik und Ideologiekritik: Metakritische Erörterungen zu Warheit und Methode', in Karl-Otto Apel, Claus von Bormann u.a. (eds), *Hermeneutik und Ideologiekritik* [Frankfurt a. M.: Suhrkamp, 1971]).

Gane, Mike (ed.), 'Special Issue: Rhetoric' *Economy and Society* (1989) vol. 18, 1989.

Gauthier, David P., *Practical Reasoning: The Structure and Foundations of Prudential and Moral Arguments and Their Exemplification in Discourse* (Oxford: Clarendon Press, 1963).

Graham, L., Lepenies, W., and Weingart, P. (eds), *The Functions and Uses of Disciplinary Histories* (Dordrecht: Reidel, 1983).

Grassi, E., 'Can Rhetoric Provide a New Basis for Philosophizing?' *Philosophy and Rhetoric* 11/2 (1978).

——— *Macht des Bildes: Ohnmacht der rationalen Sprache* (Köln: DuMont Schauberg, 1970).

——— *Die Macht der Phantasie* (Königstein/Ts., 1979).

——— *Rhetoric as philosophy: the humanist tradition* (London: Pennsylvania State University Press, 1980).

——— *Vico and humanism: essays on Vico, Heidegger, and Rhetoric* (New York: Lang, 1990).

Grimaldi, W., 'Studies in the Philosophy of Aristotle's Rhetoric', Hermes, *Zeitschrift für Klassiche Philologie* 25 (Wiesbaden, 1972).

——— 'The Aristotelian Topics' (1958), reprinted in K. Erikson (ed.), *Aristotle: The Classical Heritage of Rhetoric* (Metuchen: Scarecrow Press, 1974).

Gross, A.G., *The Rhetoric of Science* (Cambridge, MA: Harvard University Press, 1990).

Habermas, J., *The Theory of Communicative Action*, trans. T. McCarthy (Boston: Beacon Press, 1981).

Halsall, A.H. (ed.), 'La rhétorique du texte' *Texte* 8 (Toronto, Trinity College: University of Toronto, 1989).

Harvey, David, *The Condition of Postmodernity* (Oxford: Blackwell, 1989).

Hellwig, Antje, *Untersuchungen zur Theorie der Rhetorik bei Platon und Aristoteles* (Göttingen: Vandenhoeck and Ruprecht, 1973).

Hesse, Mary, *Revolutions and Reconstructions in the Philosophy of Science* (Bloomington: Indiana University Press, 1980).

Hill, Adams Sherman, *The Foundations of Rhetoric* (New York: Harper and Row, 1899).

Horner, Winifred Bryan (ed.), *Historical Rhetoric: An Annotated Bibliography of Selected Sources in English* (Boston: Macmillan, 1980).

Hunter, L., *Rhetorical Stance in Modern Literature: Allegories of Love and Death,* (London: Macmillan, 1984).

Hempel, Carl G., *Fundamentals of Concept Formation in Empirical Science, International Encyclopaedia of Unified Science,* vols I and II: Foundations of the Unity of Science, vol. II (Chicago: University of Chicago Press, 1955, 1st edn, 1952).

Howell, Wilbur Samuel, *Eighteenth-Century British Logic and Rhetoric* (Princeton: Princeton University Press, 1971).

Howes, Raymond Floyd, *Historical Studies of Rhetoric and Rhetoricians* (Ithaca: Cornell University Press 1961).

Hoyt, H. Hudson, 'The Field of Rhetoric' *Quarterly Journal of Speech* 9 (1923) pp. 167-80.

Hunt, Everett Lee, 'Rhetoric as a Humane Study' *Quarterly Journal of Speech* 41 (1955) pp. 114-17.

Husserl, Edmund, *The Crisis of European Sciences and Transcendental Phenomenology,* trans. David Carr (Evanston: Northwestern University Press, 1970). ET of *Gesammelte Werke,* vol. 6, Walter Biemel (ed.), *Die Krisis der europaischen Wissenshaften und die Transzendentale Phänomenologie* (The Hague: Martinus Nijhoff, 1954).

Ijsseling, Samuel, *Rhetoric and Philosophy in Conflict,* trans. Paul Dunphy (The Hague: Martinus Nijhoff, 1976).

Jamieson, Kathleen, *Eloquence in an Electronic Age: The Transformation of Political Speech Making* (Oxford: Oxford University Press, 1988).

Jamison R., and Dyke, J., *Rhetorik-Topik-Argumentation: Bibliographie zur Redelehre und Rhetorikforschung im deutschsprachigen Raum 1945 bus 1979/80* (Stuttgart: Frommann-Holzboog, 1983).

Jebb, Richard (trans.), Sansys, J.E. (ed.), *Aristotle's Rhetoric* (Cambridge: Cambridge University Press, 1909).

Jens, W., 'Rhetorik', in P. Mera and W. Stammler (eds), *Reallexikon der deutschen Literaturgeschichte* vol. 3 (Berlin and New York: de Gruyter, 1977) pp. 432-56.

———— *Von deutscher Rede* (München: enlarged edn, 1983).

Johnstone Jr, Henry W., 'The Relevance of Rhetoric to Philosophy and of Philosophy to Rhetoric' *Quarterly Journal of Speech* 52 (1966) pp. 41-6.

———— *Validity and Rhetoric in the Philosophic Argument* (University Park, PA: Dialogue Press of Man and World, 1978).

Jordan, John E., *Using Rhetoric* (New York: Harper and Row, 1965).

Kennedy, George Alexander, *The Art of Persuasion in Greece* (London: Routledge and Kegan Paul, 1963).

———— *Quintilian* (New York: Twayne Publishers, 1969).

268

———— *The Art of Rhetoric in the Roman World 300 BC-AD 300* (London: Oxford University Press, 1973).

———— *Classical Rhetoric and its Christian and Secular Tradition from Ancient to Modern Times* (Chapel Hill: University of North Carolina Press, 1980).

———— *Greek Rhetoric under Christian Emperors* (Princeton: Princeton University Press, 1983).

Klein, Julie Thompson, *Interdisciplinarity: History, Theory, and Practice* (Detroit: Wayne State University Press, 1990).

Klemm, David E., 'Toward a Rhetoric of Post-modern Theology: Through Barth and Heidegger' *Journal of the American Academy of Religion* LV iii (1987) pp. 443ff.

———— 'Ricoeur, Theology and the Rhetoric of Overturning' *Literature and Theology* 3/3 (1989) p. 281.

Koch, S., and Leary, D.E. (eds), *A Century of Psychology as Science* (New York: McGraw Hill, 1985).

Kopperschmidt, J. *Allgemeine Rhetorik: Einführung in die Theorie der Persuasiven Kommunikation* (Stuttgart: Kohlhammer, 1973).

Kuhn, T. S., *The Structure of Scientific Revolutions* (Chicago: University of Chicago Press, 2nd edn, 1970).

Lakatos, I., and Musgrave, A. (eds), *Criticism and the Growth of Knowledge* (Cambridge: Cambridge University Press, 1970).

Lausberg, Heinrich, *Handbuch der literischen Rhetorik: Eine Grundlegung der Literaturwischenschaft* (München, 2nd edn, 1973) 2 vols.

———— *Elemente der litarischen Rhetorik: Eine Einführung für Studierende der romanischen Philologie.* (München, 5 rev. edn, 1976).

Lawson, Hilary, *Reflexivity The post-modern predicament* (London: Hutchinson, 1985).

Leith, Dick, and Myerson, George, *The Power of Address: Explorations in Rhetoric* (London: Routledge, 1989).

Lodge, David, *The Modes of Modern Writing: Metaphor, Metonymy, and the Typology of Modern Literature* (Ithaca: Cornell University Press, 1977).

Loreau, Max, 'Pour Situer la Nouvelle Rhétorique', in Chaïm Perelman (ed.), *La Théorie de l'Argumentation* (Louvain: Editions Nauwelaerts, 1963) pp. 103-29.

Lundeen, Lyman T., *Risk and Rhetoric in Religion: Whitehead's Theory of Language and the Discourse of Faith* (Philadelphia: Fortress Press, 1972).

MacIntyre, A., *After Virtue: A Study in Moral Theory* (Notre Dame: University of Notre Dame Press, 22nd edn, 1984).

———— *Three Rival Versions of Moral Enquiry Encyclopaedia, Genealogy, and Tradition* (London: Duckworth, 1990).

McCloskey, D. N., *The Rhetoric of Economics* (Madison: University of Wisconsin Press, 1985).

———— *If You're so Smart: The Narrative of Economic Expertise* (Chicago: University of Chicago Press, 1990).

McGuire, J., and Melia, T. 'Some cautionary strictures on the writing of the rhetoric of science' *Rhetorica* 7/1 (1989) pp. 87-99.

McKeon, Richard, 'The Methods of Rhetoric and Philosophy: Invention and Judgment', in Luitpold Wallach (ed.), *The Classical Tradition: Literary and Historical Studies in Honor of Harry Caplan* (Ithaca: Cornell University Press, 1966).

Margolis, Joseph, 'Postscript on Modernism and Postmodernism, Both' *Theory, Culture and Society* 6 (1989) pp. 5-30.

————— *Science without Unity Reconciling the Human and Natural Sciences* (Oxford: Blackwell, 1987).

Mason, Jeff, *Philosophical Rhetoric The function of indirection in philosophical writing* (London: Routledge, 1989).

Maxwell, Nicholas, *From Knowledge to Wisdom A Revolution in the Aims and Methods of Science* (Oxford: Blackwell, 1984).

Meyer, Michael, *De la Métaphysique à la Rhétorique: essai à la mémoire de Chaïm Perelman avec un inédit sur la logique/rassamblés* (Bruxelles: Editions de l'Université de Bruxelles, 1986).

————— 'From logic to rhetoric', in *Pragmatics and Beyond* 7/3 (Amsterdam: J. Benjamins, 1986).

Miller, J.M., Prosser, M.H., and Benson, T.W. (eds), *Readings in Mediaeval Rhetoric* (Bloomington: University of Indiana Press, 1973).

Mirovski, P. 'The Rhetoric of Modern Economics' *History of the Human Sciences* 3 (1990) pp. 243-58.

Monfasani, John, 'Humanism and Rhetoric', in A. Rabil, Jr (ed.), *Renaissance Humanism: Foundations, Form and Legacy* (3 vols, Philadelphia, 1988) vol. 3, pp. 171-270.

Moscovici, Serge, 'Questions for the Twenty-first Century' *Theory, Culture and Society* (1990) vol. 7, pp. 1-19.

Moss, Jean Dietz (ed.), *Rhetoric and Practice* (Washington, DC: Catholic University of America, 1985).

Murphy, James J. (ed.), *A Synoptic History of Classical Rhetoric* (New York: Random House, 1972).

————— *Rhetoric in the Middle Ages* (Berkeley and Los Angeles: University of California Press, 1974).

————— (ed.), *Mediaeval Eloquence: Studies in the Theory and Practice of Mediaeval Rhetoric* (Berkeley and Los Angeles, University of California Press, 1978).

Nelson, J. S., Megill, A., and McCloskey D.N. (eds), *The Rhetoric of the Human Sciences* (Madison: Wisconsin University Press, 1987).

Neurath, Otto, 'Unified Science as encyclopedic integration', in O. Neurath, R. Carnap, and C. Morris (eds), *International Encyclopaedia of Unified Science* (Chicago: Chicago University Press, 1938) vol. I.

Newman, Cardinal John Henry, *An Essay in Aid of a Grammar of Assent* (London, 1870).

Nozick, R., *Philosophical Explanations* (Cambridge, MA: Harvard University Press, 1981).

Ogden, C. K., and Richards, I.A., *The Meaning of Meaning, a Study of the Influence of Language upon Thought and of the Science of Symbolism* (London: Kegan Paul, Trench, Trubner and Co., 1923).

Ong, Walter J., *The Presence of the Word: some Prolegomena for Cultural and Religious History* (New Haven: Yale University Press, 1967).

———— *Rhetoric, Romance and Technology: Studies in the Interaction of Expression and Culture* (Ithaca: Cornell University Press, 1971).

Overington, M., 'The Scientific Community as Audience: Towards a Rhetorical Analysis of Science' *Philosophy and Rhetoric* 10/3 (1977).

Parker, Ian, and Shotter, John (eds), *Deconstructing Social Psychology* (London: Routledge, 1990).

Perelman, C., 'Philosophie, Rhetorik, Gemeinplätze', in H.-G. Gadamer and G. Boehm (eds), *Seminar: Die Hermeneutik und die Wissenshaften* (Frankfurt a. M., 1978) p. 381.

———— 'The New Rhetoric: A Theory of Practical Reasoning', in *Great Ideas of Today 1970* (Chicago: Encyclopaedia Britannica, 1970).

———— *The Realm of Rhetoric* (London: University of Notre Dame Press, ca. 1982) trans. William Kluback, *L'Empire Rhétorique et Argumentation* (Paris: 1977).

———— *The New Rhetoric and the Humanities: Essays on Rhetoric and its Applications* (Dordrecht: Reidel, 1986).

Perelman, C., and Olbrechts-Tyteca, L., *La Nouvelle rhétorique: Traité de l'argumentation* (Paris, 1958) trans. by J. Wilkinson and P. Weaver, *The New Rhetoric: a Treatise on Argumentation* (Notre Dame: University of Notre Dame Press, 1969).

———— *Rhétorique et philosophie, Pour une théorie de l'argumentation en philosophie*, with a preface by Emile Bréhier, Bibliothèque de Philosophie contemporaine (Paris: Presses Universitaires de France, 1952).

Plato, *Gorgias* (Harmondsworth: Penguin, 1971).

Plett, H.F., *Rhetorik: Kritische Positionen zum Stand der Forschung* (Munich: Wilhelm Fink, 1977).

———— *Einführung in die rhetorische Textanalyse* (Hamburg, 4th edn 1979).

———— *Textwissenschaft und Textanalyse: Semiotik, Linguistik, Rhetorik* (Heidelberg: Quelle & Meyer, 1979).

———— (ed.), *Rhetorik* (Munich: 1977).

Popper, Karl R., *Conjectures and Refutations: The Growth of Scientific Knowledge* (New York: Harper and Row, 1968).

Poster, Mark, *The Mode of Information Poststructuralism and Social Context* (Cambridge: Polity Press, 1990).

Prelli, L., *A Rhetoric of Science: Inventing Scientific Discourse* (Columbia: University of South Carolina Press).

Raichman, John, and West, Cornel, *Post-Analytic Philosophy* (New York: Columbia University Press, 1985).

Rhetorica: a journal of the history of rhetoric (Berkeley: University of California Press, 1983ff.) pp. 1ff.

Rhetorik: ein internationales Jahrbuch (Stuttgart, 1980ff.) pp. 1ff.

Rhetorica ad Herennium (London: Loeb Classical Library, Heinemann).

Ricoeur, P., *The Rule of Metaphor*, trans. R. Czerny (Toronto, Trinity College: University of Toronto Press, 1977).

Richards, I.A., *The Philosophy of Rhetoric* (London and New York: Oxford University Press, 1936).

Rorty, Richard, Consequences of Pragmatism: Essays 1972-90 (Minneapolis: University of Minnesota Press, 1990).

———— *Contingency, irony, and solidarity* (Cambridge: Cambridge University Press, 1989).

———— *Philosophy and the Mirror of Nature* (Princeton: Princeton University Press, 1979).

Schanze, H. (ed.), *Rhetorik, Beiträge zur ihrer Geschichte in Deutschland vom 16-20 Jahrhundert* (Frankfurt, 1974).

Schanze, H., and Kopperschmidt, J., (eds), *Rhetorik und Philosophie* (Munich: Wilhelm Fink Verlag, 1989).

Schmitt, Charles B. (gen. ed.), *The Cambridge History of Renaissance Philosophy* (Cambridge: Cambridge University Press, 1988).

Schollmeier, P., 'A Classical Rhetoric of Modern Science' *Philosophy and Rhetoric* 17 (1984) pp. 209-20.

Schwartz, Joseph, and Rycenga, John R. (eds), *The Province of Rhetoric* (New York: Ronald Press 1965).

Seigel, J. E., *Rhetoric and Philosophy in Renaissance Humanism* (Princeton: Princeton University Press, 1968).

Shotter, J., 'Rhetoric and the recovery of civil society' *Economy and Society* (in press).

Shuger, Debora K., *Sacred Rhetoric: The Christian Grand Style in the English Renaissance* (Princeton: Princeton University Press, 1988).

Simons, H.W., *Persuasion, Understanding, Practice and Analysis* (New York: Random House, 1986).

———— *Rhetoric in the Human Sciences* (London: Sage, 1989).

———— (ed.), *The Rhetorical Turn* (Chicago: University of Chicago Press, 1990).

Simons, H. W., and Melia, T. (eds), *The Legacy of Kenneth Burke* (Madison: University of Wisconsin Press).

Smart, Barry, 'On the Disorder of Things: Sociology, Postmodernity and the "End of the Social"' *Sociology* 24 (1990) pp. 397-416.

Smith, Adam, *Lectures on Rhetoric and Belles-Lettres*, J. M. Lothian (ed.) (London, 1963).

Solmsen, Friedrich, 'The Aristotelian Tradition in Ancient Rhetoric' *American Journal of Philology* 62 (1941) pp. 35-50, 169-90.

———— *Die Entwicklung der aristotelischen Logik und Rhetorik* (Berlin: Weidmann, 1929).

Steinmann, Martin (ed.), *New Rhetorics* (New York, 1967).

Tarde, G., *Les lois d'imitation, Etude sociologique* (Paris: Alcan, 2nd edn, 1895).

———— *La logique sociale* (Paris: Alcan, 1895).

Toulmin, S., *The Uses of Argument* (Cambridge: Cambridge University Press, 1958).

———— *Human Understanding* (Princeton: Princeton University Press, 1972).

Tyler, Stephen, *The Unspeakable: Discourse, Dialogue and Rhetoric in the Post-modern World* (Madison: University of Wisconsin Press, 1987).

Ueding, G., *Rhetorik des Schreibens: Eine Einführung* (Kronberg/Ts., 1985).

Ueding, G., and Jens, W. (eds), *Historisches Wörterbuch der Rhetorik* (Tübingen, forthcoming).

Ueding, G., and Steinbrink, B., *Grundriß der Rhetorik: Geschichte, Technik, Methode* (Stuttgart: J. B. Metzlersche Verlagsbuchhandlung, 2nd edn rev., 1986).

Ulman, H. L., and Graves, R., *Rhetoric Textbase (Rhetoric bibliography in progress)* (Columbus: Department of English, Ohio State University, 1990ff.).

Vickers, B., *The Artistry of Shakespeare's Prose* (London: Oxford University Press, 1968).

———— 'Bibliography of rhetoric studies 1970-1980' *Comparative Criticism* 3 (1981) pp. 316-22.

———— (ed.), *Rhetoric Revalued: papers from the International Society for the History of Rhetoric* (Binghamton: Centre for Mediaeval and Early Rennaissance Studies, 1982).

Viebrock, H. (ed.), *Sozial Reform und Rhetorik* (Wiesbaden, 1984).

Wallerstein, I., 'World Systems Analysis', in Anthony Giddens and Jonathan Turner (eds), *Social Theory Today* (Cambridge: Cambridge University Press, 1987) pp. 309-24.

Warner, Martin, *Philosophical Finesse: Studies in the Art of Rational Persuasion* (Oxford: Clarendon Press, 1989).

Weaver, Richard M., *The Ethics of Rhetoric* (Chicago: Henry Regnery Company, 1953).

Weigart, A., 'The immoral rhetoric of scientific sociology' *American Sociologist* 5 (1970) pp. 111-19.

Weimer, W. B., 'Science as a Rhetorical Transaction: Toward a Non-justificational Conception of Rhetoric' *Philosophy and Rhetoric* 6/1 (1977) pp. 1-29.

Whately, Richard D., *Elements of Rhetoric* (1846) (New York: Harper and Row, 1893).

White, Eugene E. (ed.), *Rhetoric in transition: studies in the nature and uses of rhetoric* (London: Pennsylvania State University Press, 1980).

White, Hayden, *Tropics of Discourse: Essays in Cultural Criticism* (Baltimore: Johns Hopkins University Press, 1978).

Winterowd, W. Ross, *Rhetoric: A Synthesis* (New York: Holt, Rinehart and Winston 1968).

Woodman, A.J., *Rhetoric in Classical Historiography: Four Studies* (London: Croom Helm, 1989).

Woods, David, *Philosophy at the Limit* (London: Unwin Hyman, 1990).

Woolgar, S., 'Irony in the social study of science', in K.D. Knorr-Cetina and M. Mulkay (eds), *Science Observed: Perceptions on the Social Study of Science* (London: Sage, 1983).

Index

Nature, 205
New rhetoric, 2, 3; in the Renaissance,
40
Nussbaum, Martha, 199

Orality, 101
Ovid, *Metamorphoses*, 52

Pareto, Vilfredo, 101, 106
Perelman, Chaïm, and Lucie Olbrechts-
Tyteca, 2, 39 n.34, 40, 42f., 62, 96,
123
Person, 9
Petrarca, Francesco, 29, 31ff.
Philology, classical and *Germanistik*,
93
Philosophy and poetry, 197
Plato, 42, 63; *The Sophist*, 120
Politics, 164ff.
POROI project, 3
Poster, Mark, 12
Postmodern condition, 1, 1 n.2, 9 n.46
Postmodernity and rhetoric, 10, 225
Potter, Jonathan and Margaret
Wetherell, 7
Presentism, 10
Preston, R.H., 226
Probatio, 105
Pseudo-Longinus, *On the Sublime*, 112
Psychology, 4; 'mutualist' psychology,
15 n.8

Quintilian, 2, 35, 38, 80, 104, 107; *Institutio oratoria*, 27

Radcliffe-Brown, A.R., 108
'Recovery of Rhetoric', 1ff., 25, 43
Renaissance, 30, 51
Rhetorica ad Herennium, 26, 35, 40,
127
Rhetoric defined, 2; epideictic, 51; and
feminism, 203ff.; instruction in, 89;
and magic, 71 n.24; medieval, 25
n.3; occultation of, 3; and science, 9
n.44; and social science, 101ff., 167

n.13; Rhetoric of rhetoric, 61ff., 75;
professionalisation of, 62
Rhetorical inquiry, 13, 168, 224
Rorty, Richard, 11n., 53, 199
Rouse, Joseph, 241f.

Said, Edward, 7
Salazar, Philippe-Joseph, 8
Salutati, Coluccio, 97
salutatio, 28
Sartre, J.P., 196, 204
Schlegel, F., 196
Science, hard and soft, 149; social
studies of, 210
sententiae, 28
Shelley, Mary, *Frankenstein, Or, The
Modern Prometheus*, 61
Shotter, John and Kenneth Gergen, 7
Simmel, Georg, 101, 104
Smith, Adam, 11, 224
Social psychology, 15-6 n.13, 239
Sociobiology, 205, 208
Sociologie de l'imaginaire, 60, 101
Socrates, 12, 65, 124
Sophists, 2, 77
Spitteler, Carl, 89
Still, Arthur, 6
Strauss, David Friedrich, 93
Stryker, S., 251f.

Tarda, Gabriel, 101, 103
Tawney, R.H., *Religion and the Rise of
Capitalism*, 226
Taylor, Charles, 12
Techne/ars, 65, 70ff.
Thatcher, Mrs (now Lady) Margaret,
236
Toulmin, Stephen, 62
Trivium, 3, 50
Tropes, 37, 50, 165 n.5, 176, 180

Ueding, Gert, 3
Universities, 11, 87

Valery, Paul, 194